GO EAST!

STUDIES IN HUNGARIAN HISTORY

László Borhi, *series editor*

GO EAST!

A History of Hungarian Turanism

Balázs Ablonczy

INDIANA UNIVERSITY PRESS

This book is a publication of

Indiana University Press
Office of Scholarly Publishing
Herman B Wells Library 350
1320 East 10th Street
Bloomington, Indiana 47405 USA

iupress.org

© 2022 by Balázs Ablonczy

Manufactured in the United States of America

First printing 2022

Library of Congress Cataloging-in-Publication Data

Names: Ablonczy, Balázs, author. | Lambert, Sean, translator.
Title: Go east! : a history of Hungarian Turanism / Balázs Ablonczy ;
[translated by Sean Lambert].
Other titles: Keletre, magyar! English | History of Hungarian Turanism
Description: Bloomington, Indiana : Indiana University Press, [2021] |
Series: Studies in Hungarian history | Includes bibliographical
references and index.
Identifiers: LCCN 2021001566 (print) | LCCN 2021001567 (ebook) | ISBN
9780253057402 (hardback) | ISBN 9780253057419 (paperback) | ISBN
9780253057433 (ebook)
Subjects: LCSH: Pan-Turanianism. | Hungarians—Origin. | Hungarians—Ethnic
identity. | Magyars—Origin. | Ural-Altaic peoples. |
Hungary—Intellectual life.
Classification: LCC DS17 .A2513 2021 (print) | LCC DS17 (ebook) | DDC
305.894/511009—dc23
LC record available at https://lccn.loc.gov/2021001566
LC ebook record available at https://lccn.loc.gov/2021001567

CONTENTS

MAPS

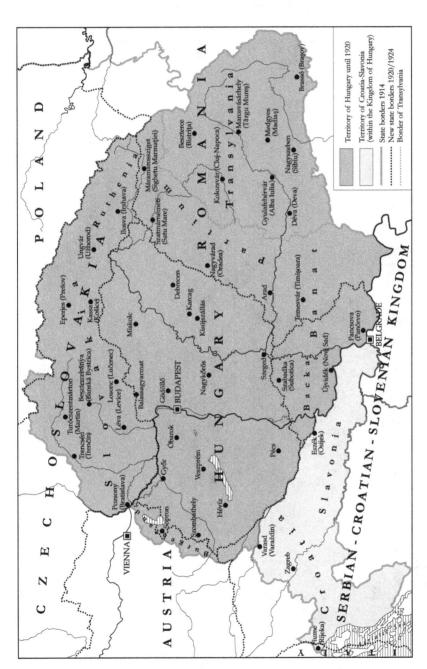

Hungary before and after the Trianon Peace Treaty in 1920 © Béla Nagy.

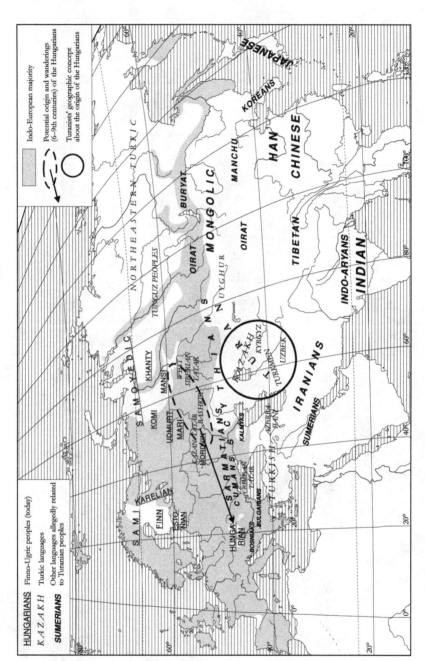

Map of allegedly Turanian people © Béla Nagy.

ACKNOWLEDGMENTS

I RECEIVED ENORMOUS HELP FROM MANY PEOPLE IN writing this book. I would above all like to thank my brother, Bálint Ablonczy, for reading the Hungarian-language manuscript with incredible speed and helping me to improve its readability.

I would also like to thank those who shared the stories of their knowledge and disciplines with me for both their time and effort and for reading parts of the text and providing me with advice and remarks. Naturally, if I did not accept some of their recommendations or did not understand them, it is solely my responsibility. I would thus like to thank Eötvös Loránd University Faculty of Humanities (ELTE BTK) professor László Kósa (ethnography), ELTE BTK professor István Vásáry (Turkology), ELTE BTK and Károli Gáspár University of the Reformed Church in Hungary Faculty of Humanities (KRE BTK) professor Katalin Keserü (art history), KRE BTK professor Miklós Sárközy (Iranian studies), University of West Hungary professor Emese Egey (Hungarian Finno-Ugric studies), National University of Public Services specialist Zoltán Egeresi, and migration expert-Turkologist Péter Kövecsi-Oláh (Hungarian-Turkish relations). I would also like to express my gratitude to Pál Ritoók of the Gyula Forster National Centre for Cultural Heritage for drawing my attention to certain authors and collections regarding the history of Hungarian architecture and to Katalin Török for showing me the letters of Tibor Boromisza kept in her care, suggesting books for me to read, and offering me enlightening insights regarding the painter during our conversation at her home in Szentendre. László Szende of the Hungarian National Museum–Archaeological Repository has honored me with twenty years of friendship and furnished me with useful advice concerning the history of Hungarian archaeology. I am particularly grateful for the help of Japan expert and former diplomat Péter Wintermantel, with whom I have been friends since our university years, for acquainting me with many correlations that I would certainly have otherwise overlooked. My friend István Papp of the Historical Archives of the Hungarian State Security supplied me with data and a list of fonds for my research. The granddaughter of István Medgyaszay, Mrs. Ládonyi Gabriella Bartha, permitted me to inspect documents kept by her family and kindly supplemented these records with stories about her grandfather.

I would like to thank those associated with many museums and public collections for their helpfulness, friendliness, and flexibility. Museum of Ethnography Ethnologic Repository director Péter Granasztói provided me with both the conditions necessary to carry out my research and professional advice. Museum employees Hanga Gebauer, Tímea Bata, and Evelin Kovács were very kind and accommodating and helped me obtain forgotten monographs. I am extremely grateful to Tatjána Kardos of the Ferenc Hopp Museum Repository for calling my attention to documents that I would not have otherwise even known existed and for assisting me with my work in many other ways as well.

I would like to thank Hungarian Geographical Museum director János Kubassek and museum papers and documents collection custodian Katalin Puskás. My reception at the museum was just as warm in the course of my work for the present book as it was when I first conducted research there fifteen years ago.

János Kalmár of the National Archives stood behind me with his customary quiet encouragement and willingness to help. National Széchényi Library Manuscript Department director Ferenc Földesi and employee Gábor Szita received my importunate requests with kindness and responded to them quickly. Hungarian Academy of Sciences Library Department of Manuscripts director Antal Babus was also very helpful, as were Katalin F. Csóka, who now works elsewhere, and Hungarian Natural Sciences Museum History of Science Collection custodian Réka Sebestyén. University Archives director Júlia Varga and her colleagues provided significant support for my work.

Dr. Enikő Juha at the University of Debrecen and National Library Manuscript Archives kindly furnished me with much help. Ágnes Sőreghy allowed me immediate access to her grandfather's papers. Déri Museum Ethnographic Archives director Dr. Márta Magyari and Art Depository director Éva Fodor showed palpable interest in my work and attempted to relieve me of administrative burdens. Debrecen Reformed College Great Library director Botond Gáborjáni Szabó and employee Dr. Teofil Kovács gave me access to requested documents in spite of the inconvenient timing; I am grateful for their flexibility. I thank Ottó Herman Museum Historical Repository director Ádám Hazag and art historian Andrea Pirint for their kindness. Hungarian National Archives–Békés County Archives director

Dr. Ádám Erdész graciously provided me with access to the unpublished parts of historian Sándor Márki's journal that dealt with Turanism. My former university classmate Gergő Sonnevend assisted me greatly with my research at the Historical Archives of the Hungarian State Security, while the employees of the institution's research room helped me overcome my digital illiteracy. I thank Hungarian Agricultural Museum Personal Historical Records Collection director Balázs Mészáros and museologist Gábor Gergely for permitting me to conduct research at this unique location. I would like to thank director László Budai and librarian Mrs. Zsolt Varga of the Gyula Krúdy Library Local History Collection in Várpalota for providing me with access to Aladár Bán's papers and for their subsequent help with my research. I wish to express my gratitude to the deputy director of the Aladár Bán Elementary School in Várpalota, Mrs. István Musits, for kindly showing me the school's exhibition regarding the poet, translator, and literary historian.

I would like to thank my colleagues Róbert Kerepeszki of the University of Debrecen Faculty of Humanities and professor Zsolt Nagy of the University of St. Thomas (St. Paul, Minnesota) for providing me with their unpublished or difficult-to-obtain manuscripts. University of Debrecen Faculty of Humanities professor Róbert Keményfi rapidly obtained needed documents and scanned them for me. I apologize if I sometimes failed to sufficiently maintain our email correspondence—it is difficult to keep pace with him.

I held a master's seminar on Turanism at Eötvös Loránd University during the spring semester of the 2015–2016 academic year. I learned very much from my students' questions, remarks, and papers at this time and am particularly grateful in this regard to Anikó Izsák, Bence Üveges, and Viktor Papp, although I would naturally like to thank all of those who patiently listened to my occasionally irreverent ramblings on Eastern thought.

I express my gratitude to Jaffa publishing house director Richárd Rados for our nearly seven years of fruitful cooperation even though I know he detests any such acknowledgment. I would also like to thank Júlia Jolsvai and Krisztina Nemes for their editing help and Melinda Támba for her administrative and logistical assistance. I don't know if they envisioned a book such as this when we first discussed the project, but in any event, I am very happy that they decided to publish it.

Although my fellow historians were surprisingly reserved about the book following its publication in Hungarian, I received warm and favorable responses from art historians, archaeologists, ethnographers, linguists,

Orientalists, and political scientists from Pécs, Szeged, and Budapest. I learned a lot during my discussions with them and attempted to incorporate their observations into the English-language edition. It would be difficult to mention all of these people by name, although those to whom I am referring surely are aware of it. Thank you.

I would also like to thank the translator of the English-language edition of the book, Sean Lambert, who not only converted the text from one language to another but also asked precise questions that helped me refine it. I am grateful to the National Bank of Hungary for its support and to Hungarian Academy of Sciences Research Center for the Humanities chief director Pál Fodor for his trust; László Borhi, Peter A. Kadas Chair Associate Professor of the Indiana University, for his help; and the people at Indiana University Press for their patience and professionalism.

Finally, I would like to thank my family—my wife, Zsófi; my daughter, Anna; and my sons, Zsigmond and András—for overlooking my frequent absences, glassy-eyed ruminations, and long hours of work at home and even during our summer vacations. However, they can now see that I was not fooling them: I was really writing.

ABBREVIATIONS

Collections are to be found in Budapest if not otherwise designated.

ÁBTL: Historical Archives of the Hungarian State Security

BFL: Budapest City Archives

BM: Ministry of Interior

BT-CsA: Tibor Boromisza Family Archives (Szentendre)

cs.: bundle

DEENKK: University of Debrecen and National Library Manuscript Archives

DMKA: Déri Museum Visual Arts Documentation Department (Debrecen)

DMNA: Déri Museum Ethnographic Archives (Debrecen)

EA: Museum of Ethnography Ethnologic Repository

EKK: Eötvös Loránd University Library Manuscript Department.

EL: Eötvös Loránd University Archives

HMA: Ferenc Hopp Museum Repository

HOM: Ottó Herman Museum Historical Repository and Fine Arts Repository (Miskolc)

KI: Képviselőházi Irományok

KN: House of Representatives Journal

MDK: Hungarian Academy of Sciences Research Center for the Humanities, Institute of Art History Documentation Center

MFM Érd: Hungarian Geographical Museum (Érd)

MMGM SZE: Hungarian Agricultural Museum, Personal Historical Records Collection

MNL BéML: Hungarian National Archives–Békés County Archives

MNL OL: National Archives of the Hungarian National Archives

MNL PML: Hungarian National Archives–Pest County Archives

MNM RAHA: Hungarian National Museum–Archaeological Repository, Papers and Documents

MTAKK: Hungarian Academy of Sciences Library and Information Center, Department of Manuscripts

MTTM TtGy: Hungarian Natural Sciences Museum, History of Science Collection

NMI: Museum of Ethnography Archives

NN: National Assembly Journal

OSZKK: National Széchényi Library Manuscript Department

PIM: Petőfi Literary Museum Manuscript Department

t: item

TTREKK: Library of the Trans-Tisza Reformed Diocese, Manuscript Department (Debrecen)

GO EAST!

1

A BATCH OF BREAD

OCTOBER 14 OF THE YEAR 1919 WAS A damp and dreary autumn day. Public services had not been functioning very well since the final years of the war, and it appeared as if nobody had cleaned the streets of Budapest at all since the Romanian occupation in early August. The prospect of catching a hansom cab seemed nearly hopeless. The few people who proceeded on foot toward the Kerepesi Avenue Cemetery slipped about on the soggy leaves that thickly covered the sidewalks and the roads within the cemetery. The group that had gathered for the funeral was composed of important people: a former House of Representatives speaker and a current state secretary appeared to pay their last respects in the name of the two major literary societies, the Kisfaludy and the Petőfi, while Dezső Kosztolányi (1885–1936), one of the renewers of Hungarian prose, represented the Hungarian Writers' Federation. Reformed bishop Elek Petri pronounced the funeral oration in honor of the deceased.[1] The city donated the burial plot. In the ring of friends, creative companions, and former comrades in arms stood the lonesome and childless widow. Newspaper reports about the funeral mourned the deceased as a master interpreter of the ancient tradition of Hungarian poetry and the apostle of Turanism. The deputy registrar of what was then the fourth district of Budapest made only the following remark regarding the cause of death in the death certificate of the resident of Bástya Street 11 who had passed away at 2:30 a.m. on the morning of October 12, 1919: "heart muscle deficiency." The deputy registrar filled out the other rubrics of the fifty-four-year-old deceased's death certificate according to regulation as well: namely, that he had been a member of the Reformed Church, that he was the son of the late András Imrey and late Krisztina Abaurer, and that Anna (Révész) Rizdorfer was his widow. With regard to the profession of the deceased, Árpád Imrey, the deputy registrar noted only that he had been an author. Then he added, as if the latter circumstance required some explanation, that "in public life the deceased is known by the name 'Zempléni.'"[2]

This is how the life of one of the peculiar figures of Hungarian literature, Árpád Zempléni, came to an end. Zempléni had an atypical career as well: he was a bank clerk who suffered continually from the malevolence and ignorance of his superiors while—contrary to numerous participants in Hungarian literary life—not having daily money worries. Working as a bank filing clerk provided a respectable, though not Croesus-like, livelihood, although Zempléni did continually lobby for a raise.[3] Following his death, Zempléni's table companions remembered him as a Falstaffian figure: "somewhat excessively easy-going, though his engagingly natural manner was that of a grandiloquent student even when he was in his fifties."[4] Zempléni was the type of guy who was fond of small Buda pubs; he expressed peremptory opinions regarding poems placed before him for judgment, and it bothered him to an extraordinary degree if somebody departed from a pub gathering in a sober state. At the same time, Zempléni was not an untalented poet: he belonged to the fin-de-siècle branch of Hungarian literary modernism, whose members (Lajos Tolnai, Jenő Péterfy, and Jenő Komjáthy) literary history frequently refers to as the "cursed generation" because of the tragedies that afflicted them and their premature deaths. Zempléni translated Charles Baudelaire, gaining a certain amount of recognition for his literary translations and poetry in early twentieth-century Hungary. His verse novel *Didó* (1901) appeared in literary compendia.[5] Zempléni's contemporaries took note of the stunning virtuosity with which he handled metrical forms. According to Mihály Babits (1883–1941), a contemporary of Kosztolányi and creator of equal standing, Zempléni "was a master of the Hungarianness of forms and words—perhaps the last great master of the old Hungarian forms of verse."[6] The greatest of the era knew and respected him.

Zempléni would nevertheless be remembered as a creator of relatively minor importance if, in 1908, his poem "Bosszú" (Revenge) had not won one of the prizes accorded by the prestigious Kisfaludy Society. Zempléni elaborated a Finnish mythological theme drawing on the research of his friend Béla Vikár (1859–1945), who was a folklorist. Zempléni's success and personal experiences guided his poetic interests into an entirely different direction. Zempléni informed his colleagues—among them Endre Ady (1877–1919), the central figure associated with the Hungarian poetic renewal and the periodical *Nyugat* (West)—of his new program: turning away from the West and "the Aryan peoples" and reviving the ancient Hungarian myths through kinship with Finno-Ugric and Asian peoples.[7] Apocalyptic worries and his image of world war between the races motivated the turnabout, as Zempléni wrote in 1908 to Andor Kozma (1861–1933), the editor of the newspaper *Pesti Hírlap* and poet who took an interest in Easternness:

> Perhaps my plans will not remain plans either. I will write, and perhaps tolerably, that which still seethes in my soul and seeks form and my planned book will be more than a simple pamphlet against the malice and unrighteousness of the Aryans. It really hurts me that the peoples of Europe still today regard us as a horde of intruding Mongol newcomers and the devil knows what else. The sobriquet *Mongol* does not hurt, but those proceedings that they are unequivocally conducting against us without distinction to language, as if they want to launch an extermination campaign following the purely paper campaign. They are also squeezing our eastern racial kin in every way, they are persecuting and exterminating them. What is to come from this? A life and death struggle between the races? A white war of extermination against the yellow? "I dream of dread and gory days, Which come, this world to chaos casting"—either that old world in the east or this new, for us dearer, one in the west, or both of them. They will bring down each other's buildings, each other's culture. They will destroy each other's fields and peoples "And we who live shall not forgive" from the Pacific Ocean to the shore of the other ocean.[8]

Zempléni eventually set down in writing that which seethed in his soul: his 1910 book *Turáni dalok* (Turanian songs) was an enormously popular success and inscribed his name definitively in Hungarian public opinion as the poet of Turanism. This remained the seminal theme of Zempléni's creative work throughout the rest of his life: he published further books dealing with Turanism and engaged in newspaper polemics regarding this concept. He had German- and English-language translations of his poems published at his own expense both before and during the First World War and also attempted to win the support of the education ministry for this endeavor. Zempléni ended a letter asking the ministry to purchase two hundred copies of his books with the following statement: "The peoples of Siberia above all have preserved the memory of the ancient Scythian religion of the old Hungarians and therefore I am trying to compensate for the lack of ancient poetry in our literature through the reconstruction of this [religion] and with this to promote the enrichment of the national spirit."[9]

Zempléni had by this time become quite sickly, complaining in his letters of persistent coughing and weakness. His physical condition deteriorated steadily during the summer of 1919. In one of his final letters,

Zempléni asked Hungarian Royal Central Statistical Office president and fellow poet Gyula Vargha, who was staying in the countryside, nothing more than to have "good wheat bread" baked for him because otherwise he would "flee from Budapest": "My dear Gyula! I am sick. Have a loaf of wheat bread baked for me and then another one. I terribly miss good bread, the bread of life. It is made for you! God be with you!"[10] It is not known whether the bread finally arrived. Zsigmond Móricz (1879–1942), who, alongside Ady, Babits, and Kosztolányi, was the fourth great figure associated with the first generation of Hungarian literary modernism, published the most touching obituary for Zempléni in *Nyugat*: "This great poet brought the legacy of the Hungarian race out from Hungarian popular culture. This great and courageous person, who disappeared entirely and in his personal life became inconsequential until slow death from starvation: behold he has risen and raised within us as well the forgotten word, to the starry heights of our race, to the Turanian stars."[11]

The memory of Zempléni was not preserved very well despite Móricz's words, although at the beginning of the 1920s, the Zempléni Table Society was established to cultivate his poetry, and articles about him appeared here and there. In 1940, a few remembrances were issued in a booklet, and his remaining works were published in the small town of Sárospatak on the twentieth anniversary of his death.[12] However, Zempléni's birth house, for example, was not preserved, even though before his death, his widow had implored former colleagues, powerful political officials, and, not incidentally, the president of the Turanian Society, Gyula Pekár, to do so ("How many times did he have to work honorably through the night in order to keep his little birth house, where—he hoped—he would find a peaceful home in his old days, and after his death he wanted to leave it to his hometown with the objective of starting a 'reading circle.' And now some Jew who has grown rich puts his business sign up on it!").[13] Although Zempléni's tomb is still today part of the national pantheon and appears in the National Cemetery database, an impenetrable thicket has grown around his remains at the Fiumei Avenue Cemetery.

In terms of magnitude and formalities, Árpád Zempléni's funeral could not compare to that of Endre Ady, who had died eight months earlier. Zempléni's literary work and, especially, public activity were part of an intellectual current that was at least as strong as that which had spurred Ady to attempt to uplift the Asian-descended Hungarian people, to democratize conditions in Hungary, and to oppose the contemporary Hungarian elite.

Fig. 1.1. Árpád Zempléni (1865–1919). Attribution: Országos Széchényi Könyvtár, Kézirattár, An. Lit. 6829.

The Eastern idea has engaged a significant segment of Hungarian intellectual public life with ever-renewing force from the beginning of Hungarian political modernity until the present day. Zempléni was the bard of rediscovering roots whose remembrance has today become threadbare; he was a poet who—although not comparable to the greats—was not at all devoid of talent and who died at a symbolic moment.

The autumn of 1919 was one of the dark moments in the modern history of Hungary. Following the loss in the world war and the postwar revolutions, amid the wave of refugees and the Romanian occupation, and in advance of a portentous peace treaty, many Hungarians could well have thought that the century-old national plan—catching up with the West and European-type modernization—had been pointless and that it was necessary to turn back toward the East, to find friends and kinfolk, to search for other models, and, thus strengthening themselves, to retaliate for every unjust injury they had suffered. This yearning imbued even such humble intellectuals as the literary scholar Frigyes Riedl (1856–1921), who, in notes made near the end of his life, produced the following contemplation in which he denounced the lack of morality in the West: "We overestimated the west. . . . The great Hungary was on the border of Asia. The Hungarian people is an Asian people. The Hungarian [people] is a people of Russia. Shall we be Russians? No! Hungarians. Back to Asia? Would this not be an ugly relapse? Shameful decadence? No! The moral ideals originating in Asia are worth more than the modern European ones. Christ, Buddhism, Kong Fuzi. . . . *Back to Asia.* This is not such a terrible motto. Indeed, in certain regards this would perhaps be progress."[14] This thought was not new. One of the first researchers of Hungarian literary Orientalism highlighted one of the fundamental characteristics of Hungarian Eastern thinking: "The ancient eastern home is the predominant concept of Hungarian Orientalism."[15] The question "Where are we from?" and the associated "What is our calling?" had aroused Hungarian public life since the beginning of the nineteenth century. Debate surrounding the contradictions connected to the Eastern origin of the Hungarians and the following of Western models intensified as thought regarding the origin of the Hungarian language progressed along with the institutionalization of the modern nation (Hungarian Academy of Sciences, National Theater, National Museum).

This book presents the history of these reflections. It would be more precise for me to write about the history of deducing the public-cultural consequences of thinking regarding the East instead of that of *Turanism*, a term that elicits a negative association of ideas, although the former description is obviously too long and rather impractical. That cultural, and even legal and political, consequences could be drawn from true or supposed ethnic origins was not at all a new phenomenon in Europe—let us just think of Gallic-French and Lusitanian-Portuguese ethnic derivation. In the central European region, there emerged in the fifteenth century, following Sarmatism as the ideology of the Polish nobility at the time of the common Polish-Lithuanian state and *Rzeczpospolita* at the time of the noble Polish republic and certain medieval chronicle antecedents, the notion that the Polish nobility (the *szlachta*) was not of Slavic origin but had descended from the mythical people of Iranian origin who had once ruled over the eastern European plains and as such had a historical right to social status. This train of thought—which from a current perspective seems rather discriminatory, besides the fact that in many respects it obviously draws from the historical outlook of humanist historiography that often looks back unnaturally to ancient roots—constituted, as analysts have pointed out, an important cohesive element of the baroque idea of the Polish-Lithuanian state alliance in the sixteenth to the eighteenth centuries insofar as it played an important role in its integration into the multinationality of the noble republic.[16] Historian and diplomat Jan Długosz (1415–1480) is customarily regarded as the originator of the term *Sarmatism*, particularly in the monumental work that he wrote until his death, *Annales Regni Poloniae*. The scholar, historian, and University of Kraków professor Maciej Miechowita (d. 1523) first elaborated Sarmatic theory in comprehensive fashion and made the initial identification of eastern Europe with Sarmatia—in the greatest detail in his work *Tractatus de duabus Sarmatis Europiana et Asiana et de contentis in eis*, printed in 1517. Sarmatism became an important component of the baroque ideology of Polish noble liberty, national independence, and the public law concepts of the nobility that constituted nearly 10 percent of the population.[17] There is an immense amount of literature regarding Polish-Hungarian intellectual connections during this period, including studies on the Hungarian reception of Sarmatism. Yet there is relatively little information available regarding possible links between Sarmatism and an important sixteenth-century book, the compendium of Hungarian noble rights entitled *Tripartitum*.[18] However, it is certain that the author of *Tripartitum*, the political official, chancellor, diplomat, and jurist István Werbőczy (d. 1541), studied for a short time at the University of Kraków in 1492. Werbőczy's work, which appeared in print in 1517, constituted one of the foundations of Hungarian thinking about public law until 1848, although it was never codified. *Tripartitum*, in addition to proclaiming the principle of the single and indivisible nobility (*una eademque nobilitas*) and drawing conclusions from the binding of the serfs to the soil and 1514 peasant war in Hungary, is interesting because it veritably canonized the Hungarian nobility's Scythian-Hun origin, which would form the basis for the authority that members of this social class exercised over the subjugated peasantry in ethnic terms. Werbőczy was able to base this determination partially on medieval Hungarian chronicle literature (primarily Simon Kézai's late thirteenth-century *Gesta Hungarorum*) and the fifteenth-century texts of the humanist historiographers, primarily of Italian origin, who had been active in the kingdom of Hungary.[19] The work of seventeenth- and eighteenth-century baroque, mainly Jesuit, historiographers emphatically helped to incorporate into church and popular convention this Hunnic tradition that proclaimed the direct descent of the Hungarians from Attila and his people.[20] It would be a mistake to trace the roots of Hungarian Turanism unequivocally to this medieval tradition, but it undoubtedly provided firm foundations for its creation.

At the same time, Turanism does not represent some kind of special Hungarian ideology—it fits into a larger intellectual trend that was significant at this time. During the great period of nineteenth-century nation building, it produced its own supranational nationalism that reacted to the existence of intellectual trends that Louis L. Snyder described as *macronationalism* (Pan-Germanism, Pan-Slavism, Pan-Turkism).[21] Within the strongly social Darwinist intellectual milieu of the second half of the nineteenth century, not taking part in the "competition of the races" entailed the danger of national failure. The latter had constituted a permanent obsession within a large segment of the Hungarian intellectual and political class since the remark that German philosopher Johann Gottfried Herder (1744–1803) made regarding the disappearance of the Hungarian nation and language in his 1791 work entitled *Ideen zur Philosophie der Geschichte der Menschheit* ("As for the Hungarians or Magyars, squeezed between Slavs, Germans, Vlachs and other peoples, they are now the smallest part of their country's population, and in centuries to come even their language will probably be lost").[22]

Russian Eurasianism signified the other circle of ideas that emerged in the region in connection to Easternness. Some of the early proponents of Eurasianism, in response to Russophobe Western scholarly trends, interiorized the attributive *Turanian* that had been attached to them in a pejorative context, and in the name of turning Russian culture toward Asia, some Eurasianist authors even broke away from their own Slavic consciousness. Although Eurasianism had some forerunners in the nineteenth century (we do not know who read their works and to what extent they read them in Hungary), the great era of this intellectual current was connected to the circle of post–First World War Russian émigrés surrounding Nikolai Trubetzkoy (1890–1938) and Pyotr Nikolaevich Savitsky (1895–1968).[23] Trubetzkoy, who is regarded as a pioneer in the field of structural linguistics, was a professor at the University of Vienna during the interwar period, although there is no information suggesting that he maintained close Hungarian connections. The venturesome Austrian aristocrat Erik von Kühnelt-Leddihn (1909–1999) introduced Trubetzkoy's viewpoints, which will be examined again later in the book, to Hungarian audiences within the influential Turanian Society.[24] However, the opinion frequently surfaced in Hungary between the two world wars, particularly within more radical Turanist circles, that—transcending the traditional anti-Russian outlook of Hungarian nationalism—Russians should be regarded as "Turanian brothers." These several elements (Sarmatism, Eurasiansim, the pan-movements, and the tradition of Hungarian Hunnic consciousness) obviously had an influence over the birth of Hungarian Turanism and can be placed into numerous internationally recognized comparisons. However, it is worth paying attention as well to endogenous Hungarian political and cultural circumstances that made the development of Turanism possible.

Today Turanism has a fairly bad reputation in Hungary. In the best case, it provides a type of ironic self-definition—in this regard it is somewhat reminiscent of the modern Polish usage of the word *Sarmatian*. However, as a political concept, Turanism is understood to represent some kind of radical right-wing agenda interwoven with Eastern elements—in part rightfully so. In spite of this, my objective is not to lament, along with the reader, at how anybody could have seriously thought what they thought or wrote about the "Turanian spearhead penetrating the body of Europe," Hungarian-Chinese kinship, the plan for a forty-meter-tall Attila statue, a Tatar scholarship program, or blood-group analysis. My fundamental intention is to understand and impart understanding. *Why* did so many—retired Hungarian Royal Police counselors, university professors, popular-song writers, lawyers, master printers, engineers, assistant bakers, landowners, stenography teachers, and painters—regard fulfilling the Eastern mission of the Hungarians to be their task? Moreover, I seek to show how they would have understood the term *Turanism*, which could have had the various following meanings:

1. Searching for the Hungarian ancient homeland in the East
2. Identifying the kin and Eastern connections of the Hungarian people—that is, simple scholarly questions
3. Drawing the political consequences from these connections (with whom shall we make alliances, and with whom shall we not?)
4. Gaining cultural and political influence, or a type of Hungarian imperialism, in the Balkans, the Middle East, and Asia Minor, as well as southern Italy, Ukraine, and all of Asia
5. Redefining Hungary's political roles of serving as a mediator of Eastern values for the West, as well as the same capacity in the opposite direction, and establishing and leading new alliances and power constellations
6. Transmitting scholarly knowledge about Asia—as both a recipient and producer
7. Attempting to create a national fine- and industrial-arts style with the help of the Turanian motifs of related peoples

8. Adapting European-transatlantic literary-artistic Orientalism in Hungary
9. Lobbying in Hungary connected to the East
10. Reforming all of Hungarian society "placed on Turanian foundations" (liberating it, for example, from the tutelage of the historical churches and incorporating the Hungarian Eastern legacy into school curricula)

These many expectations, aspirations, and plans composed the core of Hungarian Turanism, and this ideology was so successful precisely for this reason—because everybody could read into it what they wanted according to their interests. In this way, Turanism could simultaneously serve as a watchword for the postal clerk engaged in an effort to introduce the use of the Székely runic script, the Orientalist scholar, and the retired military officer lobbying for the construction of a mosque in Budapest.

At the same time, it is important to highlight that it is better not to concede to the "everything is interrelated with everything else" simplification. Not all of those who were members of the Turanian Society or other Turanian organizations were necessarily committed Turanists. Perhaps membership in such organizations was important for their career advancement, or maybe they thought it appropriate because they possessed a significant collection of Eastern artwork. At the same time, not all Turanists/activists who had drawn the political-cultural conclusions stemming from the Eastern roots of the Hungarians were members of the aforementioned organizations. Artists often found active participation in associations to be foreign to their natures even if their thinking and activity displayed Turanist characteristics. There were, additionally, solitary scholars who unambiguously proclaimed Eastern-inspired viewpoints even though they were not particularly active in the organizations of the movement. Turanism exercised an impact on numerous artists and thinkers—even if these intellectuals attempted to deny this influence during the fateful moments of the twentieth century. In order to highlight the state-political influence of Turanism, it is enough to mention the fact that between 1913 and 1944, almost every Hungarian prime minister was a member of the Turanian Society and that some of them showed significantly more than simple protocolary commitment to the organization. For example, while Regent Miklós Horthy (1868–1957) merely showed interest in the sphere of ideas associated with Turanism, in the person of law academy professor Béla Zsedényi (1894–1955), who was the chairman of the three-member National Supreme Council that performed the functions of the head of state for a short period in 1945, a devout believer in Turanist ideas served as the leader of Hungary.

The attributive *Hungarian* is an important element of the subtitle of this book, because while Japanese, Turkish, and other nations' Turanism movements are at least as important, the analysis of Pan-Turkism represents one of the common themes in the international academic world of today. This book also fills a gap: Turanist thought was omnipresent in Hungary before 1945; condemned to silence during the years of communism, its reappearance after 1990 perplexes some observers. This book describes the connections between Hungarian Turanism and that of other peoples. I also want to emphasize at the outset what this book will not be: it will obviously not be an account of Hungarian sciences (ethnography, Turkology, archaeology, history, art history); it will not attempt to explore popular anthropology connected to Hungarian ancient history; it will not be a history of the cult of the Székelys, Eastern art collecting, or foreign-policy thinking. However, it will contain some elements from all of these domains. This book is above all a *history of public sensitivity*: the attitudes that the Hungarian intelligentsia and political class maintained toward the East and the notion of Hungarian kinship with Eastern peoples and the solutions and proposals they formulated to use and make use of this consciousness of origin.

Until now rather few recapitulations of this theme with regard to Hungarians have appeared, but Pan-Turkism (the affiliation of Turkish peoples) and the history of Turkish Turanism have been subjected to an intensive degree of review within the scholarly thinking of the Atlantic world since the 1910s. Joseph A. Kessler's unpublished doctoral dissertation represented the first work summarizing the theme.[25] This work was pioneering, and the authors of Anglo-Saxon literature often relied on its conclusions. Kessler wrote his dissertation based primarily on printed works (he did not have access to information contained in manuscript collections and archives in Hungary), and thus many of his findings have today become obsolete and are in need of clarification. In 2001, Eötvös Loránd University doctoral student Ildikó Farkas defended her dissertation entitled "A turanizmus" (Turanism), which has likewise not yet been published in print, although the manuscript and the sporadically published parts of it represent the most important and most frequently cited treatment of the Turanist current of thought.[26] László Szendrei produced the most recent summary of this subject matter in a highly empathetic work based on published sources and elaborations that is shorter than the previously mentioned dissertations.[27] However, I do not agree with certain points of emphasis in the latter work: here I am thinking above all about the overvaluation of certain authors who even in their own era were considered to be peripheral. I used all three of these sources in the process of writing this book, and I learned much from them. My work differs from those of Kessler, Farkas, and Szendrei, partly in terms of focus: I extend the scope of this book from the first half of the nineteenth century all the way to the present day, mainly because neither the resurgence of Székely runic writing nor the Eastern opening policy of the Fidesz government of Viktor Orbán that came to power in 2010 can be interpreted without understanding the theoretical foundations of Turanism. The other important difference is the base of sources. In addition to the major collections of written documents in Hungary (the Hungarian National Archives, the National Széchényi Library, and the Manuscript Collection of the Hungarian Academy of Sciences), I worked in the archives of around two dozen smaller, but not at all insignificant, institutions. I am extremely grateful to those who granted me access to their private family archives or sacrificed their time in order to discuss the history and circumstances surrounding their branch of scholarship with me.

As I progressed in making my notes and organizing my thoughts about this theme, it became increasingly obvious that the elements of this tradition are still present and exercise a much greater influence than one would think at first glance. Budapest and Hungary are strewn with symbols whose origin we can discern in the Eastern idea: memorials, statues, buildings, and even school readings. This book endeavors to help in the interpretation of these symbols and to place the works and actors into a general history of ideas and intellectuals. The book will guide the reader across dictatorships, revolutions, authoritarian systems, and democracy and to locations ranging from Tibet to Argentina. It will introduce the landowner's daughter who transformed from a feminist to a blood-group analyst, a Turanist monotheistic radio technician, a theosophist who became a county chief clerk of court, a Montenegrin hotel owner, and the founder of the Budapest Agricultural Museum, who was incidentally a poet: the nearly simultaneous fabricator of world peace as well as a trench-digging machine.

It will be exciting. I promise.

Notes

1. For descriptions of the funeral of Árpád Zempléni, see *Budapesti Hírlap*, October 15, 1919, 7, and *Pesti Napló*, October 14, 1919, 4.

2. "Hungary, Civil Registration, 1895–1980," FamilySearch, accessed August 17, 2016, https://www.familysearch.org/ark:/61903/3:1:S3HT-DRD3-X1Z?i=33&wc=92QF-K6X%3A4067 8301%2C48553201%2C42189902%3Fcc%3D1452460&cc=1452460.

3. For the circumstances and conflicts surrounding Zempléni's bank employment, see the Hungarian Academy of Sciences Library and Information Center, Department of Manuscripts (hereafter, MTAKK), Ms 1020/198, Zempléni Árpád levele Vargha Gyulának, January 21, 1901.

4. János Varságh, "Apróságok Zempléni Árpádról," Kelet, October 7, 1920, 7–9.

5. For Zempléni's work, see Tamás Gusztáv Filep, "Turáni dalok," in Az ellenállás vize: Jegyzetek, kísérletek, portrévázlatok, ed. Tamás Gusztáv (Budapest: Széphalom, 1993), 14–17.

6. Quoted in Imre Bori, "Zempléni Árpád," Híd 63, no. 11 (1999): 690.

7. See Katalin Hegyi and László Vitályos, eds., Ady Endre levelezése, vol. 2 (Budapest: Argumentum, 2001), 116–17. Neither did Ady feel aversion toward certain themes and motifs connected to Easternness. See Dóra Kolta, "A Kelet-motívum újjáéledése: Orientalista motívumok Ady prózájában," Napút 12, no. 6 (2010): 103–14.

8. National Széchényi Library, Manuscript Department (hereafter, OSZKK) Fond 44/105, 1. sz., Zempléni Árpád levele Kozma Andornak, Budapest, 1908. február 12. Zempléni quoted the poems of Sándor Petőfi (1823–1849), the leader of patriotic romanticism, "Véres napokról álmodom" (I dream of gory days), and János Arany (1817–1882), "Walesi bárdok" (The bards of Wales).

9. OSZKK, Fol. Hung. 1672, Zempléni Árpád vegyes jegyzetei, 207. f. Zempléni Árpád levele Jankovich Béla vallás- és közoktatásügyi miniszternek, Budapest, 1915. május.

10. MTAKK, Ms 1020/215, Zempléni Árpád levelezőlapja Vargha Gyulának, Budapest, 1919. szeptember 23. és 1919. szeptember 25.

11. Zsigmond Móricz, "A magyar költő—Zempléni Árpád halálára," Nyugat 12, nos. 14–15 (1919): 998.

12. Mózes Rubinyi, ed., Zempléni Árpád emlékezete (Budapest: La Fontaine Társaság, 1940).

13. OSZKK Levelestár, özv., Zempléni Árpádné levele Pekár Gyulának, Budapest, 1925. január 5.

14. Riedl Frigyes hagyatékából (Budapest: Minerva Társaság, 1922), 45–47. Quoted in Miklós Szabó, Az újkonzervativizmus és a jobboldali radikalizmus története (1867–1918) (Budapest: Új Mandátum, 2003), 296n533.

15. Géza Staud, Az orientalizmus a magyar romantikában (Budapest: Terebess, 1999), 136.

16. For a survey of Sarmatism, see Andrzej Waśko, "Sarmatism or the Enlightenment: The Dilemma of Polish Culture," Sarmatian Review 27, no. 2 (1997), http://www.ruf.rice.edu/~sarmatia/497/wasko.html; and Janusz Tazbir, "Polish National Consciousness in the Sixteenth to the Eighteenth Century," Harvard Ukrainian Studies 10, nos. 3–4 (1986): 316–35.

17. With regard to the historiographical attitude, see Norbert Kersken, "Geschichtsbild und Adelsrepublik: Zur Sarmatentheorie in der polnischen Geschichtsschreibung der frühen Neuzeit," Jahrbücher für Geschichte Osteuropas, Neue Folge 52, no. 2 (2004): 235–60. For the broader discourse, see Tomasz Zarycki, Ideologies of Eastness in Central and Eastern Europe, BASEES/Routledge Series on Russian and East European Studies, no. 96 (London: Routledge, 2014), 135–44.

18. For the Hungarian reactions to Polish Sarmatism, see Endre Angyal, "Lengyel és magyar barokk," in Tanulmányok a lengyel-magyar irodalmi kapcsolatok köréből, ed. László Sziklay et al. (Budapest: Akadémiai, 1969), 211–44. For Werbőczy's sources, see László

Blazovich, "A Tripartitum és forrásai," *Századok* 141, no. 4 (2007): 1011–23; and Martin Rady, "The Prologue to Werbőczy's Tripartitum and Its Sources," *English Historical Review* 121, no. 490 (2006): 104–45.

19. István Vásáry, "'A megalkotott hagyomány'—Szittyák és hunok," *Magyar Tudomány* 175, no. 5 (2014): 566–71.

20. László Szörényi has written most recently about this: see *Hunok és jezsuiták: Fejezetek a magyarországi latin hősepika történetéből* (Budapest: Nap, 2018).

21. Louis L. Snyder, *Macro-Nationalism: A History of the Pan-Movements* (London: Praeger, 1984).

22. For a naturally much more comprehensive examination of this subject matter, see Ferenc Bíró, *A nemzethalál árnya a XVIII. századvég és a XIX. századelő magyar irodalmában* (Pécs: Pro Pannonia, 2012).

23. On the Russian Turanian self-image in the nineteenth century, see Marlène Laruelle, "La question du 'touranisme' des Russes: Contribution à une histoire des échanges intellectuels Allemagne-France-Russie au XIXème siècle," *Cahiers du Monde Russe* 45, no. 1 (2004): 241–66; and especially with regard to twentieth-century Russian Eurasianists, see Marlène Laruelle, *Russian Eurasianism: An Ideology of Empire* (Baltimore: Johns Hopkins University Press, 2008).

24. "Társasági ügyek," *Turán* 12, nos. 1–4 (1929): 60.

25. Joseph A. Kessler, "Turanism and Pan-Turanism in Hungary, 1890–1945" (PhD diss., University of California–Berkeley, 1967).

26. Among others, see Ildikó Farkas, "A turánizmus," *Magyar Tudomány* 54, no. 7 (1993): 860–68; "A turanizmus és a magyar-japán kapcsolatok a két világháború között," *Folia Japonica Budapestininensia* 1 (2001): 28–44; "A török-tatár népek turanizmusa," *Világtörténet* 28, no. 2 (2006): 52–63; "A magyar turanizmus török kapcsolatai," *Valóság* 50, no. 6 (2007): 31–48; and "A Magyar-Nippon Társaság," in *Tanulmányok a magyar-japán kapcsolatok történetéből*, ed. Ildikó Farkas et al. (Budapest: ELTE Eötvös Kiadó, 2009), 226–47.

27. László Szendrei, *A turanizmus: Definíciók és értelmezések 1910-től a II. világháborúig* (Máriabesnyő-Gödöllő: Attraktor, 2010).

2

GYÖRGY ILOSVAY WRITES A LETTER

IT ALL BEGAN ON A TERRIBLY COLD WINTER day in February 1836, when the winds, sweeping down from the Carpathians, covered the wooden Ruthenian peasant houses with snow and buried the roads. Ilosva (Irshava, Ukraine) was a village of hardly seven hundred souls located in Bereg County at the foot of the mountains three miles from Munkács (Mukachevo, Ukraine). According to Elek Fényes's 1851 statistical description, it was a "Russian village" in which there lived hardly a few dozen Reformed, Roman Catholic, and Jewish inhabitants: everybody else was Greek Catholic, that is, very likely Ruthenian. In addition, "there are a brimstone mineral spring, water mill [and] the debris of an old castle here," while the beautiful woods "provide many acorns and galls." County judge György Ilosvay was a member of the Ilosvay clan that had been in possession of the village from time immemorial, and by then, he was well beyond fifty. After having retired from his office as county judge, he in all probability spent the bleak winter and the dull evenings arranging family documents. This is when he came across a manuscript translation that his long-deceased father-in-law, Dénes Zalakapolcsi Domokos, had made. Being an educated person himself, he immediately understood its significance and sent the entire bundle of papers off in the hope of later publication—presumably to University of Pest assistant professor István Horvát. His motive was based on both patriotic and family considerations: "Although out of patriotism as well, I also felt obliged out of reverence toward the ashes of my Late Father to effectuate the future placement of them [the papers] before the world."[1] The work bore a convoluted title: *Bajad: A' Tatárok, Mungálok és Magyarok első időkbeni eredeteikről szólló értekezések* (Bayad: Discourses on the origins of the Tartars, the Mongols, and the Hungarians from the earliest times). Domokos had rendered into Hungarian the 1726 book *Histoire généalogique des Tatars*—a French-language translation, published in Leiden, of *Shajare-i*

Türk (Genealogy of the Tatars), in which the statesman and historian Abu al-Ghazi Bahadur (1603–c. 1664), to whom Domokos referred simply as Mr. Bahad, wrote about the history of the Mongol and Tatars in the seventeenth century. Abu al-Ghazi, who wrote in the Khiva dialect of the Chagatai language, based his book primarily on oral sources and earlier written works: the parts on the period following the death of Genghis Khan contain little new information and are sometimes historically unreliable, although they impart first-rate source material regarding the history of Central Asia from his era, the seventeenth century.

The book presented much information regarding the Mongol Empire that was unknown in Europe at that time, and for this reason, it spread rather quickly through the continent. Two Swedish officers who had fallen into Russian captivity during the Battle of Poltava produced the first translation of the work, initially in German. Domokos, a member of the lesser nobility who traveled to foreign countries, likely purchased the French edition during one of his trips abroad. He did not translate all of the extensive work, which had originally been published in nine volumes, contenting himself with those parts that he thought provided new data regarding Hungarian ancient history. In accordance with this, Domokos conducted some charming Magyarizations—rendering Genghis Kahn as Gyöngyös and Kublai Kahn as Kopjai—and, as far as we know, used the term *Turán* (Turan) for the first time in a Hungarian-language text to designate the Central Asian steppes extending northward from Iran. However, this translation made between 1796 and 1812 was never prepared for publication. It is not known whom Domokos spoke to about the translation or to whom he showed it, although at the time he wrote his letter, the expression *Turán* had already appeared in printed form. Domokos addressed his letter to retired military judge and Hungarian Academy of Sciences member Ferenc Kállay (1790–1861), an author of numerous works on ethnography, linguistics, and ancient history who, in an 1835 article regarding the etymology of the name Attila, used *Turán* as a geographical term pertaining to an area of variable magnitude.[2] Kállay's etymology was based on a German-language translation of a book on the history of Persia by Scottish Orientalist and diplomat John Malcom (1769–1833).[3] Editor and author István Kultsár (1760–1828) likewise referred to the 1726 edition of Abu al-Ghazi Bahadur's work in his 1803 supplementation and expansion of a history of Hungary by Ludwig Albrecht Gebhardi (1735–1802). In this book, Kultsár wrote about the subjugation of Turán in connection with the thirteenth-century military campaign of the Mongols.[4] However, it is difficult to determine whether Kultsár's use of this expression was based on the original work by Gebhardi or his own augmentation of it from a Hungarian point of view. There is other sporadic data showing that the word *Turán* was already being used in Hungary at this time, presumably also based on its appearance in western European sources.[5]

The word became current beginning in the 1830s. The political official and later director general of the Hungarian National Museum who accrued a significant collection of Eastern artworks, Ferenc Pulszky (1814–1897), expressed his viewpoints regarding the opposition between Turán and Iran in a lengthy philosophical treatise published in the periodical *Athenaeum* in 1839.[6] The use of the word *Turán* has one common characteristic in the cited works of Domokos, Kállay, Gebhardi/Kultsár, and Pulszky: it was in nearly all instances based on Western technical literature and therefore emerged in only second- or thirdhand form in the Hungarian language.

The Iran-Turan opposition that developed around the term originated in Persia sometime during the later Sasanian era between the third and seventh centuries AD in epic fragments (such as the *Khwaday-Namag*, which was put into writing around the seventh century, and other primarily eastern Iranian oral traditions) that Ferdowsi incorporated, in the vicinity of the year 1000, into a gigantic epos, the *Shahnameh* (The book of kings), a sort of Persian *Iliad*. With the *Shahnameh*, Firdausi set the Iranian national tradition prior to the Islamic conquest down in writing, and his use of the word Ṭurān established the dichotomy, placing Iran and the world beyond its limes, Turan, in opposition to one another. However, the notion of the region of Turan that existed during the Sasanian era did not necessarily designate the nomad-inhabited lands lying to the north of Iran between the Amu Darya and Syr Darya Rivers but rather Baluchistan, which today is part of Pakistan.[7] According to Ferdowsi, conflict arose among the sons of King Fereydun—Salm, Iraj, and Tur—and as a consequence of this murderous internecine war, Tur was banished. After becoming the king of all the nomads of the steppes, Tur continually attacked his father's former empire. One of Turan's mythical descendants, King Afrasiab, became the greatest sovereign of all the Turanians and the embodiment of the equestrian hero of the prairielands. Later Turkic historiographers identified the Turanians as Turks, although this name had previously pertained primarily to the eastern Iranian peoples of Central Asia. It is important to note that these peoples accepted this designation, and in fact, the quality of being Turanian did not necessarily entail negative connotations in Iranian culture. The term reached Europe via the Ottomans, for whom the Persians served as the bearers of high culture in much the same way that the Greeks did for the Romans. Thus, when interest in the East emerged in Europe in the seventeenth century, works dealing with this subject often first reached readers on the continent via the Turks. The first Western partial translation of the *Shahnameh* emanated from the pen of English Orientalist Sir William Jones (1746–1794), who had been in close connection with the Habsburg diplomat and Orientalist Count Károly Reviczky (1737–1793), himself the first European translator of the Persian poet Hafez (into Latin).[8]

These examples perhaps serve to demonstrate the fact that Persophilia constituted an inherent component of the early Hungarian image of the East. The assessment of the Turks in Hungary was contradictory at the very least. Although Hungarian public opinion later regarded Turkey's granting of refuge to Ferenc Rákóczi II and his followers, known in Hungarian as *bujdosó*, in a positive light, this attitude was still far from being general in the eighteenth century. Let's not forget that between 1787 and 1791, the Habsburg Empire was at war with the sultan and that the existence of the military frontier was a permanent reminder to all Hungarian patriots of who was threatening the borders of the country. At the same time, receptivity to Persian culture, perhaps in the form of enthusiasm for the notion of Parthian-Hungarian kinship or Persian literature, was not at all unusual during this period. Hungarian poet Mihály Csokonai Vitéz attempted desperately to obtain Reviczky's translations of Hafez during the final years of his life, even writing a poem in honor of the Persian poet and using Eastern poetic meter in his work. József Kármán also translated Persian literature, and in the 1850s, János Arany wrote about Firdausi as one of his greatest inspirations as an author. Furthermore, Arany planned to base his unwritten Csaba trilogy on the Iran-Turan opposition. There was a strikingly large number of people who showed pro-Persian sympathies and were connected to the city of Szeged within the group of Hungarian "proto-Turanists" who publicly raised the issue of the Eastern origin and kinship of the Hungarians: these people ranged from András Dugonics to János Jerney and István Maróthy, the Hungarian physician who was professionally active in Persia. The people who belonged to this group, which could still not be called Turanist, and generally all of those who took an interest in the Eastern origin of the Hungarians were able to draw on the Werbőczyist historical view that since the sixteenth century had regarded the nobility as an ethnically distinct class descended from the Scythians. For these people, identification with the steppe cultures did not cause significant difficulty.[9] The Ottoman influence contributed to this, for, as we have seen, in many cases Persian culture arrived to Hungary through Turkish (and even Western) intermediaries. We can mention Orientalism and the evolution of Eastern research in western Europe and their subsequent slow introduction in Hungary as a third factor. During the first half of the nineteenth century, the Finno-Ugric affiliation of the Hungarian language was still just an option: although János Sajnovics had already traveled through the Lapland and in 1770 published his famous *Demonstratio* in an attempt to prove the Finno-Ugric linguistic relationship, Antal Reguly, who provided the research of this linguistic affinity with true momentum, departed on his expedition only in 1839 and was unable to publish all of the results of this journey. The comparative linguistic method was likewise in its early stages of development at this time, thus providing broad leeway for the formation of various ties of kinship between peoples, not only in Hungary but also in other countries.[10]

One of the first great figures in Hungarian scholarly Eastern research, the Transylvanian Sándor Kőrösi Csoma (1784–1842), also left for the East in 1819 on a quest to find the kinsfolk of the Hungarians; however, he planned to search for them neither in Turkey nor in the presumed territory of Turan but in the mystical homeland of the Yugurs/Uyghurs farther to the east. The Székely scholar also played with the idea of Hungarian-Sanskrit name affinity. Everybody acknowledges Kőrösi Csoma's unparalleled achievements in the domain of Tibetology. During this period, domestic public opinion also focused on the scholar whose research surrounding the ancestors of the Hungarians had carried him away to distant lands: in 1833, Kőrösi Csoma was elected a member of the Hungarian Scholarly Society, the precursor of the Hungarian Academy of Sciences, and his reports appeared in the much-read Hungarian scientific press, albeit not in large number. With his astounding output, devotion, monkish asceticism, incessantly proclaimed Hungarianness, and death in a foreign land, Kőrösi Csoma became a topos of Hungarian oriental studies.[11] He was the archetype of the scholar who was ready to make any sacrifice in his search for the ancient homeland and was, moreover, a Székely originating from the "most ancient Hungarians." His character and work became a reference for Hungarian Orientalists and in a certain sense for Turanism as well, whether this pertained to a periodical, an association, or a public statue—as we will see later.

Thus, beginning in the 1840s, the term *Turán* became part of Hungarian scholarly discourse, while the fountainhead of the frequently mentioned *Turanian curse* (providing a sort of ironic self-definition) can also be found sometime during this period. Arnold Ipolyi's *Magyar mythologia* (1854) focused on the topic of the "curse" and, although he did not use the attributive *Turanian*, essentially described the meaning of this term in the chapter entitled "Ancient curse" (*Ős átok*):

> In the foreground of other national legends ethno-genetic traditions regarding the ancient division and conflict of peoples are again pressing forward, so that one people is separated from another and certain denominations of people, pushed out or forced to emigrate from among the indigenous inhabitants, conduct eternal, incessant war against one another for centuries on end. . . . Numerous legends in these immense myths bear this unique consciousness, as a sin that constitutes the unfortunate cause of the cursed life on earth; and namely the legend of the Iranian hero in which we gain the tradition of the century-long struggle of the Iranian and Turanian peoples.[12]

The term *Turanian curse* appears only in journalism published at the beginning of the twentieth century but to a massive degree at this time. The author Ferenc Herczeg likely coined this expression.[13]

In order for us to understand the priorities of the early seekers of the Hungarian ancient homeland, we must take a glance at Hungarian history. Beginning in the fifteenth century, Hungary came under increasing Ottoman pressure, which led to the tragic defeat at the Battle of Mohács and the collapse of the medieval kingdom of Hungary in 1526. The country was soon divided into three parts: the Habsburg emperors ruled the western and northern parts as Hungarian kings beginning in 1541, while the Ottoman Empire occupied the southern and central parts of the country for almost 150 years, and the principality of Transylvania came into existence on the eastern marches as a relatively autonomous Ottoman vassal state. The Habsburgs extended their sovereignty to include the entire country following the wars of liberation at the end of the seventeenth century, although their curtailment of traditional Hungarian noble liberty, attempts at centralization, and, above all, imposition of frequently excessive tax burdens often incited the Hungarians to rebellion. Following the Rákóczi-led rebellion (1703–1711), relative prosperity arrived to the country. In the 1820s, liberal-nationalist groups within the nobility began to form plans aimed at modernizing the country that clashed with the increasingly rigid conservatism of the Viennese court. This reform era led to revolution in 1848–1849 and then to a war of independence against Habsburg rule that Vienna was able to defeat only with the help of Russian czarist forces in the summer of 1849. Hundreds of people were executed in the course of the ensuing reprisals, and many thousands were thrown into prison: a significant community of Hungarian political exiles formed in western Europe and beyond the Atlantic with the former leader of the war of independence, Lajos Kossuth (1802–1894), in the forefront. Following periods of repression and, subsequently, transition, Vienna and the Habsburg sovereign, the young Franz Joseph I, were compelled to come to an agreement with the Hungarian political elite: this produced the 1867 compromise (Ausgleich) that furnished the Hungarian government residing in Pest-Buda (from 1873 in Budapest) with extensive rights. The dual monarchy came into existence, which endured until the end of the First World War in 1918 and made unparalleled economic and social modernization possible in the Hungarian half of the empire.

The Persophilia of those who took an interest in the East in Hungary gradually transformed into Turkophilia after 1848–1849. Sympathy toward Turkey grew in conjunction with the country's provision of sanctuary to Kossuth and his fellow émigrés, as well as a decrease in the perceived threat from Turkey and increase in the perceived threat from Russia and Pan-Slavists within Hungarian popular opinion. Among the manifestations of this were gestures such as a Hungarian university student delegation's presentation of a ceremonial sword to Turkish commander-in-chief Abdul Kerim in 1877, the Transylvanian formation of a legion to help the Turks in the Balkan wars, and the taking to Hungary in 1906 of the ashes of eighteenth-century rebel leader Ferenc Rákóczi II; his foster father, Imre Thököly; and their bujdosó followers who had died in exile in Turkey. The developments that were meanwhile taking place within Hungarian scholarship, which can be grouped primarily around the person and activity of Ármin Vámbéry (1832–1913), chimed with the robust pro-Turkey sentiment that had emerged within pro-independence public opinion.[14]

Vámbéry, the son of an impoverished Talmudist who died shortly after Vámbéry's birth, was in all regards a product of the nineteenth century and Hungarian liberalism. The open and intelligent native of Szentgyörgy (Svätý Jur, Slovakia), who never took the examination needed to receive his high school diploma despite the fact that he spoke around a half dozen languages with spectacular fluency, was treated as a wunderkind in Pest during the 1850s. The Hungarian intelligentsia that had been forced into silence following the failure of the war of independence was proud of the prodigiously talented Vámbéry, who had undergone the process of Magyarization, changing his surname and adopting the Calvinist religion (considered to be "pure Magyar confession"). In 1857, with the support of the prominent liberal writer and political official József Eötvös, Vámbéry made a trip to Constantinople, where he acquired extraordinarily good connections within the sultanic court. He was not yet thirty years old when he was elected a member of the Hungarian Academy of Sciences. Following his return home from Constantinople, he made two more trips to Central Asia and Persia, in disguise and under the name Reshit Efendi.[15] Vámbéry had the opportunity to travel to the Central Asian emirates before the Russian conquest and published his singular observations in highly successful books; in fact, he became at least as popular in Great Britain as he was in Hungary. Vámbéry remained until the end of his life an admirer of the British Empire, for which—as has recently come to light—he performed intelligence services as well.[16] He met with the young Theodor Herzl and through his English friends helped the Zionist movement take its first steps. Before his death, Vámbéry allegedly converted to the Baha'i faith, a universalist religion that had broken away from the Shiite branch of Islam.[17] Vámbéry wrote prolifically and well, and although he never received regular academic training, he was granted a university professorship in Budapest in 1865. However, the Catholic teachers at the university were not eager to accept among them a Jew who had converted to Calvinism: Vámbéry requested and received an audience with Franz Joseph, who then appointed him professor without the approval of the faculty. Vámbéry wrote cheerfully about this incident, referring to the Jesuit Péter Pázmány who had founded the university: "So I just screwed the priests, because the emperor appointed me and thus I am the first Calvinist to consume Pázmán's capital [purse]."[18]

Vámbéry became a founding figure in the fields of Hungarian Turkology and broadly defined Eastern scholarship; almost all of those researchers who dealt with Turkish and Arabic studies and whose names we will encounter several times in connection to the Turanist movement were his students. His influence can be felt to the present day within Hungarian Orientalism. Hungarian liberalism did not merely place Vámbéry's name on its banner—he himself believed in its early ideas. The spirit of Islam did not affect him deeply, and he was a convinced believer in the civilizing mission of the Hungarian and British nations. He regarded both the Ottomanist and Pan-Islamic modernization of the Ottoman Empire to be impracticable.

Among the new ideas, Pan-Turkism, which found its feet at the end of the nineteenth century, stood close to his thought. In an indirect manner, via his international prestige, Vámbéry became an inspiration for the birth of both Hungarian Turanism and the movement promoting the unification of the Turkic peoples. He engaged in correspondence with one of the ideologues of the movement, the Volga Tatar Yusuf Akçura (1876–1935), and near the end of his life, acknowledging the ambitions of the Russian Tatars, he encouraged the new movement in the following way: "Because if the common Turkish literary language could be successfully created among Tatars, the Kirghiz, the Sharts, the Bashkirs, the Uzbeks, and the Turkmens with the influence of Russia's more progressive Mohammedans, the possibility that, aligning themselves closer to one another, the fragments of the Turkish people now living in separation from one another would unite with one another and form a nation numbering at least 50 million souls. The excessive power of the West, though particularly of Russia, can for the time being disrupt and delay this process, though can hardly stop the final outcome."[19] Pan-Turkism originated primarily outside Turkish-language territories, and its first ideologues were Crimean or Russian Tatars (Ismail Gaspirali and Yusuf Akçura) or Azeris (Ahmed Agayev and Ali Huseynzade). This system of viewpoints suffered from the perpetual problems of how to place itself within a larger Pan-Turanist affiliation and what to do with the non-Muslim peoples who could be regarded as Turanian, such as the Hungarians, for example. In order to remedy these problems, Akçura attempted to introduce the dual concepts of Lesser Turan and Greater Turan, the former referring to that of the Muslim Turkish peoples and the latter to all Turanian peoples. However, the majority of those who propounded Pan-Turkism were not receptive to Akçura's propositions: in 1914, the poet Ahmed Hikmet declared with regard to these options that "no matter what happens, the Hungarians will remain orphans."[20]

Vámbéry's role did not assert itself quite so indirectly in the emergence of Hungarian Turanism. The "Ugrian-Turkish war" that broke out between Vámbéry and the linguists József Budenz (1836–1892) and Pál Hunfalvy (1810–1891) in connection with the publication of Vámbéry's book *A magyarok eredete* (Origin of the Hungarians) represented a decisive moment in the development of Hungarian ancient history and linguistics and, indirectly, in the entire Hungarian national consciousness.[21] Today, it is hard to imagine the milieu and the fervor generated by Budenz's article "Jelentés Vámbéry Ármin magyar-török szóegyeztetéseiről" (Report on Ármin Vámbéry's

Hungarian-Turkish word correlations) published in the periodical *Nyelvtudo-mányi Közlemények* in 1871 (in which he reacted to an article that Vámbéry had published in 1869) and the 1882 work responding to this. The ferocious battle that took place in academic journals, daily newspapers, and every existing public forum throughout almost the entire decade of the 1880s had begun. The issue of whether Vámbéry had made correct use of the phonetic accords from his previous Chagatai studies to prove that Hungarian was fundamentally a Turkic language and that the Finno-Ugric influence on it was negligible obviously concerned the general public to a lesser degree. The determination of the linguistic—and consequently ethnic—origin of the Hungarians was at stake. The debate was interwoven with scientific policy motifs (what was the place of comparative linguistics in the emerging domain of Hungarian scholarship?), the battle over the legitimacy of the very newly established Finno-Ugric linguistic affinity (Finno-Ugric linguistics was introduced as an obligatory subject at the University of Budapest in 1872), and the resentment that part of the academic world felt as a result of Vámbéry's overly facile pen, the circumstances surrounding his appointment, and the deficiencies in his training.

Even today, many regard the opposition of Budenz, a German from the German Empire, and Hunfalvy, a German from Hungary, to Vámbéry's "true Hungarian" attitude to be pro-Habsburg intrigue. József Budenz (nicknamed Yusuf) and Ármin Vámbéry (nicknamed Reshid) together kept company with Orientalist, Hungarian Academy of Sciences member, and Reformed pastor Áron Szilády (alias Harun) during their student years. Budenz himself had previously supported the notion of Turkish-Hungarian linguistic affinity, and Hunfalvy was by nature disinclined to participate in pro-Habsburg machinations of any kind.[22] The tone of the dispute was in many cases not very edifying, and Vámbéry's opponents did not refrain from personal attacks. In general, those who coalesced around Vámbéry were generally not linguists (with the exception of József Thury): among them were the anthropologist Aurél Török and the historian Henrik Marczali, while on the other side, we find primarily those associated with the emerging field of linguistics. Vámbéry eventually conceded that he had suffered defeat in this debate and that his position was for the most part incorrect. However, current scholarship recognizes the legitimacy of the question that Vámbéry had posed and numerous ideas that he had put forward: some of his word correlations proved to be enduring, although his Turkish-Hungarian word agreements are not regarded as evidence of

Fig. 2.1. One of the founding fathers of Hungarian Orientalism: Ármin/Arminius Vámbéry (1832–1913). Attribution: Magyar Földrajzi Múzeum, Germanus-hagyaték, Strelisky Lipót felvétele.

ancient kinship but of old Turkish loan words that had become part of the Hungarian language.[23]

The way in which the affair surrounding ethnic kinship and the origin of the Hungarian language had played out within scientific circles was not to everybody's liking. The aristocrat Jenő Zichy (1837–1906), an enthusiastic art collector who took an interest in the East, wrote to one of his followers after Vámbéry's defeat: "Because I must meet with You and moreover in the interest of the Concern. This is by all means necessary, because both of us find the Hunfalvy doctrines to be incorrect! and we are looking for a proper point of departure for the Hungarian Nation![24]" Count Zichy did not satisfy himself with mere protestations and promises: between 1895 and 1898, he led three expeditions to Russia (the Caucasus and the Volga regions) at his own expense, even reaching as far as China during his third expedition. Since Zichy's ambition was to make valid declarations regarding the origin of the Hungarian language, he took scholars with him on his voyages. Among them were linguist Gábor Szentkatolnai Bálint, ethnographer János Jankó, archaeologist Béla Pósta (1862–1919), and geographer Jenő Cholnoky (we will encounter almost all of these names again later in this book). The results of these expeditions (which often consisted largely of looking over Russian museum collections) were published in eight books that appeared in Hungarian, French, and German.[25]

As a result of scholarly criticism that had been voiced with regard to his first two expeditions, Zichy proved willing to take Finno-Ugric linguist József Pápay with him on his third expedition, during which the future language professor at the University of Debrecen conducted research among the northern Ostyaks. Memoirs and diaries regarding this expedition reveal that personal conflicts prevented it from becoming truly scientific in nature. The participating scholars did not get along with one another and occasionally skipped out on the entire expedition. If they did agree on something, it was to present ultimatums to Count Zichy, who showed himself to be quite parsimonious. Angry entries from the diary of Béla Pósta are rather telling: "swindle," "tourist-like journey," "dilettantism," "Zichy is getting himself worked up about absurdities," "Zichy was blowing a lot of hot air," "*faché* and reconciliation with the count" (who rushed off in offense the next morning despite this reconciliation).[26] In addition to Zichy's stinginess, the scholars resented that Zichy did not want to dig or collect, instead bargaining with antique dealers over items of uncertain origin; was fed up with his own expedition; spent his time among local aristocrats; and in the Kuban plain, suspected every heap of earth to be a *kurgan* (a tumulus over a single grave, rather widespread among nomadic peoples of the Pontic-Caspian steppe). Moreover, the count spoke disdainfully of Finnish kinship before Finnish and Russian scholars and introduced researchers who were proud of their scientific renown as if they were members of his royal household.[27] In spite of this discord, the written summary of the research done during the expedition (written primarily by Pósta) is a serious scientific work, and the participants, especially the linguist Bálint and the geographer Cholnoky, profited greatly from the journey from a scientific perspective, and their data collected appeared in their books all along their career. And there was a certain grandezza in Zichy's behavior: following the publication of the final volume of his account, he presented Pósta with a dress sword and jewels to be worn with traditional Hungarian noble attire. The Zichy expedition was not a novelty: earlier, in 1877, Béla Széchenyi had gone on a journey to the East on which he took Lajos Lóczy and Gábor Bálint. Széchenyi published the results of this expedition in a three-volume book, in exchange for which the Hungarian Academy of Sciences elected him to serve as an honorary member and the University of Budapest accorded him an honorary doctoral degree.[28] However, unlike Zichy, Széchenyi did not take finding the Hungarian ancient homeland as the mission of his expedition; instead, he conducted geological and geographical observations and collected rock and plant samples. The benefit of this expedition in terms of ancient history was that the greatly talented, although eccentric and lonely, linguist Bálint, who joined Széchenyi after making Mongolian and Kalmyk collections, became convinced of the relationship between the Hungarian and Tamil languages. In the course of Zichy's expedition, Bálint—after learning the language—became tempted by the notion of Hungarian-Kabardian linguistic affinity. Bálint, whom Vámbéry warmly supported, represented the most promising figure active in Hungarian Eastern linguistics, and he very soon received a Russian scholarship. After returning home, he became a private lecturer at the University of Budapest. Bálint supported Vámbéry's position during the "Ugrian-Turkish war." In 1879, feeling ignored and disillusioned with Hungarian scientific life, he left Hungary. It is not known precisely what Bálint did for the subsequent period of more than a decade; he lived at different locations in the Ottoman Empire before taking up residence in Athens. A public campaign emerged among the Székelys to lure Bálint back to Hungary, and as a result, he became a professor of Ural-Altaic languages at the university in Kolozsvár (Cluj-Napoca, Romania) in 1893.

Bálint was a reclusive figure who held an unrelenting hatred for the "Budapest gang," the "German race," and the entire "game of Finno-Ugric kinship," which "homeless, provincial Baltic Germans inflated so that they could become Russian academics."[29] He was a member of the circle of intellectuals that formed in Kolozsvár at the beginning of the twentieth century whose members—Béla Pósta, historian Sándor Márki (1853–1925), and geography professors Jenő Cholnoky and Vilmos Pröhle, who taught in the city during the First World War—became the vanguard of the Turanist movement and played key roles in the formulation of the ideology connected to it. Bálint is an important personality insofar as those who have rediscovered Turanism in the present day frequently want to see in him the "Turanist" man of letters who is crippled by official scholarship. Márki was the founder of the historical outlook of the Turanist circle that did not abound with historians, but it would be a mistake to regard him as a Hungarian nationalist heated by chauvinistic passions. Although Márki maintained strongly pro-independence sentiments, during the period in which he taught in Arad, he wrote sympathetically about Avram Iancu, the Romanian who led rebels against the Hungarian government in connection with the events of 1848–1849 and, with his biography, became a pioneer in changing the image of György Dózsa, transforming the leader of the sixteenth-century peasant war into a pioneer of democracy; Márki was the first person to propose the erection of a statue honoring the peasant leader. In addition to his astonishingly extensive historiographical work (he underwrote more than a thousand scholarly papers), he was also one of the pioneers in the methodology of teaching history and was a member of the Hungarian Academy of Sciences before the age of forty.[30]

In his summaries and articles published in the 1920s, Márki strove to inject Hungarian historical scholarship with the Turanist outlook and attempted to find a new approach with which to explain the Mongol conquest of 1241–1242 (which is known in Hungarian vernacular as the "Tatar invasion") and the Turkish occupation of the sixteenth and seventeenth centuries within a Turanist context.[31] The result was not convincing in every regard: in both instances, Márki highlighted the effort of Mongol and Turkish leaders to come to an agreement through which they would offer their "Turanian brothers" the possibility of alliance or, at least, allied status. At the same time, Márki attempted to portray the struggle against the Turks and the Tatars as an internecine war that stemmed primarily from the narrow-mindedness of Hungarian leaders. Moreover, he emphasized the assimilatory capability of the Hungarians, reflected in their rapid integration of the fragments of the Turanian peoples who had settled among them, as well as the significant contributions that the assimilated peoples had made to the country. Within the context of the Treaty of Trianon, it is worthwhile to regard Márki's writings about the "8,000 kilometers of tillage" stretching between Beijing and Budapest, "the granary of Eurasia," and the Turanian civilization as the basis for Mesopotamian culture as evidence of estrangement from the West.[32] Márki's endeavor is interesting because it attempted to synthesize everything that the Hungarian geographers, archaeologists, and ethnographers who looked to the East had put together, and although he did not proclaim the permanent separation from the West, he regarded his movement as a synonym for a new "purified humanity."

Among the Asian-research expeditions conducted in the period before the First World War, the two voyages that György Almásy (1867–1933), the father of László Almásy (the figure who inspired the protagonist of Michael Ondaatje's novel *The English Patient*), took to Turkestan in 1900 and 1906 deserve mention. Almásy, who also wrote a book about his journeys, nearly had to make excuses for the fact that he could not carry out extensive research regarding all aspects of Asian kinship, thus reflecting the change in expectations since the Zichy expedition: "It is not necessary for me to note that national traditions and the impelling example of those who have gone before me cannot have left me unaffected and that I too endeavored in accordance with my strength and the given situation to observe and pass judgment upon the ethnic particularities of the encountered peoples not only in a general ethnographic sense, but primarily from a special Hungarian perspective." Unable to make a decision with regard to the question of Finno-Ugric or Turkic-Tatar kinship, Almásy added, "These are very detailed questions and I remained extremely far away from contributing more valuable and abundant data to their clarification. Since the objective of our expedition moved in another direction and I was able to deal with the maze of linguistic and ethnographic questions only in passing, furtively so to speak."[33] Almásy's collections, particularly those obtained from the Kyrgyz, enriched the Hungarian National Museum Ethnographic Collection (the predecessor of the current Ethnographic Museum) with materials and knowledge that are valid to the present day. He took the young geographer Gyula Prinz, who later taught at the University of Pécs, with him on his second expedition. However, the Turanian curse unleashed its poison again here: the scholar had a falling out with the financer of the expedition, and they penetrated the heart of Asia separately. Later on Prinz—as almost all Hungarian geographers— became a member (albeit not a very active one) of the Turanian Society. Prinz was presumably one of the last people to use the term *Turan* as a descriptive concept within Hungarian scholarship: his book *Utazásaim Belső-Ázsiában: Nagy-Turán földrajzi ábrázata* (My travels in Inner Asia: Geographical features of Greater Turan) was published in Budapest in 1945.

However, not all of the Hungarian travelers were wealthy aristocrats: Benedek Baráthosi Balogh (1870–1945) was a teacher, first at a primary school and then at a state civil school. Baráthosi Balogh initially pursued a career in poetry but then happily announced to poet Andor Kozma, the editor of the daily newspaper *Pesti Hírlap*: "It was a good year ago that we did away with the rhymester in me," adding that "I am departing for Japan by way of Siberia in order to place my studies on firm foundations on the basis of the true approach. My objective is to make a pilgrimage throughout the peoples known and believed to be related to us and make this into the subject of a linguistic and historical, that is, ethnographical study."[34]

In spite of his lack of money, Baráthosi Balogh traveled through Japan, Korea, Manchuria, and the Far Eastern territories of Russia on several occasions with his wife and made collections among the Ainu, the Tunguz, and the Mongols that still form the foundation of the Ethnographic Museum's Japanese and "related peoples of Russia" materials.[35] Baráthosi Balogh financed his voyages partially through the sale of collected items and even documentation to public collections in not only Hungary but also other countries, such as the Museum für Völkerkunde in Hamburg, Germany.[36] Although Baráthosi Balogh admittedly followed Kőrösi Csoma's footsteps in his search for the related peoples of the Hungarians, his Ainu collections—which as it happens have nothing to do with Hungarian ancient history—have, for example, remained unique until the present day. He also made collections with Finno-Ugric and Samoyedic peoples, although he was not too voluminous about them: his Nenets collections, for example, have never been put in order. Baráthosi Balogh visited other related peoples as well as other scattered peoples in eastern Siberia: he was a thorough and passionate collector, though was not of explicitly scholarly temperament. He did not manage to organize his collections and even lacked the training to do so. Moreover, Baráthosi Balogh was not always so fortunate with his voyages: in 1904–1905, the Russo-Japanese War drastically restricted his movement, while during another journey, he came down with typhoid fever. In 1914, at the time of the outbreak of the First World War, the Russian authorities interned him in Khabarovsk, from where he managed only with great difficulty to return home, though his collections remained behind and were permanently lost.[37] Baráthosi Balogh was a member of the Turanian movement from the very beginning and together with Árpád Zempléni wrote a Japanese-themed play.[38] He proclaimed increasingly radical viewpoints beginning in the 1920s. His eighteen-volume (originally planned to be twenty-four volume) series of books, *Baráthosi Turáni Könyvei* (Baráthosi's Turanian books), partially reflects this transformation in his thinking.

We must not forget that the great Eastern art collections featuring Japanese, Chinese, Indian, and other Asian works of art in accordance with the fashion of Orientalism that had filtered in from western Europe originated from this period.[39] Among the first Hungarian collectors was none other than Ferenc Pulszky, who became acquainted with Eastern artists under the guidance of his uncle Gábor Fejérváry, and during his period of exile even studied the Sanskrit language. Pulszky continued to expand his collection while he served as director of the National Museum; however, at this time there still existed a unified image of the East, and thus, his collection did not focus on one region or country.[40] Attila Szemere (the son of the prime minister at the time of the 1848–1849 revolution and war of independence) traveled to Japan during the first half of the 1880s and established his art collection, which the Museum of Applied Arts in Budapest and the Ottó Herman Museum in Miskolc acquired partially through donation and partially through purchase.[41] The Moravian-born Ferenc Hopp (1833–1919) became wealthy through the manufacture and sale of optical equipment, thus enabling him to establish an art collection and build a villa on Andrássy Avenue in Budapest.

In his will, Hopp bequeathed both his four-thousand-piece collection and his villa to the Hungarian state under the condition that they be used to found an Eastern museum.[42] His idea regarding an Eastern museum had already aroused the interest of Szemere as well, but the plan was only realized following Hopp's death in 1919. The Ferenc Hopp Museum was established under the direction of art historian and important Turanist network organizer Zoltán Felvinczi Takács (1880–1964). The museum generally oversaw the nearly one-thousand-piece collection that Museum of Applied Arts founding director György Ráth left to the state, which is currently housed at the György Ráth Museum in Budapest. During the first years of the twentieth century, titular bishop and ecclesiastical writer Péter Vay (1863–1948) received a considerable amount of money from the education ministry in order to purchase primarily Japanese woodcuts for the newly inaugurated Museum of Fine Arts in Budapest during his trip to the Far East. These materials constituted the core of the Japanese exhibition at the museum that drew twenty-six thousand visitors in the year after its opening in 1910.[43] The foundation of the Déri Museum in Debrecen at the end of the 1920s represented one of the last ripples emanating from this Eastern wave. This new museum housed the partially Eastern (Japanese and Chinese) collection belonging to Viennese industrialist Frigyes Déri. This collection included the Samurai armor and swords that I often admired as a child during visits to my grandparents in Debrecen.

The appearance of the culture of Finland in Hungary initiated processes that were parallel in many respects to the Eastern vogue (and the enthusiasm that Japan's surprise victory in the Russo-Japanese War had aroused). News regarding the great sensation that the Finnish pavilion had created at the 1900 world's fair in Paris reached Hungary as well.[44] Finnish artists and architects who had previously maintained good Hungarian contacts—such as the painter and industrial artist and architect Akseli Gallen-Kallela (1865–1931) and the architect Eliel Saarinen (1873–1950), who designed the initial element of the singular body of architecture in Columbus, Indiana, the First Christian Church, in 1942—worked on the pavilion. For a significant group of Hungarian artists (such as those who worked at the art colony in Gödöllő), the Finnish example, whose renewal was based on a peasant society's traditions and the artistic reflection of this, became one to be followed. Gallen-Kallela's Hungarian friends took him to Transylvania, where the Finnish artist dazzled villagers with his astonishing cross-country skiing skills.[45] Gallen-Kallela held two greatly successful exhibitions in Budapest in 1907–1908 and illustrated Béla Vikár's translation of the *Kalevala* published in 1909. Many of those active at the Gödöllő art colony, including Ede Toroczkai Wigand, István Medgyaszay, and Sándor Nagy, later became leading Turanists. They gained much inspiration from this connection. The sudden appearance of Japan and Japanese culture on the international stage, the internationally visible renewal of Finland, and news arriving about Pan-Turkism stirred in many people the feeling that a "Turanian awakening" was about to take place in the world and that Hungary could play a role in it.

Two conditions were necessary in order for the diverse sensitivities outlined thus far to give birth to the Turanian idea and for it to assume form in Hungarian public life: a scientific framework and a political will. German-born British linguist and Indologist Max Müller (1823–1900) provided the former: in his classification formulated in the 1850s, Müller divided the languages of the world into three major groups: Semitic, Aryan, and Turanian. He examined languages in historical-linguistic and evolutionary terms and categorized them into groups based on their level of grammatical development. The Turanian language group was a catchall: any language that could not be classified as either Semitic or Aryan was placed into it. Even within this system, Müller classified Hungarian among the Finno-Ugric languages, emphasizing the nomadic character of this language family—that is, comparing historical-social categories with linguistic categories. Müller, three of whose books were published in Hungarian, personally presented his ideas in Hungary and was even elected to serve as an external member of the Hungarian Academy of Sciences in 1874.[46] However, Müller's theses quickly proved to be incorrect, and the designation Ural-Altaic was already beginning to replace the word "Turanian" in the scientific discourse in the 1890s. In any case, the scientific concept had come into existence and did not go out of fashion even after its repudiation: in his inaugural lecture delivered at the Hungarian Academy of Sciences in 1905, archaeologist Géza Nagy immediately affirmed that he still regarded the Turanian category to be useful, albeit not in a Müllerian sense, and that he always regarded "the peoples that belonged to the Ural-Altaic language family or can at least be counted among them" to be part of this classification.[47] Nagy used this category in this way throughout most of his nearly one-hundred-page work. The concept thus maintained scientific relevance for a short time following its appearance and gained wide usage in academic gazettes published in Hungary at the beginning of the twentieth century.

The scientific will existed, while the political resolve could only come from the government side. The concept of the Eastern—primarily Balkan— mission of the Hungarians appeared with increasing strength in public thought beginning in the final years of the nineteenth century. Historian and common ministry of finance official Lajos Thallóczy (1857–1916) was the prophet of the Hungarian advance into the Balkans and presence in the region. Hungarian historiography has not yet produced a scholarly work regarding Thallóczy's life, though any future biography will certainly require strong colors.[48] Thallóczy, who was born in Kassa (Košice, Slovakia) with the surname Strommer, was a friend and university companion of Sándor Márki. He started off as a historian and, although he enjoyed a nice career in the common administration of the dual monarchy, always remained devoted to his historical work: he became a corresponding member of the Hungarian Academy of Sciences in 1883, a full member in 1895, and president of the Hungarian Historical Society in 1913. His house in Vienna was a meeting place for Hungarian bureaucrats working in the imperial capital and visiting Hungarian political officials. Many of the leading figures—primarily historians and archivists—associated with the history of Hungarian Turanism, from Gyula Szekfű to István Medgyaszay, turned up at Thallóczy's residence at one time or another. The unmarried Thallóczy, who sometimes appeared in public wearing quite fantastic attire, operated the so-called Deli Büzér (Handsome stinky) club at his home on Traungasse that was mostly for men, to whom the appointed club leader, known as the Büzérnagy (Grand stinky), referred using a wide range of nicknames. An excellent female cook whom Thallóczy sent on study trips in order to learn new recipes provided the culinary delights served at the club's festive dinners. Thallóczy wrote in the club's regulations that as a matter of fundamental principle "I give wine, not beer. Nobody gets a cigar at my place, not even for money."[49] Thallóczy could transmit his sweeping momentum to other club members with iron will; he helped many and quarreled with many others. In addition, his position as department chief at the Ministry of Finance and the trusting relationship that he allegedly maintained with emperor and king Franz Joseph I guaranteed his influence.

However, Thallóczy was much more than the Hungarian enfant terrible of the imperial city. The fact that common finance minister Béni Kállay, the governor of occupied Bosnia, was Thallóczy's mentor served to strengthen the interest of the latter in Hungarian-Balkan relations. The historian-bureaucrat was convinced that the increase of Hungary's influence in the Balkans was a condition of the strengthening of the country within the dual monarchy. Thallóczy developed several plans aimed at achieving this objective. However, it is important to note that his ideas did not entail colonization: the intellectually remarkable Finance Ministry official published an anonymous concept for a Bosnian history book and played a significant role in the Albanian national movement via his connections and counsel as well.[50] For instance, Thallóczy played a noteworthy role in the formation of the cult of Skanderbeg. His name almost always appears in connection with justifications of attempts to expand influence in the Balkans that took place during the mature period of Hungarian Turanism, be it a matter of Hungarian education in Constantinople, a scientific institution, or scholarships for Bosnian, Albanian, or Bulgarian students to study in Hungary.[51] Thallóczy was killed in a train accident in Herceghalom, Hungary, in 1916 as he returned from Franz Joseph's funeral to his post in occupied Serbia, where he served as civilian governor.

Edward Said's 1978 book *Orientalism* was a paradigm-changing work in Western scholarly thinking and continues to significantly determine postcolonial criticism. In his examination of the system surrounding the West's experience of the East, Said relied primarily on English and French examples, from which he developed his ideas regarding the Orientalist scientific discourse that took place in Europe in the nineteenth and twentieth centuries and its relationship with power and, at the same time, its connections to colonialism. The author himself noted that the German Eastern outlook had remained outside the sphere of his book's investigations, not to mention the issue of the Orientalism that predominated in Vienna, which played a key role in early Eastern research, or the Central European states.[52] The objective of the Hungarian Eastern outlook—as the Hungarian proponents of Turanism could not emphasize strongly enough—was not to colonize but to weave a new network of political, economic, and cultural connections based on ethnic kinship and mutual benefit. And this is not true in this form, since the Hungarian Turanists were the ones who determined what counted as mutual benefit and there were indeed colonialist tones present within Hungarian Turanism. The Turanian idea demands at least as much analysis as Western Orientalism even if it did not start with the Rosetta Stone and Napoleon's Egyptian campaign but with Sándor Kőrösi Csoma and a bleak evening in Ilosva.

Neither can we disregard the Eastern cult of the era: the Turanist-flavored remarks of painter Tivadar Csontváry-Kosztka (1853–1919), the solitary genius of Hungarian modernism, regarding the "scions of Attila" whose mission was to "halt the destructive influence of the dissolute moral life of the Roman Empire";[53] the recurring Eastern (Indian, Japanese, Chinese, and Finno-Ugrian) motifs in the poetry and journalism of Endre Ady; and Mihály Babits's 1908 poem "Turáni induló" (Turanian march), which can be (and has been) interpreted as both a parody and a persiflage, show that the East was in fashion in Hungary during the early years of the twentieth century.[54]

Thus everything was ready by the beginning of the 1900s: debates surrounding the origin and language of the Hungarians, the program for the Hungarian advance into the Balkans and the Middle East, the requirements of a unique brand of Hungarian imperialism, the fashion of the East, the awakening of the "Turanian nations," the frameworks connected to the scientific thought of the era, the transformation of artistic thinking, and the demand for originality, for primordiality. These many threads were just waiting for somebody to weave them together.

Notes

1. Quoted in István Seres, "'Gyöngyös kám'-tól 'Batu mongol-magyar hadjárata'-ig (Abulgázi Bahadir és Rasidaddin krónikáinak első magyar kutatói)," in *A kísérlet folytatódik. II. Nemzetközi Vámbéry-konferencia*, ed. Mihály Dobrovits (Dunaszerdahely [Dunajská Streda]: Lilium Aurum, 2005), 179.

2. Ferencz Kállay, "Szónyomozások," *Tudománytár* 5 (1835): 170.

3. John Malcolm, *Geschichte Persiens von der früesten Periode an bis zur jetzigen Zeit* (Leipzig: Hartleben, 1830).

4. Lajos Albert Gebhardi, József Hegyi, and István Kultsár, *Magyar Országnak históriája*, vol. 2 (Pest, 1803), 263.

5. For example, János Hübner, ed., *Mostani és régi nemzeteket, országokat, tartományokat, városokat, emlékezetre méltó mezővárosokat, helységeket, folyókat, tavakat, tengereket, öblöket, fokokat, szigeteket, hegyeket, erdőket, barlangokat, pénzeket, mértékeket, 's t. e. f. esmértető lexicon*, vol. 1 (Pest: Trattner János, 1816), 45.

6. Ferencz Pulszky, "Irán és Turán," *Athenaeum*, no. 18 (September 1, 1839): 273–79.

7. C. E. Bosworth, "Turan," *Encyclopaedia Iranica* online, accessed on July 2, 2018, http://www.iranicaonline.org/articles/turan.

8. Michael O'Sullivan, "A Hungarian Josephinist, Orientalist, and Bibliophile: Count Karl Reviczky, 1737–1793," *Austrian History Yearbook* 45, (2014): 61–88; László Szörényi, "Perzsául a magyar költészetben," *Tempevölgy* (March 2016): 66–71.

9. See Sándor Bálint, "Maróthy István orvos, Vörösmarty diákkori barátja," Az Országos *Orvostörténeti Könyvtár Közleményei*, no. 43 (1967): 113–22.

10. For the development of the outlook regarding ancient history during this era, see Péter Domokos, *Szkítiától Lappóniáig: A nyelvrokonság és az őstörténet kérdéskörének visszhangja irodalmunkban* (Budapest: Universitas, 1998), 51–104.

11. No monograph has yet been written about Kőrösi Csoma, but there is the classical work by Theodore Duka, *Life and Works of Alexander Csoma de Kőrös* (London: Trübner, 1985). Among the literature dealing with Kőrösi Csoma, Elek Csetri's book can be recommended: *Kőrösi Csoma Sándor* (Kolozsvár [Cluj-Napoca]: Kriterion, 2002).

12. Arnold Ipolyi, *Magyar mythologia* (Pest: Gusztáv Heckenast, 1854), 348–49.

13. Ferenc Herczeg, "1904," *Újság*, January 1, 1904, 1–2.

14. No comprehensive scholarly monograph exists regarding the life of Vámbéry either. Most recently, see David Mandler, *Arminius Vambéry and the British Empire: Between East and West* (Lanham, MD: Lexington Books, 2016); and *Magyar Tudomány* 174, no. 8 (2013), published in honor of him.

15. Vámbéry described these journeys in his best-selling English-language books. See Arminius Vámbéry, *His Life and Adventures* (London: T. Fisher Unwin, 1886).

16. Ferenc Csirkés, "Nemzeti tudomány és nemzetközi politika, Vámbéry Ármin munkásságában," *Magyar Tudomány* 174, no. 8 (2013): 944–51.

17. Miklós Sárközy, "Arminius Vámbéry and the Baha'i Faith," *Bahai Studies Review* 18, no. 1 (2012): 55–82.

18. "Vámbéry Ármin levele Szilády Áronhoz: Koritnica, 1866. július 31," in *Batu kán pesti rokonai*, ed. Iván Kovács Sándor (Pozsony [Bratislava]: Kalligram, 2001), 304.

19. Ármin Vámbéry, "A tatárok kultur-törekvései," *Budapesti Szemle* 35, no. 131 (1907): 369, 376.

20. Quoted in Péter Oláh, "A török és a magyar turanizmus kapcsolata a 20. század első felében," *Keletkutatás* (Spring 2012): 75. With regard to Pan-Turkism, see the already classic work: Jacob M. Landau, *Pan-Turkism: From Irredentism to Cooperation* (London: Hurst&Company, 1995): 7–73. (With a special reference to Vámbéry already in the introduction.)

21. For details regarding this dispute, see János Pusztay, *Az "ugor-török háború" után* (Budapest: Magvető, 1977).

22. For documents regarding their friendship, see Kovács Sándor, *Batu kán pesti rokonai*, 276–307.

23. See Vámbéry Ármin (1832–1913): Kelet-kutató és hagyatéka a Magyar Tudományos Akadémia Könyvtárában website, "Az 'ugor-török háború,'" accessed July 2, 2018, http://vambery.mtak.hu/hu/09.htm.

24. Ferenc Hopp Museum Repository (hereafter, HMA) Ad/5987-2016, Zichy Jenő levele Némäti Kálmánnak, Budapest, 1893. január 2.

25. Jenő Zichy, *Kaukázusi és közép-ázsiai utazásai*, vols. 1–2 (Budapest: Gusztáv Ranschburg, 1897); Jenő Zichy, *Oroszországi és keletázsiai expeditiójának beszámolója* (Budapest: 1899); and Jenő Zichy, *Harmadik ázsiai utazása*, vols. 1–6 (Budapest-Leipzig: Hornyánszky-Hiersemann, 1900–1905).

26. OSZKK, Quart. Hung. 4153, Posta Béla oroszországi naplója, 1897. október 12.–1898. május 1., especially 1897. október 12., 1898. március 19., 21., 31. And Hungarian National Museum–Archaeological Repository, Papers and Documents (hereafter, MNM RAHA) 284 .XXVIII, Posta Béla oroszországi jegyzetei, 1898. május 3-i bejegyzés.

27. See the following brief summary on the *Rénhírek* website: "Zichy Jenő gróf ázsiai expedíciói," June 4, 2010, accessed July 2, 2018, http://renhirek.blogspot.com/2010/06 /zichy-jeno-grof-azsiai-expedicioi.html.

28. Béla Széchenyi, *Gróf Széchenyi Béla keletázsiai utazásának (1877–1880) tudományos eredményei*, vols. 1–3 (Budapest: Kilián, 1890–97).

29. Museum of Ethnography Ethnologic Repository (hereafter, EA) 13148, Sebestyén Gyula hagyatéka, Levelek-B, Bálint Gábor levele Sebestyén Gyulának, Kolozsvár, 1905. november 24.

30. For his life, see Rudolf Paksa, "Márki Sándor," *Korunk* 22, no. 5 (2011): 60–65; and Ignác Romsics, *Clio bűvöletében—Magyar történetírás a 19–20. században, nemzetközi kitekintéssel* (Budapest: Osiris, 2011): 150–52.

31. For Márki's Turanist studies, see László Szendrei, ed., *Márki Sándor: Turáni tanulmányok* (Máriabesnyő: Attraktor, 2014).

32. Sándor Márki, "A turáni népek jelene és jövője," in *Márki Sándor: Turáni tanulmányok*, ed. Szendrei, 66.

33. Dr. György Almásy, *Vándor-utam Ázsia szívébe* (Budapest: Kir. M. Természettudományi Társulat, 1903), 14.

34. OSZKK, Fond 44/8, Baráthosi Balogh Benedek levele Kozma Andornak, Budapest, 1900. április 27.

35. Ethnographic Museum Archives (hereafter, NMI), Jelentés Zichy Istvánnak a Néprajzi Tár finnugor anyagáról (Krompecher Bertalan), Budapest, 1936. február 7. Baráthosi Balogh collected 664 of the 854 items in the museum's "related peoples of Russia" collection. See NMI, 22/1935: kimutatás a japán anyagról a kultuszminisztérium számára, Budapest, 1935. március 9.

36. For information regarding Baráthosi Balogh's career, see Gábor Wilhelm, "Baráthosi Balogh Benedek néprajzi gyűjtései," *Néprajzi Értesítő* 88 (2006): 131–42; Mihály Hoppál, "Egy elfelejtett magyar sámánkutató: Baráthosi Balogh Benedek élete és munkássága," *Keletkutatás* (Autumn 1996/Spring 2002): 185–202; and Eszter Ruttkay-Miklián, "Die uralischen forschungen des Ungarn Benedek Baráthosi Balogh," in *Europa et Sibiria: Gedenkband für Wolfgang Veenker*, Veröffentlichungen der Societas Uralo-Altaica 51, ed. Cornelius Hasselblatt and Paula Jääsalmi-Krüger (Wiesbaden: Harrassowitz, 1999), 373–80.

37. For a vivid summary of Baráthosi Balogh's last voyage, see NMI, 80/1917, Feljegyzés Baráthosi Balogh Benedek gyűjteményének megvásárlása ügyében (piszkozat), Budapest, 1917. június 26.

38. OSZKK, Fol. Hung. 1670. Zempléni Árpád-Baráthosi Balogh Benedek: Az aranyhalász. Japán mesejáték három felvonásban. Budapest, 1909 körül.

39. For this process, see Györgyi Fajcsák, "Keleti tárgyak gyűjtése Magyarországom, kitekintéssel Kínára, a 19. század elejétől 1945-ig, a Hopp Ferenc Kelet-Ázsiai Művészeti Múzeum tárgyainak tükrében" (PhD diss., Eötvös Loránd University, Budapest, 2005); and

Mónika Bincsik, "Japán műtárgyak gyűjtéstörténete Magyarországon a 19. század második felében—kitekintéssel a nemzetközi összefüggésekre" (PhD diss., Eötvös Loránd University, Budapest, 2009).

40. See Bincsik, "Japán műtárgyak gyűjtéstörténete Magyarországon," 52–64.

41. Péter Wintermantel, "Szemere Attila hagyatékának orientalisztikai vonatkozású anyagai," *A Herman Ottó Múzeum Évkönyve* 38 (1999): 793–814.

42. With regard to Hopp, see Györgyi Fajcsák and Zsuzsanna Renner, eds., *A Buitenzorg-villa lakója—A világutazó, műgyűjtő Hopp Ferenc (1833-1919)* (Budapest: Hopp Ferenc Múzeum, 2008).

43. Bincsik, "Japán műtárgyak gyűjtéstörténete Magyarországon," 129–30.

44. See Katalin Keserü, "Finn-kép a magyar művészeti életben a századelőn," *Hungarologische Beiträge* 1, no. 1 (1993): 209–17; and Tamás Csáki, "A finn építészet és az 'architektúra magyar lelke,' Kultúrpolitika, építészet, publicisztika a századelő Magyarországán," *Múltunk* 51, no. 1 (2006): 200–230.

45. For Gallen-Kallela's visit to Hungary, see Judith Koós, "Akseli-Gallen Kallela (1865–1931) és a finn-magyar művészeti kapcsolatok kezdetei," *Művészettörténeti Értesítő* 16, no. 1 (1967): 44–66.

46. For the relationship between Müller and Hungary, see Zegernyei, "Max Müller és a turáni átok. Nyelv és Tudomány," *Rénhírek*, July 8, 2011, accessed July 2, 2018, https://www.nyest.hu/renhirek/max-muller-es-a-turani-atok.

47. Géza Nagy, *A skythák: Székfoglaló értekezés* (Budapest: MTA, 1909), 109.

48. The following volume is the most complete work regarding Thallóczy: Dževad Juzbašić, Imre Ress, and Andreas Gottsmann, eds., *Lajos Thallóczy, der Historiker und Politiker* (Sarajevo: Akademia der Wissenschaften und Küste von Bosnien-Herzegowina-Ungarischen Akademie der Wissenschaften, Institut für Geschichte, 2010).

49. See the following excellent summary of the history of Thallóczy's club: Andrea Waktor, "'Kegyelmes Büzérnagy! . . . Én ábrándozom a bécsi szép napokról': Thallóczy Lajos és köre Bécsben," *Budapesti Negyed* 46, no. 4 (2004): 435–56, quote from 455.

50. See Krisztián Csaplár-Degovics, "Lajos Thallóczy und die Historiographie Albaniens," in *Südost-Forschungen*, vol. 68, ed. Ulf Brunnbauer and Konrad Clewing (Regensburg, DEU: Oldenbourg, 2009), 205–46.

51. For one of Thallóczy's plans in this regard, see OSZKK, Fol. Hung. 1900, II. kötet, "A Balkán félszigeten beállott változásokkal szemben Magyarország részéről követendő eljárás kulturális és gazdaság politikai téren."

52. For a larger context, see Johann Heiss and Johannes Feichtinger, "Distant Neighbors: Uses of Orientalism in the Late Nineteenth-Century Austro-Hungarian Empire," in *Deploying Orientalism in Culture and History: From Germany to Central and Eastern Europe*, ed. Johannes Feichtinger et al. (Rochester, NY: Woodbridge, Boydell, and Brewer, 2013): 148–65.

53. Gedeon Gerlóczy and Lajos Németh, eds., *Csontváry-emlékkönyv* (Budapest: Corvina, 1976), 58.

54. Éva Toldi, "Egy ellenmondásos Babits-vers: A Turáni induló," *Híd* 60, nos. 5–7 (1996): 482–90.

3

THE MOMENT

As may have become clear in the previous chapters, the concept of Turanism was connected not to organizations but rather to individuals. Nevertheless, the formation of the Turanian Society on November 26, 1910, represented a milestone in the history of Turanism: it certainly played a central role until 1918, and although it undoubtedly lost much of its influence as a result of the post–First World War revolutions and the Treaty of Trianon, it can in no way be avoided until 1945.

The day after the foundation of the Turanian Society, the newspaper *Budapesti Hírlap* (Budapest journal) published an article introducing the objectives of the organization taken verbatim from its bylaws:

> The objectives of the association are to study, present and develop the science, art and economics of Asian and European peoples that are related to us and at the same time to bring them into harmony with Hungarian interests. Therefore, the association—which upon the suggestion of Béla Vikár took the name *Turanian Society*, since it wishes to deal with those peoples whose culture is of Turanian origin—will attempt to establish spiritual colonies of sorts on the Belgian and Dutch model in China, India, Persia, Turkey and the larger part of Central Asia, naturally in accordance with our circumstances. It [the association] wishes to reach this established objective through lectures, study trips, scientific expeditions, scholarships and periodicals. It will exclude politics and religious and sectarian questions from its operations. Its activity will be scientific and it will not deal with business.[1]

Until 1916, the Turanian Society bore the "subtitle" Hungarian Asian Society, which for many would have represented a more suitable primary name for the organization. This distinction appeared in the section of the society's bylaws that stated: "The objectives of the association are to study, present and develop the science, art and economics of *Asian and European peoples that are related to us* and at the same time to bring them into harmony with Hungarian interests."[2] This shows that the society's objectives were not only espousal of kinship and drawing the associated political conclusions but also spurring general interest in Asia. In later versions of the Turanian Society's bylaws (1918 and 1928), this formulation disappeared, and working with related peoples became the organization's exclusive objective.

The new society held a general assembly one week after its foundation, at which it admitted further full members and elected its officers.[3] Pál Teleki (1879–1941), who later twice served as prime minister of Hungary, was elected president of the Turanian Society, while Ármin Vámbéry and Béla Széchenyi were chosen as honorary presidents within the organization's nine-member presidium. Among the remaining members of the presidium, we find the geographers Jenő Cholnoky, Béla Erődi, and Lajos Lóczy and the political officials Mihály Károlyi (1875–1955), who became prime minister and president of Hungary after the First World War, and László Szapáry (1864–1939), who had previously been governor of Fiume (Rijeka, Croatia) and later served as ambassador to the United Kingdom. Finally, Agricultural Museum museologist Alajos Paikert (1866–1948) was chosen to fill the post of executive president—and his office in the Budapest City Park became the organization's initial headquarters. Without the efforts of Paikert, the Turanian Society would not have survived (his diary reveals that he spent more time organizing the society's activities than he did with his own regular work) and would not have developed in the way that it did during the interwar period. Therefore, it is worthwhile to examine the person of Alajos Paikert in more depth.[4]

Paikert was born in Nagyszombat (Trnava, Slovakia) in 1866 to a military physician of Sudeten German origin who had received a title of Hungarian nobility; he studied law, as well as acquired the knowledge needed to become an agricultural scientist while attending the economic academy in Magyaróvár, and then became a teaching assistant alongside anthropologist Aurél Török during his second year at the University of Budapest. With regard to this period, Paikert noted that he could have become a man of science, either a geographer or an anthropologist just as his "two good friends" Pál Teleki and Jenő Cholnoky were, and that they would have certainly been able to resolve their possible scientific competition—which frankly says quite a lot about the museologist's self-esteem difficulties. ("Along with me, he studied law and finished the economic academy, dealt with geography, ethnography and history, liked maps and, just as I, prepared to become an Asia researcher and a scholarly investigator of serious intent.")[5] After his university studies, Paikert worked as an employee of the lobby organization for major landowners, the National Hungarian Economic Association, then became one of the organizers of the Agricultural Museum established at the Vajdahunyad Castle built in Budapest to commemorate the one-thousand-year anniversary of the arrival of the Hungarians to the Carpathian Basin. Paikert also served as the museum's museologist and, from 1923, its director.

Meanwhile, Paikert was appointed to the post of ministerial counselor, in addition to which he filled leadership positions in numerous organizations (including the Hungarian Economic Society, for which he held the office of general secretary beginning in 1908), was the editor of several periodicals (as well as the founder of the *Hungarian Economic History Review*), and organized Hungary's participation in a series of international exhibitions and conferences. The three years that he spent during his Ministry of Agriculture period working in Washington as a special correspondent, referred to simply as a "manure diplomat," exercised a decisive impact on his life. Paikert left an amazing amount of documentation behind: he melded his daily experiences together in his diaries and wrote his memoirs (in several versions), and his correspondence, sketch books, inventions, and poetry have come down to us in unusual abundance.[6] The initial and most important feature of this enormous amount of documentation is that it resonates with the thinking of a committed snob and tediously conventional mind. Paikert was undoubtedly a good father, a loving spouse, and a dependable employee. He was not among the ardent proponents of Turanism: it is hard to imagine the prematurely bald, thin, mustached, and monocle-wearing man waving his saber at the head of a nomadic cavalry troop sweeping across the steppe. Paikert did not long for Turanism to become a mass movement and for him to stand at the head of it. His world was that of the traditional Hungarian middle class with leather club chairs, chalice dinners, and tea parties at his Buda villa on Napos Avenue. It would be useful for us to see him as an exasperatingly rule-following and immeasurably refined gentleman for whom self-reflection did not figure among the most important components of his identity. Paikert regarded himself to be an exceptionally original and independent thinker at several moments of his life, for example, when, during the First World War, he identified the war of Mexico and Japan against the United States and the seizure of the Suez Canal to be conditions for winning the conflict; when he wrote a memorandum to the prime minister regarding a Hungarian viceroyalty in Libya; when, after the collapse of the Hungarian Soviet Republic, he mused about punishing Jews (then twenty-five years later hailed the foundation of Israel); when he devised a world religion; and when, in 1948, he delineated the foundations of a coming "world alliance" extending over the entire planet and praised Soviet nationality policy.[7] He did, however, renounce any monetary recompense for himself to the benefit of the Hungarian Academy of Sciences.

Although Paikert never learned a single language characterized as Turanian, he believed sincerely in the notion of Turanian-German alliance (during the First World War) and in the pathway to the future embodied in the Turanian idea (during the interwar period). He always regarded the Turanian Society to be an influential lobby group and suffered if the organization's mission offended somebody who was active within Hungarian scholarship, thus impelling him to express criticism.[8] The society could have hardly survived its early years without Alajos Paikert's energy and ambition. Paikert's precision and administrative expertise were recognized in spite of his dreadful banality (his diary reveals that he found every conversation to be *pleasant*, every meeting to be *interesting*, and every lecture to be *superb* and *greatly successful*); however, beneath this extraordinarily polished surface, there lived within Paikert enormous resentment. Addressing posterity, he wrote: "The reader is perhaps surprised that a wealthy, handsome, well-mannered young man [such as I] who is endowed with so many good qualities, received such a careful and distinguished upbringing, possesses so many excellent family and other connections and aspires toward the highest and purest ideals did not achieve more." According to Paikert, this lack of achievement resulted from the fact that he had "accommodated himself," had "spurned selfishness," and was an "idealistic individual who lived only for the common good." He admitted that "my bitterness grew continually and on several occasions I wanted to put an end to my life, which had begun so nicely." Paikert believed that shameful machinations had ruined his career: "For this I can thank the Jews!"[9]

In fact, Paikert's career progressed nicely: his name was connected to the foundation of the agricultural museum in Cairo at the beginning of the 1930s, and he was able to retire as a state secretary at the end of this career. His 1911–1912 diaries are full of entries that begin with "talks about Turanian Society affairs," and he wrote dozens of memoranda and circulars. Paikert had the nerve to stand in opposition to the president of the society: the enthusiasm of his initial diary entries about Pál Teleki quickly gave way

Fig. 3.1. The perennial Alajos Paikert. Attribution: Országos Széchényi Könyvtár, Kézirattár, 627. sz. Strelisky Lipót felvétele.

to disappointment, prompting him to note with exasperation: "To Count Pál Teleki's residence, long and detailed discussion, I state my opinion regarding his perpetual delays. The Tur[anian] Soc[iety] must succeed, even against Teleki. If he is president, let him be with us completely."[10] What was it that led Paikert to Turanism? Perhaps it was the Pan-American movement, with which he became familiar in the United States, or perhaps modernism—the incessant need for renewal—or the illusion of it.

The other important personality in the new association was Pál Teleki, the later Hungarian royal prime minister.[11] At this time, Teleki was still just a newly married father, political official, and public figure who took an interest in the East. The first decade of the Turanian Society's existence was connected closely to his name. Teleki himself never traveled to the East, collecting the material for his cartographical history of Japan primarily at western European libraries, for example. He had taken a brief "expedition" to Africa and, during the First World War, reached as far as Constantinople, and as a member of the League of Nations committee, he had traveled to Mosul in 1925. His commitment to the Turanian Society undoubtedly stemmed from personal interest. In a certain sense, Teleki was part of the generation that steeped itself in the new intellectual trends of the early twentieth century, whether they were called psychoanalysis, feminism, sociology, or cubism. Teleki was there at the beginning of the Hungarian eugenics movement: his first published writings pertained to racial hygiene, appearing in the monthly *Huszadik Század* (Twentieth century) around which the left-wing intelligentsia later coalesced. Teleki occupied himself with introducing Hungary to the field of political geography, which was just emerging at that time. His engagement with Turanism was also part of this new intellectual pursuit. Although Teleki occasionally became discouraged with the difficulties he encountered in managing the Turanian Society's affairs and conflicts and with the organization's lack of money, he played a key role in the Turanian movement from 1910 to 1918.

If we examine the members of the Turanian Society during its early years, surmise their motives for joining the organization, and take a look at their connections, we can divide them into three major groups and into further subgroups. The first major group was composed of leading public figures. The least interesting among those in this group were the ubiquitous aristocrats and political officials who regarded membership to be part of their public activity. I am thinking of such people as former governor of Fiume László Szapáry as well as Mihály Károlyi, István Tisza, and Móric Esterházy, all of whom served as prime ministers of Hungary before 1919. We find no fewer than six count Zichys, three Széchenyis, and three Telekis (among them Géza and Sándor, the father and uncle, respectively, of Pál). With few exceptions (Pál Teleki himself or former county prefect and future opera house government commissioner, foreign minister, author, and member of the upper house of parliament Miklós Bánffy (1873–1950), these men had very little to do with Hungarian Turanism. This group also included high-ranking public officials (state secretaries and ministers), such as former and future education minister Albert Apponyi, trade minister Károly Hieronymi, agricultural minister Béla Serényi, and common Finance

Ministry department chief Lajos Thallóczy, as well as other state secretaries, diplomats, and ministerial department advisors (such as Árpád Zempléni's fellow poet and Central Statistical Office president Gyula Vargha). The members of the upper-middle class and the economic-financial elite, some of them Jewish, who regarded Hungary's acquisition of Balkan and Eastern influence to be a logical strategy, belonged loosely to this group of public figures: among them were Ferenc Chorin, the founder of the Confederation of Hungarian Employers and Industrialists; József Hatvany, the manager of the Hatvan Sugar Factory; Móric Domonyi, the CEO of the Hungarian River and Ocean Navigation Joint Stock Company; bank directors Leó Lánczy and Árpád Gorove; and wholesaler Ferenc Heinrich. Moreover, those associated with the press in various rank and order can be classified in this group: Ferenc Csajthay, editor of the *Budapesti Hírlap*; Pál Hoitsy, the champion of Hungarian imperialism; Jenő Rákosi, the founder of the *Budapesti Hírlap*; Ferenc Herczeg, one of the most widely read authors of the period; and Gyula Pekár, the later president of the Turanian Society. Naturally, Árpád Zempléni belongs here as well.

The second major group consisted of members of the scientific world: among the 201 founders of the Turanian Society, we find no fewer than 19 university professors and private lecturers—not only Orientalists but also historians (Sándor Márki) and anthropologists (Aurél Török). If we add to this group later university professors, such as Mihály Kmoskó, Gyula Germanus (1884–1979), Pál Teleki, and Rezső Milleker; those who taught at other institutions of higher education (instructors from the law academies and the Eastern Academy, such as Ignác Kúnos, linguist József Pápay, or Mihály Réz, one of the ideologists for István Tisza's National Party of Work); and other people connected to Hungarian scientific life, such as those who worked at museums, archives, and scientific institutes, then we can see that this was the Turanian Society's most significant group in numerical terms. And in a certain sense, we can also classify in this group those art collectors who became members of the Turanian Society as a result of their significant collections of Eastern-themed works, such as Ferenc Hopp and Péter Vay or, from among the aristocrats, Rafael Zichy, the son of the previously mentioned Eastern traveler Count Jenő Zichy.

The third major group was composed of activists. The members of this group were, for the most part, of lower social standing and frequently worked as high school teachers, school inspectors, student teachers, postal officials, ship captains, and physicians. They often became founding members of the

Turanian Society as a result of previous travels to the East or out of personal conviction. Among such members, we have already become acquainted with elementary school teacher Benedek Baráthosi Balogh and will encounter the name of high school teacher and Estonian translator Aladár Bán (1871–1960) on many occasions later in the book. These categories are, of course, rather arbitrary. For example, the distinguished paleontologist and Albania researcher Baron Ferenc Nopcsa (1877–1933) and landowner, former diplomat, and professional gambler Miklós Szemere would rather belong to the public figure group, but at the same time, they threw themselves body and soul into the affairs of the Turanian Society. And although Béla Vikár and Gyula Pekár appear on the list of members as authors, their careers are connected so closely to the organization that they can be placed into the activist group.

The list of those who were *absent* from the register of founding members of the Turanian Society says at least as much as the roll of those who were on it: the fact that the perhaps excessively reclusive University of Kolozsvár (today Cluj-Napoca, Romania) linguist Gábor Bálint was not among the original members of the organization provides an eloquent example of this. Engineer and later state secretary Antal Szentgáli, one of the leading figures in the interwar Turanian movement, was working in the Russian Far East at this time, which may explain his absence (although physical absence did not prevent others from joining). There were also no artists among the 201 founding members of the Turanian Society—neither those who were active at the art colony in Gödöllő and who later drew close to Turanism (e.g., István Medgyaszay, Ede Toroczkai Wigand, Sándor Nagy, and Jenő Remsey) nor those who worked independently (Jenő Lechner, for example, and who will appear later in the book).

The objectives of the Turanian Society corresponding to this three-way division are largely reflected in various organizational documents. These revealed the existence of a sort of Hungarian imperialism, that is, that Hungary—which had just emerged from the 1906–1910 political crisis (unlike the still-faltering Austria)—had begun to formulate very assertive political and economic objectives in the Balkans and the Middle East, which were based to a significant degree on the German presence in the Ottoman Empire and the British presence in the East. Geographer Rezső Milleker articulated this aim in the Turanian Society periodical: "Hungary must take a prominent role in the revival of Asia Minor. . . . Our markets are here and in the Balkans"—all the more so because, according to Milleker, the Hungarians maintained no political interests in the region, unlike the Germans and the English, and thus approached its peoples as siblings. The main purpose for expansion was therefore neither political nor economic in nature, but because "we are related and they must clasp hands chiefly with kindred nations, to reach the fairest objective, the attainment of a perfect culture."[12] The goal was the formation of a local elite and its "linkage to us" as well as the creation of a market for Hungarian goods, although—as continually crops up in the pronouncements of intellectuals affiliated with the Turanian Society—one based on kinship and resurgent sympathy toward the Hungarians, not with the aim of colonization. Turanian Society president Pál Teleki himself summarized the initial years of the organization's existence: "We do not presently have colonies and we do not even strive for true colonies, but just as the enterprising manufacturers, merchants and scientists of little Belgium obtain glory and affluence for their homeland everywhere in the most distant parts of the world, we could also proceed in this manner with similar success. . . . Neither political nor sectarian, nor exclusively racial considerations guide us in these endeavors."[13] This meant that, in fact, racial (kinship) considerations indeed figured among the motives of the Turanian Society, even if not in exclusive terms. The affirmation of scientific Eastern research on the model of the frequently cited Royal Asiatic Society and the Deutsche Asiatische Gesellschaft may have been attractive for members of the scientific community in the form of publication of technical literature and periodicals and support for popularizing lectures, expeditions, and scholarly enterprises. But the research about kinship, the investigation of ethical roots was not among the principal goals of those scientific communities.

The topic of kinship and the political-cultural consequences to be drawn therefrom engaged the attention of the activists to the greatest degree. Occasionally these objectives may have coalesced with the requisites of the other two groups: for example, the provision of scholarships to the sons of the "Turanian" nations or the maintenance of connections with the elite of the nations awakening to a new consciousness. An article published in the premier issue of the periodical *Turán* in 1913 commented on this as follows: "[The Turanian Society] wants to extend a helping hand to the peoples that are related to us so that in this important period of their reawakening, one that is significant for us here in Hungary as well, they are able to acquire together with us the great scientific and economic achievements of the west. Therefore it [the Turanian Society] will strive to enable Turanian youth who yearn for education to attend our universities or our technical schools that are suitable for them here in this country."[14] More robust foreign policy objectives appeared in Alajos Paikert's zestfully proclaimed "from Dévény to Tokyo" spirit as well.[15] Turanian Society president Teleki paid homage to this notion in his 1914 executive report when he stated: "The Hungarian nation stands before a great and lustrous future and it is certain that the flourishing of the Turanians will follow the golden age of the Germans and the Slavs. The great and difficult, though glorious task awaits the Hungarians, the western representatives of this enormous awakening power (the Turanians), for us to be the intellectual and economic leaders of the 600 million Turanians."[16] Membership in the Turanian Society did not, of course, entail immediate agreement of opinion. Along with the Tisza-Károlyi conflict, the most obvious indication of this circumstance was the unrelenting and frequently malicious debate that played itself out in 1911 within the periodical of the Ethnographic Society, *Ethnographia*, regarding the connection between the ancient Hungarians and the Bashkirs. This dispute pitted the ethnographic researcher Gyula Mészáros against the archaeologist Géza Nagy, both of whom were employees of the National Museum and members of the Turanian Society. Such discord remained typical throughout the decade of the 1910s: differences in the objectives of the organization brought members with divergent motives together, and the conceptual disparities that existed between them soon manifested themselves.

In view of the great expectations, the operations of the Turanian Society did not begin smoothly. And the executive president was not the only one who was dissatisfied with the president's brooding and indecisiveness. According to ethnographic researcher and founding member Gyula Sebestyén (1864–1946), the organization operated in disorderly fashion, had no money, and lacked the will to engage in productive activity. Sebestyén complained that administration stifled all initiatives and that everything required presidential approval, noting reproachfully that the Turanian Society had failed to invite foreign Orientalists to salute Ármin Vámbéry on the occasion of his eightieth birthday. Sebestyén claimed that the official document requesting such acknowledgment had not even been prepared even though "we agreed with Teleky at the time of our recent meeting that he would translate the Hungarian-language summons into Turkish, though I still don't know anything about this. Now we are completely running out of time." The ethnographer added that other actions had not gotten underway and that he feared the Turanian Society could be left behind: "They are go-ing to carry it into effect beautifully without us. Just as with regard to the boarding school affair we have not wanted to enforce our word until now. I really fear for the Turanian Society."[17]

The official rancor clearly suggested that the University of Budapest did not want to cooperate with the Turanian Society on the birthday of the organization's copresident and wanted instead to coordinate the celebra-tion of the event entirely within its own sphere of authority.[18] An associate of the Turanian Society noted bitterly that teachers and students from the Eastern Academy, which prepared graduates to undertake practical com-mercial careers, were "protesting through their absence" from the official celebration of Vámbéry's birthday.[19] The Turanian Society yearbook that had been promised during the organization's initial meetings was never published, and the frequently floated idea of establishing a Turanian mu-seum remained a castle in the air. Although the Turanian Society did conduct educational lectures and language classes, President Teleki himself struck a self-critical note after two years of operation when he reflected on the lack of consideration given to member admission categories and the organiza-tion's excessive remoteness.[20]

However, the Turanian Society undoubtedly realized some successes as well. For example, the organization had provided support for five Hungarian expeditions by the beginning of 1914. These expeditions were conducted primarily in Asia Minor, parts of the Caucasus, and the Middle East and engaged in the collection of ethnographic, geologic, geographic, and linguistic materials. Accounts of these journeys were published for the most part in *Turán*, the periodical that the Turanian Society launched with Alajos Paikert as editor in 1913 and which can be regarded as the organization's only far-reaching achievement.[21] The Education Ministry–supported periodical was intended to appear on a bimonthly basis but was, in fact, published only three times, all in the year 1913, before the beginning of the First World War.

There already existed a scientific forum to satisfy scholarly interest in the East before the launching of *Turán*: the Bernát Munkácsi (1860–1937) and Ignác Kúnos–edited *Keleti Szemle* (Eastern review) had been published with support from the Hungarian Academy of Sciences since 1900 with the revealing subtitle "Publications on the subject of Ural-Altaic peoples and languages". The Turanian Society had to shape its publication in accordance with this. With the exception of the issues that appeared in 1918, *Turán* was always distinguished by a strange duality, publishing articles of scholarly character and quality alongside writings intended to disseminate knowledge to the general public that were often prone to dilettantism. The periodical in any case represents a first-rate source for news regarding the Turanian Society's activity. The three issues of *Turán* that appeared during its first year of publication in 1913 contained articles by the well-known German explorer and college instructor Georg Wegener, regarding the awakening of China; Rezső Milleker, regarding his trip to Asia Minor; and Zoltán Felvinczi Takács, regarding East Asian art, as well as Mihály Kmoskó's two-part study on the Sumerians.[22] They also published two articles by the painter Jenő Tóth, including one entitled "Turáni törzsek a Himaláyában" (Turanian tribes in the Himalayas), in which the author expresses unambiguous support for the notion of kinship between the peoples of northern India and the northern Finno-Ugrian peoples based on such conclusive arguments as the fact that both the former (Rajputs, Gurkhas, Sikhs, and Magars) and the latter peoples ate meat. Tóth, who was an artist (painter) by profession, asserted in this article that "our ancient past is tightly connected to them, which shall cast light upon the important question of the place from which we Hungarians originate," thus establishing a tradition regarding Hungarian ancient history that has maintained some influence to this day.[23] The second issue of *Turán*, published in 1913 shortly after the death of Ármin Vámbéry, opened with an elegy that Árpád Zempléni wrote in honor of the father of the Turanian idea.

Turanian Society president and *Turán* managing editor Pál Teleki set the tone for the periodical in an article published in its first issue. Teleki—in somewhat unusual fashion for the president of an ambitious organization—emphasized in the article that he did "not want to provide a program" but nevertheless identified the cultivation of a new generation of scholars dealing with the East as the Turanian Society's most important task. Teleki identified the organization's mission as follows: "To study these people, their customs, language and history, to investigate their lands, the past and future of their lands; to seek them out and call upon them, their youth, to come among us in order so that we may become acquainted and gain respect for one other, to draw strength from the common memory of the past and the common interests of the present; to utilize our geographical situation in order to press forward with our industry."[24] In the same issue, editor Alajos Paikert affirmed the emphasis on sympathy-based colonization:

"Asia is now for us Hungarians a territory to be conquered, though neither with the blade of a sword nor through the oppression and exploitation of the people who live there, but quite to the contrary, through fraternal support and productive work and with the weapons of technology, science and art shall we acquire there benefits and truly good friends for ourselves and for our nation. Progressing along this road we shall attain the glory of the great old times and the realization of the dreams of our ancestors: the Magna Hungaria."[25] From Paikert's perspective, such expansion connected the past to the present and Hungarian nation building to the network of relations with kindred peoples: according to this outlook, Hungary would become great through the use of its relations with peoples in Asia as a means of penetrating the continent based on the new concept of kinship that was opening enormous vistas for the Hungarians, not the old logic of colonization. Or, as an intransigent, racist Turanist wrote very gracefully after the First World War, the motto to be followed was "to colonize with love."[26] The fact that an editorial note stating that the Turanian Society sharply distanced itself from the "economic exploitation" stemming from imperialism and supported "economic strengthening based on reciprocity" was attached to articles published in later issues of *Turán* shows that this attitude was not the result of a single outburst of emotion.[27]

It must be added that *Turán* was not the only periodical that served as a vehicle for the propagation of the Turanian idea. Writings that expressed sympathy with Turanism initially appeared in many periodicals, ranging from the Freemason *Világ* to István Tisza's *Magyar Figyelő*. Many Turanists additionally appeared among the authors who contributed to *A Cél* (The target), the early Hungarian racialist organ published under the auspices of Miklós Szemere and his associates.[28]

The few years in which the Turanian Society operated before the beginning of the First World War in any case provided it with the opportunity to become acquainted with the procedures associated with organizational life during the era: holding lectures, conducting Turkish- and Russian-language courses, foraging for money, and establishing contacts with foreign individuals and organizations with similar interests, such as the Tatar-born apostle of Turanism, Yusuf Akçura, and his associates, the periodical *Türk Yurdu* (Turkish homeland), and the organization Türk Ocağı (Turkish Hearth).

That the thinking of official Hungarian circles was also changing and that Turanist ideology had begun to function as a rhetorical device is clearly shown in the report that ethnographic researcher Gyula Mészáros, an important though somewhat difficult-to-manage Turanist from the early period, published regarding his 1912 journey to Turkey and Asia Minor. According to Mészáros's account, the materials he had gathered during this voyage were important not only from a scientific perspective but also for the Hungarian National Museum, which was, with its support and acceptance of his collection, "fulfilling a national mission when it attempts to preserve for everlasting time all the treasures of our kindred peoples here in Budapest, the capital city of the most advanced Turanian race, the Hungarians."[29] The Turanian Society had ambitious plans at the beginning of 1914: the foundation of a Turanian boarding school, the promotion of the Budapest mosque issue, the launching of further expeditions, the establishment of foreign and domestic branches, the organization of a Turanian exhibition, and even an international congress in Budapest.[30]

However, the war swept all of these plans away. Many of the leaders of the Turanian Society (including Pál Teleki) joined the army, and publication of *Turán* was suspended due to paper restrictions. The organization nevertheless continued to function, albeit on low throttle, holding lectures and even language courses. There were relatively few indications that Turanism might still emerge as a strong and influential current of thought within Hungarian public life. It appeared to be simply one of the worthy and interesting spheres of thought from the early twentieth century that gave rise to a short-lived Turanian association. The years from 1916 to 1918 were nevertheless regarded as the Turanian Society's golden age: this period served as the subsequent frame of reference for everything and largely determined the types of programs that the organization could launch and what kind of attention it received from the government even at the time of the Second World War. During this two-year interval, hundreds of young scholarship recipients arrived in Hungary in order to study at educational institutions in the country, Hungarian scholars plied the roads of the Balkans and Asia Minor in the course of expeditions, Hungarian businessmen attempted to obtain markets in the allied "Turanian" states, a Hungarian scientific institute opened in Constantinople, exhibitions were held, and street names were christened. Eastern thinking appeared with primal force, and for a broad strata of public opinion, this represented the moment of initial contact with thinking about the East.

As a result of the entry of Turkey and Bulgaria into the war, the government of István Tisza decided to emphasize Hungary's presence in the Balkans and to therefore reactivate the Turanian Society, indeed, to essentially endow the organization with governmental responsibilities. This course of action was, in fact, compatible with the Hungarian administrative practice that had been gaining ground since the 1910s of delegating the government's social tasks (i.e., handling affairs related to Hungarians residing in foreign countries) to associations that were subject to strict oversight and kept on a financial lead. According to Alajos Paikert's diary, meetings and talks regarding the reorganization of the Turanian Society were held almost incessantly by late 1915. Paikert himself wrote very enthusiastically to Árpád Zempléni in November of that year: "The Turanian idea is spreading continually, now not only in theory, but in most serious practice as well. The Hungarians stand before a great future, but only if they stick together and work for one another rather than against one another."[31]

At a general assembly held at the Hungarian Academy of Sciences on May 2, 1916, the Turanian Society was reconstituted as the Turanian Society–Hungarian Eastern Cultural Center. At the same time, a new organization called the Hungarian Eastern Economic Center was formed under the leadership of economist Kálmán Balkányi (1883–1965), who later served as president of the Hungarian Cobden Federation and was one of the legendary personalities associated with interwar Hungarian Freemasonry. The two institutions operated within the framework of the Eastern Federation, which the government filled with such prominent National Party of Work figures as Prime Minister István Tisza himself, the Austro-Hungarian joint foreign minister István Burián, *ban* (governor) of Croatia Iván Skerlecz, and cabinet ministers Imre Ghihllányi and János Harkányi.[32] The history of the Hungarian Eastern Economic Center has remained largely unresearched, and no organizational documents have survived. The head of the economic center recorded only his anecdotal observations regarding doing business with the Turks, emphasizing that corruption and nepotism were part of everyday commercial life in the East, which was based on what he kindly called a *buddy system*, to which it was very difficult to gain access without knowledge of local conditions.[33] Within the leadership of the Hungarian Eastern Economic Center, one finds the big guns of Hungarian major industry and bank capital. The organization published its own communiqués; held lectures at its headquarters on Andrássy Avenue in Budapest; proudly referred to its network of correspondents, archives, and language courses; and dispatched delegations to Turkey and the Balkans that were led by its most active leaders, including banker Leó Lánczy, lawyer Géza Magyary, and organizational leader Kálmán Balkányi himself.

This Hungarian Eastern Economic Center did not emerge from nowhere: it had been known earlier as the Hungarian-Bosnian and Herzegovinian Economic Center, which at once represented a suitable vehicle for supporting Hungarian aspirations vis-à-vis the provinces that had been annexed in 1908 and continued to occupy a transitional status between the Austrian and Hungarian halves of the dual monarchy. However, the long-range plans of the organization were aimed not merely at making economic inroads but at "strengthening economic and cultural relations" between Hungary and "eastern countries that are allied and maintain fraternal relations with us." The Hungarian Eastern Economic Center thus advocated the foundation of the Orientalist institute (and the affiliated Vámbéry library) at the University of Budapest as well as the sending of "missions composed of superior technical and scientific men" to the East in order to establish permanent scientific institutions there on the French and German model.[34] In 1918, the organization established its Hungarian-Russian committee in preparation for the Treaty of Brest-Litovsk and stood ready to conduct trade even with Bolshevik-led Russia. This naturally did not take place, and problems occurred in connection to theoretically feasible courses of action as well. For example, German military authorities were reluctant to allow emissaries from the Hungarian Eastern Economic Center to enter occupied Romania, which German capital regarded as its preserve and tolerated competition only with significant difficulty.

The rise in the prestige of the Turanian Society–Hungarian Eastern Cultural Center was reflected immediately in the location of the organization's offices in the upper-house wing of the Hungarian Parliament Building, where they remained until 1945. The Education Ministry, which determined the course of the operations of the Turanian Society–Hungarian Eastern Cultural Center, placed functionaries at the organization's disposal, thus essentially creating a small bureau composed primarily of high school teachers under the direction of prime ministerial state secretary Kuno Klebelsberg's confidant Artúr Benisch (Némethy following the Magyarization of his name).[35] The leadership of the organization also underwent a fundamental transformation: Béla Széchenyi became president, while no fewer than seven copresidents served under him, including Lajos Thallóczy, the civilian governor of occupied Serbia who was one of the main figures involved in

Hungarian Balkan studies, and Klebelsberg, who from his position as state secretary was able to pull many strings from the background. Pál Teleki became just one of a half dozen vice presidents, while Alajos Paikert was also relegated to this rank, and there was thus a chance that such professional and public authorities as Mór Déchy or Ignác Goldziher might be able to curb the previous executive president's hyperactive dilettantism and often capricious methods. Zoltán Felvinczi Takács, the first director of the Ferenc Hopp Museum and a seasoned veteran of the Turanian movement, wrote the following in the early 1930s about the drawbacks of Paikert's activity while acknowledging his administrative talents:

> Alajos Paikert, whose will always prevailed as it were within the Turanian Society, from the very beginning proclaimed these and similar ideas [here Felvinczi Takács was referring to the motto "from Dévény to Tokyo" and the notion of six hundred million Hungarians], which inevitably entailed the sterility of the Turanian movement that he himself had promoted and the collapse of the Turanian Society. With his declared support for Miksa Müller's old theory, according to which all non-Aryan and non-Semitic peoples are Turanian, he has alienated the Hungarian scientific world from both himself and the Turanian Society—the linguists to such a degree that those among them who bring their names into circulation in connection to the Turanian Society place themselves outside the gates of the Hungarian Academy of Science and the University of Budapest.[36]

The diary entries of internationally acclaimed Hungarian Orientalist Ignác Goldziher suggest that such relegation to the background did not necessarily succeed: "At the insistence of Count Pál Teleki, who visited me at my home, I agreed to take part in the cultural center. I was elected president of its linguistic section. However, I was only able to put up with this honor for a short time. The members are unceasingly dilettante and I felt their saucy chatter to be unbearable after two meetings and could do nothing else than announce my resignation. And this they were glad to accept."[37] One must add for the sake of fairness that by every indication Goldziher's journal constituted a type of therapy in which the deeply depressed scholar attempted to vent the pent-up frustration he felt toward his environment (colleagues, religious community, and political officials). Therefore, his remarks regarding the foundation of the Eastern centers ("useless," "unprepared") can be regarded as the reflections of general ill humor.

Pál Teleki became a member of the working committee that conducted operative affairs along with Gyula Pekár and writer Miklós Bánffy, the author of *The Transylvanian Trilogy* and later foreign minister. The cultural center established departments (periodical and book publishing, linguistics and ethnography, history and archaeology, etc.) that planned the organization's professional operations.[38] Some of the artists and, above all, architects who appeared as members of the center's art department, such as Károly Kós (1883–1977) and Ignác Alpár, had taken an interest in the Eastern idea and relations with the East. At the initiative of the Turanian Society, Museum Boulevard in Budapest was renamed Sultan Mehmed Street at the end of 1915 (while in Constantinople, a Hungarian Brothers Avenue was dedicated in return), and the Muslim religion was recognized in Hungary at this time.[39] The restoration of the Tomb of Gül Baba (a Muslim pilgrimage site built in Budapest during the period of Turkish rule in the sixteenth and seventeenth centuries), the ceremonial return of the dervish's mortal remains to the *türbe*, and the foundation of the Hungarian-Turkish Friendship Society in 1917 were all important manifestations of the Turkish-Hungarian brotherhood in arms.[40] Moreover, a military exhibition was held on Margaret Island in Budapest in 1917 and 1918 that, although not associated with the Turanian Society, clearly projected the leitmotifs of the organization to the general public. In addition to ethnographic materials that Ignác Kúnos had collected from Tatar prisoners of war (POWs) in Hungary, the exhibition presented the folklife of Serbia in buildings that were designed for the most part by architect István Medgyaszay.[41] Other prominent artists such as sculptor Ferenc Medgyessy also participated in the implementation of the buildings for the exhibition. We will encounter all of their names later in this book.

The research of Orientalist Ignác Kúnos leads us to an important question pertaining to the cultural center, one that Hungarian historical literature has completely neglected, of collections and anthropological examinations conducted among POWs during the First World War. Beginning from the first years of the war, more than 1.3 million Russian soldiers fell into Austro-Hungarian captivity. The presence of soldiers of "Turanian origin" among these prisoners aroused great enthusiasm within Hungarian scientific life. Scholars who were associated to a greater or lesser degree with the Turanian Society (Ignác Kúnos, Béla Vikár, and Bernát Munkácsi, among others) were participating in the anthropologic-ethnographic study of Russian POWs even before 1916. Austro-Hungarian military leaders and scientific societies strongly supported the conduct of such *Kriegsvolkskunde* (wartime folklore research). Kúnos, for example, eagerly described the collections he gathered at the POW camp in Eger (Cheb, Czech Republic): "I have been here since yesterday and at work since this morning. The material is abundant, the result will be magnificent. I have 8,000 people at my disposal, all kinds of Tatars, Cherkess, Avars, Ossetians, etc."[42]

Kúnos, who served as the director of the Eastern Academy in Budapest, worked at the Eger POW camp together with musicologist Robert Lach and anthropologist and physician Rudolf Pöch, among others.[43] Their work, which in the majority of cases grew out of German colonial research, in many regards represents a transition to the National Socialism–generated skull and racial examinations. Although Hungarian research appears to have focused on ethnography and linguistics, University of Budapest professor Mihály Lenhossék, in fact, carried out such examinations among the prisoners, reporting his findings in a German-language article published in *Turán*.[44] Since the era of Russian voyages had come to an end for Hungarian researchers, the examination of such "home-delivered" Turanism seemed to be an obvious course of action.[45] The cultural center organized an expedition to POW camps in 1916, providing monetary support for the travels of its members and petitioning the military leadership to permit them to move freely among the prisoners.[46] Aladár Bán also engaged in research among the prisoners. Such investigations could have been solidly topical from an ethnographic standpoint as well, although there were some who drew more far-reaching conclusions from the presence of the large number of Turanian prisoners at the camps: in 1918, the cultural center requested that the prisoners of Tatar nationality at camps in Bohemia be transported to Hungary. In fact, Turanian Society officials had previously entertained the idea of forming a "Turanian legion," which can justifiably be relegated to the world of Turanian fantasies.[47]

The relaunching of *Turán* represented the cultural center's other major endeavor. The organization's growing financial opportunities made it possible to publish ten issues of the periodical per year. The task of editing *Turán* was taken away from Paikert (from whose viewpoints the new editorial staff once distanced themselves in a note[48]) and first given to ethnographic researcher and translator Béla Vikár and then to Pál Teleki, who assumed the position of editor in chief beginning in 1918.[49] The young Turkologist Gyula Németh (1890–1976) was appointed to serve alongside Teleki as editor: together the two of them completed most of the editorial work on the periodical. Among the other editors of *Turán*, we find the geographer Gyula Prinz, Count Miklós Bánffy, Béla Vikár, art historian (and Teleki's childhood playmate) Zoltán Felvinczi Takács, and historian and later director of the Hungarian National Museum István Zichy.[50] The issues of *Turán* published in 1918 and 1919 stand out conspicuously from those published in other years in terms of length, quality, and contributing authors. Teleki maintained a serious ambition to transform *Turán* into a respectable scientific forum, and in the middle of 1918, he noted with satisfaction that he had succeeded in this endeavor:

> The periodical had begun to lose all of its scientific qualities when I finally blew a fuse at a working-committee meeting, as a result of which I had to draw the consequences and take the work upon myself. Most of them vacillated at this time as well. Many did not believe that it would be possible to make something of it, while many feared for their scientific reputation; in short very few came along with me entirely for the sake of the objective. I can actually thank foreigners for the fact that we nevertheless managed to carry through with this thing at a European level. Now Hungarian scientific circles also recognize that it is a good thing.[51]

It was remarkable not only that *Turán* managed to overcome the reticence of the Hungarian scientific world in order to recruit a high-quality corps of writers (not solely Hungarian) but also that in spite of the ongoing world war, the periodical reacted keenly to the reverberations of scientific life even in enemy countries without any hint of insult or aggressive intent. *Turán* mourned the death of the great French Sinologist Edouard Chavannes,[52] wrote in not-at-all-unfavorable terms about an article that American historian and political theorist Lothrop Stoddard published regarding Pan-Turanism,[53] and reviewed the *Geographical Journal*[54] as well as the works of British[55] and American[56] scientists. The periodical reported on the activities of the reinvigorated Turanian Society, noting sadly that paper restrictions had prevented the organization from sufficiently publicizing its educational lectures on Balkan and related peoples, thus resulting in poor attendance. (One of the leaders of the Turanian Society wrote dejectedly: "But even in this way all of this is still a regrettable symptom of the fact that we do not see beyond our own hedgerows in spite of the world war.")[57]

One of the secrets of *Turán*'s relative success was that chief editor Teleki gave free rein to Gyula Németh, who, while still quite young in 1918, became an ordinary public professor at Budapest University and the heritor of Vámbéry's departmental chair, which he retained for nearly a half century. The leading modern-day Hungarian Turkologists belong to the last generation of Németh's students. Teleki loyally took the rap when the young titan criticized or returned articles that had been submitted by mature and influential scholars. Teleki himself drove away trade school teacher Lajos Sassi Nagy, an old proponent of fundamentalist Turanism who had wanted *Turán* to pay for the publication of one of his pamphlets. When the elderly insurance officer János Galgóczy, one of the early advocates of Hungarian-Sumerian linguistic kinship, submitted an article to the periodical and Németh straightforwardly rejected it on the grounds that it was not worthy of publication, Teleki attempted to mollify his fellow editor ("in view of the unselfish character of the old gentleman and his endeavors might it not be possible to slip it [the article] in somewhere in greatly abbreviated form?),[58] but Németh was unyielding. When ethnographer Gyula Sebestyén became involved in polemics with Németh, Teleki not only defended him but also immediately counterattacked:

> I regret that I am not in a position to disavow Németh's response to the exceedingly sharp accusations that were much sharper than his. . . . It is very difficult for us here in Hungary to conduct anything in the scientific domain. I am compelled with certain resentment to tell this to the vice president of one of our scientific sections as well. Throughout the course of all of the work I have done as part of the TS [Turanian Society], I have rather felt an absence of support from our scientific circles, in particular the sections, every single one of the sections.[59]

This referred unambiguously to Teleki's opinion regarding the work ethic of his colleagues. The flow of correspondence between Teleki and Sebestyén unsurprisingly ran dry: the latter, one of the most influential figures in the field of Hungarian ethnography, obviously did not appreciate the rebuke, especially not from someone who had expressed praise for him in the periodical *Ethnographia* during the early stages of his career.

Despite the wartime collapse, *Turán* published issue 9–10 of 1918, which, like a message in a bottle cast into the ocean, included a report on one of the cultural center's expeditions to Asia Minor. In 1917–1918, the Turanian Society initiated a succession of research expeditions, including a mission to southern Russia under the leadership of paleontologist Kálmán Lambrecht[60] and a voyage to the Balkans that included geographers Lajos Lóczy and Albert Pécsi and entomologist Ernő Csikí.[61] One of the final groups of Turanian Society–sponsored researchers departed for Constantinople on September 21, 1918, in order to conduct geographic, ethnographic, and botanic observations in the interior portions of Anatolia and to collect as many rocks, plants, and other items as possible.

The leader of this voyage was Jenő Lénárd, the author of the enormous Hungarian-language work introducing Buddhism, *Dhammó*, and at this time a committed Turanist. Lénárd had written to Zoltán Felvinczi Takács in 1914: "Perhaps we, the new human culture, will put new wine into old skins under the intellectual leadership of the Hungarians at the head of our Asian kindred peoples."[62] Among the members of the expedition was the ethnographer and Hungarian National Museum Ethnographic Repository employee István Györffy (1883–1939), who later became a professor at the first department of ethnography at the University of Budapest and one of Hungarian ethnography's main institution-founding figures. His reports provide us with a description of this hardship-filled expedition. Before the voyage, Györffy procured 3,000 krone' worth of sugar cubes with the help of Teleki, since this was not an easy task at a time when the Austro-Hungarian Monarchy was converting to a ration card system. He believed that the sugar might serve as a form of currency to be exchanged for objects of ethnographic value after hearing that the inhabitants of Anatolia were exceedingly wary of all types of money.

The expedition did not begin well: baggage had to be continually discarded, then some of the pack animals had to be cut loose as well, and members of the research mission became sick one after another, including Captain Lénárd himself. Locals received the Austro-Hungarian expedition with deep mistrust, and it was hardly possible to make collections. The news of the collapse at the end of the war reached Györffy and his colleagues amid such circumstances deep inside Anatolia. They then returned to Constantinople, where they were interned. Several officers abandoned the group and attempted to get home on their own. Györffy and the others finally made it back to Hungary by way of Fiume after having passed through the Aegean and Adriatic Seas in a decrepit boat that the passengers themselves had to repair along the way. The voyage placed a great strain on Györffy, whose lack of medication to treat his painful kidney disease prompted him to take morphine, to which he became addicted for a time. Moreover, his entire collection remained behind in Constantinople—not to mention his three crates of sugar cubes. Györffy's recapitulation of the undertaking was not too auspicious: "The results of the expedition did not stand in proportion to the care and exertion that I invested in it."[63] The ethnographer obtained the collected objects, photographs, and notes from the trip only years later.

Györffy is not by any means the only Karcag-born scientist who appears in this story: Gyula Németh was also born in this town in the Trans-Tisza region of Hungary that constitutes one of the centers of the Greater Cumanian identity and even built itself up to be the capital city of "steppelandism" (*pusztaiság*)—a designation that has remained current until the present day.[64] Although Györffy distanced himself from official Turanist organizations after 1919, he maintained his belief in the importance of the Eastern origin of the Hungarians and the cultural ramifications of this until the end of his life. Ethnography represented the science of ancient history par excellence during this era. Györffy himself, although an intuitive and programmatic scholar who possessed an amazingly broad range of knowledge, did not really perceive the process of embourgeoisement that had taken place within peasant society and regretted the weakening/disappearance of peasant culture. In a short book summarizing his viewpoints published shortly before his death in 1939, *Néphagyomány és nemzeti művelődés* (Folk tradition and national culture), Györffy envisaged the integration of Hungarian middle class and folk culture based on a folk tradition that served in direct terms to carry forward the Eastern legacy of the Hungarians and that was further strengthened through the arrival of subsequent Eastern settlers (Cumans, Pechenegs, etc.). He proposed that this elevation of folk culture to the level of national culture and the preservation of folk tradition be carried out based on the Japanese and Finnish models. Györffy urged the implementation of such initiatives as the teaching of folk tradition in all domains of education, from notary training schools to military academies; instruction in the Old Hungarian runic script; the foundation of an independent ethnographic museum; and the construction of an open-air museum.[65] These endeavors received backing from the man who was serving as education minister at this time—none other than Pál Teleki, who himself expressed strong support for the establishment of an outdoor ethnographic museum during a speech outlining ministry policy in 1938.[66] However, the first open-air museum in Hungary was opened only in 1967, north of Budapest in the town of Szentendre.

Although the cultural center did not participate directly in the initiative to establish a Hungarian institute in a foreign country, it was certainly present among the supporters of the first such institute, which opened in Constantinople in 1916. The notion that Hungary or the dual monarchy would need an Eastern research institute for scientific purposes had emerged many years earlier. Jenő Zichy referred to this idea as early as the end of the nineteenth century, while Kolozsvár university archaeology professor and prominent member of the city's Turanist intelligentsia Béla

Pósta advocated the foundation of the Eastern Archeological Institute in Mesopotamia beginning in the early 1910s.[67] Pósta was good friends with the controversial Gábor Bálint, whose views regarding linguistic kinship exercised a significant influence on his ideas. Pósta designated one of his students to become the director of the proposed institute, while he counted on a young theologian and historian of religion who had completed his university degree in Kolozsvár (although he was working in Debrecen), Zsigmond Varga, to interpret Sumerian and other cuneiform scripts. We shall encounter Varga's name again: he played a key role in the foundation of the concept of Hungarian-Sumerian affinity after 1945. However, the student whom Pósta had intended to become the director of the Mesopotamian institute fell on the Russian front during the early days of the First World War, thus taking the proposed institute off the agenda for a time. However, Pósta did not give up the fight and, even at the very end of the war, declared that the future Hungarian archaeological mission would be located in the city of Nusaybin in Upper Mesopotamia, to which a Hungarian archaeological expedition would travel following the end of "hostilities."

However, promising research connected to Hungarian-related themes, particularly Hungarian ancient history, involved more than archaeology. Certain states had begun to establish research institutes in foreign cities that were important from the perspective of national history in the first half of the nineteenth century: the German Archaeological Institute established in Rome in 1829 represented the first such institute. During the second half of the century, similar German, French, and British institutes and missions were founded one after another in Rome, Athens, Cairo, and Jerusalem, while Russian and German bodies were later established in Constantinople. In 1909, Kuno Klebelsberg, who served all along as one of the primary supporters of such an initiative, comprehensively described the mission of the Hungarian institute in a letter to Lajos Thallóczy, including details such as the arrangement of rooms in the future Hungarian House and the collection of books at its library. The thirty-year-old ministerial advisor concluded his letter to the powerful Finance Ministry department chief with the caveat "for the time being we must keep quiet about our beautiful plan precisely in the interest of its success."[68]

Klebelsberg slated Imre Karácson, a Catholic priest, a church historian, and an Orientalist who was already conducting research in the Ottoman capital, to become the director of the new institute. Karácson had himself already played with the idea of establishing such an institute: "I have begun to seriously think that since I receive a benefice, I will immediately get a house here and found an *Institut hongrois* such as the Russians have."[69] However, Klebelsberg was merely preaching to the choir with Thallóczy, since the historian firmly believed in the necessity of Hungary's mission in the Balkans and the Middle East. During the Balkan Wars, Thallóczy wrote a memorandum regarding the creation of the institutional system required to implement Hungarian Balkan policy in which he presented a series of proposals, which included the introduction of Balkan languages at the postsecondary and even secondary levels of the educational system, the establishment of a Balkan customs union, the construction of a mosque in Budapest, and the foundation of a Hungarian gymnasium in Constantinople. The idea of establishing a Hungarian institute in Constantinople gained new momentum with the promotion of Klebelsberg to the position of state secretary at the Education Ministry and, subsequently, the office of the prime minister in 1916. Klebelsberg, who during the Horthy era became a highly influential education minister, not only became the executive vice president (and de facto head) of the institute established in November 1916 but also selected one of his relatives (instead of Karácson), the archaeologist-art historian Antal Hekler, to serve as its director, an appointment that provoked some displeasure within intellectual public opinion.[70]

In early 1917, Hekler traveled with the institute's first scholarship to Constantinople, where in a rented building he began operating the first Hungarian scientific institute located in a foreign country (the Berlin institute opened a few weeks later). Among the small number of people who received scholarships to study at the institution, we find the archaeologist Géza Fehér (1890–1955), one of the Turanian Society's fellow travelers who became an outstanding authority on the Bulgarian-related aspects of Hungarian ancient history and was an employee of Hungary's legation in Sofia during the interwar period. Architect and author Károly Kós was among the first scholarship recipients and wrote his 1918 book *Sztambul* based on his experiences in Constantinople. An analyst of the work that Kós did during his stay in the city emphasized that the architect of the Werkeletelep district in Budapest, the Budapest Zoo, and other acclaimed buildings did not imbue his book with the motifs of Turanism (in so far as he wanted to avoid any attempt to demonstrate the superiority of the Westernized culture of Hungary and to suggest that the Hungarians were approaching their "Turkish brothers" with civilizing intent) and did not particularly strum the chords of fraternity either.[71] Kós's identification with Turkish architecture and culture in many respects resembled his relationship with Transylvanian folk culture: he expressly feared the impact that the West might exercise on them. At the same time, he completely identified the constructed East with the Hungarian past and therefore accepted certain premises of Hungarian Eastern thinking.[72] While Kós received a scholarship to study at the institute essentially so he could avoid performing military service, he nevertheless participated actively in the institute's activities, holding lectures, leading excursions, and conducting research and drawing, until his departure in 1918 to design Archduke Joseph August's hunting lodge in Görgény (Gurghiu, Romania).[73]

The Hungarian institute in Constantinople was forced to confront many difficulties: disruptions in the supply of provisions, the surliness or outright malice of Turkish authorities, and even the sudden death of one of the participating scholars.[74] The institute nevertheless attempted to carry out far-reaching scientific activity: scholarship holders and foreign guests presented lectures, conducted research, and published scientific articles.

Although the Hungarian Scientific Institute of Constantinople (HSIC) was dependent on the Ministry of Religion and Public Education and received its financial support—which was almost always inadequate and late in arriving—from the budget of the Hungarian government, correspondence and other documents reveal that the Hungarian Eastern Cultural Center exercised a significant informal influence over the institute. On the one hand, *Turán* quickly became the institute's "official gazette," reporting on its activities and providing a forum for its publications.[75] Cultural center representatives (primarily Miklós Bánffy and Pál Teleki) occasionally appeared personally at the institute, and on these occasions, director Antal Hekler could not thank them enough for their support ("In Teleki we have a strong and reliable source of support," Hekler wrote in the spring of 1918).[76] On the other hand, prominent Turanians associated with the Hungarian Eastern Cultural Center, above all Miklós Bánffy, played a key role in selecting a new director for the institute after Hekler was appointed to serve as an ordinary public professor at the University of Budapest in 1918. For the many candidates who aspired to attain this position, their meeting with the government commissioner in charge of the Hungarian Royal Opera House was of the utmost importance. ("As I have learned from István Zichy, Bánffy desires the meeting with the professor. Over the coming days I will pay a visit to Zichy or write to him in relation to this matter."[77])

The authorities responsible for selecting the new director of the HSIC finally chose the young historian Gyula Szekfű (1883–1955), who accepted the post only after much urging. Szekfű, who denounced Turanism in extremely sharp terms a decade and a half later, even published a French-language article in *Turán* in early 1917, perhaps in an attempt to portray himself as an authority in the domain of Hungarian-Turkish relations in this way as well.[78] Szekfű demurred that he was unfamiliar with the Turkish language (which was true), maintained nearly impossible demands (he wanted to simultaneously receive two salaries through 1918), and was extremely touched by his own fate when he had to have a tailcoat made for himself in order to meet the dress requirements for his new assignment.[79] However, the collapse at the end of the First World War swept away both the appointment and the wardrobe update. In the autumn of 1918, the HSIC moved to its intended permanent location in Constantinople, and the letter from the director connected to this event casts light on the manifold talents of the architect who had designed the decor for Hungary's final royal coronation: Hekler decreed with regard to the new building that "Kós will bring the bed sheets himself."[80] However, the scholarship recipients never returned, and the HSIC was soon closed. The institute's collection of books was donated to the Apostolic Nunciature, and in early January 1919, secretary Zoltán Oroszlán became the last staff member to leave Constantinople and return to Hungary.[81] During the 1920s, the Hungarian government toyed with the idea of reopening the HSIC: in fact, the institute's budget heading continued to exist until 1923, and its subsequent elimination was closely connected to the reorganization of the Turanian Society's finances.

The balance sheet of the HSIC was at the very least mixed. Although at the beginning there had been planned archaeological digs in Asia Minor (this is one of the reasons that Hekler, who had also received training as an archaeologist, was appointed director of the institute), these excavations were never carried out. Furthermore, due to the wartime conditions, there were no true Turkologists or Byzantinologists among the institute's scholarship recipients. Although the HSIC recruited such scholars in the autumn of 1918, they were unable to travel to Constantinople due to the wartime collapse. The Hungarian scientific institute that had been founded and begun operations in the Ottoman capital amid extremely unfavorable circumstances constituted the first—and rather poorly organized—attempt to establish an Eastern scientific presence and was the logical continuation of all that had taken place in connection to Hungarian-Turkish relations since the time of the Russo-Turkish War. At the same time, the institute complemented the activities of the Turanian Society and satisfied its long-standing demand for an independent and rational mouthpiece for Hungarian Balkan policy.

However, all of these activities were dwarfed by the cultural center's most significant undertaking: the scholarship enterprise. The education of "Turanian youth" represented one of the long-held ambitions of the Turanian movement, having already appeared in Lajos Thallóczy's previously mentioned memorandum.[82] Beginning with the 1916–1917 academic year, hundreds of young Turks, Bulgarians, Bosnians, and even Tatars and Albanians studied in Hungary with the generous support of the Education Ministry and the Trade Ministry—and under the strict subordination of the former. The cultural center expropriated similar, previously existing initiatives, such as the Julian Society's Bosnian action that had been functioning since 1911 or the Bulgarian action of the city of Temesvár (today Timișoara, Romania), and began to conduct them as its own undertakings.[83] In July 1916, the cultural center sent a teacher to Constantinople in order to provide scholarship recipients who were preparing to go to Hungary with instruction in the Hungarian language. (The language instructor, Gyula Avar, managed to begin teaching only ten months later and was able to operate with such a low degree of efficiency that he soon discontinued his work. In his report, Avar offered a rather bitter appraisal of his failure.)[84] A total of 186 Turkish students, around 80 Bulgarian and Bosnian students each, and 11 Tatar students traveled to Hungary to study primarily at institutes of secondary education and technical (agricultural and industrial) schools, although some of them attended universities and economic academies. In addition to the primary centers of education in provincial Hungary such as Győr, Kassa, Debrecen, Szeged, Kolozsvár, Temesvár, and Szabadka (Subotica, Serbia), these "red-fezzed Turks or characteristically garrulous Bulgarian students" appeared at smaller locations such as Hajdúböszörmény and Csáktornya (Čakovec, Croatia) as well.[85] The provision and management of these students as well as the mediation of their conflicts consumed a significant portion of the cultural center's energy. The students had difficulty learning the Hungarian language, adapting to the climate, and dealing with school discipline, and cultural center officials used every means at their disposal to prevent money from being sent to them because they feared that it would be used for illegitimate purposes. We surprisingly do not really find references to problems surrounding

Muslim religious regulations, for which the cultural center had attempted to prepare the schools that received the students. The main difficulties were connected rather to alcohol consumption, gambling, relations maintained with unauthorized persons that served to undermine classroom discipline, minor cases of theft, and leaving without permission.[86] Around 340 scholarship recipients attended educational institutions in Hungary through this program over the course of two and a half academic years, and during the 1920–1921 academic year, 52 Turkish students were still studying in Hungary in spite of the wars and revolutions that had taken place; some were still in the country even in the middle of the 1920s.[87] The cultural center also attempted to provide students with internships; thus, those who were studying to become agriculturalists were often sent to work at large estates or agricultural plants.

It is difficult to assess the results of this scholarship program. At the least, the idea seemed to be logical, and moreover, the Turkish state covered a significant portion of the related expenses. Documents reflect concern for the students, the compiled dossiers reveal expended effort, and the certification registers exhibit personal progress.[88] However, in many instances, these records indicate a lack of preparation, language ability, and special civilizational knowledge among students as well. The process of selecting those who would receive scholarships was not problem-free either and above all was not devoid of improvised and even authoritarian elements. Hungarian-Turkish relations in the 1920s nevertheless show that Turkish students who had studied in Hungary in many instances provided assistance to Hungarian diplomats or organizations. The results of the program were at the very least contradictory, and due to the program's discontinuation, it ultimately proved to be a dead-end street. In any event, the idea clearly reflects the fundamental attitude that sprang from the Hungarian consciousness, according to which the Hungarians, as the most developed Turanian nation, would civilize those that were less developed.

"Here everything is purely about interest in the East," the hypercritical Ignác Goldziher noted in his diary in August 1916.[89] This heightened interest and, above all, the hundreds of thousands of krone in government support brought not only recognition to the cultural center but also, during the First World War, the first expressions of disapproval. This criticism pertained primarily to the scientific and conceptual validity of Turanism. The most serious attack from this perspective came from somebody who had been associated with the Turanian Society from the very beginning: Gyula

Germanus, one of the legendary figures associated with Hungarian Orientalism who at this time worked as an instructor at the Eastern Academy.[90] In 1912, Germanus offered his services to the Turanian Society and even participated in its early activities.[91] The fact that Germanus's attack on Turanism, which was later published in reprint, originally appeared in *Magyar Figyelő*, the periodical associated with the intelligentsia that was close to Prime Minister István Tisza, served to heighten the degree of threat that it posed to the movement.

Germanus's thirty-page polemic was published in two parts in the first half of 1916 with a fairly significant Orientalist critical apparatus.[92] In the first part of his discourse, Germanus sharply criticized the usage of the term *Turanian* to denote an ethnic group, arguing that this designation never signified a standard classification and applied rather to a way of life. Germanus noted that the word was used in reference to both Aryan and non-Aryan peoples and that such imprecision "provides the opportunity for misunderstanding." Germanus then disparaged Hungarian Turanists with the remark that "commensurate to their powers of imagination they operate with the number of 300–700 million Turanian souls."[93] In the second part, Germanus—while demonstrating the inaccuracy of the classification Turanian based on the example of the ancient Parthians—tore apart Max Müller's theory pertaining to the existence of a Turanian language family, pointing out that use of the term was not at all symmetrical, namely, in Turkey, where it designated the solidarity of "full-blooded Turks" that Turkish nationalists were using precisely against Christians during this period and thus included neither the Hungarians nor the more distant peoples such as the Finns or the Japanese. Germanus pronounced a merciless final verdict, one that established the main direction of later criticism toward Turanism: "In Hungary the catchword 'Turanian' is understood to mean something completely different—the universality of Asia, which finds expression in the slogan of the Turanists 'from Dévény to Tokyo.' They idealize Asia and yearn with morbid enthusiasm to return to Asia, while they forget that the Hungarian nation has been living in Europe for a thousand years, clings with innumerable roots to European soil and can thank its survival only to the fact that coming from Asia it was able to become European."[94]

In these articles, Germanus characterized the reasoning of the Turanists to be quite simply a house of cards. It is not known what prompted Germanus to form this judgment, which in fact served to harm his career opportunities. In 1915 and over subsequent years, Germanus conducted several government missions to Turkey that were either covert or shrouded in secrecy, and he perhaps thought that his protectors would defend him from the boundless wrath of the Turanians.[95] Alajos Paikert wrote to Kolozsvár university professor Sándor Márki urging him in no uncertain terms to deliver some kind of riposte and that *"unpatriotic* is the gentlest expression" he could use to qualify Germanus's articles criticizing Turanism.[96] Márki unenthusiastically mentioned Paikert's request in his diary and at the same time shed light on one of the eternal scourges of Hungarian Turanism: "But this is perhaps not my task after all. Here somebody who is acquainted with eastern languages is needed."[97] In the subsequent issue of *Magyar Figyelő*, art historian Zoltán Felvinczi Takács published a response to Germanus, who had attacked him personally in his previous articles. Although Felvinczi Takács presented his case elegantly, his lack of familiarity with Eastern languages forced him to refer only to secondary sources, and the main arguments he advanced in support of the affinity of the Turanian peoples—"the debate has not yet been settled" and "why not?"—did not really resonate with elementary force. This affair incidentally nullified any chance that Germanus may have had of ever working at the HSIC; thus, the effort he made in 1918 scurrying from door to door in an attempt gain an appointment to the institute was in vain.[98]

Author and journalist Zoltán Szász struck out at Turanism in terms that were one register lower in *Pesti Hírlap* (in which he did not use Germanus's work) and in *Nyugat* (in which he did). Szász's objections were not so scientific in nature, focusing rather on skepticism regarding the ideological prerequisites of Turanism. The author cautioned against the racial outlook connected to the entire Turanist idea as well as against drawing final conclusions from the condition of linguistic isolation. In the article published in *Pesti Hírlap*, Szász wrote that the most important thing to remember was that "culturally we resemble the most cultivated people of Europe." Szász continued: "Because it is not racial and, especially, linguistic affinity, but the cultural community that joins developed, cultivated and self-aware people together. The cultured Hungarians stands much closer to the cultured Aryan German than to the purest Turanian-blooded Asian indigenous inhabitant."[99] Szász employed more irony and verbal devices to repeat his previous theses in the article published in *Nyugat*, though in this instance he charged that Turanism was not only anti-Western and anti-Slavic but also anti-Semitic ("Turanism has already become a group slogan against that culture which is for the most part of Aryan character, though for them is primarily disseminated and proclaimed by Semites"),[100] as was shown in certain writings and pronouncements (e.g., in Mihály Kmoskó's articles).[101] But antisemitism was not characteristic of either the Turanian Society or the cultural center as a whole during this period in any case.

Alajos Paikert and Árpád Zempléni reacted to Szász's assertions in articles that appeared in *Pesti Hírlap*.[102] Statements of this type also compelled the leading members of the Turanian Society to respond. Both Pál Teleki and Jenő Cholnoky commented on the pronounced arguments in issues of *Turán* published in 1917 and 1918, attempting to deflect the accusation that Turanism was based on unscientific ideas by emphasizing that *Turan* was primarily a geographical rather than racial term.[103] Teleki and Cholnoky contended that *Turan* was a synonym for the Asian steppe, which had placed its stamp so strongly on the people who lived there or had originated from there that one could justifiably refer to them as the "peoples of Turan." Teleki characterized the Turanian plain as a "cultural foundry" that, like the great river valley civilizations, shaped the peoples that had "wandered there" and had "hardened and amalgamated into new form there and disseminated their culture."[104] This reasoning worked temporarily but did not resolve the issue of kinship (because if the landscape molds, then there can be no blood or linguistic relationship).

Although the collapse of Austria-Hungary at the end of the war buried all of the ambitious plans, 1916 and 1918 represented an exceptional period in the history of Hungarian Turanism: the new idea managed to transform itself into a comprehensive public movement and met with the main current of Hungarian nation building as well as the public demand for triumphant Hungarian imperialism. Strong government support provided the Turanian Society and cultural center with unprecedented financial opportunities. Intellectuals traveling with special military permits on the Balkanzug that had replaced the Orient Express and frequenting salons in Sofia and Constantinople; expeditions surveying the landscape from the steppes of southern Russia to Albania and the semidesert of Anatolia, fulminations sent to rural school headmasters regarding Turkish scholarship recipients, volumes of *Turán* that were fifteen centimeters thick, the gentle leafage on trees along Sultan Mehmed Avenue—all of these gave rise to the notion that the Hungarian nation had entered a new era, that following the post-1867 period of reconstruction the time for expansion had arrived. Hungary would become the point of reference not only for the dual monarchy but also for the Balkans and even the Middle East—their Paris, Berlin, and London, the metropolis of the Turanian peoples, the new Samarkand. This illusion was to last for hardly three years; it was followed by a painful awakening.

Notes

1. *Budapesti Hírlap*, November 27, 1910, 16.
2. National Archives of the Hungarian National Archives (hereafter, MNL OL), Belügyminisztérium, általános iratok, 3855. cs. 5. t. VII. kútfő, 160138. sz. a Turáni Társaság alapszabálya, 1911. július 28.
3. "A Turáni Társaság tagjainak névsora," Budapest, n.d. [1911].
4. For Paikert's diary, see OSZKK, Oct. Hung. 1445 Paikert Alajos naplója, 1911; for the first three months of the year 1911 (January-March), we can find no less then thirty-three entries mentioning activities related to the Turanian Society.
5. Museum of Hungarian Agriculture, personal records collection, Paikert Alajos hagyatéka, I.248, 1329–1338. Paikert Alajos: Életem, 120. f. (this part did not appear in the printed version of his autobiography).
6. See the following important study regarding Paikert's career-building and mate-selection strategies: György Kövér, "'Minden tekintetben megfelelő combinatio . . .' Egy keresztény középosztályi fiatalember párválasztási dilemmái a 19–20. század fordulóján," in *Biográfia és társadalomtörténet* (Budapest: Osiris, 2014), 351–72.
7. For the plans Paikert and others made during the First World War, see Ignác Romsics, "A magyar birodalmi gondolat," in *Múltról a mának* (Budapest: Osiris, 2004), 121–22, 144–47. For the memorandum Paikert wrote to Prime Minister István Tisza, see Hungarian Agricultural Museum, Personal Historical Records Collection (hereafter, MMGM SZE), Turán-feliratú mappa: Paikert Alajos memoranduma, Budapest, 1916. július 10. For his expressions of antisemitism in 1919, see MMGM SZE, Turán-feliratú mappa: Paikert Alajos memoranduma, Budapest, 2012.21.1, Paikert-hagyaték, Turáni Társaság feliratú mappa, Paikert Alajos: Újjáéledés, 4. f.: "Implanting Jewry in the place of the Christian Hungarian nation is possible in Hungary only by way of shameful deception and mass murder, thus those who attempt this must be treated as every respectable state treats traitors and murderers." For his post-1945 plans, see MTAKK, Ms 10234/2 Paikert Alajos levele Voinovich Gézának, az MTA főtitkárának, Budapest, 1948. január 14. és 27. Attached to this letter is his twenty-eight-page manuscript "Világbéke" (World peace).
8. "Why have you been so silent and why do you keep yourself so distant from the Turanian Society?" (OSZKK Fond 121/471, Paikert Alajos levele Németh Gyulának, Budapest, 1915. március 13).
9. MMGM SZE, I.248, 1329–1338. Paikert Alajos: Életem, 120. ff. and 89. f.
10. OSZKK Oct. Hung. 1445/I, Paikert Alajos évről évre szóló kis naplója, 1911. november 7.
11. For the time that Teleki spent engaged in Turanism, see Balázs Ablonczy, *Pal Teleki (1879–1941): The Life of a Controversial Hungarian Politician* (Wayne, NJ: CHSP, 2006), 29–31, 36–39.
12. Rezső Milleker, "Kis-Ázsia gazdasági viszonyai," *Turán* 1, no. 1 (1913): 43.
13. Pál Teleki, *A Turáni Társaság eddigi és jövendő működése: Megnyitó beszéd az 1914. január 31-i közgyűlésre* (Budapest: s.n., 1914), 9.

14. *Turán* 1, no. 1 (1913), 51.

15. Dévény (Devín, Slovakia) is currently a borough of Bratislava. Before 1918, the settlement represented the Western gateway of the kingdom of Hungary. It was likewise a symbolic location for the Slovak national movement. Shortly after Dévény became part of Czechoslovakia following the First World War, Czechoslovak officials ordered the removal of a monument that had been erected in 1896 to commemorate the one-thousand-year anniversary of the Hungarian arrival to the Carpathian Basin. For information regarding Dévény's role in national discourse, see Varga Bálint, *Monumental Nation: Magyar Nationalism and Symbolic Politics in Fin-de-siècle Hungary* (New York: Berghahn, 2016), 47–72, 213–40.

16. Teleki, *A Turáni Társaság eddigi és jövendő működése*, 9.

17. MNL OL K 1384, 1. cs. 1. t. 26. f. Sebestyén Gyula levele Paikert Alajosnak, Budapest, 1912. február 24.

18. Ibid., 1. cs. 2. t. 1912. dosszié, hivatalos levelezés, Fröhlich Izidor rektor levele a Turáni Társaságnak, Budapest, 1912. március.

19. Ibid., 18. f. Marzsó Lajos hetijelentése, 1912. február 3–10.

20. Teleki, *A Turáni Társaság eddig és jövendő működése*, 3–4.

21. Ibid., 5–6; "Hírek," *Turán* 1, no. 2 (1913): 107–8; Imre Timkó, "Turáni népek az Arál-Kaspi síkságon," *Turán* 1, no. 3 (1913): 143–55.

22. György Wegener, "Khina ébredése," *Turán* 1, no. 2 (1913): 69–85; Dr. Zoltán F. Takács, "Kölcsönhatások a távol Kelet művészetében," *Turán* 1, no. 3 (1913): 170–77; Mihály Kmoskó, "A sumírek," *Turán* 1, no. 1 (1913): 15–27; Mihály Kmoskó, "A sumírek," *Turán* 1, no. 3 (1913): 123–42.

23. Jenő Tóth, "Turáni törzsek a Himaláyában," *Turán* 1, no. 3 (1913): 169.

24. Pál Teleki, "Bevezető a 'Turán' című folyóirathoz," in *Válogatott politikai írások és beszédek*, ed. Balázs Ablonczy (Budapest: Osiris, 2000), 11.

25. Alajos Paikert, "Ázsia jövője," *Turán* 1, no. 1 (1913): 14.

26. MNL OL P 2256, személyi fondtöredékek, 6. doboz, 36. t. Gálocsy Árpád iratai, 1–5. f. Előterjesztés a Kettőskereszt Vérszövetség Elnöki Tanácsához a turanizmus tárgyában, 1923. július 19.

27. For this editorial note, see Antal Penigey, "A Kelet gazdasági meghódítása c. cikkéhez," *Turán* 1, no. 2 (1913): 88.

28. For the Turanism of *A Cél*, see Ibolya Godinek, "Fajvédő eszme *A Cél* című folyóiratban," *Valóság* 57, no. 2 (2014): 40–42.

29. NMI 36/1912, Mészáros Gyula jelentése török és kisázsiai útjáról, Budapest, 1912. május 22.

30. Pál Teleki, "Bevezető," *Turán*, no. 1 (1913), 5–6; *A Turáni Társaság eddig és jövendő működése*, 8.

31. OSZKK, Levelestár, Paikert Alajos levele Zempléni Árpádnak, Budapest, 1915. november 26.

32. Kessler, "Turanism and Pan-Turanism in Hungary," 138–39, 144.

33. Kálmán Balkányi, *Arcok, harcok, kudarcok* (Budapest: Pesti Lloyd Társulat, 1934), 68.

34. *Mit kíván a Magyar-Keleti Gazdasági Központ* (Budapest: Márkus Samu Könyvnyomdája, 1916), 1, 4.

35. "Társasági ügyek," *Turán* 2, no. 10 (1917): 480.

36. HMA, A 3337/0-8 Felvinczi Takács Zoltán turáni témájú kézirattöredéke, undated.

37. Ignác Goldziher, *Napló*, ed. Sándor Scheiber (Budapest: Magvető, 1984), 347.

38. For a list of the departments, see "Társasági ügyek," *Turán* 2, no. 1 (1917): 70–72.

39. Miklós Szalai, "Az 1916. évi VII. törvénycikk," *Történelmi Szemle* 52, no. 4 (2010): 593–601.

40. Gábor Ágoston and Balázs Sudár, *Gül baba és a magyarországi bektasi dervisek* (Budapest: Terebess, 2002), 77–79.

41. András Hadik, "Hadikiállítások Lembergben és a Margitszigeten," lecture presented on September 20, 2017, at the István Medgyaszay Memorial Conference held at the Hungarian Academy of Arts in Budapest; and Ferenc Potzner, *Medgyaszay István* (Budapest: Holnap Kiadó, 2004), 137–42.

42. Eötvös Loránd University Library Manuscript Department (hereafter, EKK), H 272/27, Kúnos Ignác levelezőlapja Simonyi Zsigmondnak, Eger (Csehország), 1915. július 17.

43. Britta Lange, *Die Wiener Forschungen an Kriegsgefangenen 1915–1918*, Veröffentlichungen zur Sozialanthropologie 17 (Vienna: Verlag der ÖAW, 2013), 119.

44. Mihály Lenhossék, "Anthropologische Untersuchungen an russischen Kriegsgefangenen finnisch-ugrischer Nationalität," *Turán* 2, no. 3 (1917): 136–51.

45. For the linguistic research done at the camp, see "Társulati ügyek," *Keleti Szemle* 16 (1915/1916): 255–63, and *Keleti Szemle* 17 (1916/17): 225–32.

46. NMI 259/1916, Sebestyén Gyula levele a Néprajzi Múzeumnak, Budapest, 1916. szeptember 7. With regard to the freedom of movement of researchers at the camps, see OSZKK, Fond 121/471, Németh Gyula hagyatéka, Paikert Alajos levele Németh Gyulának, Budapest, 1916. március 1.

47. MNL OL P 1384, 4. cs. 1918–1919-es ügyviteli iratok. 2121/1918, Mayer Károly miniszteri tanácsos levele a Turáni Társaságnak, Budapest, 1918. szeptember 6. The German consul general reported about the idea of a Turanian Legion based on his interview with Gyula Pekár: Archiv des Auswärtigen Amtes (Berlin), Gesandtschaft Budapest, Karton 140, P47—Turanische Frage, Fürstenberg an Auswärtigen Amt, Budapest, 1915. december 17.

48. "A szerkesztőség megjegyzése Alois v. Paikert 'Der turanische Gedanke' c. cikkéhez," *Turán* 2, nos. 4–5 (1917): 191.

49. With regard to Vikár's work as editor of *Turán*, see Ildikó P. Varga, *"Finnország leglelkesebb diplomatája itt több mint 50 éven keresztül": Vikár Béla levelei* (Kolozsvár [Cluj-Napoca]: Erdélyi Múzeum Egyesület, 2017), 204–6.

50. The everyday routine of editing *Turán* can be partly reconstructed to some degree in correspondence between Teleki and Németh: OSZKK, Fond 121/640, Németh Gyula hagyatéka, Teleki Pál levelei, 1918–1937, especially Teleki Pál levele Németh Gyulának, 1918. április 27. and 1918. szeptember 13.

51. Ethnographic Museum, Ethnological Archives, 13148, Levelek T, 5207. sz Teleki Pál levele Sebestyén Gyulának, Budapest, 1918. július 3.

52. "Edouard Chavannes," *Turán* 3, nos. 1–2 (1918): 125.

53. T. Lothrop Stoddard, "Pan-Turanism," *American Political Science Review* 11, no. 1 (February 1917): 12–23; and Teleki Pál, "Folyóiratszemle," *Turán* 3, nos. 6–7 (1918): 416–17.

54. For example, *Turán* 3, no. 5 (1918): 314–18; and *Turán* 3, nos. 6–7 (1918): 424–27.

55. Jenő Horváth, "Seton-Watson R. W.: The Rise of Nationality in the Balkans," *Turán* 3, no. 8 (1918): 412–14.

56. For example, Julius Germanus, "Herbert Adams Gibbons: The Foundation of the Ottoman Empire," *Turán* 3, no. 8 (1918): 491–96.

57. "Társasági ügyek," *Turán* 3, no. 4 (1918): 272.

58. OSZKK Fond 121/640, Teleki Pál levele Németh Gyulának, Budapest, 1918. április 27.

59. EA, 13148, Levelek T, no. 5207. Teleki Pál levele Sebestyén Gyulának, Budapest, 1918. július 3. For details regarding this dispute, see Gyula Németh, "A nagyszentmiklósi kincs körül," *Turán* 3, nos. 3–4 (1918): 265–67; "A nagyszentmiklósi kincs körül II," *Turán* 3, no. 5 (1918): 325–29; Gyula Sebestyén, "Nyílt levél a főszerkesztőhöz," *Turán* 3, no. 5 (1918): 329–31; and Gyula Németh, "Válasz Sebestyénnek," *Turán* 3, no. 5 (1918): 331–32.

60. Dr. Kálmán Lambrecht, "Tanulmányok Ukrániában," *Turán* 3, nos. 9–10 (1918): 541–64.

61. The results of this expedition were published during the interwar period as well: Ernő Csiki, *Csiki Ernő állattani kutatásai Albániában*, vol. 1, Balkán-kutatások I, 1 (Budapest: MTA, 1923); *Csiki Ernő állattani kutatásai Albániában*, vol. 2, Balkán-kutatások I, 2 (Budapest: MTA, 1940); Ludwig [Lajos] Lóczy, *Geologische Studien im westlichen Serbien*, Balkán-kutatások 2 (Berlin: Walter de Gruyter, 1924); and Pál Teleki and Ernő Csiki, eds., *Adatok Albánia flórájához / Additamenta ad floram Albaniae*, Balkán-kutatások 3 (Budapest: MTA, 1926).

62. HMA A 2601/6.1, Lénárd Jenő levele Felvinczi Takács Zoltánnak, Eszék (Osijek), 1914. szeptember 5.

63. NMI 162/1919, Györffy István jelentése kisázsiai gyűjtőútjáról, Budapest, 1919. február 20.

64. For an ethnographic approach to the Greater Cumanian identity, see Miklós Szilágyi, "A nagykun öntudat," *Regio* 7, no. 1 (1996), 44–63.

65. For more about Györffy, see László Kósa, "Györffy István öröksége," in *Nemesek, polgárok, parasztok* (Budapest: Osiris, 2003), 404–23.

66. For Teleki's education ministry policy speech, see *Képviselőházi Napló 1935–1940*, vol. 19, session held on June 11, 1938, 647.

67. Zoltán Pallag, "Pósta Béla és a magyar keleti archeológiai intézet terve," in *A Debreceni Déri Múzeum Évkönyve 2002–2003*, (Debrecen: Déri Múzeum, 2003): 117–32; and Zoltán Vincze, *A kolozsvári régészeti iskola a Pósta Béla-korszakban (1899–1919)* (Kolozsvár [Cluj-Napoca]: EME, 2014), 470–71.

68. Quoted in Norbert Nagy, *A Konstantinápolyi Magyar Tudományos Intézet története (1916–1918)*, Balkán Füzetek 7 (Pécs: PTE TTK FI Kelet-Mediterrán és Balkán Tanulmányok Központja, 2010), 17.

69. OSZKK, Fol. Hung. 1900: Karácson Imre: Török–magyar oklevéltár (1533–1789) 27. f. beledolgozva Karácson Imre levele Thallóczy Lajosnak, n.d. [1911 előtt]. For more about Karácson, see György Csorba, "Történész a történelem viharában: Karácson Imre az 1908–1911 közötti törökországi eseményekről," *Keletkutatás* (Spring 2012): 87–101.

70. For information about Hekler, see Árpád Miklós Nagy, "Hekler Antal (1882–1940). Pont—ellenpont. Hekler Antal, a klasszika archeológus," *Enigma* 13, no. 47 (2006): 161–77.

71. Yavuz Sezer, "Hungarian Orientalism, Turanism and Karoly Kós's *Sztambul* (1918)," *Centropa* 7, no. 2 (2007): 136–52.

72. For a survey of Kós's entire career, see Anthony Gall, *Kós Károly műhelye/The Workshop of Károly Kós* (Budapest: Mundus, 2002).

73. For information regarding Kós's time in Constantinople, see Samu Benkő, ed., *Édes Idám! Kós Károly levelei feleségéhez. 1911–1918, 1946–1948* (Kolozsvár [Cluj-Napoca]: Polis, 2011), 39–152.

74. Peter Ralbovszky, a Catholic priest and Byzantinologist, died of a heart attack while bathing in the sea. For the circumstances surrounding Ralbovszky's death, see Benkő, *Édes Idám!*, 93.

75. "A Konstantinápolyi Magyar Tudományos Intézet közleményei," *Turán* 3, no. 4 (1918): 231–41; and *Turán* 3, nos. 6–7 (1918): 391–95.

76. BTK Művészettörténeti Intézet, Adattár, MDK C-I-76/40, Hekler Antal: Személyes emlékek. In this source: Hekler Antal levele ismeretlennek, Konstantinápoly, 1918. május 12.

77. EKK, G 628, Németh Gyula levele Szekfű Gyulának, Budapest, 1918. augusztus 14.

78. Jules Szekfű, "Tableau de la domination turque en Hongrie," *Turán* 3, no. 3 (1918): 129–43.

79. OSZKK, Fond 121/607, Szekfű Gyula levele Németh Gyulának, Ötösbánya (Rudňany), 1918. augusztus 9.

80. Egyetemi Levéltár, 401/a, Oroszlán Zoltán hagyatéka, 2. doboz, Hekler Antal levele Oroszlán Zoltánnak, Budapest, 1918. szeptember 1.

81. Nagy, *A Konstantinápolyi Magyar Tudományos Intézet története*, 31.

82. OSZKK, Fol. Hung. 1900: "A Balkán félszigeten beállott változásokkal szemben Magyarország részéről követendő eljárás kulturális és gazdaság politikai téren," Emlékirat Thallóczy Lajostól, n.d.

83. Jenő Gy. Szécsi, "A Turáni Társaság nevelési akciója," *Turán* 4, (1921): 66–73.

84. MNL OL, P 1384, 2. doboz 2. t. általános ügyviteli iratok, 810–11, f. Avar Gyula jelentése, Budapest, 1917. szeptember 12.

85. Szécsi, "A Turáni Társaság nevelési akciója," 67.

86. For detailed reports on these transgressions, see, for example, MNL OL P 1384, 2. doboz 2. t. általános ügyviteli iratok, 398. f. Donavell János levele a Magyar Keleti Kultúrközpontnak, Temesvár, 1917. július 31.

87. MNL OL K 28, Miniszterelnökség, Kisebbségi és Nemzetiségi Osztály iratai, 211. doboz, 208biz/1922. sz., 391–95, f. Pekár Gyula elnök éves jelentése, Budapest, 1922. május 27.

88. One can find detailed information regarding Bosnian students at the Hungarian Geographical Museum (Érd), Archives, Registry "Turáni Társaság, Bosnyák tanulók személyi adatai, 1917–1918."

89. Goldziher, *Napló*, 346.

90. For Germanus's career, see Adam Mestyan, "Materials for a History of Hungarian Academic Orientalism: The Case of Gyula Germanus," *Die Welt des Islams* 54, no. 1 (2014): 4–33; and Adam Mestyan, "'I Have to Disguise Myself': Orientalism, Gyula Germanus, and Pilgrimage as Cultural Capital, 1935–1965," in *The Hajj and Europe in the Age of Empire*, ed. Umar Ryad, Leiden Studies in Islam and Society, vol. 5 (Leiden: Brill, 2017), 217–39.

91. MNL OL P 1384, 1. cs. 2. t. 1912-dosszié, hivatalos levelezés, Germanus Gyula levele Paikert Alajosnak, Budapest, 1912. október 17; and OSZKK, Oct. Hung. 1445 Paikert Alajos naplója, 1911. január.

92. Dr. Germanus Gyula, "Turán," *Magyar Figyelő* 6, no. 1 (1916): 405–20; and Dr. Germanus Gyula, "Turán II," *Magyar Figyelő* 6, no. 2 (1916): 23–37.

93. Germanus, "Turán," 419–420.

94. Germanus, "Turán II," 37.

95. Mestyan, "Materials for a History of Hungarian Academic Orientalism," 13–14.

96. MTAKK Ms 5164/378, Paikert Alajos levele Márki Sándornak, Budapest, 1916. március 23.

97. MNL Békés Megyei Levéltára XV. 33. (Xerox-tár) 251. tétel Márki Sándor naplója 1873–1925. 1916. március 27.

98. OSZKK, Fond 121/223, Germanus Gyula levele Németh Gyulának, Lőcse (Levoča), 1918. augusztus 15. illetve augusztus 29.

99. Zoltán Szász, "Turánizmus," *Pesti Hírlap* 37, November 12, 1915, 5.

100. Zoltán Szász, "Turánizmus," *Nyugat* 9, no. 16 (1916): 267–75.

101. For Kmoskó's reference to the Jewish origin of certain western European Sumerologists, see Mihály Kmoskó, "A sumírek—Babylonia hely- és néprajza," *Turán* 1, no. 3 (1913): 127. However, antisemitism became a dominant element in Kmoskó's thought only after 1916. For more on this, see István Ormos, *Egy életút állomásai: Kmoskó Mihály (1876–1931)* (Budapest: METEM, 2017), 216–18.

102. Árpád Zempléni, "Turanizmus (Válasz Szász Zoltán úrnak)," *Pesti Hírlap*, November 21, 1915; "Turanizmus," *Pesti Hírlap*, November 14, 1915, 16.

103. Jenő Cholnoky, "Túrán," *Turán* 3, no. 1 (1918): 25–43; and Pál Teleki, "A Turán földrajzi fogalom," *Turán* 3, no. 1 (1918): 44–83.

104. Pál Teleki, "Táj és faj," in *Válogatott politikai írások*, ed. Ablonczy, 26.

4

SILVER AGE

THE AUSTRO-HUNGARIAN MONARCHY LOST THE WAR AT THE end of 1918, but the armistice signed at the Villa Guisti near Padua on November 3 settled the fate of an empire that had already fallen apart. Whereas just a half year previously armies of the empire had stood deep inside Ukraine, the Balkans, and northern Italy and had forced Romania to conclude a separate peace, by this time, Austro-Hungarian troops were streaming back from the front in disorderly fashion. On October 16, the monarch, Charles I (for the Hungarians, Charles IV), attempted to avert the looming catastrophe through the federalization of his empire; however, almost the entire Hungarian political elite rejected this and instead wanted to transform the monarchy into a personal union before renouncing the 1867 compromise at the very end of the month. Meanwhile, on October 28, the foundation of Czechoslovakia was proclaimed in Prague, and Croatia also announced its secession. Count Mihály Károlyi formed a government in Budapest, composed of social democrats, left-wing bourgeois radicals, and Independence and '48 Party representatives who had formed the official opposition to the previous regime. Then on November 16, 1918, the people's republic was declared. Count Károlyi (who was earlier a member of the Turanian Society's leadership) served as Hungary's head of state beginning in January 1919. In addition to the military collapse, public security deteriorated to a tragic degree: soldiers returning from the front and criminal elements robbed and looted, the economy went into a freefall, and nationalities (Slovaks, Serbs, Romanians, and Transylvanian Saxons) living in Hungary declared their secession from the country at various popular assemblies. The armies of the successor states soon began to penetrate the territory of the previous kingdom of Hungary, and by the beginning of 1919, the majority of the country had come under Serb, Czechoslovak, and Romanian occupation.

A new ultimatum from the representative of the Entente in Hungary prompted the Budapest government to face the fact that these territories would likely be detached from the country and, indeed, that further territories would likely be occupied; therefore, on March 21, 1919, the government resigned and transferred power to the Hungarian Soviet Republic, composed of members of the newly formed Communist Party and left-wing social democrats. Under the leadership of Béla Kun, who had just returned home from Soviet Russia, this new state began to implement the Soviet-type transformation of society with lightning speed and made abundant use of violence in doing so. The Hungarian Soviet Republic initiated two military campaigns in order to regain control over the occupied parts of the country. The Northern Offensive quickly liberated the eastern part of Upper Hungary that had been occupied by Czechoslovakia, and Hungarian troops withdrew from this territory only under pressure from the Entente and the Paris Peace Conference. The so-called Tisza Offensive was then launched against the Romanian army at the end of July 1919, which ended in total collapse and the failure of the communist experiment: the Romanian army occupied Budapest and the northern part of Transdanubia.

Following a short-lived social democratic government, a right-wing cabinet came to power in Budapest. Then on November 16, 1919, after the withdrawal of Romanian troops, the former Austro-Hungarian vice admiral Miklós Horthy arrived to the city from the anticommunist stronghold of Szeged at the head of the National Army, which provided the naval officer with indispensable assistance in gaining the necessary support in the National Assembly to win election to the post of head of state (regent) of Hungary on March 1, 1920. Horthy's name came to designate the political system that characterized his governance in Hungary, which lasted until 1944. The Horthy regime retained the formal elements of parliamentarianism but was strongly autocratic and inconsistent in its observance of civil liberties. Among the pillars of this regime were strong anticommunism, revisionism, and, at times, antisemitism. On June 4, 1920, the Horthy-appointed government was compelled to sign the postwar peace treaty pertaining to Hungary at the Grand Trianon palace in Versailles. In accordance with this treaty, 67 percent of the territory and 57 percent of the population of the earlier kingdom of Hungary that composed the Hungarian part of the Austro-Hungarian monarchy were attached to new countries. More than three million ethnic Hungarians became citizens of foreign states. A deluge of refugees streamed from the lost territories into what remained of Hungary, the prime minister of which in 1920–1921 was Pál Teleki, the former president of the Turanian Society. The economic, political, and military collapse had produced an enormous shock within Hungarian society: the new government was forced to struggle with Hungary's new status as a small state and all of the consequences of economic upheaval (hyperinflation, rationing, disruptions in the supply of provisions, housing shortages, refugees) while establishing the foundations of the new state.[1]

Although the Turanian Society wanted to make itself appear to be a resolutely anti-Bolshevik organization that stood in opposition to "left-wing destruction," its everyday activities in 1918–1919 and the documents pertaining to them show a slightly different picture.[2] Turanian Society deputy president Gyula Pekár nearly wept as he implored Károlyi to receive him so that he could acquaint him with his plans regarding the Eastern Cultural Center: however, Pekár complained in a letter written in late 1918 that "I was never lucky enough to gain admission [to Károlyi's office]."[3] Following Béla Széchenyi's death in December 1918 (precisely kept organizational cashbooks show that a 400-krone wreath was purchased for his grave) and after the Turanian Society was permitted to operate in regular fashion after 1919, Gyula Pekár again became the organization's president, a position that he retained until his death in 1937.

In a memorandum written at the end of 1918, Pekár—still as deputy president—defined the Eastern Cultural Center's primary aim as follows: "Hungary, as the Turanian people that has acquired western culture to the greatest degree, is called upon to be the mentor of our more backward racial kin and the Turanian peoples." Pekár wrote with regard to the streamlining of organizational objectives that "the modest Albanian action was of political character and was intended to ensure that not only Austrian interests prevail in Albania, but Hungarian ones as well." The Turanian Society's deputy president concluded that the Albanian action therefore had to be discontinued, although the situation regarding the Bosnians was not so clear-cut: "It may be in our political interest to nourish these antagonisms [within the new Yugoslav state]." However, since the students who arrived in Hungary were very poor and thus required full financial support, Pekár asserted that "it is nevertheless our opinion that amid the completely changed circumstances the significant expenditures that must be appropriated for this action do not stand in proportion to its anticipated benefit."[4] The deputy president noted that this action could nevertheless not be ended until it had run its course. Pekár characterized the Turanian

Society's newly established Tatar contacts as utopian and concluded that Tatar students should thus be sent home. He believed that the organization's Bulgarian relations should be maintained, although only if the Bácska and the Banat regions, including the city of Temesvár, remained part of Hungary. Finally, Pekár recommended that the scholarship action be preserved in connection with Turkish students on the grounds that sending them home would be problematic.

Pekár's complaints regarding the scholarship recipients eventually paid off: on March 21, 1919, the government approved a motion from Prime Minister Dénes Berinkey (also a member of the Turanian Society) to not only provide the Eastern Cultural Center with its usual 50,000-krone prime ministerial subvention but also grant the organization an exceptional 100,000-krone remittance to cover "the most necessary expenses of the young people from the east." Although Finance Minister Pál Szende strenuously opposed the proposal to furnish this support, the prime minister's intention prevailed.[5]

The Hungarian Soviet Republic that came to power on the very day on which the Berinkey government approved this funding was not totally hostile toward the Turanian Society, which later attempted to create the impression the Bolsheviks had persecuted members of the organization and had forced them to vacate their premises. Although it is true that the József Cserny–led Lenin Boys (the political terror unit of the Hungarian Soviet Republic) were permitted to occupy their offices in the Hungarian Parliament Building, the Eastern Cultural Center received another office space elsewhere in the building and thus were by no means put out on the street. However, some of the center's documents did indeed fall victim to the office relocation and the malevolence of Hungarian Soviet Republic authorities. Although some of the Turanian Society's leading personalities obviously opposed the objectives of the commune, this did nothing to change the fact that the president of the Revolutionary Governing Council, Sándor Garbai, personally supported the provision of Turkish students with state assistance through the organization and that the Turanian Society received 50,000 krone despite certain resistance from the people's commissariat for foreign affairs.[6] The socialist-communist government, in a display of interest in the problem, founded the Eastern Socialist Party, published its Turkish-language periodical *Kelet* (East), and attempted to organize those who sympathized with left-wing ideas using the Turanian Society's infrastructure. This was not difficult in light of the fact that during these lean times those who stood up in support of the government received an abundant monthly allowance of between 300 and 400 krone.[7]

The situation turned around with the collapse of the Hungarian Soviet Republic. In the autumn of 1919, the Turanian Society was very slowly able to resume regular official operations even if it was not permitted to immediately move back into its appropriated offices. The appointment of Gyula Pekár to the position of state secretary at the Ministry of Religion and Public Education provided the process with significant impetus; in fact, Pekár served as the Friedrich government's minister without portfolio in charge of maintaining contacts with the Entente missions in Budapest, which is why he insisted on being addressed as *Minister* Pekár in all existing forums until the end of his life. Over the following decade and a half, the activities of the Turanian Society were closely intertwined with this athletically built man who spoke a half dozen languages and who was rumored to have posed, before the loss of his curly locks, as the model for the accessory figure depicting the Herculean medieval hero Miklós Toldi on the statue of poet János Arany in the garden of the National Museum in Budapest. (The daughter of future Turanian Society president Béla Széchenyi, Alice, served as the model for the other accessory figure that sculptor Alajos Stróbl placed on the statue, one depicting Toldi's fictional true love, Piroska.[8]) Pekár carefully collected clippings of published material containing criticisms of him, such as the comments—which, although savage, did not lack a certain inventiveness—of author Dezső Szabó (1879–1945), one of the main figures associated with Hungarian literary expressionism.[9] Szabó characterized Pekár as a "literary Szamuely" (a nickname borrowed from the sanguinary communist deputy people's commissar for the interior), a "noxious Slovak mediocrity" (referring to his origin), and a "furnitureless newcomer" who "in a more muscular culture could only be a literary joke."[10] Following his years as a lawyer, Pekár spent the definitive period of his life in Paris and was a member of painter Mihály Munkácsy's circles, and his editors wanted to build his writing career based on his hussar novellas regarding Lieutenant Dodo.

Although Pekár never caught up to Ferenc Herczeg, an author who originated from the Banat region, in terms of popularity, he did become a noted literary figure in Hungary at the beginning of the twentieth century. He also served as the president of a dozen associations, including the Kisfaludy Society beginning in 1901 and the Petőfi Society beginning in 1920; a parliamentary representative loyal to István Tisza; and a member of the Hungarian Academy of Sciences beginning in 1911. The books of notes kept among Pekár's papers preserved at the National Széchényi Library in Budapest clearly show how during the war his interests shifted from French, Breton, and Russian themes to the subjects of kindred peoples and Turanism.[11] Pekár wrote some literary works on these topics without significant success. (His novel *Attila* represented one such work.) As a result of the important position Pekár filled at the Film Industry Foundation, he gained the good fortune of having some of his works made into films.[12] As the president of the Petőfi Society, the conservative literary association named after the romantic poet Sándor Petőfi, Pekár played a central role in official cultural life, appearing almost everywhere and, by his own account, serving as the president of at least a dozen organizations and filling leadership positions in several others.[13] He was frightfully convinced of his own importance, and his lack of imagination, permanent social engagements, commitment to hierarchy, and political connections guaranteed that there would be no commotion within the Turanian Society. Pekár, together with Alajos Paikert, founded the Foreign Affairs Society, an organization for those interested in Hungarian foreign policy that published the periodical *Külügyi Szemle* (Foreign affairs review).

Under Pekár's presidency, the membership of the Turanian Society stagnated in number, and although some attempts were made to establish branches in provincial Hungary, the organizational hierarchy became entrenched.[14] Aside from a few loyal members who spoke at Turanian Society events almost every year, the membership of the most important organization associated with the Turanian movement was composed primarily of retired military officers, stenographers, and high school teachers. Although this did not mean that the Turanian Society had no influence, its level of authority during this period was not close to that which it had exercised between 1916 and 1918. A 1937 membership list provides us with information regarding the regular members of the Turanian Society: despite the decline in the association's prestige, twenty-seven of its ninety-nine regular members were college instructors, university professors, or private lecturers, most of whom were not, incidentally, involved in fields of study connected to the East.[15] We also find among the members four former, current, or future prime ministers (Sándor Simonyi-Semadam, István Bethlen, Kálmán Darányi, and László Bárdossy). In 1937, only one-quarter of the Turanian Society's members lived at locations outside Budapest. Particularly in the 1930s, we find many collectivities among the simple and supporting

Fig. 4.1. Turanian Society president Gyula Pekár (third from the right) holds forth before an audience that includes Archduke Joseph August of Austria (first on the left). FORTEPAN © 2010–2014 under Creative Commons CC-BY-SA-3.0 license, Zoltán Katona.

members of the Turanian Society, such as that composed of members from communities with a significant number of German inhabitants (Dunabog-dány, Budaörs, Solymár, and Kunbaja). Since one can hardly presume that ethnic Germans would have shown any particularly enthusiasm for Turan-ism, more comprehensive research will be required in order to determine if those who became members of the Turanian Society did so collectively based on the example of the local elite or if they were perhaps civil servants (teachers, notaries, magistrates) who maintained an individual interest in Magyarization.

Following the collapse at the end of the First World War and the shock of the Treaty of Trianon, there emerged a social demand for Turanism: within the beaten and humiliated society of Hungary, particularly its middle class, appeared a receptivity to an ideology that called not for expansion but for turning away from the West and striking back. The expression *Turán* became part of everyday language, not only in politics and culture but also in commerce; however, Turanism managed to benefit from this situation to only a limited degree. At the same time, the Turanian Society, which represented the main current of Turanism (and had restored its original name), split into three parts.

Documentation regarding precisely what occurred within the Turanian Society in 1920 and 1921, during which time this split took place, is somewhat scanty. We are therefore forced to rely mostly on fragmentary documents and decipher articles published in the periodical *Turán* in the manner of a Kremlinologist in order to determine the causes of this schism. On the one hand, President Gyula Pekár, yielding to the spirit of the age, did not refrain from making remarks bearing antisemitic connotations. For example, Pekár articulated his opinion during a September 1919 presentation on Turanism at a meeting of the Hungarian National Defense Association (Magyar Országos Véderő Egylet; founded by Gyula Gömbös and associates) that three great families of peoples had always struggled against one another throughout the course of history—the Aryans, the Turanians, and the Semites. According to the president of the Turanian Society, the latter "have played the role of blacksmith in history. They have always forged revolution."[16] As a result of such statements and the sharply antisemitic public mood, all of the Jewish Orientalists—with the exception of the prominent linguist Bernát Munkácsi—and members of the upper-middle class among the Turanian Society's members distanced themselves from the organization.[17] A certain antisemitism permeated the activities of the Turanian Society during the interwar period: applicants of Jewish origin were excluded from the 1924 engineer action in Turkey,[18] some organizational officials searched for Jewish ancestry in order to knock their rivals out of competition for positions,[19] Jews were not automatically accepted as members of the organization but first had to receive approval from the board of directors,[20] and Jews who participated in the society's language courses were not recommended to official organizations;[21] however, none of these measures were ever made public. The changing times are reflected in the fact that in the 1940s one of the accusations that intransigent Turanists lodged against the Turanian Society was that it had not expelled its Jewish, half Jewish, and Freemason members.[22]

The decline in the public prestige of the organization is revealed in the disappearance of government ministers and academy presidents from among its honorary members, who by this time were in the very best case ministerial counselors or, on occasion, state secretaries. The nearly collective withdrawal of all Orientalists from the Turanian Society did not serve to improve the movement's reputation, and during Pál Teleki's presidency, the Kőrösi Csoma Society and the organization's periodical, *Kőrösi Csoma Archívum*, were established. The leading article published in the first issue of *Kőrösi Csoma Archívum* explicitly defined the periodical as the successor of *Turán* and identified its program as the conduct of Eastern research from a Hungarian perspective. ("Our program is the field of Eastern research, which especially interests the Hungarians by virtue of their ancient history and geographical situation.")[23] The newly launched periodical was able to do this with relative ease because *Turán* was struggling with serious financial difficulties, and its subsequent issues were published in significantly reduced form only in 1921. The merger of the Hungarian Academy of Sciences Asian Committee into the new Eastern research society also served to strengthen the position of the new organization.[24] Pál Teleki never assumed any other functions within the Turanian Society, and although he was ritually commemorated at all the organization's significant events, the former and future prime minister made it clear that his departure had been the result of a conscious decision. In 1937, Teleki inadvertently received an invitation to a meeting of the Turanian Society's board of directors, which he returned with the following request: "I ask you to please delete my name, because I cannot participate there as well and a board of directors is a working organization, thus there is no sense in me taking the place of somebody else who would be willing to work."[25] Paikert, who always looked on Teleki with hidden envy, was sad to see him leave: "I always regretted that we did not stay together more closely in public life, working together on the major problems of the day."[26]

While Paikert returned in the prime of his life to the leadership of the Turanian Society alongside Pekár, the intransigent Turanians founded the Hungarian Turan Alliance.[27] The members of this new organization fell into four categories: committed followers of Árpád Zempléni from the Zempléni Table Society; those who had been associated with various counterrevolutionary groups, including a surprisingly large number of women, under the leadership of Gyöngyi Békássy, who will appear later in the book; intellectuals affiliated with the radical independence party (that was in opposition during the dual monarchy era); and finally some of those who had belonged to the Jenő Cholnoky–Benedek Baráthosi Balogh faction that had split away from the Turanian Society. The Hungarian Turan Alliance launched a periodical called *Kelet* (East) with Baráthosi Balogh as its editor in chief. After the first issue, the title *Kelet* was dropped because there had gradually appeared contributors who were almost totally unfamiliar with the tastes of the radical Turanists (liberal political officials who counted as "Jews") and the periodical began to proclaim rather muddled viewpoints that nevertheless pointed in the direction of national democracy.

The division of labor between the three wings of Turanism—the Turanian Society, the Hungarian Turan Alliance, and the Kőrösi Csoma Society—cannot be clearly determined, particularly with regard to the first two organizations. In late 1920, Gyula Pekár and Alajos Paikert wrote a memorandum to Prime Minister Teleki in which they asserted that the framework of the Turanian Society had proven too narrow to satisfy the great interest in Turanism; therefore, it seemed necessary to implement an expedient distribution of tasks. They thus attempted to more clearly define the various spheres of organizational activity at a joint meeting of the three associations. This meeting produced the following arrangement: the primary objectives of the Turanian Society would be to maintain "social and political contacts" with Turanian states, to oversee the "Turanian upbringing of children" (whatever this might mean), to organize expeditions, and to retexture economic relations; the mission of the Kőrösi Csoma Society would be to carry out "eastern scientific research and the elaboration and publication of its findings as well as scientific research on the past and present of Turanian relations in the spirit of Sándor Kőrösi Csoma and the other major Turanian scholars"; and the task of the Hungarian Turan Alliance would be "to make all of these labors accessible to the greater Hungarian public, to draw the broader strata of society into the sphere of Turanian propaganda and to strive to conduct the popular diffusion of the Turanian concept within a broad channel."[28] They furthermore requested that the three Turanian associations be allocated 250,000 krone in annual support. In order for us to comprehend the magnitude of this sum of money during this period of high inflation, we should know that the request four months later for 100,000 krone in funding for the relaunching of *Turán* elicited an indignant response from Prime Minister István Bethlen ("I naturally consider the request for assistance of such a large sum amid the state's present financial circumstances to be unfulfillable"),[29] and the Turanian Society was thus compelled to accept one-quarter of the solicited amount. However, subsequent cooperation between the three organizations based on this agreement proved to be sporadic: the Kőrösi Csoma Society had nothing to do with the Turanian Society and the Hungarian Turan Alliance, failing not only to share information with them but also to

Fig. 4.2. Two geographers: Pál Teleki, former president of the Turanian Society (first from the left), and Jenő Cholnoky, grand vizier of the Hungarian Turan Alliance (in traditional Hungarian costume on the right), receive Archduke Joseph Francis of Habsburg, future patron of the Turanian Society, at the entrance of the Hungarian Academy of Sciences (1922). FORTEPAN © 2010–2014 under Creative Commons CC-BY-SA-3.0 license, Tamás Cholnoky.

even acknowledge their existences. Moreover, collaboration between the Turanian Society and the Hungarian Turan Alliance was limited for the most part to a few joint events and articles published in *Turán*.

At the very beginning of the 1920s, the Hungarian Turan Alliance appeared to be in position to assume the leading role within the Turanist movement in Hungary. The Hungarian Turan Alliance's followers were more committed, the initiatives of the organization were more innovative, and its radicalism was more compatible with the public mood that prevailed in Hungary in the early 1920s. Geographer Jenő Cholnoky became the newly founded organization's grand vizier (president). The Kolozsvár and, subsequently, Budapest University professor who had emerged from the circles associated with Lajos Lóczy was not famous for his moderate temperament, a personal quality that manifested itself in his social viewpoints as well: even before 1918, he was known for his sharply antisemitic pronouncements.[30] Cholnoky did not refrain from making tasteless remarks as grand vizier of the Hungarian Turan Alliance either, as the racialist daily *A Nép* (The people) regularly demonstrated in its reports. (The most plastic of these was a January 1922 article regarding one of Cholnoky's lectures that contained blatant antisemitic references in its title: *Lecherous Budapest Needs Golem, Lili Grün, 'Originality' and Purpleness* [*Gólem, Grün Lili, "eredetiség" és lilaság kell a buja Pestnek*].) At the same time, as an author Cholnoky was wonderfully descriptive, extraordinarily readable, and extremely prolific, though somewhat monomaniacal, and held as many as three or four popularizing lectures per week in addition to carrying out his workplace obligations. Cholnoky's audience adored him because he was a man of mettle who spoke passionately and without scientific jargon. He was also a member, even president, of a series of associations; among these (besides the Hungarian Geographical Society), the Balaton Society and the Hungarian Tourist Association stood closest to his heart. In addition, Cholnoky was an avid photographer who was able to bring passion even to moderation: as the result of the tragic lives of his brothers, the writers László and Viktor, he quit drinking alcohol and became a committed teetotaler.[31] Cultivation of the Hungarian language also counted as one of his manias. Cholnoky's passion was reflected in an article he published in his capacity as grand vizier of the Hungarian Turan Alliance, regarding the organization's program. In this article, he reflected on the humiliation of the Treaty of Trianon and his own experience of being driven out of Kolozsvár: "Miserable freebooters and rabble with a dark past are riding roughshod over the hallowed ground of our thousand-year homeland and bands of rogues hurtled upward from slavery are kicking around the scions of princely families that reach back all the way to the tales of the Scythian world. Turan cannot be humiliated and disgraced for long! Life or death, but the sunbeam, the people of the steppes and the children of the homeland of unlimited freedom cannot tolerate shackles and stigma. Life or death, but Turan cannot be held in slavery!"[32]

The Hungarian Turan Alliance had been founded and the organization's bylaws adopted ten days before the publication of this writing. According to its founders, the alliance's principal objective was to promote "through the development of the consciousness of our racial character the strengthening of the moral and material foundation of the Hungarians and the establishment of relations with our kindred Turanian peoples in the domains of culture and economy"—a sentence that with the exception

of the initial clause could have appeared in any previous Turanian document.[33] One novelty of the bylaws was that they had to define the meaning of the still little-known Turanian terminology used to designate the
organization's various offices for the benefit of the Interior Ministry officials who were responsible for authorizing its operations. According to
these definitions, the president was known as the *nagyvezér* (grand vizier),
the secretary as the *szövetségnagy* (alliance chief), the recorder as the *rovó*
(notcher), and the chief cashier was the *kincstartó* (treasurer). The Hungarian Turan Alliance adopted the Turanian Society's use of specialty sections
and wanted to make innovations primarily in relation to the assessment
of Turanism.[34] The new alliance established a press office and launched a
journalism course that it hoped to later expand into a journalism college.
It also instituted organizations (called *tribes*) at locations outside Budapest:
the Pusztaszer Tribe organized in the city of Szeged, for example, proved to
be so viable that it outlived its parent organization.[35] The Hungarian Turan
Alliance held some of its lectures jointly with the Turanian Society.[36] The
letter that ministerial advisor István Dessewffy, the chief recorder from
Sáros County who had fled to Hungary following its annexation to Czechoslovakia, provides an excellent reflection of the broad array of organizational undertakings. Dessewffy wrote in reference to an unfinished statue
that was to be erected below Buda Castle following its completion:

> Not long ago I saw in the studio of the sculptor Dankó [Damkó], our fine arts
> chief council member, a statue that he is making of John of Capistrano. The
> statute is pretty, but rather brutally conceived. The hoary friar is stepping with
> a cross in his hand on the naked body of a Turk who holds the Turkish horse-
> tailed, crescent-mooned holy standard in his hand. The standard is also tram-
> pled into the ground. Being familiar with the enormous sensitivity of the Turks,
> I consider it to be out of the question that the statue will not cause the greatest
> degree of bitterness among them, especially now, at a time when they are waging
> a life-and-death battle. Fortunately, however, the situation can still be helped if
> they put something else in the Turk's hand besides the Turkish holy insignia.
> Perhaps the face could made to be Jewish-like and then we could tell the Turks
> and comment on the matter in our newspapers at the time of the unveiling as
> well that the statue in fact represents the victory of faith over destruction. In
> short, the hand is the hand of Isaiah, the voice is the voice of Jacob. In my opin-
> ion, it is completely unnecessary to turn the Turks against us.[37]

The statue was eventually erected with the Turkish warrior and the horse-
tailed flag under the friar's feet, while Dessewffy soon indignantly resigned
from his offices because his reform plans had been swept aside and he had

not been reelected to his main post. However, his presumption regarding the statue was not groundless in spite of its morbidity. The tower of the elephant house at the Budapest Zoo, for example, had to be taken down during the First World War because its mosque-like form offended the sensibilities of Hungary's Turkish ally—a perceived affront to which the Turkish consul general in Budapest gave voice.[38] A similar occurrence took place in 1936: on the 250th anniversary of the liberation of Buda Castle, the Turkish envoy to Budapest could not complain enough about the anti-Turkish overtones of the connected celebrations and protested vehemently against the inscription on a statue of Pope Innocent XI (also one of József Damkó's works) that had been erected to mark the occasion.[39] At other times, the Hungarian Turan Alliance's diplomatic sensitivity was not so acute. In 1923, the Foreign Ministry sent a letter to Grand Vizier Cholnoky requesting that the alliance organize with the greatest possible degree of tact a "sympathy ceremony" in connection to the Kantō earthquake because it would be a shame if the speakers were to humiliate the kindred Turanian people of Japan by holding forth on the end of the country's great-power status.[40]

As is generally this case with radical organizations, there are always some who are more genuine than others. The differences sparked a sharp conflict in early 1923. Indications of this conflict had already multiplied: not only the radical Dessewffy was dissatisfied, but the humble scholar Zoltán Felvinczi Takács was also subjected to attack, first from students participating in the journalism course and then from the fine arts chief council, the members of which—notably chairman and sculptor, György Zala—had "remarked with indignation that Zoltán Takács, whose activity as part of the journalism course we incidentally also regard with concern, had intervened in a hostile manner on behalf of the destructive press in his [Chairman Zala's] noble struggle surrounding the Venice exhibition [and its Hungarian pavilion]." The fine arts chief council therefore requested that "the case be examined most vigorously from a Turanian perspective and for the Zoltán Takács affair to be brought before an appropriate forum because we consider it to be preposterous that Zoltán Takács be allowed to seemingly operate with us though continually work against us." Felvinczi Takács, the director of the Ferenc Hopp Museum, took offense at the attacks and withdrew from the Hungarian Turan Alliance.[41] Felvinczi Takács long thereafter remained a member of the Turanian Society, though after realizing that the organization's activities tended to revolve around themselves, he founded the Eastern Alliance (Keleti Szövetség) in 1932. Felvinczi Takács's connection to Turanist institutions essentially came to an end after his friend Pál Teleki appointed him to serve as a professor at the university in Kolozsvár following the return of northern Transylvania to Hungary in 1940.[42]

However, the real uproar began within the Hungarian Turan Alliance only at the time of its general assembly, which in organizational terminology was called an *ősgyűlés* (ancestral assembly), in early 1923. A group of members who were primarily from Budapest presented a list of candidates to oppose the Jenő Cholnoky–led official candidates for office. The assembly, which was convened at the former House of Representatives building in Budapest (today the Italian Institute), degenerated into a bitter free-for-all, requiring the police official who was present to break up the meeting.[43] The leader of the opposition camp was Budapest audit commissioner, author, and founding president of the Hungarian National Literary Association (a relatively minor literary society), István Kornai ("original name Kralován," the beleaguered grand vizier immediately noted in an attempt to contextualize Kornai's foreign origin). Kornai could not really keep track of the number of associations to which he belonged either, although it is certain that most of them were pro-independence in orientation and the young city-hall audit-office junior clerk had been reprimanded for lèse-majesté previously, in 1899.[44] It was thus easy to frame the conflict with the leadership of the Hungarian Turan Alliance within the context of the opposition between legitimists and those who wanted to freely elect a king that intersected Hungarian public life during this period—and the grand vizier himself was among the members of the organization who attempted to do just this.[45] Cholnoky's opponents made it clear that although the majority of them were indeed proponents of freely electing the Habsburg Charles IV as king, they had formulated the list of opposing candidates primarily as a result of the grand vizier's leadership methods. Kornai and his followers charged that Cholnoky neglected his duties and had introduced new members to the organization in irregular fashion and that official records were inadequate. The committee meeting that the Hungarian Turan Alliance held at the University of Budapest's geographic institute a few days following its general assembly again devolved into such a fracas that the dean had to come out of his office to reestablish order.[46] Members of the opposing camps scuffled and expelled one another from the organization. Some Budapest newspapers expressed a certain schadenfreude in their reports on the fray, which bore rather unoriginal titles such as "The Turanian Curse" and assorted variations thereof[47] (although László Cholnoky defended his brother in an article that appeared in the liberal-bourgeois radical newspaper *Világ*[48]). On March 2, 1923, the daily *Budapesti Hírlap* published a list of members who had been expelled from the Hungarian Turan Alliance that is interesting because it contains the names of a former interior minister, a writer, a professional diplomat, a globe-trotting drawing teacher, a young poet, and a printing-house official. On the one hand, this list reflects the heterogeneous character of the organization, while on the other, it includes quite a few people who played a role in the resurgence of radical Turanism in Hungary during the Second World War.[49]

Although Cholnoky and his faction managed to solidify their position at the head of the Hungarian Turan Alliance, the organization began to disintegrate rapidly and by 1924 ceased to conduct substantial operations. Members of the alliance either joined the Turanian Society or scattered in various directions, becoming active in such proxy organizations as the Society of Hungarians, the Kuruc Alliance, the Mátyás Hollós Society, the Hungarian-Indian Society, or the Hungarian-Turkish Association (these shall be mentioned again later). In the early 1930s, one of the central figures associated with far-right organizational activity in Hungary, the metallurgical engineer Árpád Gálocsy (1864–1934), attempted to resurrect the Hungarian Turan Alliance. Gálocsy tried to convince candidates for membership to forgive one another for past offenses and create anew an old alliance "that would stand on the foundation of the self-contained existence of the Turanian race." Furthermore, he insisted that the revived organization "would never be inclined, never be prepared to rate the particular, uncharitable and materialistic benefits of the West over the legitimate interests of the Turanian East and the universal, ancient and eternal values of Asia."[50] However, either Gálocsy did not manage to reconcile the discord between potential members of the recast Hungarian Turan Alliance, or the latter were unwilling to accept his authority; in any event, Gálocsy's interests soon turned in another direction, and he died not long after his unsuccessful effort to reconstitute the organization.

The Turanian Society could breathe a sigh of relief: one of its serious rivals had fallen by the wayside. The Turanian Society consolidated its operations at the time of the Hungarian Turan Alliance's dissolution in 1924. The society not only began to receive permanent state support and regularize the pay of its officials but also relaunched *Turán* and, thanks to the good offices of the government, was allocated 1 percent of the revenue of the Corvin Cinema in Budapest until 1927.[51] This period recalled the Turanian Society's golden age between 1916 and 1918, notably when the Turkish government sought the services of Hungarian engineers and agriculturalists in order to help rebuild and modernize Turkey. The Turanian Society carried out the task of recruitment for this effort, albeit with much more limited success than it had a few years previously.[52] In the late spring of 1924, the first twenty Hungarian engineers traveled to Turkey as part of the program. However, this action did not come off very well: a group of these engineers returned to Hungary due to insufficient preliminary information, the lack of a prior contract, the change in climate, difficulties adjusting to Turkish food, and various unfulfilled expectations.[53] Others were threatened with legal action after their wives began collecting signatures in order to improve their conditions, which provoked understandable tension among Turkish government officials. Hungarian diplomatic representatives in Constantinople urged the Turanian Society to proceed with caution as a result of the rather negative response of the Turkish government, while a Hungarian Commerce Ministry official sent the following, somewhat reproachful, communiqué to the organization: "Based on information received from the H. Roy. [Hungarian Royal] Foreign Ministry, I herewith most emphatically draw the kind attention of the cultural center to the fact that similar movements are to be provided with moral support exclusively in the event that it is conferred with the knowledge, official cooperation and leadership of the H. Roy. commercial affairs and H. Roy. foreign affairs government [ministries]."[54] In its reply to this communiqué, the Turanian Society strenuously attempted to vindicate itself and made promises of all kinds.

The stream of Hungarian specialists into Turkey continued in spite of this even if not under the direction of the Turanian Society. Among these specialists were some who became members of the organization after returning to Hungary. For example, Hungarian authorities found it expedient to conjure away ethnographer Gyula Mészáros, who had fought a duel with Alajos Paikert before 1918, due to his key role in the French franc counterfeiting scandal that erupted at the end of 1925. (Certain people involved in Hungarian political life counterfeited a significant number of 1,000-franc banknotes during the first half of the 1920s in order to gain revenge for France's role in formulating the stipulations of the Trianon peace treaty.[55])

Mészáros maintained very good Turkish connections, including, according to rumors that circulated at this time, with President Mustafa Kemal
Atatürk. Thus, it seemed to be self-evident for Mészáros to make his way
toward the city of Ankara. Here he received a commission to establish the
local ethnography museum: therefore, when a journalist from the newspaper *Magyarság* called on Mészáros in the new capital of Turkey, he was able
to report, in elegiac tones, on a new Hungarian success and the affirmation
of Hungarian talent in a foreign country in spite of the fact that "at one time
they were talking a lot about" the protagonist of the article.[56] At the beginning of the century, Mészáros was considered to be a promising young
ethnographer: even Vámbéry patronized him, and his Chuvash and Bashkir collections received considerable recognition.[57] However, due to his ad-
venturistic lifestyle and other affairs to which he was connected, Mészáros
dropped out of scientific circles, and although he remained a member of
the Turanian Society, he no longer played an active role in the organization.
Following his return to Hungary in 1932, Mészáros worked on the National
Monument Committee and then became a teacher at the Eastern Trade
College established in Újvidék (Novi Sad, Serbia) during the 1943–1944 academic year. Mészáros's scientific interests had by this time become palpably
out of the ordinary, turning toward "folk history" (*néptörténet*): in 1944, he
wrote that "I had to break with the manufacturing of history based on pure
fictions that has existed until now (Hóman, Gyula Németh and his associates) and finally had to turn toward folk-history realities."[58] After emigrating to Turkey and, subsequently, the United States, Mészáros subscribed to
this mythical, prehistorical orientation.[59] The head of Hungarian military
intelligence, General István Ujszászy, testified during captivity following
the Second World War that Mészáros and his Turanian friends had assisted
intelligence agents during the war and placed saboteurs behind Soviet lines
in the Caucasus. It is not known how valid General Ujszászy's claims were
in this regard, but it is certain that audacious activity of this type was not
foreign to Mészáros's character.[60]

The Turanian Society conducted another government-supported action during the interwar period: in 1937, Minister of Religion and Public
Education Bálint Hóman (1885–1951), who nine years later was condemned
to life in prison for war crimes, asked the association (of which he had been
a member since 1917 and for which, at this time, he was a copresident) to
serve as a partner in a Hungarian-Finnish student exchange.[61] However,
only ten students were able to participate in the exchange, which cost a

rather expensive 220 pengő (around one month's pay for lower-middle-class people), and the financial irregularities that surrounded the action as well as an article that the noted writer János Kodolányi published about it in the periodical *Kelet Népe* (People of the East) led to the dismissal of the Turanian Society's secretary and the replacement of General Secretary Frigyes Lukinich.[62] All in all, one can say that the management of government-supported actions based on the 1916–1918 model was fairly weak. If the organization transcended the comfortable boundaries of the lecture–language course–social dinner–periodical publication quadrangle, it generally ended up failing.

The demise of the rival Hungarian Turan Alliance prompted the leaders of the Turanian Society to make an effort to extend its activities to provincial Hungary: beginning in 1925, the society attempted to found organizations in the cities of Baja, Nagykőrös, Szeged, Debrecen, Pécs, and Szentes.[63] However, this undertaking ended in almost complete failure: branches of the Turanian Society began actual operations at only two of these six locations and even the established organizations disbanded after just a few years. Lacking the firm support of local notabilities and intellectuals who were in contact with the Turanian Society, there was no chance of even forming the intended provincial chapters. The fundamental cause of this failure was generally the post–First World War existential difficulties of the middle class: as a result of their dwindling financial means, members of this class had considerable difficulty maintaining the previously existing network of local associations and therefore in many cases did not even attempt to institute the new organizations of the Turanian Society.

In fact, associations featuring the attributive *Turanian* functioned at numerous locations in Hungary, though maintained extremely diverse objectives and often did not even operate according to the ideology of Turanism. One such Turanist organization was active in Diósgyőr, while teacher Vilmos Pröhle started another called the Turanian Circle in Nyíregyháza that included members of the local elite. The Turanian Circle initially proclaimed the motto of *racial kinship*, but it was one of many similar organizations in interwar Hungary that in the course of its operations embraced causes that did not necessarily have anything to do with Turanism, ranging from name Magyarization to the struggle against "destruction" and sponsoring lectures on bacteria. These objectives could be intermixed as well: for example, in 1922 Debrecen school principal Lajos Ady received the following invitation from the Turanian Circle in Nyíregyháza to present a lecture regarding his late brother, the acclaimed poet Endre Ady: "We would particularly wish to see emphasized the ancient Hungarian features that can be found in the poet's personality and poetry as well as the things for which the Hungarian nation can thank Endre Ady, because we can-not permit that destruction appropriate his great spirit for itself."[64] The Budapest-based Turanian Society's attempt to establish branch organiza-tions in provincial Hungary produced temporarily positive results at two locations—in the cities of Nagykőrös and Balassagyarmat.

In Nagykőrös, the successful initiative to launch a Turanian association depended primarily on the will and support of Mayor Dezső Kázmér and the organizational work of journalist and local historian Béla Galántai Fekete. In Balassagyarmat, the local chapter of the Turanian Society began operations following the conclusion of what was known in organizational jargon as the "provincial action."[65] The key figure in the Balassagyarmat-based Turanian organization, local financial directorate audit officer Márton Vargyassy, dealt intensively at this time with the Székely past, notably the origin of the Székelys and the Old Hungarian runic script (rovásírás), and during the second half of the 1930s, he published writings on the subject of the presumed kinship between the Hungarians and the Sumerians as well.[66] Thanks to Vargyassy's organizational activities and the involvement of local high school teacher and jack-of-all-trades Antal Both, the Balassagyarmat branch of the Turanian Society formed in October 1930. The elite of the city constituted the core of the organization: both the mayor and the county prefect joined the new chapter, the membership of which was composed primarily of lawyers, local functionaries, entrepreneurs, and those associated with local public education. The new Turanian Society branch organization began its operations with great momentum, holding weekly lectures in which members presented information regarding subjects ranging from Turanian hunting (the mayor of the city addressed this topic) to the Sumerians and Buddhism. Lectures about the Palóc subgroup of Hungarians that reside in the region in which Balassagyarmat is located attracted the greatest amount of interest. However, as a result of a lack of lecturers, the Balassagyarmat chapter of the Turanian Society soon began to repeat previously examined topics, while one of the main local organizers, Antal Both, did not understand the objections of the central organization in Budapest to his proposed lecture on Hungarian-Hebrew linguistic kinship.[67] Two circumstances sealed the fate of the Balassagyarmat branch of the Turanian Society: first, Márton Vargyassy was transferred away from the city, and we soon find him working as the organizer of the Hargitaváralja Symbolic Székely Community in Pesterzsébet; second, the methods of the retired military officer who had been elected to serve as president of the chapter induced the local intelligentsia to withdraw from the organization, thus causing it to essentially cease operations by 1933.

In the middle of the 1930s, the Turanian Society experimented with a medical sciences section as well. Among those who were responsible for this initiative were physicians who had visited Finland or Estonia and based on their experiences in these countries advocated the exchange of medical practitioners and the holding of professional conferences.[68] Since one of the founders of the medical sciences section of the Turanian Society, University of Debrecen professor of medicine Endre Jeney, was one of the pioneers of Hungarian blood-type research, the new section adopted the name Hungarian Blood Research Society as well. This immediately compelled another founder of the Turanian Society's medical sciences section, Dezső Gaskó, to publish an article in the newspaper *Pesti Napló* (Pest journal) in which he explained that the Hungarian Blood Research Society maintained no racial mission and had nothing whatsoever to do with the Jewish question.[69] However, since the intentions of the Hungarian Blood Research Society were ambiguous and, moreover, as one of the most striking figures associated with the Hungarian racial-protection movement, the entomologist Lajos Méhely (1862–1953), was among its founders, nearly twenty physicians who were regarded as "Jews," such as Sándor Korányi and Béla Purjesz, soon ceased to participate in the activities of the new section of the Turanian Society. Although the subsequent operations of the section did not serve to confirm the initial suspicions (and Méhely did not become a member), aside from a few organizational tours and reform proposals, there is no more information available regarding its activities. However, Turanian blood-type research, itself of very dubious pedigree, exercised an influence on others who were close to the Turanian Society. As early as 1934, the longtime radical Turanist Gyöngyi Békássy indicated that she was prepared to present her "blood-type theory" to the general public. Turanian Society director Péter Móricz referred Békássy to the medical sciences section, which must not have received the radical Turanist with too much enthusiasm since she finally had to publish her work, *A vércsoportok kutatásának faji jelentősége* (The racial significance of research on blood types), in 1938 at her own expense.[70]

It is worthwhile for us to take a quick look at the person of Gyöngyi Békássy. She was born in 1893 with the Christian name Flóra, the daughter of a landowner. Békássy was the sister of the diplomat László Békássy and became one of the central figures in the Hungarian feminist movement. She was the vice president of the Feminist Youth Group and, along with her mother, organized the congress of the International Woman Suffrage Alliance held in Budapest in 1913 that was attended by the most influential suffragettes of the era.[71] During the 1910s, Békássy entertained poet and author Mihály Babits, feminist Róza Bédy-Schwimmer, and other distinguished Hungarian progressives at her house in the village of Óbarokpuszta located west of Budapest. After the post–First World War revolutions, Békássy changed her Christian name and, evidently, her world outlook as well, and together with her previously mentioned brother, she found her place on the outer fringes of the Turanian movement. Her 1920 book, *A turáni eszme* (The Turanian idea), is one of the first works belonging to the modern ancient-history tradition that attempted to synthesize all of the prevalent theories regarding the ancient home of the Hungarians and served as the archetype for Tibor Baráth's book *A magyar népek őstörténete* (The ancient history of the Hungarian peoples) published in the 1960s and 1970s.[72]

In addition to peoples who were perhaps actually related to the Hungarians, Békássy considered not only the Etruscans, the Basques, and the Celts to be Turanians but also the Aztecs and the Sumerians. According to Békássy, the "yellow-raced" Turanians had spread out from Atlantis to populate all of the territories where these people lived. This notion was even too much for a majority of those who adhered to the Turanist movement, and thus, Békássy's book did not elicit much commentary. From time to time, Békássy published letters in various forums associated with the Turanian movement, and she was a member of the Hungarian Turan Alliance as well. Her letters, which are composed in an unmistakably distinctive style, reflect no doubts and make no appeals. In 1928, Békássy launched her own gazette, the "journal of the strong, uncompromising, pure Hungarians," *Hadak Útja* (Path of the armies). This periodical did not survive for very long—there is no evidence showing that it appeared after 1929. *Hadak Útja* was a strange mixture, publishing sectarian Turanist writings, a Christmas issue written by children in order to entertain family members, and articles characteristic of women's lifestyle magazines—for example, one entitled "Healing diets." In addition to Turanist movement activists such as Ferenc Zajti (1886–1961), Adorján Magyar (1887–1978), and Benedek

Baráthosi Balogh, a conspicuously large number of women published articles in the periodical, which Gödöllő-based artist Sándor Nagy, an old friend of Békássy's family, occasionally illustrated. Békássy recruited colleagues from among those who had been involved in the women's branch of the early Christian Socialist movement as well as feminists who, like her, had changed course and women who later became prominent counterrevolutionaries. The career of Gyöngyi Békássy, who in the 1930s became one of the leaders of the Hungarian Girl Scout movement and published writings that attracted little interest, typifies the search for intellectual pathways that occurred in Hungary in the early twentieth century, particularly the quest of those who explored many different avenues and eventually ended up adhering to a rather extreme ideology and whose fate was in any event not predetermined.

The Turanian Society was able to make true innovations with regard to radio broadcasts. Beginning in 1929, Hungarian Radio aired a Turanian-themed presentation every month from September through May. The first year of these Hungarian Radio broadcasts included the following lectures: General Tivadar Galánthay Glock on the Tartars, designer and architect Ede Toroczkai Wigand on the Turanian traditions in Hungarian folk architecture, Vilmos Pröhle on Emperor Meiji, architect Jenő Lechner on the Turanian spirit of Hungarian folk art, Jenő Cholnoky on the Turanian plain, Aladár Bán on Estonia, and Péter Móricz on Turkey. Although the number such lectures broadcast on Hungarian Radio later decreased, they nevertheless provided the Turanian Society with a singular opportunity to disseminate its ideas.[73]

The Turanian Society was, therefore, not really able to step outside the circle it had drawn around itself: the association's activities revolved around the publication of *Turán*, the organization of language courses, the holding of lectures—mostly with the same lecturers—receiving "Turanian" visitors, and perhaps conducting foreign study trips. Those who wanted to inject dynamism into the activities of the Turanian Society generally suffered bitter experiences regarding the acceptance of their ideas. In the late 1920s or early 1930s, painter Dezső Mokry-Mészáros approached the "Turanian Association" with a plan to hold a Turkish exhibition, but Director Péter Móricz brusquely showed him the door. Mokry-Mésáros noted angrily: "The same old song, nobody stands up for the national causes: we are disintegrating here in the middle of the damn big continent of Europe, and if it is this way, then we deserve it."[74]

Fig. 4.3. Expressions of frightful boredom: meeting of the Turanian Society's board of directors (1938). Sitting at far left: Lajos Marzsó and László Bendefy; in the first row, from the left: Ubul Kállay, Alajos Paikert, and Ernő Kovács-Karap. Attribution: Magyar Földrajzi Múzeum, Cholnoky-hagyaték, Kaulich Rudolf felvétele.

This communications failure is illuminating because during the inter-war period Hungarian society was receptive to Turanism as a catchword. Regent Miklós Horthy not only took an interest in Turanism (in 1930, he asked for documents regarding the subject)[75] but also, from time to time, even attended Turanian-type lectures, and it is a known fact that his special train was given the name Turán.[76] Although during the 1920s the governing party occasionally mentioned Turanism in the National Assembly in slogan-like terms, really only those backbenchers dealt seriously with the movement and, in 1925, formed a group known as the "Turanian Bloc." The parliamentarians known to have been associated with this group, which according to Gyula Pekár numbered forty members, were primarily second- and third-rank representatives from the governing party, although there were also some who were affiliated with the Racial Protection Party that had split away from it. The Turanian Bloc's demonstrable activity was limited to a few speeches in the National Assembly.[77] Turanism as a political ideology appeared emphatically within the Racial Protection Party that later prime minister Gyula Gömbös (1886–1936) founded in 1923, although the latter had known nothing about the Turanian movement until obtaining relevant information and documents from the Turanian Society in 1919–1920.[78]

Rejection of Turanism appeared early—and not only on the political left. The legitimist (Habsburg supporter) György Pallavicini, a childhood friend of Pál Teleki, stated during polemics in the National Assembly with Gyula Gömbös: "Because what is this Turanism? I really esteem the Turanian race, there may be a certain amount of this race in me as well. And if we do not want to remain a truncated Hungary, and we do not want to . . . then we must not attribute too much importance to this Turanism and not make it into a political watchword that scares off the detached parts [of the country] in which we are in a minority vis-à-vis the nationalities."[79] In the 1930s, references to Turanism in the National Assembly occurred either in the form of derisive jeers from representatives or as simple oratorical embellishments.[80] The negative coverage in the press regarding the Turanian monotheists (who will soon be discussed) was largely responsible for this. The attributive *Turanian* appeared in a positive or interpretative milieu predominantly in the remarks of representatives who belonged to the Arrow Cross Party or to the right wing of the governing party. One such Arrow Cross Party representative was Imre Palló, who remained faithful to the ideology even after his post–Second World War emigration to Argentina, where he served as the president of the Turanian Academy in Buenos Aires and was a regular contributor to the periodical *A Nap Fiai* (Sons of the sun).[81] The leader of the Arrow Cross Party, Ferenc Szálasi, himself turned toward the interpretative framework of Turanism relatively late: as a result of his Catholicism, the Arrow Cross leader had regarded Turanism with aversion because of its association with paganism, and only when he sought contacts with the Japanese legation in Budapest in 1943–1944 did he request materials regarding Japan's "Turanian popular movement." However, Szálasi found it important to note that the Turanian associations in Hungary were "in Jewish hands." Arrow Cross Party official Kálmán Hubay also emphasized the "foreignness" of Hungarian Turanian organizations during a speech in the National Assembly.[82]

The attributive *Turanian* turned up in a completely different segment of Hungarian public life as well: the writer Dezső Szabó, who was largely responsible for forming the outlook of the populist movement that maintained the political objective of elevating the Hungarian peasantry, transformed the range of meanings associated with the word *Turanian* according to his own taste and began to use the term in his writing. According to Szabó's interpretation, the word *Turanian* meant "ancestral, pure-blooded Hungarian," and through it, he aimed to promote the interests of the Hungarians who were oppressed in their own country. However, after his initial enthusiasm at the very beginning of the 1920s, Szabó began to make rather disdainful statements about racialists and their Turanism.[83] The young members of the Miklós Bartha Society adopted Szabó's interpretation when they discussed the concept of the Turanian-Slavic peasant state.[84] This met with sharp disapproval from Gyula Szekfű. This historian, who before 1918 occasionally appeared in forums that were close to the Turanian Society, in the 1920s and 1930s became the most committed critic of Turanism in Hungary, and the periodical that he edited, *Magyar Szemle* (Hungarian review), regularly published articles disparaging the movement.[85] Moreover, the populists turned amicably toward the Scandinavian, and within it the Finnish, model—and not only for reasons of kinship. The democratic character and high level of development of the northern model and the dynamism of the Balkan peasant states (such as Bulgaria) filled the populists with sympathy that regularly manifested itself in the periodicals associated with populist literature. Following in Dezső Szabó's footsteps, author László Németh, who was incidentally exceptionally critical of Turanism, was a dedicated believer in Central Europe–Balkan cohesion designated in the "most-punte-silta" trinity. If the populist movement had any foreign-policy conception whatsoever, it rested on the following three pillars: the communal example of the northern peasant democracies, Central European "fraternity," and kinship with other peoples. Turanism likely exercised an influence on populist intellectuals in spite of their criticism of the movement and during this period their viewpoints corresponded partially to Hungarian public opinion that was turning away from western Europe and its models.

The Turanians did not find much scope for action in either the domestic or foreign political domain in spite of the fact that after the collapse of the proletarian dictatorship, the Hungarian Royal Foreign Ministry always managed to place officials, frequently the heads of the Press and Culture Department, in the leadership of the organization. Those who directed the press policy of Horthy-era governments of Hungary (László Bárdossy, Béla Ángyán, Zoltán Gerevich, Lajos Villani, Zoltán Baranyai, Antal Náray, and

Domokos Szent-Iványi [1898–1980]) were members of the Turanian Society's leadership at one time or another. The Hungarian envoys accredited to "Turanian" states (Bulgaria, Finland, Turkey, and Estonia) routinely became members of the Turanian Society even if they did not participate intensively in its activities. The organization published a memorandum referring to the head of the nationality department of the Prime Minister's Office, Tibor Pataky, as one of the greatest supporters of its undertakings. Moreover, at the end of the 1930s, Pataky become the Turanian Society's honorary president. Particularly in the early 1920s, representatives from the Turanian Society were invited to attend the Foreign Ministry's propaganda meetings and were selected to serve as members of official Hungarian government delegations: in 1930, Aladár Bán traveled to Finland and Estonia with Minister of Religion and Public Education Kuno Klebelsberg, while in 1933 Gyula Pekár accompanied Prime Minister Gyula Gömbös to Turkey. Prominent members of the Turanian Society met with high-ranking foreign guests when they visited Hungary: General Tivadar Galánthay Glock, one of the organization's jacks-of-all-trades, was in this way able to acquaint the presumably spellbound Prime Minister İsmet İnönü with his Turkish-language shorthand system.[86]

Accredited diplomats from the "Turanian states" regularly appeared at the Turanian Society's events in Budapest as well. However, personal connections did not end here. Retired Hungarian diplomats also undertook roles in the Turanian Society, such as Péter Móricz, the former consul in Constantinople (Istanbul), Adrianople (Edirne), Trebizond (Trabzon), and Rusçuk (Ruse) who served as director of the organization for almost a decade. In addition, we find Vilmos Pröhle and Ödön Hollós, Japan's honorary consul in Budapest, as well as others such as Mihály Jungerth-Arnóthy, Hungary's envoy to Estonia. In 1944, Jungerth-Arnóthy reached one of the highest offices that a career diplomat could possibly attain with his appointment to the position of permanent deputy to the foreign minister. Jungerth-Arnóthy's career predestined him to become a true "Turanian diplomat": after 1920 he served as Hungary's envoy in Tallinn, Helsinki, and Ankara. Jungerth-Arnóthy was a former collaborator of Lajos Thallóczy's and a steadfast member of the Turanian Society, and he even presented lectures when he had enough time to do so. However, he did not comment too enthusiastically in his memoirs on the long period of time he spent living among the kindred peoples to the north: "I sat for 12 years in an impossible climate, literally *kalt gestellt* [put into the cold]."[87] Turanism's penetration of the Hungarian diplomatic apparatus is clearly reflected in the fact that several members of the Turanian Society obtained positions as cultural or press attachés, such as archaeologist Géza Fehér in Sofia and Jenő Habán (the brother-in-law of Hungarian-Nippon Society president István Mezey) in Tokyo.

Despite the participation of so many government officials and notwithstanding the demands of the intransigent Turanists, Hungarian foreign policy never turned in a Turanian direction. Diplomats from the Hungarian Foreign Ministry in Budapest continued to look toward London, Paris, Rome, Berlin, and perhaps Moscow and Washington: these were the reference points that determined the orientation of Hungary's foreign relations. They did not make foreign-policy decisions based on presumed Japanese, Finnish, or Turkish kinship. The notion of kinship with the Turanian peoples surfaced within catchphrases that were generally proclaimed during the first five minutes of a meeting or a dinner in order to initiate conversation. Thereafter, the traditional system of diplomatic methods and reasoning pushed factors related to kinship aside. In 1933, the Hungarian military attaché posted in Ankara wrote with regard to his negotiating tactics: "I initially steered the discussion toward the question of our racial kinship in order to bring us a little closer to one another."[88] Meanwhile, the government used the Turanian organizations in order to conduct propaganda that turned out to be useful, though was never intended to elevate Turanism or the Eastern mission of the Hungarians in general to the level of official ideology.[89]

Through one of the transfigurations of Turanism and the notion of kinship, the Turanian Society was able to grasp public attention and receive concrete governmental tasks. The idea of kinship had started primarily in Finland in the name of affinity between the Finns, the Estonians, and the smaller Finno-Ugric peoples. In 1921, the first Finno-Ugric education congress was held in Finland. Although amid the difficult circumstances that prevailed in Hungary at this time only five Hungarians were able to attend the conference, among them was high school teacher Aladár Bán, one of the stalwart members of the Finno-Ugric branch of the Turanian movement and the author of the first translation of the Estonian national epic *Kalevipoeg* into Hungarian.[90] An account of the event that appeared in *Turán* (and was presumably written by Bán) recommended that a greater number of Hungarians participate in future such congresses. In 1924, Pál Teleki and Károly Kogutowicz led a delegation of three dozen scholars and students to Tallinn to attend the next education congress, which now referred to itself as a "Pan-Finno-Ugric" event. After the end of the congress in Estonia, the members of this Hungarian delegation traveled to Finland as well, reaching as far as the Lapland.[91] These experiences represented a decisive event in the life of Pál Teleki, who was struggling with severe depression after recovery from a serious illness. Following his trip to Estonia and Finland, Teleki became a committed supporter of the notion of Finno-Ugrian kinship, and Finnish-Hungarian relations began to occupy a significant role in his political ideas as well. In 1928, Teleki brought the Finno-Ugric congress to Budapest. Nearly eleven hundred Finns and Estonians attended this congress, during which delegates divided into four sections and held discussions regarding common themes. Among the Hungarians who attended this congress were numerous intellectuals who belonged to the Turanian Society, while Gyula Pekár served as president of the literature section. In addition to the official events, delegates participating in the Budapest Finno-Ugric congress engaged in other activities, such as going on day trips and visiting museums, which permitted Teleki to expand his network of Turanist connections.[92]

Teleki edited a book published on the occasion of the congress entitled *Finnek, észtek—A magyarok északi testvérnépei* (Finns and Estonians— The northern kindred peoples of the Hungarians), for which he wrote the foreword and provided some of his own photographs to use as illustrations. Those who wrote the articles published in this book included both Teleki's students and colleagues as well as noted Turanist intellectuals who were receptive to the Finno-Ugric idea: law professor István Csekey (who was at this time teaching at the University of Tartu), Aladár Bán, Zoltán Felvinczi Takács, Elemér Virányi (University of Tartu Hungarian-language instructor and later general secretary of the Turanian Society), high school teacher József Faragó, and University of Helsinki Hungarian-language instructor Gyula Weöres (all of whom were members of the Turanian Society). In his foreword for the book, the cover of which displayed a famous painting by Finnish painter Akseli Gallen-Kallela, Teleki wrote: "Words and grammatical structures prove that we are the branches of a single tree. After a thousand years we have found one another again, brother and brother have recognized each other. And along with the evidence of linguistics, today we feel their entire world to be close to ours."[93] The next congresses took place in Helsinki (1931) and Tallinn (1936). The subsequent congress would have again been held in Budapest in 1941, but it was canceled due to the world war and the Soviet occupation of Estonia. Education minister

Klebelsberg also saw the potential benefits of strengthening the feeling of Finno-Ugric kinship. In an article that appeared in *Pesti Napló*, Klebelsberg evaluated the trip he had taken with Aladár Bán to Estonia and Finland. In this article, in which Klebelsberg occasionally indulged in pathetic, romanticized discourse that what characteristic of his writing (claiming, e.g., that Estonian and Finnish households listened with affection to Hungarian Gypsy music broadcast on the radio), the education minister made the following important remark that was obviously intended to distance Turanism from politics: "Politicians invented Pan-Slavism, Pan-Germanism and, more recently, the Anglo-Saxon idea and Spanish South American Pan-Iberism. In direct contrast to this, scientists discovered Finno-Ugric linguistic kinship."

Klebelsberg furthermore announced a plan to coordinate Finno-Ugric research: "The Budapest, Debrecen, Dorpat [Tartu], Helsingfors [Helsinki], Pécs and Szeged universities will carry out research in the fields of linguistics, ethnography and common ancient history according to a jointly established plan and division of labor and to lead this research we will organize national committees from Estonia, Finland and Hungary, the delegates of which will form a fraternal international council. Thus the six Finno-Ugric universities will appear before world scholarship as an organized working group in the fields of linguistics, ethnography and common ancient history."[94] Although the stipulated universities did not conduct coordinated research as Klebelsberg had envisioned, the Finno-Ugric national committee was established and operated continually in the 1930s and 1940s under the leadership of the Hungarian linguists Zoltán Gombocz and, subsequently, Miklós Zsirai (likewise a member of the Turanian Society). Moreover, Klebelsberg concluded a cooperation agreement with the University of Tartu that resulted in a student exchange between Hungary and Estonia that determined the course of Finno-Ugric studies in the two countries and provided ammunition to the generation of scholars that emerged in 1945.[95] And following Kelebelsberg's visit to Estonia and Finland in 1930, he initiated the introduction of a "kinship day" at schools in Hungary. This event, which generally occurred on the third Saturday of October, entailed recitals and celebrations that were designed to strengthen the feeling of Finno-Ugric affinity at state civil elementary and high schools. The first such "kinship day" was held at the Wesselényi Street Elementary School in Budapest under the direction of a prominent member of the Turanian movement, Sándor Ispánovits.[96] Similar proceedings took place until 1943, and the idea was revived in 1991.

One of the great shortcomings of the interwar Finno-Ugric kinship movement was that due to the isolation of the Soviet Union, it could not open toward related peoples living in that country. Furthermore, it was unable—and frankly unwilling—to transform cultural cooperation into political cooperation. In Finland, even the most pro-Hungarian political figures among those associated with the idea of Finno-Ugrian kinship that had developed in the nineteenth century (such as government official, diplomat, and university professor Eemil Nestor Setälä [1864–1935]) did not regard Turanism to be a viable alternative. Setälä, who served for a time as Finland's envoy to Hungary, maintained contacts with even the more radical Turanists, although he refused to move forward in the direction they considered to be desirable and restricted cooperation with them to the linguistic and cultural domains.[97] The Finns did not really want to extend their *heimotyö* (Finno-Ugric kinship work) carried out in the spirit of *heimoaate* (the concept of Finno-Ugric kinship) to the Asian peoples. Whereas Finnish intellectuals were receptive to certain elements of Ural-Altaic kinship, officials in Helsinki rigidly rejected the notion that their language and people could be connected to the Mongols or the Turks—not to mention the Japanese, Chinese, or other Southeast Asian countries.[98]

In Estonia, this relationship was more ambivalent and with such an opinion within the authoritative circles of the "big" Hungary, a portion of the Estonian cultural sphere was more receptive. This openness may have contributed to the fact that in the newly independent Estonia, which was struggling with a lack of university intellectuals and wanted to free itself of Baltic German cultural dominance, there was a demand for members of the Hungarian intelligentsia in the cultural sphere. Although not many Hungarian intellectuals took up residence in Estonia, Kecskemét law-academy instructor István Csekey, who later became a law professor at the universities in Szeged and Kolozsvár; geography professor Mihály Haltenberger; and language instructor Elemér Virányi all taught at the University of Tartu, while industrial artist and ceramicist Géza Jakó and conductor Zoltán Vásárhely worked temporarily at Tallinn University. Tihamér Tuchányi, a stalwart member of the Turanian Society and, subsequently, the Hungarian Turan Alliance, sought a position as a history professor at the University of Tartu, but his application was rejected.[99] Hungarian-language departments and institutes were established at the University of Tartu in 1923 and at the University of Helsinki in 1926. Estonian and Finnish students also received scholarships to study at Hungarian universities and on more than one occasion enjoyed the hospitality of the

Eötvös Collegium that operated under the direction of curator Pál Teleki. Among these students was Alo Raun, who learned to speak fluent Hungarian during his period of study in Hungary before fleeing to the United States after the Second World War and finding employment as a professor at Indiana University. The Hungarian students who received scholarships to study in Estonia later constituted the core of the generation of scholars who dealt with Finno-Ugric linguistics (György Lakó, Béla Kálmán, and others) and after 1945 acquired the most important positions in the field of Hungarian linguistics.[100]

Cooperation with the Turanian Society and the Finno-Ugric kinship movement was generally a political expectation of those who worked as Hungarian-language instructors in foreign countries. Many of these instructors became leading figures within this movement after returning to Hungary. Finno-Ugric kinship work involved everything from Lutheran pastoral meetings to student exchanges and the revision of textbooks.[101] An important aspect of this movement was that either intentionally or unintentionally, it did not diverge sharply from mainstream Turanism, and with its help, the Turanian Society was able to demonstrate its usefulness to the government. The marriage between Turanism and Finno-Ugric kinship lasted until 1945 and was not necessarily the product of compulsion, a circumstance that is reflected in the fact that more than 1,500 pieces dealing with Finno-Ugric themes were published in the periodical *Turán*, the majority of them between the two world wars.[102] Hungarian Radio and newsreels shown at cinemas in Hungary disseminated an increasing number of programs and amount of news pertaining to Finns and Estonians (as well as to smaller Finno-Ugric peoples). In her book regarding Hungarian-Finnish-Estonian relations during the interwar period, Emese Egey counted fifty-seven Hungarian Radio programs and seventy-two newsreels regarding Finno-Ugric topics, a large portion of which originated from the years of the Second World War but also include an abundant number of reports regarding the Finno-Ugric cultural congresses.[103] Finno-Ugric friendship did not manifest itself merely in words: for example, during the wave of pro-Finnish sympathy in Hungary during the 1939–1940 Winter War, a Hungarian legion was raised and sent amid great secrecy to fight in Finland—one of Prime Minister Pál Teleki's private actions that served to fray the nerves of Hungary's professional diplomats.[104] Although this Hungarian legion, which was composed of eager volunteers from the Hárshegy Scout Park in Budapest as well as a considerable number of extreme right-wing activists, only became deployable after the end of the Soviet-Finnish conflict, the fundamental idea lying behind the initiative was already present in Pál Teleki's world outlook and incipient Turanism as he admired the Imatra Waterfall in Finland and marveled at the choruses "singing into" the red empire at the Soviet-Estonian border in 1924.[105]

Perceiving the expectations of the greater political sphere, the Turanian Society subtly retuned its message: the organization dropped the designation Hungarian Eastern Cultural Center in 1928 before assuming the title Hungarian Association of Kindred Peoples (Magyar Néprokonsági Egyesület) in 1931, placing emphasis on the Finnish, Estonian, Bulgarian, and Turkish "lines" after the latter year.[106] In exchange for subsidies and acceptance of "guidance," the Turanian Society received broad prerogatives and a privileged place within Hungarian organizational life. The revving up of work related to kinship led in the final third of the 1930s to the conclusion of a series of mutual friendship and/or cultural agreements with countries regarded as being Turanian. The stated justification for textually identical Hungarian-Estonian and Hungarian-Finnish cultural and intellectual cooperation agreements signed in 1937 following the treaties that Hungary concluded with Germany and Italy emphasized the thousand-year relationship between the peoples in question and the need for their rapprochement, though scrupulously avoided reference to Turanism or organizations associated with this movement. These agreements called for the initiation of student exchanges and scholarship programs, promised to permanently introduce "kinship days" and enumerated significant episodes in Hungarian-Estonian and Hungarian-Finnish relations, from the work of Antal Reguly to the holding of Finno-Ugric cultural congresses and the establishment of a Hungarian department at the University of Tartu. Hungary's National Assembly enacted these agreements without debate.[107]

However, the agreement regarding Hungarian-Japanese mutual friendship and intellectual cooperation concluded in February 1941 made some waves. Tibor Törs, the rapporteur of the law connected to the agreement, mentioned by name those organizations that would be primarily responsible for maintaining contacts between Hungary and Japan in the future: the Nippon Society, the Kőrösi Csoma Society, the Hungarian Eastern Society, and the Turanian Society. During remarks regarding the bill in the National Assembly, Endre Baross mentioned his experiences as a prisoner of war following the First World War, while Minister of Religion and Public Education Bálint Hóman spoke of "kinship extending along a single branch" between the Hungarians and the Japanese and largely repeated the train of thought contained in the justification of the proposed legislation.[108] This agreement, which compared to other such pacts was conspicuously terse, was finally enacted as Law I of 1940. The next agreement in this series was the Hungarian-Bulgarian treaty regarding intellectual cooperation concluded in 1941. Governing-party representative János Makkai, the rapporteur of the associated bill, referred to the Hungarians and Bulgarians as "two peoples of common origin" in his introduction of the proposed law, while Hóman declared during his remarks that "an ancient connection of kinship exists" between the two peoples, since their ruling classes had once been affiliated with a single (Onogur-Turkish) nation—an idea that not all Hungarian Slavic specialists accepted.[109] Makkai furthermore expressed the hope, one reflecting an old Turanist motif, that through the conclusion of similar agreements the Middle East "will become a cultural focal point" for Hungary. The justification for the parliamentary bill pertaining to the agreement was more moderate, referring to Hungarian-Bulgarian kinship, though specifically mentioned neither Turanism nor the organizations that actively promoted the movement.[110]

All of these measures related to high politics were taken at a time when the Turanian Society was going through a period of serious internal shocks. The director of the Turanian Society, Péter Móricz, died in late 1936, shortly after the organization celebrated the twenty-fifth anniversary of its foundation. In early 1937, the managing editor of *Turán*, Aladár Bán, took offense at something and not only resigned from his editorial position but also withdrew from the Turanian Society altogether. Bán eventually rejoined the Turanian Society but refused to reconsider his resignation as managing editor of the organization's periodical. Three months later, on August 19, 1937, Turanian Society president Gyula Pekár died unexpectedly. Alajos Paikert wrote, following Pekár's death, that "over the past few years he was my best friend, one whom could be trusted and who was neither selfish nor false as most of the others are" and mourned the deceased president of the Turanian Society as a "man with a golden heart" and an "honorable, open and frank Hungarian gentleman."[111] Painter József Lajos Torbágyi Novák, one of the Turanian Society's reliable troopers, wrote in a letter of condolence that "the great loss [of Pekár] seems to be irreparable. And it is nearly impossible to imagine the Turanian Society without the monumental personality of our departed president."[112] Pekár's body lay in repose at the Museum of Applied Arts in Budapest and was accompanied to its final

Fig. 4.4. Issue of *Turán* published to commemorate the twenty-five-year anniversary of the foundation of the Turanian Society. Attribution: Owned by author.

resting place with state honors and buried at the Kerepesi Avenue Cemetery a few hundred meters from the grave of Árpád Zempléni. Following Pekár's death, a third high-ranking official departed from the ranks of the Turanian Society: General Secretary Frigyes Lukinich, who had incessantly badgered his powerful patrons to transfer him to Budapest from his dreary post in Székesfehérvár, was dismissed after legal proceedings were initiated against him on suspicion of financial misconduct. High school teacher and National Finno-Ugric Committee secretary Elemér Virányi, who had previously worked as a Hungarian-language instructor at the University of Tartu, replaced Lukinich as the general secretary of the Turanian Society. The other vacant offices were filled through the appointment of author and retired police counselor Gábor Gergelyffy to the position of director and the selection in December 1937 of the geographer Jenő Cholnoky to serve as the both organization's president and the editor of *Turán*. With regard to the latter post, Cholnoky later wrote in somewhat self-exonerating fashion that "Unfortunately there were few contributors, therefore I had to write a lot [of articles] myself."[113]

Cholnoky's editorship of *Turán* immediately manifested itself in the form of fulminations regarding Hungarian-language grammar and style that appeared on the inside of the front cover of the periodical, specifically the incorrect usage of the reflexive pronoun, the increasing inclination to reduce the demonstrative pronoun to the truncated form *e*, and the growing prevalence of verbs that he considered to be Germanic in origin. Cholnoky, as always, arrived like a hurricane. Cholnoky had been on bad terms with Pekár during the final years of the former Turanian Society president's life, and after becoming the head of the organization, he quarreled with Alajos Paikert as well (though they eventually reconciled). The light dinners that served as the occasion for consultations among the members of the Turanian Society's leading officials moved a short distance from Gyula Pekár's home to that of Jenő Cholnoky in the eighth district of Budapest. Archduke Joseph Francis of Austria, the chief patron of the Turanian Society, subsequently began attending these so-called snuppers (*ucsora*), thus confirming the suspicion among some Turanists that the organization's new president was a legitimist. However, the appearance of Joseph Francis at these events unfortunately obliged the Turanian Society to publish the archduke's book of poetry entitled *Tűzhelyek* (Hearths), and the most committed organizational leaders were even compelled to sit through a recital of the volume's choicest selections.

The Turanian Society's membership grew significantly during Cholnoky's presidency, rising from between 300 and 400 in the 1930s to 562 in the spring of 1943.[114] Around 100 more people joined the organization over the subsequent year. Moreover, *Turán* appeared with increasing frequency as a result of a steady increase in government support; however, during the entire existence of the periodical from 1913 to 1944, it appeared four times in a single year only once—in 1942. Although the Turanian Society undertook some initiatives during the Second World War, such as the organization of a legion among Turanian prisoners of war, the settlement of Estonian intellectuals in Hungary, and a few other similarly fantastic endeavors, its operations were fundamentally restricted during this period, just as those of other associations in Hungary. During the wartime years, The Turanian Society expended most of its energy on the commemoration of the one-hundred-year anniversary of the death of Sándor Kőrösi Csoma and the wrangling that occurred in connection with the erection of a statue in honor of the celebrated Orientalist.[115] Under Cholnoky's leadership, the Turanian Society launched language courses in Esperanto and Chinese. However, the dreams that the organization had maintained during the First World War seemed to be very remote: as a result of the fact that Germany allowed no outside interference in the internal affairs of the territories it had occupied, making contact with the Estonians or the Turkic peoples of Russia became impossible. Establishing cultural institutes, conducting expeditions, and awarding scholarships were out of the question as a result of the war. In 1941, the conspicuously right-wing Stádium Publishing House issued Turanian Society general secretary Elemér Virányi's book *A finn-ugor népek élettere* (The living space of the Finno-Ugric peoples), which served as a manifesto for the radical wings of the Turanist and Pan-Finno-Ugric movements. Virányi, who dated the foreword of *A finn-ugor népek élettere* "the days of the liberation" of Tallinn and Viipuri (Vyborg) in August 1941, dedicated his book to Árpád Zempléni. In this work, Virányi first offered a somewhat ideological, though fundamentally sound, introduction of the Finno-Ugric peoples who lived in or near the Soviet Union. The author then presented his main proposal, advocating the organization of all "peoples of Finnic race" living in the area between the Karelian Isthmus and the Ural Mountains as part of the "great Eurasian reorganization" that was taking place at that time. Virányi urged that these peoples be converted to Christianity and steered away from Eastern Orthodoxy, at least in the direction of newly founded national Orthodox denominations, that the Latin script be introduced to write their languages in place of the Cyrillic script, and that the new intellectual elite of these peoples be trained in Helsinki, Budapest, and Tartu. Virányi's ideas thus resembled to some extent the policies of the Turanist movement during the First World War.[116] The final, enigmatic sentences of this book reveal that the author did not exclude the possibility of establishing some kind of non-Russian state framework for these peoples (the Mari, the Mordvins, the Mansi, the Khanty, and the others):

> The Russian people and its leaders have proven incapable, regardless of the system of government they have followed, to carry out the duties connected to putting this area in order. Thus new powers must be sought, those which will likely be more qualified to find a more successful solution to these questions. In this

way, the sons of the Finno-Ugric tribes that live in the Volga-Ural region and are preparing for revival will in the future receive the noble task of cooperating not only in the precise and factual mapping of this territory, but to build a new and durable cultural, economic, social and political order as well.[117]

Others in addition to Virányi harbored notions connected to population movement and sometimes involving the foundation of new state structures. Retired education-ministry state secretary Pál Petri, one of the coryphaei of the Finno-Ugric movement, wrote a memorandum to Prime Minister László Bárdossy regarding medical professor Endre Jeney's proposal that Estonian intellectuals be settled in the Subcarpathian region of northeastern Hungary. Although the outbreak of war between Germany and the Soviet Union had prevented the possible implementation of Jeney's proposed resettlement of Estonians, Petri believed that the reach of this plan might be extended: "After that we cannot know how the fate of our other linguistic kin—the Mordvins, the Cheremisa, the Voguls, the Ostyaks and the more or less kindred Turkish-Hungarian peoples—might develop. Might there be a question in connection to the removal of other nationalities from Hungary of settling our racial kin here? Will there not be people with our Hungarian blood living in foreign countries who can populate territories of the country that might be left empty?"[118] This idea contains reflections of several wartime Hungarian obsessions, each of which would merit an entire book: the expulsion of national minorities living in Hungary to beyond the Carpathian Mountains; the linkage of population movements to the repatriation of Hungarians living in foreign countries, particularly the United States; and the resettlement of "our racial kin" in Hungary. All of these notions were cloaked in the garb of Finno-Ugric kinship.

Pál Petri was one of the leaders of an organization that before the Second World War represented a dangerous rival to the Turanian Society in its own domain of activity: the Hungarian-Finn Society that had been formed in Budapest in September 1937. Former justice minister Emil Nagy became the president of the newly formed Hungarian-Finn Society, while Elemér Virányi served briefly as the organization's executive president. A similar association had existed within the National Alliance of Hungarian University and College Students in the early 1920s. Virányi had been the president of this student association, while Iván Nagy—who as a ministerial advisor was one of the Turanian Society's most active new cadres at the time of the Second World War—played a significant role in the organization as well. In December 1937, just three months after the foundation of the

Hungarian-Finn Society, the Hungarian-Estonian Society was established in Budapest with Pál Petri as president, Iván Nagy as executive president, and former University of Tartu Hungarian-language instructor József Györke, who became the director of the National Széchényi Library in Budapest after the Second World War, as secretary. This diverse array of associations disconcerted officials at both the Prime Minister's Office and the Foreign Ministry, particularly at the time of the Winter War, when they engaged in a stunning amount of activity, some of which served to hamper each other's operations. The list of programs that these associations held in Hungary in January and February 1940 contained in the papers of Finno-Ugric Cultural Committee member István Csekey kept at the Hungarian Academy of Sciences Library reveals the intensity of the efforts that the small number of Hungarian Finnophiles made at this time:

January 11, 1940: the Turanian Society's Finnish concert at the Vigadó Concert Hall on behalf of the Finnish Red Cross.

January 13, 1940: the Hungarian-Finnish Society's arts and literature evening on behalf of the Finnish Red Cross at the Music Academy. Such superstars of the times as Pál Jávor and Zita Szeleczky perform in the program and National Theater director Antal Németh will give the opening speech.

January 21, 1940: in Szeged, the Calvinist Circle's visual presentation entitled Landscapes of Finland.

January 23, 1940: Hungarian Women's Chamber Orchestra at the Music Academy and the Forrai Chorus's concert on behalf of the Finnish Red Cross.

January 27, 1940: The Nagykőrös Song and Music Association is organizing a Hungarian-Finnish evening at the cultural house in Nagykőrös. Performing will be violinist Alice Felvinczi Takács, the daughter of Zoltán Felvinczi Takács and otherwise a member of the Hungarian Women's Chamber Orchestra.

January 28, 1940: in Szeged, the Dugonics Society's recital session with Finnish themes.

February 7, 1940: in Budapest, the committee meeting of the Finnish-Hungarian Society at Aulich Street 7 in the fifth district.

February 9 and 16, 1940: Jenő Cholnoky's lectures in Budapest on "The Scientific Foundation of the Turanian Idea."

For five weeks beginning on February 13, 1940, Iván Nagy will give ten lectures entitled "Finland and Its Peoples" with projected pictures and phonograph records at the Múzeum Boulevard building of the Budapest faculty of humanities.

February 19, 1940: concert at the Vigadó Concert Hall sponsored by Finnish envoy Onni Talas with the performance of Ernő Dohnányi among others on behalf of the Finnish Red Cross.

February 26, 1940: the Baross Women's Camp will hold a concert with the participation of the Palestrina Chorus on behalf of the Finnish Red Cross at the headquarters of the Baross Federation (Múzeum Street 17). Alice Felvinczi Takáts will perform here as well.

February 28, 1940: the Turanian Society will hold a gala meeting at the Budapest University on Estonia's national holiday. István Csekey, Béla Vikár, and Elemér Virányi will give presentations.

February 28, 1940: (yes, on the same day), the Hungarian-Finnish Society's general assembly at the Gellért Hotel.

Such events could obviously not continue to be held with such frequency. Although there was ardent sympathy toward the Finns in Hungary, the relevant associations all required financial support, paper, venues, and so on, which they generally sought from the government. Therefore, an attempt was made to "concentrate" the operations of the associations: in 1939, an official from the Prime Minister's Office wrote optimistically: "We believe that this movement—albeit somewhat falteringly—will sooner or later be successful. A little official pressure would help a lot in any case."[119] In early 1939, a meeting was held at the Prime Minister's Office regarding the expected results of the cooperative efforts of the associations.[120] Subdued criticism of the Turanian Society's operations emerged during this meeting as well. Alajos Paikert vigorously rejected this criticism and declared that he intended his association to play a primus inter pares role. Those participating in the meeting eventually reached an agreement regarding some kind of interassociational coordination, though they palpably did not manage to settle all their differences. The events that took place in late 1939 provide a clear reflection of this circumstance. Rectification of this situation—as with so many others—was postponed until the end of the war after one association or another resisted the intermittent centralization efforts.

New publications served to forcefully promote the Finno-Ugric kinship movement: the periodical *Északi Rokonaink* (Our northern kin) launched in 1939; the book *Finnország 1940* (Finland 1940) published in 1940; the Dezső Gaskó– and Iván Nagy–edited volume *Finn-magyar kapcsolatok* (Finnish-Hungarian relations) appeared in 1943; and periodicals and books of a similar nature published in Finland (such as the yearbook *Heimotyö*). In certain instances, the authors of these publications did not avoid using slogans of the "forward to the Urals" type. Radical members of the kinship movement envisioned a woodland empire along the border of Europe and Asia that would adjoin the *Provincia Japonica*, as well as the new Greater

Finland and Turanian dominance in Eurasia.[121] The Turanist interpretation of the Second World War as a struggle of the Turanian peoples living in the vicinity of the Bolshevik-Russian empire against evil represented a very easy-to-explain motif, one that furthermore corresponded to the aversion toward Pan-Slavism that had constituted an element of Hungarian nation-building since at least the time of Miklós Wesselényi (1796–1850), author of some pamphlets with anti-Pan-Slavic tones.[122]

The Turanian Society faced serious challenges not only from the Finno-Ugric kinship faction but also from its own radicals. Radical and for the most part fairly young Turanists from an organization called the Turanians of Hungary Friendship Circle (Magyarországi Turánok Baráti Köre) revived the Hungarian Turan Alliance in April 1938.[123] A veteran of the Turanist movement, engineer and retired state-secretary Antal Szentgáli—who served as the first president of the Hungarian-Nippon Society and composed one of the several Turanian anthems that were in circulation at this time—played the main role in the reconstitution of the Hungarian Turan Alliance. Those who assisted Szentgáli in this endeavor included both fellow diehards who had been involved in the Turanian movement since the early 1920s as well as members of the new generation of Turanians, such as László Túrmezei and publisher László Reé as well as Ferenc Forrai and his son Sándor, both of whom were members of the association's Grand Council.[124] (Sándor Forrai [1913–2007], a stenography teacher who went blind in the 1950s, became one of the apostles of the movement to renew the Old Hungarian script in the 1970s and began promoting the broadly defined notion of Sumerian-Hungarian linguistic and genetic kinship in the 1990s.) Among the members of the reconstituted Hungarian Turan Alliance, we find prominent advocates of radical Turanism such as Ferenc Zajti, Gyöngyi Békássy, and Lajos Sassi Nagy.

However, conflict soon emerged among the leaders of the alliance: traveler and geography writer Viktor Keöpe resigned from his post as alliance chief in September 1939, complaining that he could no longer tolerate Grand Vizier Szentgáli's unrealistic plans, authoritarian leadership style, and frequent improvisations.[125] Keöpe's grievances appear to have had some factual basis: the fragmentary documentary sources available regarding the operations of the Hungarian Turan Alliance at this time constitute a repository of utterly fantastic ideas. In addition to the plan to raise a legion of Turanian prisoners of war, Public Education subleader Ferenc Zajti proposed the construction of a Turanian Peoples' Levente[126] and Student Dormitory next to the Tomb of Gül Baba[127] and a Hungarian Cultural History Museum and Exhibition Hall in the Buda Hills.[128] The alliance also promoted the plan that had first emerged more than a decade earlier to erect a gigantic statue of Attila the Hun in Budapest.[129] The Hungarian Turan Alliance sought to establish close relations with either the National Alliance of Hungarian Racial Protectors (Magyar Fajvédők Országos Szövetsége) or the Turanian Society in order to break out of its isolation. The Hungarian Turan Alliance's attempted rapprochement with the Turanian Society provided László Túrmezei, whose original surname was Mihalovits, with the opportunity to clarify his role in the melee that had taken place at the University of Budapest between members of the alliance's opposing camps nearly two decades earlier. Túrmezei's letter to Turanian Society president Jenő Cholnoky is interesting because it shows how Turanists who had surnames that were not of Hungarian origin were forced to defend themselves from accusations—often from other Turanists—that they were not of purely Hungarian origin: "I have never claimed to be a pure-blooded Hungarian in the strict sense of the word. In connection to the Turan movement, I have left the public decision regarding this question to science. I had myself objectively examined at the University of Budapest Anthropological Institute as well as by specialists who are not affiliated with it. I received a certification from the Anthropological Institute regarding the results of the examination. According to this, I am Hungarian. I have never been a Slav."[130] Túrmezei's letter also reveals the primary objections that intransigent Turanists maintained toward the Turanian Society: "I propose that you rid the Society of Jews, half-Jews, freemasons and the like. This above all else. Then relax your totally scientific stance a bit."[131] The Hungarian Turan Alliance addressed memoranda to the government with regard to the Csángós, recommending that they left in place and that a scholarship program be started for them.[132] Members of the Hungarian Turan Alliance advocated for the establishment of a Turanian Party, a Turanian World Federation, a Hungarian-Manchukuo Chamber of Commerce, a Hungarian-Nippon Travel Agency, and a Turanian People's Academy; the construction of a Turanian Exhibition Hall; the holding of an Olympics of Turanian Peoples; and the introduction of a Turanian curriculum in public schools.[133]

Meanwhile, the Hungarian Turan Alliance insisted on maintaining its independence and schemed to evade the government's attempt to unite the various kinship associations. Those who formulated these plans, however unrealistic they may have been, in many cases held significant offices: among the members and leaders of the Hungarian Turan Society were a former county prefect, the former director of the National Museum, a parliamentary representative and a county chief recorder. The member of the organization who held the latter position, Lajos Blaskovich, was the right-hand man of Pest County subprefect László Endre, who was executed for war crimes in 1946, as well as the editor of the periodical *Teozófia* (Theosophy)—facts that provide further evidence of the degree to which the various doctrines were intertwined at this time. Blaskovich, who served as the Hungarian Turan Alliance's "planning subvizier," published a biography of Sándor Kőrösi Csoma on the one hundredth anniversary of the renowned Hungarian Orientalist's death in 1942.[134] The book, in fact, served as a vehicle for Blaskovich to promote his ideas regarding kinship between the Hungarians and certain peoples in North India and Scythian-Indian-Hun continuity as well as to portray Kőrösi Csoma as an anti-Bolshevik hero and celebrate him as a champion of Turanian racial excellence. Moreover, Blaskovich extended the range of Hungarian kinship in the direction of Mesopotamia in space and back to the first human couple and the Genesis flood in time.[135] The author also traced the origin of Greek and Sumerian legends to ancient Turanian mythology, thus laying the foundation for a tradition that surfaced among Hungarian émigrés after the Second World War. Finally, he offered a Turanist interpretation of the existing political situation: "Those marching together with the Aryan-Turanian (German, Italian, Japanese) peoples of the Axis Powers are almost exclusively peoples of Turanian race. The third mighty Turanian state has been born amid flames in the spirit of the rising sun of Japan: North China. And the new empires of the Turanian peoples are being born from the hell of Bolshevism on the continent of seething India and the fiery South."[136] In spite of the ambitious plans, the activities of the Hungarian Turan Alliance for the most part followed the cultural evening–afternoon tea–piano concert trajectory that was customary for associations in Hungary.

In May 1942, members of the Hungarian Turan Alliance became fed up with Szentgáli's despotism and chose ministerial advisor and Racial Protection Party director Miklós Majthényi, who had formerly served as the mayor of the city of Kecskemét, to replace him as the organization's grand vizier.[137] A parallel may be drawn between this change in leadership and the Turanian Society's election in April 1944, shortly after the German occupation of Hungary, of the diplomat and former student of Pál Teleki,

Domokos Szent-Iványi, to the position executive president (veteran members of the organization cheerfully affirmed that "we got a good catch with Szent-Iványi")[138] in the hope that he would eventually succeed the aging Jenő Cholnoky as president. Examining these two changes in leadership, it is difficult to dismiss the notion that the Szent-Iványi–led, anti-German though noncommunist Hungarian Independence Movement (the true influence of which is debated) and the illegal Hungarian Community, which was organized partially on a nationalist basis and regarded freemasonry as its organizational model (and of which Miklós Majthényi was a staunch member) were attempting to extend their influence within the associational sphere and broaden the reach of national, noncommunist, anti-German resistance.

Hungary, although it concluded various treaties of alliance with Nazi Germany beginning in 1939, attempted to stay out of the Second World War. In fact, in September 1939 Hungary received refugees who had fled from Poland following the German invasion of the country and permitted them to travel on to western Europe. Pál Teleki, the first president of the Turanian Society and an enthusiastic supporter of the Hungarian kinship movement during the interwar period, served as the prime minister of Hungary at this time (1939–1941). German victories at the beginning of the war and, chiefly, Hungary's reacquisition with Italian-German arbitration of some of the territories lost via the Treaty of Trianon between 1938 and 1941 pushed the country toward active alliance with Germany. In April 1941, Hungary participated in the Axis invasion of Yugoslavia, an action that raised moral dilemmas that drove Prime Minister Pál Teleki, the former founder of the Turanian Society, to suicide. Under the guidance of Teleki's successor, László Bárdossy (a former member of the Turanian Society), Hungary joined the war against the Soviet Union in June 1941 and then declared war on Great Britain and the United States. However, the British and US air forces did not bomb targets in Hungary until 1944, and the Hungarian population lived in relative peace in spite of the war on the eastern front. Although a series of anti-Jewish laws had been enacted between 1938 and 1941, Jews in Hungary were comparatively secure, the country's parliament continued to function, and though subjected to heavy censorship, opposition newspapers were permitted to appear. This situation changed radically on March 19, 1944, when Nazi Germany invaded Hungary after discovering that the Hungarian political elite had been attempting to establish contacts with Great Britain and the United States. The Germans placed a staunchly right-wing government in power and, with the help of the Hungarian public administration, deported a significant proportion of Hungary's Jewish population in a period of just a few weeks as Regent Horthy remained in office. Then began the Allied bombing of Hungary and essentially the entire Hungarian army was sent to fight on the eastern front under German command. The Turanian Society's leadership change took place amid these circumstances in the spring of 1944.[139]

Under the direction of Domokos Szent-Iványi, prominent right-wing and extreme right-wing figures were removed from the Turanian Society's leadership, including former Prime Minister László Bárdossy; historian and former minister of religion and public education Bálint Hóman; propaganda minister István Antal; Interior Ministry state secretary László Endre, who was responsible for the deportation of Jews from Hungary; and collaborationist government press secretary Mihály Kolosváry-Borcsa. Szent-Iványi later wrote: "I wished to continue this cleansing operation."[140] Yet he did not explain how and under what circumstances the specified people had gained positions of leadership within the Turanian Society in the first place, although we do know that László Endre and Mihály Kolosváry-Borcsa became members of the organization during the latter half of the Second World War. However, there was no longer enough time to purge the leadership—if there indeed there even existed the true intention to do so. The Turanian Society and the Hungarian Turan Alliance essentially ceased to operate in the summer of 1944, from which time the organizations produced no more written documents and the periodical *Turán* was no longer published. At this time, members of the Turanian Society and the Hungarian Turan Alliance were preoccupied with their own survival. The Soviet Red Army crossed the expanded borders of Hungary in August 1944 and passed into the post-Trianon territory of the country the following month. Following the royal coup in Romania, Horthy and his entourage concluded that the time to act had arrived: the regent dismissed the collaborationist government, appointed a trusted military officer to replace Döme Sztójay as prime minister, and initiated secret armistice negotiations with the Soviet Union. Domokos Szent-Iványi traveled to Moscow with an illegal Hungarian cease-fire delegation in September 1944. On October 15, the elderly Horthy announced on the radio that Hungary would leave the German alliance and conclude a truce with the Soviet Union as a representative of the Allied powers. This prompted Nazi Germany to play its trump card: following some minor street skirmishes, German officials forced Horthy to resign and appointed the leader of the extreme right-wing

Arrow Cross Party, Ferenc Szálasi, to serve as the head of a new government. Szálasi then had himself installed as head of state as well. Soon thereafter, Szálasi fled before the Soviet advance toward Budapest in the direction of Germany. The Red Army siege of the city began on Christmas Eve 1944. Turan had arrived to Budapest.

Notes

1. See Ignác Romsics, *Hungary in the Twentieth Century* (Budapest: Osiris–Corvina, 1999), 89–123.

2. For the Turanian Society's version of the period of collapse at the end of the First World War and the postwar revolutions, see Lajos Marzsó, "A Turáni Társaság működése 1918–1921-ben," *Turán* 4 (1921): 64–66.

3. MNL OL K 28, 211. doboz, Pekár Gyula Károlyi Mihálynak, Budapest, 1918. december 4.

4. Ibid., 853–1920. Memorandum a Magyar Keleti Kultúrközpontról. Budapest, 1918. november 25.

5. Ibid., Szende Pál pénzügyminiszter Berinkey Dénes miniszterelnöknek, Budapest, 1919. január 30.

6. Ibid., 2389/1919. előterjesztés a Forradalmi Kormányzótanácsnak, Budapest, 1919. április 12.

7. Kessler, "Turanism and Pan-Turanism in Hungary," 162–63; MNL OL P 1384, 4. cs. 1918–19-es ügyviteli iratok, 579/1919.: a Partie (sic: correctly: Parti in French) Socialiste d'Orient átirata a Magyar Keleti Kultúrközpontnak, Budapest, 1919. április 23.

8. In fact, Pekár's self-satisfied posturing irritated Stróbl so much that he did not finally use him as the model for the statue of Toldi: see Béla Debreczeni-Droppán, "Toldi buzogánya," Hungarian National Museum's blog, March 21, 2017, accessed July 22, 2018, https://mnm.hu/hu/cikk/toldi-buzoganya.

9. This collection is preserved among Pekár's papers kept at the National Széchényi Library in Budapest: OSZKK, Fol. Hung. 2769.

10. Dezső Szabó, "A Nemzeti Színház," *A Nép*, May 12, 1921, 1.

11. OSZKK, Fond 139/2, Pekár Gyula hagyatéka (unarranged), "Thémák és gondolatok."

12. Ibid., 139/3 Fond: the 1931 film *A szép Pongráczné krinolinja* (The beautiful Mrs. Pongrácz's crinoline) and the 1937 film *A kölcsönkért kastély* (The borrowed castle) were based on Pekár's works.

13. For information regarding Pekár's public activities and work as a state secretary, see OSZKK, An. Lit 4739 Pekár Gyula egyesületi tisztségei.

14. According to Turanian Society records, the organization had 242 members in 1921 and 367 members in 1932.

15. MNL OL P 1384, 9. doboz, 1937-es ügyviteli iratok, "Primusz István fiókjából," taglista, n.d. [István Primusz was secretary of the society, relieved of his duties for financial irregularities in 1937].

16. OSZKK Analekta 4743, Pekár Gyula előadása a turáni kérdésről, 1919. szeptember 6.

17. Although Munkácsi published no articles in *Turán*, he did appear occasionally at Turanian Society meetings and events. See the list of those who attended the association's

October 21, 1933, meeting in the following source kept at the Hungarian Geographical Museum in Érd (hereafter, MFM Érd): "Turáni Társaság vendégkönyvei, 1932–1935."

18. MNL OL P 1384, 6. doboz 1924, általános ügyviteli iratok (Files Lajos Herman, Elemér Tolnai).

19. For research done to uncover the Jewish origin of *Turán* editor Aladár Bán, see MTAKK 4711/475, Virányi Elemérnek, a Turáni Társaság főtitkárának levele Csekey Istvánhoz, Budapest, 1938. április 16.

20. MNL OL P 1384, 11. doboz, 5. t. a Vidéki akció iratai, Balassagyarmat, Móricz Péter ügyvezető elnök levele Both Antalnak, Budapest, 1931. február 13.

21. Ibid., 11. doboz 2. t. 1942-es ügyviteli iratok, a Turáni Társaság levele a vezérkari főnökségnek, (s.d., but probably in October 1942).

22. Ibid., Turmezei László levele Gergelyffy Gábor igazgatónak, Budapest, 1942. február 15: "I recommend that you rid the Society of Jews, half Jews, freemasons and the like."

23. "Olvasóinkhoz," *Kőrösi Csoma Archívum* 1, no. 1 (1921): 1.

24. "Társulati ügyek," *Keleti Szemle* 19, no. 3 (1920–1922): 2.

25. MNL OL P 1384, 9. doboz, 286/1937. Teleki Pál levele Pekár Gyulának, Budapest, 1937. február 23.

26. MMGM SZE, I.248, 1329–1338, Paikert Alajos: Életem, 197. (This statement was not included in the Rózsa Takáts–published Paikert memoires.)

27. For the Hungarian Turan Alliance's program, see Dr. István Dessewffy, "A Magyarországi Turán Szövetség céljai és működése," *Turán* 4, (1921): 74–76.

28. MNL OL, K 28, 211. doboz, 169–1921. Pekár Gyula és Paikert Alajos jelentése Teleki Pálnak, Budapest, 1920. december 21.

29. Ibid., Bethlen István levele Teleki Pálnak, Budapest, 1921. május 24.

30. The best examples of such pronouncements were those that Cholnoky made in response to the questionnaire on "the Jewish question" initiated by the left-wing periodical *Huszadik Század* in 1917. See "Jenő Cholnoky" in *A zsidókérdés Magyarországon: A Huszadik Század körkérdése*, 2nd ed. (Budapest: Társadalomtudományi Társaság, 1917), 71–76.

31. Cholnoky described his abstinence from alcohol in his autobiography. See "Cholnoky Jenő önéletrajza," *Vár Ucca Tizenhét* (Veszprém) 6, no. 2 (1998): 187–339.

32. Jenő Cholnoky, "Turán," *Kelet* 1, October 7, 1920, 4.

33. Petőfi Irodalmi Múzeum, Aprónyomtatványtár, Any 77.3/30, A Magyarországi Turán Szövetség Alapszabályai, elfogadva 1920. szeptember 26-án.

34. Ibid.

35. The Turanian organization in Szeged was still organizing lectures in 1930. See "A Turán Szövetség előadása," *Délmagyarország*, March 9, 1930, 13.

36. For information regarding these joint lectures, see "Turáni előadások. Szervezi a Turáni Társaság és Magyarországi Turán Szövetség," *Turán* 4 (1921): inside front cover.

37. MFM Érd, Cholnoky-hagyaték, 5. doboz, 1921–1923-as levelek, Dessewffy István levele Cholnoky Jenőnek, Budapest, 1922. január 6. (John of Capistrano [1386–1456] was an Italian Franciscan friar and inquisitor who shortly before his death led a crusade along with János Hunyadi against the Ottoman forces that were invading Hungary.)

38. "Bonyodalmak az állatkerti dsámi körül," *Pesti Napló*, August 7, 1913, 7–8; and "Szekula Gyula felszólalása," *Fővárosi Közlöny*, May 19, 1917, 916.

39. Zsolt Nagy, "In Search of a Usable Past: The Legacy of the Ottoman Occupation in Interwar Hungarian Cultural Diplomacy," *Hungarian Studies Review* 42, nos. 1–2 (Spring-Fall, 2015): 39–40.

40. MFM Érd, Cholnoky-hagyaték, 3. doboz, tudományos és hatósági levelek 1923, Vest Fedor levele Cholnoky Jenőnek, Budapest, 1923. szeptember 14.

41. HMA A4702, Felvinczi Takáts Marianne: Felvinczi Takáts Zoltán életrajza. n.d.

42. Ibid., A4268/1-5, Felvinczi Takáts Zoltán önéletrajzának piszkozata, n.d. (1947–1948 körül).

43. "A turáni ellenzék kizárja a nagyvezért, a nagyvezér pedig az ellenzéket," *Az Est*, February 28, 1923, 2; and "Feloszlatták a Turán Szövetség gyűlését," *Pesti Hírlap*, February 20, 1923, 4.

44. PIM V. 4131/182/1, Kornai István felségsértési ügyének iratai, 1899.

45. At the same time, Kornai himself made a list of those in the opposition camp who—according to him—were of Jewish or German origin (PIM, Any 77.3/31, a törzsgyűlés szavazólapja, with Kornai's remarks on it).

46. "A Magyarországi Turán Szövetség válsága," *Pesti Hírlap*, February 27, 1923, 4.

47. "A turáni átok," *Az Est*, February 20, 1923, 1.

48. László Cholnoky, "Turáni emlék," *Világ*, February 21, 1923, 7.

49. "A Turán Szövetség kizárta rentienskedő tagjait," *Budapesti Hírlap*, March 2, 1923, 5.

50. OSZKK, Fond 446, Turáni dolgozatok 2, a Magyarországi Turán Szövetség egyezséglevele, Budapest, 1931. július 13.

51. MNL OL, P 1384, 11. doboz, 6. t., "Corvin Mozgó" feliratú dosszié.

52. Ibid., 7. doboz, 1925–1931, "Törökországi mérnökakcióval."

53. Ibid., 6. doboz, általános ügyviteli iratok 1924, 161/1925. a Turáni Társaság válasza a kereskedelmi minisztériumnak, Budapest 1925. április.

54. Ibid., 6. doboz, 891/1925, a kereskedelmi minisztérium szigorúan bizalmas átirata a Turáni Társaságnak. Budapest, 1924. okt. 31.

55. David Petruccelli, "Banknotes from the Underground: Counterfeiting and the International Order in Interwar Europe," *Journal of Contemporary History* 51, no. 3 (2016): 507–30.

56. A. E., "Látogatás az angorai etnográfiai muzeumban, melyet Mészáros Gyula rendez be," *Magyarság*, July 8, 1928, 7.

57. For information regarding Mészáros's Chuvash and Bashkir collections, see Ágnes Kerezsi, "Mészáros Gyula baskír gyűjteménye a Néprajzi Múzeumban," *Néprajzi Értesítő* 96 (2014): 75–98.

58. OSZKK, Fond 170, Bendefy László hagyatéka, Levelezés L-M, Mészáros Gyula levele Bendefy Lászlónak, Újvidék, 1944. február 6.

59. Gyula Mészáros, *A másfélezeresztendős magyar nemzet: Néptörténelmi tanulmány* (New York: New York-i Magyar Irodalmi Kör, n.d.).

60. György Haraszti, *Vallomások a holtak házából—Ujszászy István vezérőrnagynak, a 2. vkf. osztály és az Államvédelmi Központ vezetőjének az ÁVH fogságában írott feljegyzései* (Budapest: Corvina-ÁBTL, 2007), 510–11. (Following the communist revolution in Budapest in 1919, the first thing that Mészáros did was to take one of the Hungarian National Museum Ethnographic Repository's revolvers, which he never returned [NMI 21/1919, Seemayer Vilibald múzeumigazgató tanúsítványa, 1919. március 26]).

61. "Szakosztályi ülések," *Turán* 20–21, nos. 1–2 (1937–38): 33.

62. MNL OL, P 1384, 9. doboz, 912/1937, a Turáni Társaság levele Lukinich Frigyesnek, a Társaság főtitkárának, Budapest, 1937, október 1. és Kodolányi János: Harmadszor Finnországban. *Kelet Népe*, September 1–7, 1937.

63. For documents pertaining to the foundation of these branch organizations, see MNL OL P 1384, 11. doboz 5. t., a "Vidéki akció iratai."

64. PIM V 2400/1, a nyíregyházi Turáni Kör levele Ady Lajosnak, Nyíregyháza, 1922. január 30.

65. MNL OL P 1384, 11. doboz, 5. t., "Balassagyarmat, 1930–1933"-dosszié; see here the member's list and Vargyassy Márton levelei Pekár Gyulának, Balassagyarmat, 1930. október 2., 1930. október 12.

66. For the latter, see Márton Vargyassy, "A szumir kérdés," *Hargitaváralja*, September 24, 1936, 12–13.

67. Ibid., 11. doboz, 5. t., "Balassagyarmat, 1930–1933"-dosszié, Both Antal levele Móricz Péternek, Balassagyarmat, 1931. február 12. Both wrote in early 1931 as follows: "I would really wish to know why the headquarters would not have approved my Hebrew lecture, whereas the Turanian origin of the entire vocabulary of the Classical Hebrew language is so evident that we should be happy about this fact rather than refuse to clarify the question."

68. Ibid., 11. dob. 3. t. az Orvostudományi Szakosztály iratai, 1934–42.

69. S. F., "Milyen célkitűzéssel indul a Magyar Vércsoportkutató Társaság?" *Pesti Napló*, February 25, 1934, 39.

70. MNL OL P 1384, 8. dob. 385. f. 645/1934, Békássy Gyöngyi levele Móricz Péternek, Óbarok, 1934, október 28. Móricz válaszfogalmazványa ugyanott, 386. f.; and Gyöngyi Békássy, *A vércsoportok kutatásának faji jelentősége* (Budapest: Reé, 1937).

71. See the special issue of the periodical *A Nő és a Társadalom* (The woman and society) published regarding the congress on April 20, 1913, that included a short article by Békássy ("Az ifjúsági bizottság" [The Youth Committee]), 67.

72. Gyöngyi Békássy, *A turáni eszme* (Budapest: Göncöl, 1920).

73. MNL OL P 1384, 13. cs. 8. t. Móricz Péter ügyvezető alelnök jelentése az 1930, évi közgyűlésen, n.d. [november 29.]. According to this and other sources, the Turanian Society maintained this opportunity as late as the year 1937.

74. Ottó Herman Museum Historical Repository-Miskolc (hereafter, HOM), Képzőművészeti Adattár, Mokry-Mészáros Dezső hagyatéka, Mokry-Mészáros Dezső levele Boromisza Tibornak, n.d.

75. MNL OL Mikrofilmtár, X 4253, 8936. doboz, a kormányzói kabinetiroda iratai, Teleki Pál levele ismeretlennek (vélhetően Györffy Istvánnak), Budapest, 1930. február 23.

76. For information regarding Horthy's visit to a Turanian Society–sponsored event, see "Szakaroff Konstantin volt orosz tábornok előadása," *Turán* 14, nos. 1–4 (1931): 61.

77. With regard to the formation of the National Assembly's Turanian Bloc, see the following source: MNL OL K 28, 211. doboz, 308biz/1925, Pekár Gyula levele Prónay György államtitkárnak, Budapest, 1925. május 23.

78. MNL OL P 1384, 5. cs. általános ügyviteli iratok, 1919–1924, 121/1920. Gömbös Gyula levele a Turáni Társaságnak, Budapest, 1920. április 21.

79. "A Nemzetgyűlés 1921. december 30-i ülése," *NN 1920-1922*, volume 14, 245.

80. Social democratic representative Ferenc Reisinger, for example, referred to "Turanian laziness" during a speech he made in the National Assembly (*KN 1935-1940*, volume 22 [March 13, 1939], 356).

81. "The divine mission of this nation, honored house, is to develop the other kind of culture inherited from the eastern ancestors and with the help of the acquired European culture to graft the fertile branch of the ancient Turanian idea onto the European Christian and current National Socialist culture" (*KN 1939-1944*, volume 7, October 11, 1940, 100).

82. *KN 1939-1944*, volume 1, June 17, 1939, 224.

83. For this initial enthusiasm, see Dezső Szabó, "A turánizmus," *Élet és Irodalom* 1, no. 1 (1923): 14–22.

84. Ildikó Farkas, "A turánizmus," *Magyar Tudomány* 54, no. 7 (1993): 866–67.

85. See Gyula Szekfű, "A turáni-szláv parasztállam," *Magyar Szemle* 5, no. 3 (1929): 30–37; and Gyula Németh, "A magyar turánizmus," *Magyar Szemle* 11, no. 1 (1931): 132–39.

86. MNL OL, P 1384, 13. cs., 8. t., Móricz Péter ügyvezető alelnök jelentése, Budapest, 1931. november 27.

87. Mihály Jungerth-Arnóthy, *Moszkvai napló*, edited by Péter Sipos and László Szűcs (Budapest: Zrínyi, 1989), 92.

88. MNL OL, K 63 a külügyminisztérium politikai osztályának iratai, 114. cs., 15/1 tétel, 102/53–1933. sz., Jelentés a japán katonai attaséval folytatott beszélgetéséről, 1933. szeptember 15.

89. For the Eastern idea in Hungarian foreign policy, see Balázs Ablonczy, "'Lándzsahegy,' néprokonság, small talk—Turanizmus és keleti gondolat a két világháború közötti magyar külpolitikai gondolkodásban," in *Magyar külpolitikai gondolkodás a 20: Században*, ed. Pál Pritz (Budapest: Magyar Történelmi Társulat, 2006), 87–106.

90. Fennofil, "Az első Finn-ugor Tanügyi Kongresszus turáni vonatkozásai," *Turán* 4 (1921): 37–44.

91. For information regarding Hungarian participation in Finno-Ugric cultural congresses, see Anssi Halmesvirta, *Kedves rokonok: Magyarország és Finnország 1920–1945* (Budapest: Cédrus Művészeti Alapítvány-Napkút, 2014), 20–173.

92. See the following source for documents regarding the Museum of Ethnography: NMI 122/1925, Teleki Pál levele Bátky Zsigmondnak, 1925. november 20. Bátky Zsigmond levele Teleki Pálnak, 1925. december 18. Teleki Pál levele Bátky Zsigmondnak, Budapest, 1926. január 4.

93. Pál Teleki, "Ajánlás," in *Finnek, észtek—A magyarok északi testvérnépei* (Budapest: Királyi Magyar Egyetemi Nyomda, 1928), 5.

94. Count Kuno Klebelsberg, "Testvérnépek hazájában," *Pesti Napló*, June 1, 1930, 3.

95. Péter Pomozi, "A tartui egyetem és Magyarország," *Zempléni Múzsa* 3, no. 3 (2003): 21–22.

96. "Hírek," *Turán* 13, nos. 1–4 (1930): 65.

97. MNL OL Mikrofilmtár, X 9062, Eemil N. Setälä levelezése 31134. tekercs, Baráthosi Balogh Benedek levele Eemil Setälä-nek, Budapest, 1930. február 25. Letters from Sándor Ispánovits, Béla Vikár, and Aladár Bán Aladár can also be found here.

98. Enikő Szij, "A finnugor néprokonsági eszme az 1920–30-as években," in *Őstörténet és nemzettudat 1919–1931*, ed. Éva Kincses Nagy (Szeged: JATE Magyar Őstörténeti Kutatócsoport-Balassi, 1991), 72–88.

99. MNL OL, P 1384, 6. doboz általános ügyviteli iratok, 1924, 970/1924, a Turáni Társaság ajánlása Turchányi Tihamérnak, 1924. november (draft).

100. András Bereczki, "A két háború közötti magyar-észt kapcsolatok történetéről," *Jogtörténeti Szemle* 6, no. 1 (2004): 58–67; and Emese Egey, *A két világháború közötti magyar-finn-észt kapcsolatok történetéből: Társasági, diplomáciai, katonai együttműködés*, Specimina fennica Savariae 15 (Szombathely: NYME SEK Uralisztikai Tanszék, 2010), 45–50.

101. Egey, *A két világháború közötti magyar-finn-észt kapcsolatok történetéből*.

102. Emese Egey and Enikő Szíj, eds., *A Turán című folyóirat 1913, 1917–1918, 1921–1944 finnugor mutatója* (Budapest: Tinta, 2002).

103. Egey, *A két világháború közötti magyar-finn-észt kapcsolatok történetéből*, 141–52 and 171–91.

104. Gábor Richly, "Magyar katonai segítségnyújtás az 1939–40-es finn-szovjet háborúban," *Századok* 130, no. 2 (1996): 403–44.

105. On Teleki's 1924 trip to Finland and Estonia, see Halmesvirta, *Kedves rokonok: Magyarország és Finnország 1920–1945*, 66–89.

106. MNL OL P 1384, 13. cs. 8. t.: 1932. december 2-i közgyűlés, Móricz Péter ügyvezető elnökhelyettes jelentése.

107. *KI 1935–1939*, volume 8, 469–70. The Hungarian-Estonian and Hungarian-Finnish agreements regarding intellectual cooperation were enacted into laws XXIII and XXIX, respectively, in 1938.

108. *KN 1939–1944*, volume 1, 222, 227–28. For the justification connected to this law, see *KI 1939–1944*, volume 1, 14.

109. *KN 1939–1944*, volume 10, 301, 303.

110. *KN 1939–1944*, volume 10, 301–3. For the justification of Law XVI of 1941 pertaining to the Hungarian-Bulgarian agreement, see *KI 1939–1944*, volume 6, 521. Moreover, a Bulgarian university institute was opened in Budapest in 1943.

111. OSZKK, Levelestár, Paikert Alajos Pekár Gyulánénak, Budapest, 1937, szeptember 18; and MMGM SZE, I.248, 1329–38. Paikert Alajos: Életem, 93.

112. MNL OL P 1384, 9. doboz, 872/1937. Torbágyi Novák Lajos a Turáni Társaságnak, Budapest, 1937. szeptember 21.

113. "Cholnoky Jenő önéletrajza," *Vár Ucca Tizenhét* 6, no. 2 (1998): 293.

114. MNL OL K 28, 212. doboz, 412. t., Gergelyffy Gábor jelentése a Turáni Társaság közgyűlésén, 1943. április 9.

115. For the Turanian Society's effort to settle Estonian intellectuals in Hungary, see MNL OL K28, 205. doboz, 389. t. Magyar-Észt Társaság, 1941-A-18204, Jeney Endre memoranduma a Magyar-Észt Társaság elnökéhez, Petri Pálhoz, Debrecen, 1941. március 17. For the idea of organizing a legion among Turanian prisoners of war, see MNL OL P 2249, 10. sorozat, a Magyarországi Turán Szövetség iratai, 2. t. Sándor László levele a Szövetségnek, Gödöllő, 1941. október 20, and MNL OL, K 28, 211. doboz, 412. t. 20436–1941. Túrmezei László Bárdossy László miniszterelnöknek, Budapest, 1941. július 30. For correspondence regarding the statue of Sándor Kőrösi Csoma, see MFM, Cholnoky-hagyaték, 7. doboz, a Kőrösi Csoma Sándor-szoborral kapcsolatos külön dosszié, fénymásolatok (1942–43).

116. Elemér Virányi, *A finn-ugor népek élettere* (Budapest: Stádium, 1941).

117. Ibid., 199.

118. MNL OL K 28, 205. doboz, 389. t., 21233/1941. Petri Pál memoranduma Bárdossy László miniszterelnöknek, Budapest, 1941. augusztus 9.

119. MNL OL K 28, 211. doboz, 412. t. 15804/1939. előterjesztés, 1939. április.

120. Ibid., 1939-L-16086, Jegyzőkönyv a néprokonsági egyesületek közös, parlamentben tartott értekezletéről, Budapest, 1939. február 17.

121. Enikő Szíj, "Pánfinnugor és antifinnugor elméletek, mozgalmak," in *125 éves a budapesti finnugor tanszék*, ed. Péter Domokos and Márta Csepregi (Budapest: ELTE Finnugor Tanszék, 1998), 145–52.

122. See Miklós Wesselényi, *Szózat a' magyar és szláv nemzetiség' ügyében* (Pest: Ottó Wigand, 1843).

123. Few source documents regarding the Turanians of Hungary Friendship Circle have survived. I discovered an invitation from this association among the papers of architect István Medgyaszay. See the Medgyaszay collection (private), Társaság-mappa: Magyarországi Turánok Baráti Köre meghívója 1936. február 19-re, a budapesti Pázmány Péter Tudományegyetem természetrajzi előadótermébe: Nagy Ivánnak, a Nemzetpolitikai Társaság elnökének előadására a "A külföldi magyarság szerepe rokonnépeink kapcsolódásában."

124. MNL OL P 2249, 10. sorozat, 2. t. a Magyarországi Turán Szövetség ősgyűlésének szavazólapja, 1940. június 24.

125. Ibid., 1. t. Keöpe Viktor levele az MTSZ vezéri tanácsának, Budapest, 1939. őszelő (szeptember) 28.

126. The government of Hungary launched the Levente movement in 1921 in order to provide young men between the ages of twelve and twenty-one with obligatory paramilitary and athletic training. Organizations associated with the movement operated under dual military and civilian leadership, while their instructors were generally retired military officers. The Levente movement served as a means of circumventing the ban on military conscription imposed on Hungary via the 1920 Treaty of Trianon.

127. Gül Baba was an eminent Ottoman Bektashi dervish who died in Buda shortly after the armies of Suleiman the Magnificent captured the city in 1541. The tomb (*türbe* in Turkish) of Gül Baba subsequently became an important Muslim pilgrimage site. The issues of renovating the tomb—which was partially destroyed in 1690, a few years after the reincorporation of Buda into the Kingdom of Hungary—and settling its status have emerged regularly since the second half of the nineteenth century as part of the process of Hungarian-Turkish rapprochement. A comprehensive renovation of the Gül Baba's türbe was completed in 2018.

128. Ibid., 1. t. 1942. május 31. közgyűlési jegyzőkönyv és OSZKK, Fond 446, Turáni Társasággal összefüggő iratok, 1. doboz, Zajti Ferenc: Memoranduma a Turáni Népek Levente és Diákotthona a Gül baba türbénél, a Naphegyen emelendő Magyar Kultúrhistóriai Múzeum és kiállítócsarnokról, Budapest, 1943.

129. References to the planned Attila statue appear frequently in Turanian Society documents beginning in the middle of the 1920s: MNL OL P 2249. 10. sorozat, 1. t. Reé László szövetségnagy jelentése, 1940. március 18.

130. MFM, Cholnoky-hagyaték, 5. doboz, 1941-es dosszié: Túrmezei László levele Cholnoky Jenőnek, Budapest, 1941. április 19.

131. MNL OL P 1384, 11. doboz, 2. t. Túrmezei László levele Gergelyffy Gábor igazgatónak, Budapest, 1942. február 15.

132. The Csángós are a Hungarian ethnographic group living beyond the Carpathian Mountains in the region of Moldavia who speak an archaic form of the Hungarian language. The Catholic faith of the Csángós has prevented them from assimilating with the Eastern Orthodox Romanians, who constitute a significant majority of the population in this region lying beyond the traditional area of Hungarian settlement. The estimated number of people belonging to this Hungarian ethnographic group does not exceed a few tens of thousands.

133. A Turanian party under the leadership of painter Dezső Mokry-Mészáros and his friends actually existed for a short time: MNL OL K 149, Belügyminisztérium, reservált iratok, 81. doboz, 4. t. 6407/1940. Mészáros Dezső festőművész bejelentése a Turáni Magyarok Pártjáról. Budapest, 1940. február 1. See MTA BTK Művészettörténeti Intézet, Művészettörténeti Adattár, Mokry-Mészáros Dezső hagyatéka, MDK, C-I-39/1-6. dosszié, a Turán-magyarok Pártjának nyilatkozata, 1940. április. 9. For the other plans, see MNL OL P 2249 10. sorozat, 2. t. n.d. (július 1), Kakas Koppány András javaslata a Magyarországi Turán Szövetségnek.

134. Lajos Blaskovich, *Őshaza és Kőrösi Csoma Sándor célja* (Budapest: Stádium, 1942).

135. Ibid., 46–89.

136. Ibid., 221–22.

137. MNL OL P P 2249, 10. sorozat 1. tétel, Beszámoló a Magyarországi Turán Szövetség 1942. évi működéséről.

138. MMGM SZE, 2012.21.1, Paikert-hagyaték, Napló 1944. május 3–1945. május 8. 1944. június 29-i bejegyzés.

139. Romsics, *Hungary in the Twentieth Century*, 204–16.

140. MNL OL, Belügyminisztérium iratai, XIX-B-1-h, 131. cs. 490655/1948, Szent-Iványi Domokos levele a belügyminisztériumhoz, Budapest, 1945. augusztus 14.

5

SZÉKELYS, PAGANS, AND HUNTERS

A S WAS MENTIONED PREVIOUSLY IN THIS BOOK, IT would be a mistake to regard all those who were members of Turanian organizations to have been committed Turanists. At the same time, there were many people who were not members of such organizations who solemnly believed in the importance of the Turanist program.

Following the first breakup of the Hungarian Turan Alliance in 1923, most of the organization's members returned to the Turanian Society, though many others chose to take different paths. Between 1923 and 1938, proxy associations that at first glance did not appear to have anything to do with the Turanian movement served to ensure the continuity of radical Turanism. The programs of these associations espoused distinctly Turanian principles, and their members were unequivocally Turanists of the more radical type. The Society of Hungarians that formed as the Hungarian Turan Alliance was falling apart in 1923 and, for many years, appeared to be nothing more than a conventional Budapest social club. Among the twenty-five members of the Society of Hungarians were the painter-librarian Ferenc Zajti; the architect István Medgyaszay; the entomologist Gyula Krepuska; the teacher and Japanese interpreter Tihamér Turchányi; the painter Aladár Fáy; the metallurgical engineer Árpád Gálocsy; the ministerial advisor István Dessewffy, whose viewpoints regarding the John of Capistrano statue at Buda Castle have already been cited; and the entire Baráthosi Balogh family. Miklós Majthényi, the final president of the Hungarian Turan Alliance, served as the fledgling organization's secretary. The presence of Krepuska, Turchányi, Fáy, Gálocsy, and the Baráthosi Baloghs within the Society of Hungarians represent an unmistakable indication that the organization was oriented toward the East.[1] There is no evidence showing that the Society of Hungarians engaged in any notable activity: the organization held its meetings at the editorial office of the previously mentioned periodical *A Cél*, and members occasionally expressed the desire to elevate the status of research surrounding Hungarian ancient history to its proper place within Hungary's system of higher education. The Society of Hungarians attempted to obtain support for Zajti's 1929 trip to India and emphasized that "we must resurrect the decayed Hungarian national feeling, national consciousness and pride in order to again make our nation capable of working to build the future"—a notion that was not expressly Turanian in nature, though the correct interpretation of these words has been guaranteed by the composition of the organization.[2] The Society of Hungarians then shifted course during the 1930s: during this decade, the society admitted several hundred new members, including a large number of retired ministerial advisors in addition to such notable people as the sculptor Ferenc Medgyessy and the geographer Jenő Cholnoky.[3]

The Hungarian-Indian Society was founded in early 1930 with essentially the same official personnel as the Society of Hungarians.[4] The leader of the Hungarian-Indian Society, Ferenc Zajti, inspired his friends to join the organization following his return from India.[5] Members of the Hungarian-Indian Society included everybody who maintained an interest in the political expression of Eastern kinship, from the engineer and retired state secretary Antal Szentgáli and Alajos Paikert to former National Assembly representative Ernő Kovács-Karap. Among the leaders of the new organization were ethnographer István Györffy and honorary Hungarian consul to India and Hungarian military-aviation pioneer colonel István Petróczy. Former county prefect and National Assembly Turanian Bloc leader Zoltán Mokcsay and Debrecen theology instructor Zsigmond Varga (1886–1956) served as provincial representatives for the Hungarian-Indian Society. However, not everybody was eager to accept proffered official positions within the society. For example, Ervin Baktay (1890–1963), one of the central figures associated with Indian studies in Hungary who was on rather bad terms with Ferenc Zajti, firmly refused to become a member of the Hungarian-Indian Society's committee: "My conception of things regarding India is based on extensive study and in certain regards differs so greatly from the [Hungarian-Indian] Society's conception, which is undoubtedly identical to that of his [Zajti's], that at this time I see no possibility of my working together with the Society effectively and with genuine enthusiasm."[6] The Hungarian-Indian Society's Turanist orientation manifested itself in rather explicit form when organizational president Zajti declared that "every single member of the Society should in both the public and private sphere explain the Society's objective, which is not to establish contacts with the Indo-Aryans, but to maintain relations with Turanian kin living in India."[7] However, this aim did not correspond to that stated in the organization's bylaws, which placed emphasis on building Hungarian-Indian cultural and economic relations. There is very little data regarding the operations of the Hungarian-Indian Society: available information shows that the organization attempted, for example, to undertake cooperation with regional agricultural chambers in Hungary in order to increase the country's exports to India.[8] This data suggests that the Hungarian-Indian Society engaged in public activity for the final time during the 1935 Attila celebrations.[9] It is in any case certain that by the year 1937 István Medgyaszay had trouble coming up with a way to prove to authorities in the eleventh district of Budapest that the Hungarian-Indian Society had in fact been dissolved.[10]

There is sporadic evidence during this period of the operation of some insignificant Hungarian-Turkish associations, while the Hungarian National Alliance established a Bulgarian-Hungarian committee under the leadership of the ubiquitous Smallholders' Party parliamentary representative general Tivadar Galánthay-Glock at this time as well. The Hungarian-Nippon Society founded in 1924 was the biggest and longest-operating Turanian proxy organization. Before the First World War, interest in Japan among Hungarians was largely confined to art collectors, one or two determined researchers, and those belonging to certain religious groups (such as the Jesuits). Several thousand Hungarian prisoners of war (POWs) gained a glimpse of the Japanese world as a result of their contact with Japanese imperial troops while in captivity in Siberia and their return to Hungary via Japan. Amid the isolation and boredom of confinement, interaction with Turkic or Mongolian peoples in Siberia served to spark the imaginations of many Hungarian POWs. High school teacher József Németh, the father of the distinguished author and playwright László Németh (1901–1975), was the most well known of these Hungarian POWs. While interned at a camp located beyond Lake Baikal in the summer of 1917, József Németh came down with a case of POW melancholy that manifested itself in the form of "Turanian musings": "The Turanian 'suppositions' that had been at work within me for years suddenly brought me under their spell. I no longer even know what my theory was, but during the month of September I lived under the permanent belief that I had uncovered an ancient language from which all European (Indo-Aryan) and Ural-Altaic languages and even Chinese and Indian could be derived."[11]

It is not surprising that some Hungarian POWs who had already been oriented toward the East became receptive to the notion of fostering Japanese-Hungarian relations or even of explicitly propagating the concept of kinship. Although researchers have determined that the Japanese held only around two thousand Hungarian POWs in Siberia at the end of the First World War,[12] those who laid the groundwork for the foundation of the Hungarian-Nippon Society emerged from among this relatively small number of POWs. These POWs included the key figure in the Hungarian-Nippon Society: the lawyer István Mezey, a native of Szabadka (Subotica, Serbia) who directed the operations of the organization for two decades. Mezey, who had taken an interest in the East even before the war, wrote to art historian Zoltán Felvinczi Takács from captivity in Siberia just before returning home: "From the land of the ancient Hungarians to the New Hungary!"[13] (The fact that Japanese soldiers had killed three fellow Hungarian POWs who had attempted to escape from the camp in which they were held evidently did not serve to dampen Mezey's enthusiasm.) Following his return to Hungary, István Mezey became involved in a broad range of Turanian initiatives, and although Antal Szentgáli became the president of the Hungarian-Nippon Society, Mezey was the one who coordinated the activities of the organization throughout its existence.[14] Among those who held office within the Hungarian-Nippon Society, we find both some less committed figures, such as former prime minister Sándor Simonyi-Semadam, whose gravitation toward the East was reflected in the architecture of his villa in Budapest, and prominent Turanists who had come into contact with Japan in one way or another, such as Tihamér Turchányi, Zoltán Felvinczi Takács, and Vilmos Pröhle.

Vilmos Pröhle descended from a family of Prussian origin that had been engaged in the management of estates and had provided Hungarian Lutheranism with several outstanding intellects. Pröhle, who initially earned his living as a high school teacher before becoming a university professor, was at once a language genius, a convinced antisemite, a National Assembly representative, an Arab-language instructor for rabbinical students in Budapest, a Volksdeutscher, and "an old Hungarian nationalist"—as one of his daughters, an avid member of the Volksbund[15] women's organization in Budapest, wrote to the führer.[16] Pröhle made several research trips to the Ottoman Empire and the Turkish-inhabited regions of Russia. In addition to Turkish, he had mastered Japanese, Arabic, and Hebrew; could read in Chinese; and wrote poetry in Greek. However, Pröhle's investigations of

Uralic languages and Japanese kinship published in the periodical *Keleti Szemle* during the First World War had placed him at odds with part of the Hungarian linguistic community.[17] Pröhle taught at the universities in Kolozsvár and Debrecen before becoming director of the Eastern Asian Institute that had essentially been established for him at the University of Budapest. Here Pröhle held very few classes in Japanese and Turkish: in fact, most of his students were seminarians from the rabbinical-training institute who had enrolled in Arabic language courses at the university. Some have asserted that he kept a gold-plated arrow cross or a dedicated image of Hitler on the entryway wall at his home in the Lágymányos district of Budapest, although others have denied this claim.[18] Pröhle's wife died in 1922, leaving him to raise their seven children alone. It is not known if his well-documented financial and drinking problems originated during this period. Pröhle served as the honorary Japanese consul in Budapest for a short time in the middle of the 1920s, although he traveled to Japan for the first time only in 1928. However, by this time, the Eastern world had already drawn Pröhle, who was still teaching at a high school in provincial Hungary and specializing in sciences and modern languages, into its magic circle. With regard to his meeting with Russo-Japanese War hero general Nogi Maresuke in 1911, Pröhle wrote: "I will always count this day as among the happiest of my life."[19] The "unimaginably impractical" Pröhle participated in every Turanian undertaking in Hungary for three entire decades. According to the legendary Indiana University professor Denis Sinor, who had studied under Pröhle, the only conclusion that could be drawn from an examination of his former teacher's career was that "people are contradictory and unfathomable."[20]

The Hungarian-Nippon Society generally operated according to the same model as other similar organizations in Hungary during this period, holding lectures, hosting evening parties, receiving Japanese guests who were visiting Budapest, and organizing a Japanese festival. In 1936, the society began publishing a periodical entitled *Távol Kelet* (Far East) with support from a Japanese foundation. Although many Turanists participated in the activities of the Hungarian-Nippon Society, the organization always emphasized the role that the Siberian POWs had played in its inception, thus establishing a certain distance from the Turanian Society, which had been founded in 1910. The foundation of the Hungarian-Nippon Society was never in doubt despite this fact. The active members of the Hungarian-Nippon Society included Japanese teacher Yuichiro Imaoka, who had become acquainted with Benedek Baráthosi Balogh during the latter's trip to Japan before the First World War. Imaoka traveled to Hungary in 1922 during a trip to Europe and ended up staying in the country for almost a decade. During this time, Imaoka learned how to speak Hungarian fluently and published the work *Új Nippon* (New Nippon), for which he received a distinguished government award. His translations, books, and articles examine the course of Hungarian-Japanese relations until well beyond the Second World War. After returning to Japan, Imaoka found employment at the Japanese Foreign Ministry and published many popularizing works and language books, including a Japanese-Hungarian dictionary. Imaoka's homemade New Year's greeting cards are a nearly essential component of the legacy of any Turanist who was active at this time.[21]

Although, as previously described, the attempt of the Turanists to expand their operations to locations outside Budapest was not necessarily successful, associations and circles of Turanist character did exist in cities—and even towns and villages—in provincial Hungary. We shall take a look at two such provincial Turanian circles—those in the cities of Miskolc and Debrecen.

The presence in the rapidly growing industrial city of Miskolc, located in northeastern Hungary, of the Lutheran law academy that had moved from Eperjes (Prešov, Slovakia) following the Treaty of Trianon, high schools, the intelligentsia connected to the heavy industry located in neighboring Diósgyőr, and municipal infrastructure provided a sufficient foundation for the establishment of a series of social organizations. In October 1931, the Miskolc daily newspaper *Magyar Jövő* (Hungarian future) published an article regarding a small group of people in the city who dealt with the Old Hungarian script and Turanist themes but had not formed an official organization.[22] According to this report, museum director Andor Lészih, painter Dezső Mokry-Mészáros, and local civil engineer and water master Dezső Verpeléti Kiss met at the Borsod-Miskolcz Museum under the direction of Verpeléti Kiss in order to investigate the Old Hungarian script.[23]

The Old Hungarian script (which, according to linguist Klára Sándor, who has done comprehensive research on this writing system, would more accurately be described as the Székely script)[24] began to penetrate the Hungarian public consciousness as a result of articles and books—notably *Rovás és rovásírás* (Runes and runic scripts) and *A magyar rovásírás hiteles emlékei* (Authentic remnants of the Hungarian runic script)—that folklorist and literary historian Gyula Sebestyén published in the first two decades of the twentieth century. The Székely cult that emerged in Hungary following the Treaty of Trianon served to reinforce this trend. The renaissance of the Old Hungarian / Székely script in Hungary during the interwar period was closely connected to the Turanian movement: Turanists regarded this script as an authentic pagan writing system that, even more importantly, had been preserved by the "purest" Hungarian ethnic group, the Székelys. The modernization of the Old Hungarian script and the propagation of its public and everyday usage thus became a cherished project of the movement. Scientific opinion regarding the origin of the script has remained divided to this day. Discounting those who espouse completely fanciful explanations of the Old Hungarian script's genesis (that it descended from the Sumerians, Huns, Hittites, etc.), specialists on this writing system can be classified into three main groups according to their theories regarding its origin: literary scholars who believe that the script is nothing more than a humanist invention from the fifteenth and sixteenth centuries and is thus, in fact, a sham;[25] those including Klára Sándor who maintain that the parent of the Székely script can probably be found in either the Onogur or the Avar writing system; and finally those (among them many Turanist scholars) who have contended that the roots of the script can most likely be traced to the Turkic languages of Inner Asia.[26] At the turn of the century, the Old Hungarian script, with which only a small group of scholars had been familiar until that time, entered the public sphere: sculptor János Fadrusz, for example, used the script to inscribe his memorial honoring Töhötöm (one of the seven chieftains of the Hungarians at the time of their arrival to the Carpathian Basin in the late ninth century) erected in Zilah (Zalău, Romania) in 1902, thus initiating a wide-ranging public debate regarding the public usage of the writing system.

Dezső Verpeléti Kiss, who later came up with his own runic writing system, told the enthralled journalist who wrote the previously mentioned *Magyar Jövő* article that the objective of his group was to have the writing system of the "Sumerian tribes of Turanian origin" used to adorn the National Museum in Budapest and other public buildings in Hungary and to encourage artists to use the script to sign their works (painter Dezső Mokry-Mészáros soon thereafter began to do so and himself devised a runic writing system). This newspaper article attracted unexpectedly sharp interest: not only did local Boy Scouts ask Verpeléti Kiss to teach them the Old Hungarian script, but the Catholic national daily *Nemzeti*

Újság (National newspaper) and certain county newspapers reprinted the piece.[27] Although there is evidence that the Hungarian Scout Association had previously dealt with the Old Hungarian script, the organization began to focus on this writing system only in the 1930s. (In fact, the Hungarian scouting movement primarily used the script that Verpeléti Kiss had developed on Turanian foundations.)

Verpeléti Kiss was a member of the Turanian Society and presented the book he had written in runic script at one of the organization's meetings in 1935.[28] In a letter written in a somewhat exalted tone a number of years earlier, the spirited water master had described himself as "an avid and self-sacrificing warrior for the Turanian Idea that will redeem the destructive contagion that has oozed to the surface amid the vapors from the west."[29]

Verpeléti Kiss corresponded with Miskolc local historian Lajos Marjalaki Kiss (1887–1972) and likely became personally acquainted with him as well.[30] After the First World War, Marjalaki Kiss fled from the Transylvanian town of Abrudbánya (Abrud, Romania), where he had taught at a state civil high school, to Miskolc, where he became a successful textbook author during the interwar period. Meanwhile, he poured out a steady stream of articles and books regarding the local history of Miskolc and its environs and even conducted archaeological excavations near the city. During the years he spent teaching in Transylvania, Marjalaki Kiss not only traveled throughout the Székely Land but also carried out research in the vicinity of Abrudbánya and came into contact with the Transylvanian archaeological school via Kolozsvár university Turanist professors Béla Pósta and Árpád Buday.[31] In 1929, Marjalaki Kiss published his treatise *Anonymus és a magyarság eredete* (Anonymus and the origin of the Hungarians [Anonymus was a medieval chronicler who at the end of the twelfth century or very beginning of the thirteenth century wrote about the origin of the Magyars]), first as an article in the Miskolc daily newspaper *Reggeli Hírlap* (Morning news) and then as a book. The subtitle of this work, *Visszhang Zajti híradására* (Response to Zajti's information), reveals that the Miskolc local historian also wanted to in some way elaborate Ferenc Zajti's ideas regarding Hungarian-Indian kinship. In his slim volume, Marjalaki Kiss did not refute the partial Turanian ancestry of the Hungarians, though claimed that this origin applied to only a small percentage of the Hungarian population. According to the author, the Ugric "ancient people" had inhabited the Carpathian Basin much earlier and, surviving many invasions, spread throughout the area from the Volga to the Danube. Árpád, as the leader of

a small number of Turanian warriors who carried out the Hungarian conquest of the Carpathian Basin, "breathed the national genius into the silent,
languid multitude."[32]

Marjalaki Kiss thus did not deny the Turanian origin of the
Hungarians, though attempted to modify its proportions. This notion
in fact served to instrumentalize intellectual history: on the one hand, it
trumped the theory of Daco-Roman continuity heralded in Romanian
political circles, placing the Hungarians in the Carpathian Basin before
the Romanians; on the other hand, it inverted the István Werbőczy-
initiated Hunnic consciousness of the nobility, depicting the peasantry as
the bulwark of the Hungarians in the Carpathian Basin. One of the great
Hungarian modern realist writers, Zsigmond Móricz, expressed great
enthusiasm for Marjalaki Kiss's ideas primarily for this reason. Moreover,
the respected progressive periodical *Nyugat* published Marjalaki Kiss's
discourse, albeit in significantly modified form.[33] The writer and journalist
Géza Féja, who belonged to the Hungarian populist movement, as Móricz
did, praised Marjalaki Kiss's *Nyugat* article in a review published in the
periodical *Előörs* (Vanguard).[34] The authors Gyula Illyés ("I am a longtime
believer in your theories") and Ferenc Móra ("I can for my part espouse
such a convincing viewpoint with no reservations")[35] expressed support for
Marjalaki Kiss's hypotheses, as did—even more surprisingly—numerous
directors of museums located in towns and cities in provincial Hungary
ranging from Szentes to Veszprém.[36] The latter phenomenon was not
necessarily a reflection of unscientific attitudes and procedures: during
this era, committed intellectuals who had attained a significant degree of
knowledge but whose fundamental training pointed in a different direction
often served as the directors of the newly founded municipal and county
museums. Although many of them had completed National Museum-
sponsored or university-sponsored courses in archaeology, they still had to
fight against the contextualization of their excavations. Furthermore, they
may have often felt that officials from the major scientific institutions in
Budapest looked down on their work and disparaged their opinions. As a
result of their radical novelty, Marjalaki Kiss's theories seemed to represent
a suitable vehicle for investing experiences on the ground with meaning
and filling the gaps in interpretation.[37] Decades later, the Orientalist Gyula
Germanus also upheld the ideas of Marjalaki Kiss, whom he depicted as
having continued the work of Ármin Vámbéry.[38] The Turanists Adorján
Magyar, a resident of Montenegro, and—many years later—László Bendefy

(1904–1977) (one of the propagators of the Turanist tradition during the communist era) also congratulated Marjalaki Kiss for his courage.[39] Marjalaki Kiss himself believed that the majority of archaeologists and ethnographers had accepted his viewpoints even though "conservative linguists have not."[40] No evidence indicating that Marjalaki Kiss was a Turanist in an organizational sense has been discovered so far. Though inasmuch as he drew political and social conclusions from the partial Eastern origin of the Hungarians (the Hungarian presence in Transylvania and the primacy of the Hungarian peasantry over the nobility), Marjalaki Kiss is, in any event, worthy of mention.

It is not known how much Marjalaki Kiss drew on the book *A szkíta-magyar kontinuitás elméletének jogosultsága a turáni szellem keretében* (The legitimacy of the theory of Scythian-Hungarian continuity within the Turanian intellectual framework) that Debrecen museum conservator János Sőregi (1892–1982) published in Karcag in 1927. This short book also endorsed the idea of continuity between the Scythians and the Hungarians. Sőregi earned a degree in law and then, in the course of his activity as an amateur local historian, became acquainted with ethnographer István Győrffy, who secured a position for him at the Debrecen Municipal Museum, the predecessor of the current Déri Museum. Although Sőregi sympathized with the various Turanian organizations that functioned in Debrecen, he never joined the local chapters of either the Turanian Society or the Hungarian Turan Alliance. He was, however, a member of the loose network of intellectuals that was composed of employees of the Debrecen Municipal Museum (Director István Ecsedi, for instance), artists (sculptor Ferenc Medgyessy and painter Tibor Boromisza [1880–1960]), and local city officials. The members of this group regarded Hungary's official interwar historical outlook with skepticism, were staunch cultural Protestants and anti-Catholics, idolized the nearby Hortobágy steppe, and worshipped the ancient Hungarian herder and peasant culture that they were convinced was pure-blooded Turanian in character. The work of István Ecsedi provides a prime example of this.[41] Ecsedi not only produced some of the earliest and best descriptions of the Hortobágy but also played a key role in the development of tourism in Debrecen as well as in the latter steppe located just to the west of the city.

János Sőregi spent nearly two years studying at the Collegium Hungaricum in Vienna on a Hungarian state scholarship. However, he abandoned the theme that archaeology professor András Alföldi had handed down to him and instead collected data pertaining to Scythian-Hun-Hungarian continuity. Sőregi's book on Scythian-Hungarian kinship was primarily a survey of Hungarian and international literature regarding this topic. In this book, Sőregi defended Géza Nagy's Scythian-Turanian affiliation against the "hair-splitting, constrained etymologization" of German scholars and examined the correlations between the "national idea" and archaeology based on German, Czechoslovak, and Romanian examples. Moreover, the author argued that the defense of the homeland began physically in the lower strata of the soil and chronologically before the arrival of the Hungarians to the Carpathian Basin. Finally, he urged that archaeology should be transformed into a national science in the Turanian spirit, asserting that "it is our firm conviction that the theory of Scythian-Hungarian continuity formulated according to the Turanian spirit will signal the arrival of a new era in Hungarian archaeology."[42] Although Sőregi, who considered archaeology to be an extension of nation building, adopted only an indirect position with regard to the question of autochthony, he attempted to serve Hungarian archaeological science through the demonstration of the nationalist orientation of the archaeology of other nations and—prolonging the presence of the Hungarians in the Carpathian Basin to 2,500 years—the substantiation of Scythian-Hun-Hungarian kinship. Professor Alföldi was not at all pleased with the treatise that Sőregi had published, thus souring relations between them and preventing the latter from pursuing a university career. Sőregi recalled with regard to his monograph that "the domestic Swabians and Pan-German vassals bludgeoned it, while those souls who felt themselves to be Hungarian acknowledged and endorsed every line." Sőregi later identified the Gyula Szekfű–edited leading conservative-liberal monthly *Magyar Szemle* in which archaeologist Nándor Fettich had criticized his theses as one of the primary public platforms in which these "Pan-German vassals" were able to propagate their ideas "in a Swabian spirit."[43] Among those who supported Sőregi was his mentor, István Györffy, who had previously worried that the twenty months that the former spent in Vienna might serve to diminish his "Hungarian spirit." Györffy expressed relief after the appearance of his protégé's book, declaring, "I read it with great delight and subscribe to it to the very last line. There was a very great need for this [book]."[44]

Despite limited financial resources, the city of Debrecen and its museum underwent cultural expansion during this period under the visionary leadership of Mayor István Vásáry. After opening a new building in 1929, the Déri Museum's previously modest collection became the best in Hungary outside the city of Budapest.

Standing on the square in front of the museum were four allegorical statues sculpted by Debrecen native Ferenc Medgyessy (1881–1958): *Tudomány* (Science), *Művészet* (Art), *Régészet* (Archaeology), and *Néprajz* (Ethnography). Although Medgyessy had moved away from Debrecen before the turn of the century, he remained firmly present in the life of the city and its surrounding communities through his artworks. Medgyessy adhered zealously to certain ideas that the previously mentioned group of Debrecen intellectuals espoused regarding the Asian origin of the Hungarians, shared the alienation they felt toward interwar "Neo-Baroque" Hungarian society, and occasionally used elements from the Old Hungarian script on his works. Medgyessy, whose friends referred to him as the "little Mongolian khan," proudly recounted, during a birthday party held for István Ecsedi at the Déri Museum warehouse, how he had once fallen asleep at a state ceremony and begun to snore loudly: "Let them perform a white-horse sacrifice or a shaman song for me instead of *Missa solemnizes* and then I won't doze off."[45] Medgyessy enthusiastically read Ferenc Zajti's works regarding ancient history[46] and Gábor Lükő's writings on *Völkerpsychologie*[47] and maintained such deep hostility toward the Catholic Church that, to the consternation of the Greek Catholic deacon, he omitted the cross from the tomb he made for his prematurely deceased friend, the artist Miklós Káplár.[48] The development that took place in the city of Debrecen during this period (construction of the Nagyerdei Stadium, the indoor swimming pool, the first crematorium in Hungary, etc.) went hand-in-hand with the growth in tourism at the nearby Hortobágy steppe. Debrecen Municipal Museum director István Ecsedi and other members of the local intellectual circle to which he belonged participated in an effort to expand tourism at the Hortobágy based on authentic pastoral culture that resulted in a steady increase in the number of visitors to the enormous steppe, which had been placed under the ownership of the city.[49] János Sőregi wrote in his journal that large numbers of "Turanian visitors"—Japanese, Finns, Bulgarians, and Turks—traveled both individually and in groups to Debrecen, where they flocked to the municipal museum and waited in line to tour the Hortobágy.

The development of tourism in and around Debrecen entailed a conscious strategy to depict the city as the capital of the Great Hungarian Plain and of true-born Hungarians. This strategy was reflected in the *nomenklatura* of the municipal museum as well. István Győrffy recommended one of his students, Gábor Lükő, to János Sőregi for employment at the museum with the following words of praise: "born scholar, good Calvinist boy." In Győrffy's eyes, being a native of the Great Hungarian Plain and a member of the Calvinist Reformed Church were the greatest possible guarantees of moral and professional reliability. Lükő naturally got a job at the Debrecen Municipal Museum, where Győrffy personally introduced him to his new colleagues. In 1935, following István Ecsedi's unexpected death the previous year, János Sőregi became the director of the Déri Museum, a position that he held until 1950. The first thing that Sőregi did as director of the museum was to move Ferenc Medgyessy's statue *Turáni lovas* (Turanian horseman) to a central location (in the first-floor domed hallway). Although János Sőregi was the only member of his group of Debrecen intellectuals to publish a book regarding the steppe-Asian-Hungarian correlation, their collective sensibilities could be placed somewhere in between the ancient-history concept of the official Turanists and the instrumentalized idea (Turanian = peasant) of creators associated with the populist movement. This intellectual sensibility never became fixed doctrine, but within the context of the most purely Hungarian Protestant major city in Hungary, it implied negative attitudes toward the Habsburgs and Germans, the rejection of Catholic-hued political forms, the idealization of Hungarian peasant and above all herdsman culture, and a return to some kind of "Turanian" culture (that belonging to the world of the Asian and European steppes).

Aside from Budapest, the cities of Szeged and, later, Debrecen and Kolozs-vár served as the hotbeds for the growth of "proto-Turanism." During the interwar period, another municipality became a center for Eastern thought in Hungary: Gödöllő, the location of Regent Horthy's summer residence. Gödöllő, which at this time had not yet attained the administrative rank of *city*, was the seat of the homonymous district that during the interwar period was led by László Endre, one of the central figures in the Hungarian extreme right-wing movement who after 1938 became a county subprefect and in 1944 served as Interior Ministry state secretary in charge of deporting Hungarian Jews.[50] Gödöllő hosted the 1933 World Scout Jamboree and was the site of a well-known colony of artists, including some whose commitment to Turanism will be examined later in this book. The noted historian Sándor Márki died in Gödöllő, while Imam Abdüllatif, the spiritual leader of the Muslims of Hungary, lived in the town. Gödöllő was also a popular place of residence for retired military officers, many of whom were members of various Turanian organizations or participated in the publication of Turanist periodicals.

Radical Turanists gravitated toward the dynamic Gödöllő district leader László Endre, who had introduced numerous modern social welfare measures and in the 1920s and 1930s was considered to be one of the most up-and-coming political officials on the extreme right.

For example, former elementary school teacher who became an editor of Turanist periodicals and Gödöllő resident Béla Szépvizi Balás (1871–after 1943) frequently turned to Endre for support, requesting the resources necessary to obtain a publication permit and seeking patronage for his protégés. The productive though untalented Szépvizi Balás edited his Turanist publications in Gödöllő—first his yearbook *Napkönyv* (Book of days) in 1925–1926 and then his periodical *Napsugár* (Sunbeam) from 1927 to 1929. Szépvizi Balás was not a member of the major Turanian associations, which attempted to maintain a suitable distance from him. Turanian Society president Gyula Pekár, for example, politely rebuffed Szépvizi Balás's various invitations and requests for personal meetings.[51] However, well-known Turanists ranging from Benedek Baráthosi Balogh to László Túrmezei appeared among the contributors to Szépvizi Balás's publications. One might most accurately describe the foundation of the Gödöllő publisher's intransigently right-wing worldview as "eschatological, racialist Turanism." Szépvizi Balás, who frequently expressed antisemitic viewpoints, believed that Turanism would give rise to some new historical era that would establish the conditions necessary to avoid the Final Judgment. In his yearbook, Szépvizi Balás posed the question "What is the Turanian idea?"—to which he responded: "The consciousness of the accession of historical times." The author defined this historical era as one that would engender a consciousness of unity among the Chinese, Mordvins, Estonians, and Voguls who had spread out from the Pamir Mountain plateau and give rise to the ideology of a new Asian epoch. Szépvizi Balás wrote in this yearbook article: "The Turanian races that will rule on Earth based on law descending from God must also pass through a spiritual or physical Torrent of Fire—or both—before the Turanian race can become the master of the purified, renewed Earth. However, this activity is not too distant."[52]

Szépvizi Balás's muddled syntax, fuzzy ideas, and peculiar worldview that even fellow racialists regarded as soft and unorthodox did not serve to distinguish him from any of the large number of other unsuccessful and ill-humored publishers who were active in provincial Hungary at this time. However, Szépvizi Balás's Turanism was noteworthy in one regard: even in his very early works, he connected his Turanian ideas to the cult surrounding the historical region of Transylvania, particularly the Székely Land, which Hungary had lost via the Treaty of Trianon in 1920. In 1943, Szépvizi Balás published a mythical history of the Székelys entitled *A székely nemzet története a Kr. e. 1200-tól, a Kr. u. 1562-ig* (The history of the Székely Nation from 1200 BC to AD 1561), while those authors whose works were rooted in the literary cult of the Székelys and who have justly or unjustly passed into oblivion contributed to his publications. In 1932, Szépvizi Balás launched *A Székelység* (The Székelys) in Gödöllő after having published a similar periodical, *Székely Szó* (Székely word), in Budapest eleven years earlier. This new periodical, which Szépvizi Balás published for six years, helped construct the mythical Székely Land that continues to exercise a significant influence on the thinking of the Hungarians of Hungary regarding the Hungarians of Transylvania. The boundary between Turanism and Székely consciousness was relatively narrow during the interwar period as well, and some Turanists indeed transcended this dividing line: among those who ranged back and forth between the politics of the Asian origin of the Hungarians and Székely identity politics, albeit at contrasting intellectual levels, were postal official Márton Vargyassy, retired military officers László Sándor and Gyula Máté-Törék, lawyer Miklós Endes, University of Debrecen professors István Rugonfalvi Kiss and Jenő Darkó, University of Szeged professor Lajos Szádeczky-Kardoss, and the leaders of a host of Székely associations.[53]

Although the Székely cult originated long before the First World War, at the very latest with the publication in 1868 of Balázs Orbán's book *A Székelyföld leírása* (Description of the Székely Land), the building of this cult gained true momentum with the flight of a large number of Hungarian refugees from Transylvania to Hungary following the Treaty of Trianon. The Székely Land and the Székelys became increasingly strong components on the mental map of Hungary as a result of the "Székely himnusz" (Székely anthem) composed in 1921, the activity of Székely student associations and the various organizations that emerged from them, the appearance of the Székely script in the public sphere, the increasingly popular Catholic pilgrimage site near Csíksomlyó (Şumuleu Ciuc, Romania), the proliferation of Székely fashion, and the highly read works of József Nyirő and Áron Tamási. "Székely anthem" composer György Csanády initiated the annual presentation of a Székely mystery play of sorts entitled *Nagy Áldozat* (Great sacrifice), in which several hundred members of the Association of Székely University and College Students, primarily young men, divided into thirteen clans reconfirmed their loyalty toward the Hungarian nation and the Székely people.[54] This secretive ceremony, which took place in May or June in the wooded Zugliget district in the Buda Hills, was frequently denounced as an anti-Christian pagan sacred mystery that included the sacrifice of a white horse. This event was ominously conflated in Hungarian public opinion with the activities of a controversial group known as the Turanian monotheists.

There is sporadic evidence of attempts to organize a Turanian religion in Hungary in the 1920s, although the established Church of Turanian Monotheists began to receive publicity only during the middle of the 1930s.[55] In 1934, newspapers reported for the first time that a church practicing pagan rites had formed in Budapest under the leadership of forty-some-year-old lawyer Zoltán Bencsi (who had changed his surname from Bencsik in order to make it sound less Slavic) and vegetarian restaurant owner and former Unitarian pastor Károly Köröspataki Kiss. This church conducted its first palpable public action—a Turanian funeral held on the eastern outskirts of Budapest—in July 1934, about two months after its foundation.[56] The Hungarian press embraced this news with perceptible enthusiasm amid the uneventfulness of late summer, thereby drawing the attention of the authorities to the Turanist congregation.[57] In September 1934, the new church launched its own periodical entitled *Turáni Roham* (Turanian charge). Graphic artist Gyula Szörényi designed the masthead for this periodical, which was published on newsprint ten times a year. Zoltán Bencsi generally wrote the lead articles for *Turáni Roham*, the primary named contributors of which were high school teacher Sándor Hajnóczy, eccentric ancient-history researcher and resident of Montenegro Adorján Magyar, feminist and author Gyöngyi Békássy, and retired police captain András Dajka. Dajka, whose relentless opposition to the Habsburgs and the Catholic Church led him to the Turanist movement, later became associated with the Hungarian Turan Alliance. Dajka's fierce anti-Habsburgism manifested itself in his attempt to build a cult surrounding the person of Ignác Martinovics, the leader of the Hungarian Jacobins executed in 1795 who later became one of the ideological prototypes of the Hungarian communist system. The relationship between the various Turanist factions is reflected clearly in the fact that an article published in the official bulletin of the Hungarian Turan Alliance, which was not exactly known for its political moderation, stated with regard to *Turáni Roham* that "we should not read it, because we might develop a fancy for paganism."[58]

Although Bencsi denied during interviews that he was an antisemite, police reports indicate that there was a significant overlap between his church and certain early Hungarian National Socialist parties, and articles published in *Turáni Roham* espoused virulently antisemitic viewpoints.[59] The new sect established branches at several locations, such as the town of Orosháza in southern Hungary, the Budapest suburb of Csepel, and several districts of the capital city. The leaders of these branches were given the title *bonc* (bonze), while the head of the entire church—Zoltán Bencsi—was known as the *főtáltos* (chief shaman). Although the Bencsi-led church never sacrificed a white horse as was so frequently claimed, the Budapest daily newspaper *Népszava* (People's word) reported in April 1936 that farmer András Jankó of Orosháza had had the local bonze initiate his newborn child into the Turanian monotheist church in a ritual that entailed cutting incisions into both sides of the infant's face with a knife.[60] This story created a great sensation, appearing even in foreign newspapers and prompting Hungarian commentators to lament that a few fanatics had again been able to present Hungary in a bad light. However, a more thorough investigation of the matter revealed that nobody had harmed the infant and that a photographer had spread jam on the newborn's face in order to enhance the spectacle of the bloodless rite.[61] The local chief magistrate nevertheless sentenced the organizers of the Orosháza branch of the Turanian monotheists to two months in jail.

In addition to lawsuits involving Bencsi and legal actions that certain chief magistrates initiated against members of his sect, the Budapest press focused significant attention on the Turanian church's construction of a so-called Pagan Tower on Aranyhegy (Gold hill) in the Óbuda district of Budapest.[62] The person who was responsible for building the tower was retired ministerial advisor Farkas Szász, the owner of several houses in the city of Budapest. In 1933, thus before the foundation of the Church of Turanian Monotheists, Szász had initially planned to erect a four-story observation tower in honor of the seven chieftains who had led the Hungarian tribes to the Carpathian Basin. A somewhat uncomprehending journalist for the daily newspaper *Budapesti Hírlap* identified "happiness" as the motive for building the planned tower.[63] In late 1934 or early 1935, Szász modified his plans in order to include the participation of the Turanian monotheists, who inaugurated the tower on July 7, 1935, in defiance of an official prohibition. The church thereafter frequently conducted rites and ceremonies at this tower.[64] The Turanian monotheists certainly lacked the

Fig. 5.1. The Pagan Tower in Budapest (today). Attribution: Solymári (2015), under Creative Commons CC-BY-SA-4.0 license.

financial resources necessary to cover the 30,000-pengő cost of building the tower; thus, they probably formed some kind of partnership with the eccentric Szász, who defined himself as a "pagan." The planning architect attempted to seize through legal channels the emoluments of those who did not pay for the expenses of construction.[65] The mystery and unique history surrounding the Pagan Tower—which still stands, though it has fallen into partial ruin—has made it the subject of perpetual interest that is reflected in the dozens of video recordings and blog posts that have been published on the internet. Farkas Szász died in 1942 at the age of eighty-six. His funerary monument at the Fiumei Avenue Cemetery in Budapest depicts an ancient Hungarian warrior and is located just a few hundred meters from the grave sites of a number of other people mentioned in this book. All roads evidently lead to this place.

Relations quickly soured between Turanian monotheist leaders Zoltán Bencsi and Károly Köröspataki Kiss: in 1937, Bencsi excommunicated Köröspataki Kiss on the grounds that his sole objective was to "rescue the Churches of Jesus." Soon thereafter, an article exposing Köröspataki Kiss's former affiliation with the Freemasons was published in *Turáni Roham*.[66] Bencsi stated that the specific reason for which he had excommunicated Köröspataki Kiss from the Church of Turanian Monotheists was that the latter had published a book of religious instruction for members of the congregation. One might presume that Bencsi was referring to the book *A turáni egyistenhívők egyszerű istentiszteletének szertartása* (The simple religious ceremony of the Turanian monotheists) that an author writing under the name *Batu* published in 1936. The author stipulated in this short volume that the Turanian monotheists should conduct their religious rites outside on a hill if possible, though in the event of bad weather their divine services could be held in a tent. Moreover, Batu noted that a metal basin was needed for the sacrificial fire and that all congregants with the exception of the old and the sick should stand during religious ceremonies.[67] Finally, Batu wrote that Turanian monotheist liturgy required "an old-fashioned Turanian scimitar," a familiarity with the works of Benedek Baráthosi Balogh and Ferenc Zajti, and the accentuation of the charitable activities of the Mitsui Bank of Japan. The Church of Turanian Monotheists used the doggerel published in *Turáni Roham* for both its religious observances and prayer texts. Zoltán Bencsi likely published the book *Ősi hitünk* (Our ancient faith) regarding the dogma of the Church of Turanian Monotheists in response to Batu's work.[68] In this book, Bencsi attacked the Christian churches and identified conflict rather than mercy or compassion as the primary means of upholding the truth. Bencsi furthermore postulated that the ancient homeland of the Turanians was located between the Tigris and Euphrates Rivers and that the ancient Hungarian religion was older than any other faith (naturally including Judaism) and therefore should be accorded certain rights. In a short segment of the book containing an analysis of Hungarian society, the chief shaman asserted that Protestants were more receptive than Catholics to Turanian doctrine because they were brought up in a more wholesome manner and their upper classes were not so cosmopolitan.[69]

The Interior Ministry did not ban the Church of Turanian Monotheists, but it did closely monitor its activities and issued confidential orders to district administrative organizations to use every means at their disposal to act against its members. The Interior Ministry also launched a profusion of official procedures aimed at stifling the activities of the Turanian monotheists.[70] In 1938, Chief Shaman Bencsi published a work that appeared to be a novel entitled *Koppány-e vagy István?* (Koppány or István?).[71] Graphic artist Gyula Szörényi, who designed the covers for this book and all other Turanian monotheist publications, is the father of iconic Hungarian rock music singer Levente Szörényi (b. 1945), the composer of the genre-founding 1983 rock opera *István, a király* (Stephen, the king) that featured the same central theme as Bencsi's 1938 work—that King Stephen's adoption of Christianity had entailed pragmatic benefits, though had undermined the essence of the Hungarian character. In addition to catechisms and newspaper articles, Bencsi thus used popularizing literature as a means of depicting conflict between "Western" Christianity and the superior Eastern Hungarians based on diametrical opposites.

According to a post published on the website falanszter.blog.hu in 2011, thousands of Turanian monotheists were drafted into labor battalions during the Second World War and sent to the eastern front (along with Hungarian Jews).[72] This claim circulated widely on the Hungarian-language internet, although there is no evidence showing that the Turanian monotheists—who never numbered more than a few hundred—actually served in labor battalions (initially set up for Jews) during the war. The emergence and activity of the Church of Turanian Monotheists in fact seem to have been connected much more closely to the sectarianization that occurred on the Great Hungarian Plain as a result of the crisis that was taking place within peasant society than to the fulfillment of any real spiritual need. The ideas of Zoltán Bencsi and his followers did not resurface to a significant degree in Hungary following the country's postcommunist transition to democracy. However, in 2010, the Ősi Örökségünk Alapítvány (Our Ancient Legacy Foundation) began circulating a periodical entitled *Zsarátnok* (Embers) that republishes selections from Turanian monotheist publications and relevant articles from the Hungarian émigré press.

In 1937, the assistant notary in the small town of Komádi in eastern Hungary launched a monthly entitled *Atilla* that published articles pertaining to Turanism and the Church of Turanian Monotheists. Many of those who wrote articles for the Turanian monotheist periodical *Turáni Roham* also contributed to *Atilla*, which regularly published Zoltán Bencsi's editorials and literary works. The editors of the new Turanist monthly declared that they had chosen the title *Atilla* for the publication in order to compensate for the fact that in 1935 the Hungarian nation had not suitably commemorated the anniversary of the birth of Attila the Hun. *Atilla* published writings by second- and third-rate Turanist writers and others, primarily officials working in the lower levels of public administration, who, after emigrating to western Europe or North America following the Second World War, formed the new generation of authors who dealt with topics related to the origin and ancient history of the Hungarians.

In a certain sense, the bark of the Church of Turanian Monotheists was bigger than its bite. However, the activity of this church happened to coincide with a scandal surrounding the book *A magyar társadalom turanizálása* (The Turanization of Hungarian society): the author of this work, Balatonfüred deputy notary Elek Berei Nagy, was charged with blasphemy and incitement against the Catholic Church in a case that went all the way to Hungary's supreme court, the Curia.[73] News regarding the monotheists and the legal proceedings surrounding Berei Nagy's book may have prompted many contemporary observers to worry that a Turanian pagan movement was developing in Hungary. This could explain the reason for which the Turanian Society made a strenuous effort to publicly distance itself from radical Turanists. In 1934, former prime minister István Bethlen wrote a letter to Gyula Pekár in which he asked the president of the Turanian Society to take action aimed at suppressing the Church of Turanian Monotheists: "For my part, I do not consider this movement [the Church of Turanian Monotheists] to be serious at the present stage, though I nevertheless draw your attention to it and request that you exert influence within your sphere of authority in order to paralyze this inopportune cult."[74] The Turanian Society reported the activities of the Church to the Ministry of Religion and Public Education and asked the ministry to protect the word *Turanian* from unwarranted attacks. After the failure of this initiative, the Turanian Society turned to the interior minister with essentially the same, rather exacting, request.[75] The organization's petition to the minister complained that Catholic circles had subjected the Turanian movement to the "sharpest possible attacks," adding wistfully that "the objective truth of the information that we have issued has neither appeased the notable public figures who have expressed themselves on behalf of Hungarian Catholicism nor has it restrained the activities of extreme elements aimed at promoting neo-paganism."[76]

The Turanian Society carefully collected all articles that were published in Hungarian print media regarding the Church of Turanian Monotheists. These writings reveal that Catholic newspapers and periodicals indeed gave voice to unrestrained condemnation of the church and that somewhat later Lutheran publications did likewise, though to a slightly more moderate degree. Those affiliated with recognized churches in Hungary always detected in Turanism the slight odor of brimstone. The Reformed Church had already concluded in the early 1920s that Turanism was a dangerous movement. In 1921, Reformed pastor Gyula Muraközy warned that "Christianity stands not for the blurring and blunting of national characteristics, but in their coordinated expansion. It is to be feared that the grand idea of Turanism has exhausted itself here and like a derailed train will become mired in the sands of ancient paganism."[77] The Reformed press, primarily the *Kálvinista Szemle* (Calvinist review), endorsed this point of view.[78] In order to deflect accusations of anticlericalism, Turanian Society officials, notably the organization's chief patron, Archduke Joseph Francis of Austria, enthusiastically supported the plan of the Hungarian province of the Jesuit Order to establish a scientific institute in Turkey. The Turanian Society, in fact, provided Jesuit priest János Vendel with a scholarship to finance his first trip to Turkey in 1930 in order to lay the groundwork for this highly secret undertaking. For political reasons, this initiative remained shrouded in obscurity and was exposed to light only with the publication of research regarding the proposed scientific institute in 2015.[79]

There existed within the Turanist movement a very minor Christian current that attempted to reconcile ideas regarding kinship with the principles of Catholicism.[80] The periodical *Turáni Nép* (Turanian people) published in the city of Miskolc with varying degrees of regularity for at least a decade beginning in 1933 served as the main forum for the Christian orientation. The editor of *Turáni Nép*, hunting writer, plant breeder, and Third Order Franciscan friar Gaszton Lublóváry, occasionally tried, with rather unconvincing results, to place his Turanist viewpoints on a theological foundation.[81] The churches remained rather reticent toward Turanism, and the ironic comments that Catholic high dignitaries made regarding the movement's sacrifice of white horses or paganism coincide in a peculiar way with the communist criticism of Turanism after 1945.[82]

Criticisms of Turanism based on science and scientific policy were generally published in the Gyula Szekfű–edited conservative-liberal monthly *Magyar Szemle*. The archaeologist Nándor Fettich, the Iranianist László Gaál, the literary historian János Győry, the mysterious contributor who wrote articles under the pen name R-k, and chief editor Szekfű himself delivered the most powerful blows against Turanism in the pages of *Magyar Szemle*.[83] In 1931, the Turkologist Gyula Németh, a member of the Turanian Society who was becoming increasingly removed from the organization but had not severed all of his Turanist connections, wrote the most analytical and empathetic article published in *Magyar Szemle* regarding Turanism.[84] Németh's article became one of the basic texts for scholarly literature dealing with Turanism, and his train of thought regarding the movement has exercised a significant influence on those who have researched this topic. In this writing, Németh adopted a lenient stance toward the scientific misconceptions of the Turanian movement and did not presume that Hungarian society would be receptive to a Turanist revision of history in connection to such events as the Battle of Mohács, for example.[85] Németh minimized the greater public impact of the movement: "Turanism as a political and economic concept is for the time being unrealistic. It fosters illusions, makes us inclined to daydream and diverts attention from our more important problems."[86] Articles criticizing Turanism also appeared in the periodical *Széphalom*, which was published in Szeged under the editorship of local university professor Béla Zolnai. The latter wrote articles denouncing Béla Szépvizi Balás's books using the pen name Péter Garázda, which is particularly interesting if one considers that Pál Teleki, the founder of the Turanian Society and a friend of the editor, traced his origin to the Garázda clan.[87]

The Turanian Society found itself in a rather vulnerable position amid this storm. The organization was careful to adhere to the requirements of science and scholarship, although it would have been rather difficult to contradict former members who had reached such high office. Moreover, its government funding depended on the benevolence of certain individuals whose anger it was not advisable to provoke. Therefore, the Turanian Society largely ignored criticism and attempted to reduce its exposure to attack. For example, in 1937, the Turanian Society demanded that Benedek Baráthosi Balogh remove the organization's name and logos from the cover of his long series of Turanian books on the grounds that the preface regarding "the falsifications of official history teaching" might offend Minister of Religion and Public Education Bálint Hóman, a longtime member and copresident of the Turanian Society.[88] Intransigent Turanists had long regarded Hóman, an occasionally abrasive historian, with scorn and hostility. Former Premonstratensian priest Jenő Csuday (1852–1938) was one of the most persistent critics of Hóman. Csuday, who published many works of Hungarian history, lobbied against Hóman's alleged "falsifications" and "anti-national historical outlook" in meetings with László Endre and mercilessly denounced him in articles published in *Turáni Roham* and *A Cél*. Hóman endured these attacks in silence for a couple of years before responding to them in a letter to the editor of the latter periodical that varies in tone from that of the offended scholar to the frustrated careerist:

> I do not care about the attack itself. Over the past two years I have become used to the Csuday-Gálocsy-Baron Hatvani [*sic*] (Deutsch) triad assuming the mantles of racialism and radical Bolshevism to criticize and denigrate my works that contradict the old liberal-revolutionary historical perspective and meanwhile doing everything they can, twisting and distorting, to mock my national sentiments. I will not deign to turn to the courts because of them. If Mr. Gálocsy and Mr. Hatvani can offer proof of their expertise and competence and if Csuday is able to exonerate himself of the unrefuted and certainly irrefutable accusation of plagiarism lodged against him 30 years ago . . . perhaps there might be a question of judicial proceedings. However, until then—to quote your words—"my only dignified response is contempt."[89]

The recipient of Hóman's letter, herpetologist, entomologist, and Hungarian Academy of Sciences member Lajos Méhely, became one of the prominent figures associated with racial biology in Hungary near the end of a respectable scientific career.[90] Méhely expressed criticism of mainstream Turanism on several occasions, believed that acceptance of Western culture was self-evident, and condemned the Turanist inclination to chase illusions. Méhely's Turanism was rooted in the militant Hungarian racial consciousness, which he referred to as "the true Turanian ideal that blazes in the Hungarian soul."[91] However, Méhely very quickly found common ground with more extreme Turanists in the form of uncompromising antisemitism. Criticism of Hóman, such as that published in the Méhely-edited *A Cél*, always emerged outside the system and thus may have offended the historian government minister but presented no threat to him.

There existed another organization within the somewhat complex network of Turanist groups that is often mixed up with the Turanian Society and the Hungarian Turan Alliance as a result of both its name and opera-tions. The former military officer, leader of the opposition Racial Protec-tion Party, and future prime minister Gyula Gömbös founded the National Association of Turanian Hunters in 1927.[92] However, pro-Habsburg legiti-mists under the leadership of General Secretary János Bartha who had al-ways sharply opposed Gömbös gained control over the National Association of Turanian Hunters and elected the former envoy of Hungary to Poland, Count Iván Csekonics, to serve as the organization's president. As prime minister, Gömbös sought to avenge this takeover by requesting that the in-terior minister ban the organization.[93] Retired infantry general Árpád Sipos succeeded Csekonics as president of the National Association of Turanian Hunters in 1938. Under Sipos's leadership, the organization, which had been only nominally Turanist throughout its first decade of existence, assumed a curious character that could be described as a combination of militia, athletic club, intelligence bureau, and underground anti-German resistance group. Among those who joined the National Association of Turanian Hunters after Sipos became its president were retired military officers, including Captain Vilmos Tartsay, Lieutenant General János Kiss, and future Kállay-cabinet minister of defense general Vilmos Nagybaczoni Nagy. These men became martyrs of the Hungarian anti-Nazi resistance in 1944.

Then, following the outbreak of the Second World War, cadres from other Turanist organizations acquired official positions within the National Association of Turanian Hunters, and dyed-in-the-wool Turanists began to appear among the contributors to its publications.[94] Former Hungarian Turan Alliance official Viktor Keöpe became editor of the National Association of Turanian Hunters yearbook in 1943. Keöpe, an explorer and successful travel guide writer who vigorously defended the theory of Székely-Manchu kinship in a polemic with Jenő Cholnoky carried out in the Turanian Society periodical *Turán*, recruited prominent Turanists ranging from Lajos Barátosi Lénárt and Gyöngyi Békássy to Ferenc Zajti and Zoltán Bencsi to contribute articles to the yearbook.[95] These intransigent Turanists appear to have provided the National Association of Turanian Hunters with fresh content to supplement the organization's somewhat stale radical proindependence rhetoric. The true objectives of the National Association of Turanian Hunters were preparation for armed conflict and opposition to Nazi Germany, as reflected in organizational deputy president Aladár Baráti Huszár's explicit condemnation of the proclaimed "European new order." According to the bylaws of the National Association of Turanian Hunters, the main objective of the organization was to "cultivate ancient national virtues, racial cohesion and the sentiment of unselfishness and to promote the physical development of the Hungarian race." The specific activities of organization identified in these bylaws included the protection of grain fields, "gendarme auxiliary services," and "intelligence gathering" of an unspecified nature. The members of the National Association of Turanian Hunters were provided with the opportunity to purchase sport shooting pistols from the organization.[96]

After 1941, the National Association of Turanian Hunters launched a feverish campaign to establish branch organizations in provincial Hungary, primarily in territories that the country had recovered over the previous three years. According to a report issued in May 1942, the National Association of Turanian Hunters maintained twenty-one branch organizations—twelve in territories reacquired from Yugoslavia, three in areas regained from Romania, and only six within the borders of post-Trianon Hungary.[97] The Turanian hunters organized spectacular parades, including a "national-defense day" procession in Zombor (Sombor, Serbia) that included several hundred participants and was the subject of a Hungarian newsreel report.[98] The public activities of the National Association of Turanian Hunters could have hardly been ignored in the villages and small towns of the Bácska region, which had been reincorporated into Hungary in 1941. The organization's uniforms—pert olive-green hunting hats with a feather sticking out from the back, yellowish-green sleeved sport shirts, and knee-length shorts—were a cross between an early Robin Hood film costume and a rather unimaginative outfit for the *Magic Flute* character Papageno.[99]

It is not too difficult to envisage the fate of this group that held large public assemblies in a region in which ethnic tension was even much higher than it was in other parts of Hungary. Nor is it difficult to imagine what the stipulated organizational activities of "intelligence gathering" and "gendarme auxiliary services" might have entailed in an area in which the Serb Partisan (essentially Chetnik) movement was active. However, it was the anti-German rhetoric of the National Association of Turanian Hunters that first aroused the disapproval of authorities. Shortly after German military forces occupied Hungary on March 19, 1944, the Interior Ministry banned the organization on the following grounds: "It [the National Association of Turanian Hunters] conducted covert activity aimed at overturning the internal order of the country and acting against the interests of the war effort and in this way attempted to steer the country's foreign political situation toward crisis, thus jeopardizing state security and public order."[100] The Interior Ministry confiscated the movable property of the National Association of Turanian

Hunters; transferred its assets to the association that provided support to war invalids, widows, and orphans; and instructed police officials to carefully monitor any activity that might be aimed at reconstituting the organization. National Association of Turanian Hunters members captain Vilmos Tartsay and lieutenant general János Kiss were executed for their participation in anti-German resistance, while the organization's deputy president and former mayor of Budapest Aladár Baráti Huszár was deported to the Dachau concentration camp, where he died in early 1945. General Vilmos Nagybaczoni Nagy was imprisoned but survived—unlike many members of the National Association of Turanian Hunters who remained in the Bácska region of southern Hungary after it came under the control of the Tito-led Yugoslav Partisans in October 1944. The Partisans launched a manhunt for those affiliated with the organization as a result of their visibility and varying degrees of participation in the underground war. The label "Turanian hunter" was nearly synonymous with "Arrow Cross" in the Bácska region during this period. Many members of the National Association of Turanian Hunters were interned, imprisoned, tortured, and, in numerous instances, executed without any official inquiry during these "cold weeks and months." The issue of rehabilitation and compensation for the victims of these reprisals continues to stir controversy among the Hungarians of Serbia to this day.[101]

Notes

1. OSZKK, Fond 446, Turáni dolgozatok 1, a Magyarok Társasága alakuló ülésének jegyzőkönyve, Budapest, 1923. július 25.

2. Ibid., a Magyarok Társasága közgyűlési jegyzőkönyvei, 1929. február 22. és 1930. május 16.

3. Ibid., Turáni dolgozatok 2. a Magyarok Társasága taglistája, 1936. május.

4. For Hungarian-Indian Society documents, see OSZKK, Fond 446, Turáni dolgozatok 2, Magyar-Indiai Társaság alakuló közgyűlésének jegyzőkönyve, 1930. május 23; the Medgyaszay collection (private), Társaság-album: a Magyar-Indiai Társaság alakuló ülésének jegyzőkönyve, 1930. január 20; and Medgyaszay collection, a Társasággal kapcsolatos levelezés 1931–1937.

5. See the following critical biography of Ferenc Zajti: Miklós Sárközy, "A szittya Zarathustrától a gudzsárokon keresztül az ind Jézusig—Zajti Ferenc mint orientalista," in *Okok és okozat: A magyar nyelv eredetéről történeti, szociálpszichológiai és filozófiai megközelítésben*, ed. Marianne Bakró-Nagy, Hungarian Academy of Sciences Department I series (Budapest: Gondolat Kiadói Kör, 2018), 77–109.

6. HMA, Ad/5988-2016, Baktay Ervin levele a Magyar-Indiai Társaságnak, Budapest, 1930. március 28.

7. OSZKK, Fond 446, Turáni dolgozatok 1, a Magyar-Indiai Társaság alakuló ülésének jegyzőkönyve, Budapest, 1930. január 20.

8. Medgyaszay collection, India album, Zajti Ferenc és Medgyaszay István (Magyar-Indiai Társaság) levele a Tiszántúli Mezőgazdasági Kamarának, 1931. január 10.

9. MNL OL K 148, belügyminisztérium elnöki iratok, 950. doboz, 17. t. Meghívó a Magyar-Indiai Társaság Turáni Attila ünnepére, 1935. június.

10. Medgyaszay collection, Society album, Medgyaszay István bejelentése a XI. kerületi elöljáróságnak, Budapest, 1937. szeptember.

11. József Németh, *Hét év (1914–1921)* (Budapest: Magvető, 1993), 228.

12. Kondó Maszanori, "A szibériai magyar hadifoglyok és Japán," in *Tanulmányok a magyar-japán kapcsolatok történetéből,* ed. Ildikó Farkas et al. (Budapest: Eötvös, 2009), 177–85.

13. HMA, Felvinczi Takács-hagyaték, Mezey István levelezőlapja Felvinczi Takács Zoltánnak, 1920, nyár.

14. For the history of the Hungarian-Nippon Society, see Ildikó Farkas, "A Magyar-Nippon Társaság," in *Tanulmányok a magyar-japán kapcsolatok,* ed. Ildikó Farkas et al. (Budapest: Eötvös, 2009), 226–46.

15. The Volksbund was an organization established in 1938 for the Germans of Hungary. Under the leadership of Franz Basch (1901–1946), the Volksbund—as other German organizations in central and eastern Europe during this period—became a tool of Nazi foreign policy. After the end of the Second World War, the Volksbund was disbanded, and its leaders were prosecuted as war criminals.

16. Bundesarchiv (Berlin-Lichterfelde), Reichskanzlei, R 43-II/1504, Hilde Pröhle levele Adolf Hitlernek, Budapest, n.d. [1944].

17. Wilhelm Pröhle, "Studien zur Verleichung des Japanischen mit den uralischen und altaischen Sprachen," *Keleti Szemle* 17, nos. 1–3 (1916–17): 147–83; and Toru Senga, "Bálint Gábor, Pröhle Vilmos és a japán-magyar nyelvhasonlítás története," *Magyar Nyelv* 90, no. 2 (1994): 200–207. For more information regarding Pröhle, see István Ormos, "Adalékok Pröhle Vilmos alakjához," *Keletkutatás* (Spring 2012): 33–65.

18. Ormos, "Adalékok Pröhle Vilmos alakjához," 58.

19. MTAKK Ms 5164/883, Pröhle Vilmos levele Márki Sándornak, Konstantinápoly, 1911. július 21.

20. Dénes Sinor, "Emlékezés Pröhle Vilmosra," *Magyar Nyelv* 91, no. 1 (1995): 102–3.

21. For information regarding Imoaka, see Yuko Umemura, *A Japán-tengertől a Duna-partig. Imaoka Dzsúicsiró életpályája a magyar-japán kapcsolatok tükrében* (Budapest: Gondolat, 2006).

22. "Az ősrégi magyar rovásírásnak lelkes művelői vannak Miskolcon," *Magyar Jövő,* October 11, 1931, 5.

23. For details on this group and its immediate intellectual environment, see Andrea Pirint, "Mokry asztala: Rovásírók Miskolcon a két világháború között," in *A rovás megújítói: Mokry-Mészáros Dezső és Verpeléti Kiss Dezső,* ed. Tamás Rumi (N.p: Rovás Alapítvány, 2018), 4–50.

24. Klára Sándor, *A székely írás nyomában* (Budapest: Typotex, 2014).

25. The literary historian Iván Horváth is the most vigorous advocate of this viewpoint. See the following writing, in which he refines his earlier categorical assertions to some degree: Iván Horváth, "A székely rovásírás és a latin-magyar ábécé," in *A magyar irodalom történetei,* vol. 1, ed. Mihály Szegedy-Maszák (Budapest: Gondolat, 2007), 36–48.

26. For a summary of the research conducted on the Old Hungarian/Székely script, see Tiziano Tubay, *A székely írás kutatásának története* (Budapest: OSZK, 2015).

27. "A Magyar Jövő cikke nyomán a miskolci ifjúság fel akarja eleveníteni az ősi rovásírást," *Magyar Jövő*, October 25, 1931; and "A székely rovásírás szerelmesei," *Nemzeti Újság*, November 25, 1931. See also Béla Dornyai's article in the Salgótarján weekly *A Munka* (Work) on December 8, 1934.

28. "Társasági ügyek," *Turán* 18, nos. 1–4 (1935): 77.

29. OSZKK, Fond 446, Turáni dolgozatok 2, Verpeléti Kiss Dezső levéltöredéke ismeretlennek, Verpelét, 1922. november 6.

30. Correspondence between Verpeléti Kiss and Marjalaki Kiss can be found at the Historical Repository of the Ottó Herman Museum (hereafter, HOM), 73.911.2, Marjalaki Kiss Lajos levelezése 2, Verpeléti Kiss Dezső levelezőlapja Marjalaki Kiss Lajosnak, Miskolc, 1935. március 14.

31. Marjalaki Kiss wrote in detail about this in his memoirs: HOM, 74.176.1, Marjalaki Kiss Lajos: Emlékezések. n.d. (these memoirs were written sometime in the 1960s).

32. Lajos Marjalaki Kiss, *Anonymus és a magyarság eredete* (Miskolc, Miskolci Könyvnyomda, 1929), 35.

33. Lajos Marjalaki Kiss, "Új úton a magyar őshaza felé [Új eredet-teória.]," *Nyugat* 23, no. 1 (1930): 899–913.

34. *Előörs*, July 12, 1930, 16.

35. HOM, 73.911.2, Illyés Gyula levele Marjalaki Kiss Lajosnak, Tihany, 1962. szeptember 8; 75.53.2, Móra Ferenc levele Marjalaki Kiss Lajosnak, Szeged, 1929. április 14.

36. HOM, 76.344.1, Csallány Gábor levele Marjai Kiss Lajosnak, Szentes, 1929. május 21; 75.53.3, Rhé Gyula veszprémi múzeumigazgató Marjalaki Kiss Lajosnak, Veszprém, 1929. április 18.

37. Not many people have dealt with the intellectual history of Hungarian archaeology. For the contributions made to Hungarian ancient history during this period, see Péter Langó, *Turulok és Árpádok: Nemzeti emlékezet és a koratörténeti emlékek* (Budapest: Typotex, 2017), 42–46.

38. HOM, 73.911.2, Marjalaki Kiss Lajos levelezése 2, Germanus Gyula levele Marjalaki Kiss Lajosnak, 1957. április 21. Vámbéry explored similar themes in the following posthumously published book: *A magyarság bölcsőjénél* (Budapest: Athenaeum, 1914), particularly 89–103.

39. HOM, Bendefy László levelei Marjalaki Kiss Lajosnak, Budapest, 1963. február 17 and 28; and Magyar Adorján levelei Marjalaki Kiss Lajosnak, Zelenika, 1929. augusztus 2 and 13.

40. HOM, 74.176.1, Marjalaki Kiss Lajos: Emlékezések, 6.

41. See István Ecsedi, *A bolgárok földjén: Útirajzok* (Debrecen: Tiszántúli Könyv- és Lapkiadó Rt., 1929); *A Hortobágy puszta és élete* (Debrecen: Debreczen Sz. Kir Város Könyvnyomda-vállalata, 1914).

42. János Sőregi, *A szkíta-magyar kontinuitás elméletének jogosultsága a turáni szellem keretében* (Karcag: Kertész József könyvnyomdája, 1927), 66.

43. University of Debrecen and National Library Manuscript Archives, Sőregi János hagyatéka, Ms 13/17, Napló 1924–1927, 1348–49.

44. Ibid., Ms 13/102, Sőregi János: Emlékeim és feljegyzéseim régi barátaimról, pártfogóimról, és hivatali elődeimről II: szigeti Györffy István. Györffy István levele Sőregi Jánosnak. Budapest, 1928. január 4.

45. Ibid., Ms 13/39, Sőregi János: Feljegyzéseim Medgyessy Ferenc szobrászművészről.

46. Ibid., 1939. december 24.

47. Ibid., 69: 1945. március "említette még Lükőről, kinek a Magyar lélek formái c. könyve annak idején igen kedvére való volt". ["He mentioned Lükő, whose book, *Forms of the*

Hungarian Soul, he was very fond of this time"]. Gábor Lükő's (1909–2001) personality will be an important one to make some kind of oriental sensibility alive in communist Hungary: see chapter 8 of this book.

48. Ibid., 19.

49. István Balogh, *Ecsedi István élete és munkássága*, Folklore and Ethnography 20 (Debrecen: KLTE Néprajzi Tanszék, 1985), 89–90.

50. For more details on Endre, see Zoltán Vági, "Endre László: Fajvédelem és bürokratikus antiszemitizmus," in *Tanulmányok a Holokausztról*, vol. 2, ed. Randolph L. Braham (Budapest: Balassi, 2002), 81–154.

51. OSZKK Letters Archives, Pekár Gyula levele Szépvizi Balás Bélának, Budapest, 1923. december 2.

52. Béla Szépvizi Balás, "Mi a turáni gondolat?" in *Napkönyv –Turáni képes naptár és évkönyv*, vol. 1, ed. Balás Szépvizi Balás (Gödöllő: self-published, 1925), 47.

53. For information regarding the interwar Székely movement, see Balázs Ablonczy, "Székely identitásépítés Magyarországon a két világháború között," in *Székelyföld és a Nagy Háború. Tanulmánykötet az első világháború centenáriuma alkalmából*, ed. Zsolt Orbán (Csíkszereda [Miercurea Ciuc]: Csíkszereda Kiadóhivatal, 2018), 467–85.

54. György Csanády, *A májusi nagy áldozat* (Budapest: Szefhe, 1941).

55. Vilmos Pröhle himself allegedly tried to establish a Turanian religion: see Ormos, "Adalékok Pröhle Vilmos alakjához," 57.

56. M. M., "Pogány temetés Rákoscsabán," *Pesti Napló*, July 31, 1934, 6.

57. N. A., "Beszélgetés a táltossal," *Magyarország*, July 26, 1934, 15; "Az újpogányság délibábja," *Nemzeti Újság*, July 26, 1934, 9.

58. "Mit olvassunk?" *Turáni Értesítő*, June 2, 1939.

59. Mihály Mészáros, "A turáni egyistenhívő szekta nyilvános istentiszteletének főpróbája," *Pesti Napló*, August 7, 1934, 8; see MNL OL K 149, BM reservált iratok, 168. doboz, 1936-7-12372: csendőrnyomozói jelentés a turáni egyistenhívőkről, 1936. november 4.

60. "Hadúr és társai," *Népszava*, April 16, 1936, 1.

61. "Vér helyett lekvárral keresztelték meg az újszülött csecsemőt a turáni egyistenhívők," *Békésmegyei Közlöny*, April 24, 1936, 3.

62. László Petur, "Pogány magyarok vezérkara egy pesti kiskocsmában," *8 Órai Újság*, June 26, 1935, 7.

63. Miklós Diószeghy, "A boldogság tornya épül az Aranyhegyen," *Budapesti Hírlap*, July 28, 1933, 5.

64. Gábor Tenczer, "Ennél izgalmasabb torony nincs Budapesten," index.hu, February 21, 2015, https://index.hu/belfold/budapest/2015/02/21/a_turani_atok_sujtotta_pogany-torony/.

65. "Perlik a pogánytornyot," *Magyarország*, June 13, 1934, 15.

66. *Turáni Roham*, November 14, 1937.

67. Batu, *A turáni egyistenhívők egyszerű istentiszteletének szertartása* (Budapest, 1936), 3–4.

68. Bencsi Zoltán, *Ősi hitünk* [Our Ancient Faith] (Toronto: Magyar Church of Canada, 1987).

69. Ibid., 13, 59.

70. For information regarding these official measures, see Mihály Szécsényi, "Virrasztó Koppány és társai: A turáni egyistenhívők és a hatalom az 1930-as évek második felében," in *Felekezeti társadalom—felekezeti műveltség*, ed. Anikó Lukács, Rendi társadalom—Polgári társadalom 25 (Budapest: Hajnal István Kör–Társadalomtörténeti Egyesület, 2013), 350–52.

71. Zoltán Bencsi, *Koppány-e vagy István?* (Budapest: Gyarmati Ferenc könyvnyomtató műhelye, Atilla Urunk 1504, esztendejében [1938]).

72. "Gigantikus Attila-szobor és a Koppány torony: turáni építészet Budapesten," falanszter.blog.hu, June 22, 2011, https://falanszter.blog.hu/2011/06/22/gigantikus_attila _szobor_es_koppany_torony_turani_epiteszet_budapesten?layout=1.

73. "A Kúria felmentette Berei Nagy Eleket," *Budapesti Hírlap*, February 23, 1936, 17.

74. MNL OL P 1384, 8. doboz, 507/934, Bethlen István levele Pekár Gyulának, Budapest, 1934. május 14.

75. Ibid., 492/1934, a Turáni Társaság beadványa belügyminiszterhez, Budapest, 1934 augusztus.

76. Ibid.

77. Quote from Csaba Fazekas, *Kisegyházak és szektakérdés a Horthy-korszakban* (Budapest: TEDISZ-Szent Pál Akadémia, 1996), 151n19.

78. See "A turánizmus veszedelme," *Kálvinista Szemle* 2, December 10, 1921, 411; and Jenő Sebestyén, "A turanizmus képtelenségei," *Kálvinista Szemle* 5, April 5, 1924, 117.

79. Antal Molnár, "A Szentszék, a magyar jezsuiták és egy törökországi tudományos intézet alapításának terve (1930–1934)," in *Magyarország és a Szentszék diplomáciai kapcsolatai 1920–2015*, ed. András Fejérdy (Budapest: Balassi Intézet–Római Magyar Akadémia–METEM, 2015), 173–210.

80. For an example of this effort to harmonize Turanism and Catholicism, see György Illés, *A katolikus turáni eszme hőse és vértanuja: Wilfinger József magyar apostoli hithirdető élete és működése Kínában* (Szombathely: Szombathelyi Papnövendékek Szent Ágoston Egylete, 1936). Illés himself was forced to recognize that the subject of his book, Catholic missionary József Wilfinger, had never used the word *turáni* (Turanian) in any of his written works, although he asserted that his activity corresponded closely to the mission of the Hungarian Catholic Church to convert "pagan racial kin."

81. In this regard, articles on the Csángós, a Hungarian Catholic people living to the east of the Carpathian Mountains in Romania, and their origin are the most persuasive. See "Elhagyatott magyarság—Moldva, Bukovina, Besszarábia," *Turáni Nép*, December 24, 1933, 2. For Lublóváry's argument that Turanism is not a question of religion and that the Turanian race is a creation of God, see Gaszton Lublóváry, "Fogalomzavar," *Katolikus Ösvény*, June 30, 1935, 4.

82. For the Catholic criticism of Turanism, see Gyula Avar [Gogolák Lajos], "Miért veszedelmes a turanizmus?" *Vigilia* 1, no. 1 (1935): 178–86; and g-y, "dr. Bencsi Zoltán: Ősi hitünk," *A Fehér Barát* 2, no. 3 (September 1939), 45–46. For the Catholic hierarchy's criticism, see "Grősz püspök a pozitív kereszténység ellen," *Esti Kurír*, September 11, 1938, 2.

83. See R-k, "Az orthodox turanizmus," *Magyar Szemle* 30, no. 6 (1937): 182–85; János Győry, "Turánizmus után exotizmus," *Magyar Szemle* 26, no. 3 (1936): 276–78; László Gaál, "Műkedvelők a magyar őstörténeti kutatásban," *Magyar Szemle* 12, no. 7 (1931): 262–72; Gyula Szekfű, "A turáni-szláv parasztállam," *Magyar Szemle* 5, no. 1 (1929): 30–37; and Nándor Fettich, "Szkíták-szittyák," *Magyar Szemle* 4, no. 12 (1928): 338.

84. Gyula Németh, "A magyar turánizmus," *Magyar Szemle* 11, no. 2 (1931): 132–39.

85. On August 29, 1526, armies under the command of King Lajos II of Hungary, a scion of the Jagiellonian dynasty, encountered Suleiman the Magnificent's invading Ottoman forces near the village of Mohács in southern Hungary. The Battle of Mohács ended with the total defeat of Hungarian forces and the death of King Lajos and represented the beginning of the period of Ottoman dominion in Hungary. This battle has become a synonym for national tragedy in the Hungarian collective consciousness.

86. Gyula Németh, "A magyar turánizmus," 138.

87. Péter Garázda [Béla Zolnai], "Turáni kótyag," *Széphalom* 3, nos. 3–4 (1929): 144–47.

88. MNL OL, P 1384, 9. doboz, 1937-es ügyviteli iratok, 621/1937. a Turáni Társaság levele Baráthosi Balogh Benedeknek, Budapest, 1937. június 7.

89. Magyar Természettudományi Múzeum, Tudománytörténeti Gyűjtemény, Personalia, PM/45, Méhely Lajos hagyatéka, Hóman Bálint levele Méhely Lajosnak, Budapest, 1932. március 1.

90. For more information regarding Lajos Méhely, see Attila Kund, "Méhelÿ Lajos és a magyar fajbiológiai kísérlete (1920–1931)," *Múltunk* 57, no. 4 (2012): 239–89.

91. Lajos Méhely, "Turáni eszmény – turáni agyrém," *A Nép*, January 14, 1923, 8.

92. MNL OL K 149, 168. doboz, 1937-4-10039. rendőri jelentés, Budapest, 1937. március.

93. Ibid., 1933-7-2029. Gömbös Gyula levele Keresztes-Fischer Ferenc belügyminiszterhez, 1933. április 10.

94. See Viktor Keöpe, ed., *Turáni Vadászok Évkönyve 1943* (Budapest: National Association of Turanian Hunters, 1943); and László Sütő-Nagy, ed., *Turáni Vadászok Évkönyve 1944* (Budapest: National Association of Turanian Hunters, 1944).

95. A fragment of Keöpe's autobiography can be found at the following location: MFM, Hagyatékok, Keöpe Viktor: Tanáréveim. n.d. 110. For details regarding Keöpe's debate with Cholnoky regarding Székely-Manchu kinship, see Jenő Cholnoky, "Keöpe Viktor: A magyar ház kínai rokonsága," *Turán* 20–21, nos. 5–6 (1937–38): 116–17; Dr. Viktor Keöpe, "Helyreigazítás," *Turán* 20–21, nos. 7–10 (1937–38): 155–57; and Jenő Cholnoky, "Megjegyzések Keöpe Viktor dr. helyreigazításához," *Turán* 20–21, nos. 7–10 (1937–38): 157–58.

96. Keöpe, *Turáni vadászok évkönyve 1943*, 177. The National Association of Turanian Hunters cashbook is the only organizational document kept at the Hungarian National Archives. The data in this cashbook regarding those who paid membership fees and those who purchased organizational yearbooks and pistols would merit a separate prosopographical analysis: MNL OL P 2249, 47. sorozat, 15. doboz, 2. t., a TVOE pénztárkönyve 1943–1944.

97. MNL OL K 150, a belügyminisztérium általános iratai, 3859. cs. 5. t. VII. kútfő, a TVOE névváltoztatás iránti kérelme a belügyminiszterhez, Budapest, 1942. május 7.

98. "Turáni vadászok nemzetvédelmi napja," *Magyar Világhíradó*, no. 1025, October 1943. Film híradók Online, accessed on August 19, 2018, https://filmhiradokonline.hu/watch.php?id=5184.

99. Bylaws of the National Association of Turanian Hunters, Keöpe, *Turáni vadászok évkönyve 1943*, 177.

100. MNL OL K 150, a belügyminisztérium általános iratai, 3859. cs. 5. t. VII. kútfő, 171910. sz., a belügyminisztérium körirata a rendőrkapitányoknak, Budapest, 1944. március 31.

101. For the contention surrounding the issue of rehabilitation, see Emma Zagyva-Mérey's letter to the editor, "Az 1944–45-ös tragédia áldozatai rehabilitációjának tisztaságáért," *Vajdaság Ma*, September 23, 2013, accessed on August 19, 2018, https://www.vajma.info/cikk /olvasok/147/Az-1944-45-os-tragedia-aldozatai-rehabilitaciojanak-tisztasagaert.html; "'Golyót kapsz a fejedbe'—Halálosan megfenyegették Bozóki Antalt," *Délhír*, March 18, 2014, accessed on March 19, 2018, http://regi.delhir.info/delvidek/magyarsag-koezelet/22301-2014-03-19 -07-52-53; and "Tiltakozás a fasiszta Horthy rezsim kollaboránsainak—Magyarországról kezdeményezett—rehabilitásiós [sic] eljárásai ellen," Peticiok.com, 2015, accessed on August 19, 2018, https://www.peticiok.com/120986.

6

EVERYDAY LIFE AND HOLIDAYS
IN TURANIA

IN ORDER FOR US TO UNDERSTAND HOW THE terms *Turan* and *Turanian*—
which were rarely used during the first half of the nineteenth century
and were familiar primarily among specialists after that time—became
commonly used expressions during the first half of the twentieth century,
we should take a look at everyday life in Hungary during the Horthy era.
How did the designation Turan and its derivatives first gain acceptance
and then become banal and even hackneyed? What exactly did these words
mean, and how did those artists who emphasized the Eastern origin of the
Hungarians and the preservation of their Asian legacy use them?

One version of the Turanian idea appeared at the fundamental level
of everyday life—schools—through the initiative taken under Minister of
Religion and Public Education Kuno Klebelsberg to introduce the previously
mentioned kinship days at institutions of both lower and higher secondary
education in Hungary. The same motive that had served as the inspiration
for the kinship days at high schools and state civil schools prompted the
government to establish the paramilitary Levente Associations, which
devoted an entire special issue of its periodical *Levente* to the subject of
Turanism in the early 1930s. Moreover, tens of thousands of people attended
so-called kinship evenings that the Religion and Public Education Ministry
instituted on an experimental basis. In March 1936, crowds of nearly fifty
thousand people turned up for such kinship evenings held in Fejér County
in central Hungary (including thirty-two thousand young men who
belonged to the Levente Associations and whose participation was not
really optional)—at least according to a somewhat exultant account of these
events that Turanian Society general secretary Frigyes Lukinich published in
Turán.[1] However, Turanist groups were dissatisfied with government efforts

to promote Turanism despite Klebelsberg's kinship days, the subsequent attempts of the Religion and Public Education Ministry to support the movement under the direction of Bálint Hóman, and the presence of the Turanian Society on Hungarian Radio.

The establishment of a "Turanian curriculum" represented one of the permanent demands of these groups during the interwar period.[2] The Turanian Society devised such a curriculum, which Gyula Pekár asked Kuno Klebelsberg to introduce at schools in Hungary in a 1925 memorandum.[3] The steady emphasis that radical Turanists placed on the development of a Turanian curriculum compelled the Turanian Society to deal with this initiative.[4] In the Turanian curriculum formulated by Turanian Society specialists, *Turan* represented a geographical term, although it could be used in reference to related peoples even if they lived outside this region. The Turanian Society specialists expressed caution with regard to Japanese and Chinese kinship, arguing that a distinction must be made between topics to be incorporated into the Turanian curriculum and topics that should be elaborated in reference books. According to these experts, introduction of the Turanian curriculum was especially important with regard to the following subjects: language and literature, history, geography, and art. Moreover, they advocated the urgent launching of instruction in the Turkish language at certain upper-level commercial schools. The Turanian Society specialists advocated the teaching in schools of the music, vocal culture, ornamental motifs, anthems, tales, mythology, and history of the Turanian peoples, specifically the Finnish and Estonians, as well as the geography of the countries in which they resided. With regard to the history of the Turanian peoples, those who devised the curriculum recognized that the negative effects of the Hungarian-Ottoman wars fought from the middle of the fourteenth century to the end of the seventeenth century "cannot be overlooked," although they believed that subsequent positive developments in Hungarian-Turkish relations counterbalanced these negative effects: "The tone of voice used in reference to the Turks should be tempered and the beneficial effects [of Ottoman rule] should be highlighted (e.g., that the Turks tolerated our language and religion and defended us from the oppression of the Viennese court). The old antagonism began to fade after the time of Ferencz Rákóczi II and since then relations between the two nations have become increasingly unperturbed and friendly."[5] However, the government did not accept this proposed Turanian curriculum and instead attempted to incorporate the concept of kinship into public education through the publication of reference works, book donations, and the organization of various events.

Although the education ministry did place the *Kalevala* in the national school curriculum, acquaintance with the Finnish national epic had in fact been required for teachers at state civil schools since the beginning of the 1920s. The *Kalevala* has remained part of the school curriculum in Hungary ever since this time, even during the communist period.[6] The review and mutual revision of textbooks represented one of the cardinal points of the 1937 Finnish-Hungarian cultural agreement, although it was not implemented as a result of the Second World War.[7] Intransigent Turanists produced their own Turanian curriculum as well. This proposed curriculum, which presumably took form in the early 1930s, explicitly supported the notion of Hungarian-Japanese kinship, advocated for the compulsory study of Turanian languages, and recommended that emphasis be placed on Turanian species of plants and animals within the natural sciences.[8] These uncompromising Turanists occasionally added the teaching of the Old Hungarian alphabet to their proposed school curricula. This subject, which the Hungarian Scout Association had already begun to teach to its members, was actually introduced at a few schools in Hungary at the time of the Second World War, partially at the recommendation of ethnographer István Györffy.[9]

The theme of Turanism appeared in children's literature as well, though not at a very high standard: in 1938, István Eszes and Rózsi E. Csurgói, who attempted to establish an organization called the Turanian Bibliophiles Book Service during the Second World War, published a work entitled *Turáni Napmesék* (Turanian sun tales) that did not exactly become part of the canon of Hungarian-language juvenile literature. In 1931, László Gyomlay had attempted to incorporate the topic of kinship into the genre of Boy Scout novels that was popular in Hungary during the interwar period with his book *Turáni vándorok* (Turanian wanderers). In this work Gyomlay, who died in the custody of the communist political police in 1951 following interrogation connected to the show trial of Catholic archbishop József Grősz, introduced related peoples to the reader through a fictional account of the travels of a Hungarian scout troop to Bulgaria and Turkey. Former National Museum chief conservator and radical Turanist Zoltán Szilády harshly criticized *Turáni vándorok* in a review that appeared in the periodical *Protestáns Szemle* (Protestant review) in 1932, charging that Gyomlay's book reflected a total lack of familiarity with the countries in which it took place and failed to accurately depict the lives of their inhabitants.[10]

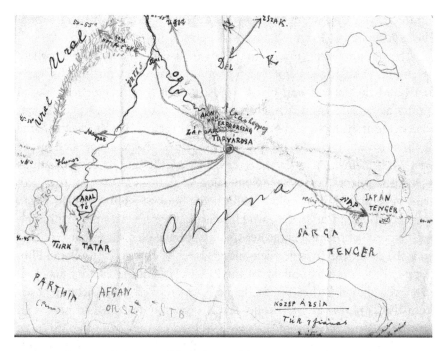

Fig. 6.1. Andor Kozma's drawing of the diffusion of the Turanian peoples. Attribution: Private collection, used with permission.

The absence of high-quality literature dealing with Turanian themes and intended for the general public is even more conspicuous. Among published Turanist works, only Andor Kozma's 1922 epic *Turán* (Turan) bears a certain degree of literary merit in its attempt to maintain the lyrical tradition of Árpád Zempléni. Those who wrote under the trademark of Turanism generally lacked the talent to avoid being classified as mere sectarian authors. Writers like the populist author János Kodolányi, who explored kinship themes during this period, frequently expressed extremely critical views vis-à-vis the Turanian movement.[11] In 1944, Mária Kiszely, who had gained recognition through her biography of Cosima Wagner, published a book with the allegorical title *Turániak* (Turanians). In this rather trite and repetitive work, the author attempted to portray nine hundred years of Hungarian history through the story of the descendants of King Stephen's valiant Turanian knight and to explore the concept of the "Turanian curse" through the presentation of a family history. Kiszely's book, which takes place primarily at a citadel called Turan Castle that is located alongside the

Turanka River and overlooks New Turan Town, received little attention. The expected great Turanian novel was never written.

The designations *Turan* and *Turanian* began to appear everywhere in Hungary during the interwar period, particularly during the early 1920s and the second half of the 1930s. Regent Miklós Horthy's special train was called Turán, while József Schuler manufactured pencils and compasses at his factory in Budapest under this label. Turán was the name of a nonextant movie theater in central Budapest that was operated by the poet Mrs. Elemér Papp-Váry Szeréna Sziklay, the author of the famous irredentist poem "Hitvallás" (Confession of faith), and her husband, an army general.[12] In 1921, Sziklay published a book of poetry entitled *Turán legendája* (Legend of Turan), which presumably served as the inspiration for the name of the movie theater that had been called the Edison Cinema until the American inventor demanded that it be changed. The Turán Film company's 1921 advertisement for the Excelsior Canning Factory may well have been shown at the Turán Cinema,[13] which likely used fuel purchased from the Turán Coal and Wood Trade Company (established nearby in 1920) to heat its furnace and might have used carpets from the Turanian Carpet Weaving Company (founded in 1923) to cover the floors of its foyer.[14] The Turán Consignment and Trade Company,[15] the Turán Domestic and Foreign Trade Company,[16] and another Turán Cinema, this one located in the village of Körösladány in eastern Hungary, also began to operate at this time. The Budapest Company Registration Court soon concluded that too many companies were using the word *Turán* and its derivatives in their names. The registration court commissioner, who also served as a deputy state secretary, initially rejected the name of the previously mentioned Turanian Carpet Weaving Company on the following grounds:

> I do not consider the attributive *Turanian* in the company name to be acceptable. The word Turan is a designation referring to the peoples of common Asian origin, a family to which the Hungarians belong. It is precisely for this reason that several associations and institutions have recently formed under this name as a means of pointedly emphasizing the ancient origins of the Hungarian nation and fostering national sentiment and racial cohesion. . . . Therefore, in consideration of the great significance of the word Turan, I am of the respectful opinion that it is hardly permissible for a trade company engaged in the production and marketing of carpets to use the attribute Turanian in its name.[17]

The commissioner added in this judgment that there were some companies, notably the Turan Hungarian National Domestic Industry Cooperative, that strove to "promote and develop the internal domestic industry based on old Turan-Hungarian folk art" and were thus able to legitimately use the words *Turan* and *Turanian* in their names.

Perhaps even more importantly, future prime minister Gyula Gömbös and the Hungarian National Defense Association had been behind the 1922 foundation of the Turan Hungarian National Domestic Industry Cooperative. In addition to Gömbös, geography professor and Hungarian Turan Alliance grand vizier Jenő Cholnoky served on the cooperative's board of directors. However, this enterprise apparently never engaged in serious activity and did not even submit data regarding its financial results in 1922. When officials asked Cholnoky to provide them with records regarding the official proceedings of the Hungarian National Domestic Industry Cooperative, he responded angrily in a letter that "I was never given an active role and they [cooperative leaders] did not even attempt to invite me to general meetings."[18] In 1921, another concern with a strong political tailwind, the Turanian Goldsmith Workshop, prepared to issue a "relic medallion" in cooperation with the National Refugee Affairs Office and to allocate part of the revenue derived from sales of the medallion to programs providing assistance to refugees who had fled to Hungary from territories that had been annexed to neighboring states via the Treaty of Trianon.[19] However, the Budapest company court rejected the National Refugee Affairs Office's application to register its associated enterprise under the name Turanian Goldsmith Workshop on the following grounds: "The circumstance that it [the company] is producing a medallion that will presumably be distributed throughout the country still cannot serve as a reason for supplementing the name of the entire workshop with [the word] Turanian, which embraces not only the Hungarian race, but related races as well."[20] Although in 1922 the Interior Ministry had promised the Turanian Society and the Hungarian Turan Alliance that their approval would be required for every request to use the term *Turan* and its derivatives in registered company names, this pledge was largely ignored. During the interwar period and at the time of the Second World War, the adjective *Turanian* was used in the names of everything from shoe factories to heavy tanks and construction projects. In 1928, a small thoroughfare and connected square on the outskirts of Budapest were rechristened Turan Street and Turan Square.[21] The cities of Kecskemét and Nagykőrös and the town of Fonyód on the southern shore of Lake Balaton each had a Turan Street as well. The first street in Hungary to have been endowed with the

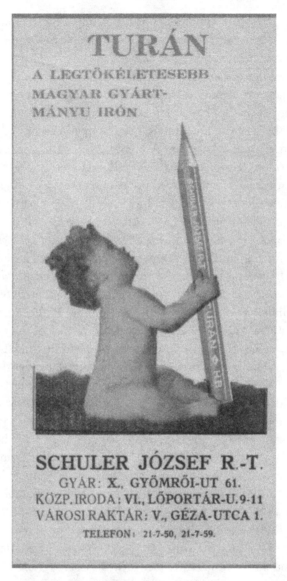

Fig. 6.2. Poster for the pencil Turán. Attribution: Owned by author.

name Turan—in 1909—appears to have been in the Kerekestelep district of the city of Debrecen.[22]

The history of the owner-occupied apartment building on Eszék Street in the eleventh district of Budapest called the Turan Court is illuminating in certain respects. The 1928 documentation pertaining to the foundation of this residential cooperative contains no reference to the motive for using the designation Turan in its name, thereby suggesting that the term had become so commonplace that it was no longer necessary to justify its usage.[23] Among the residents of this building, which was completed in 1931, one finds a relatively large number of intellectuals affiliated with the Lutheran Church. One might speculate that the choice of the name Turan Court was intended to emphasize the Hungarianness of occupants who belonged to a church that was widely considered to be the least "Hungarian" of all the religious denominations active in Hungary—though there is no evidence supporting this hypothesis. It is also possible that the relatively large proportion of Lutherans among the residents of the Turan Court was due to the fact that many civil servants lived in the district of Budapest in which the building was located and that Lutherans were overrepresented within the Hungarian civil service. In this case, there was likely no connection between the name Turan Court and its large number of Lutheran occupants. Sculptors Béla Ohmann and Lajos Mátrai Jr. produced the reliefs *Turáni vitéz-avatás* (Turanian warrior initiation) and *Űzik az Aranyszarvast* (Pursuing the golden stag) that appear to this day on the facade of this owner-occupied apartment building. The inner part of the eleventh district of Budapest, which in many ways served as a counterpoise to the largely Jewish middle class–occupied city neighborhood of Újlipótváros (New Leopold Town), was the location of numerous buildings in addition to the Turan Court that featured ancient Hungarian, Hunnic, and Asian design elements, such as the Árpád Court, the Hunnia Court, and the Sun Court.[24] Such residential "court" buildings are a distinctive element of the cityscape in this section of the eleventh district that appears nowhere else in Budapest.

The designer of the Sun Court, István Medgyaszay, was one of the most original Hungarian modernist architects. Medgyaszay worked for a time at the Gödöllő Art Colony, as did many of his fellow artists who were interested in the East and ancient Hungarians. Ferenc Márton, one of the most prominent painters of works depicting Székely themes during the interwar period, produced the sgraffiti that adorns the Sun Court as well as the Medgyaszay-designed "urban houses" and Reformed Baár-Madas High School in Budapest. Márton, a native of the Székely Land, worked as an illustrator for the daily newspapers *Magyarság* (Hungarianness) and *Új Magyarság* (New Hungarianness) and designed the cover illustration for Béla Szépvizi Balás's previously mentioned yearbook *Napkönyv*. Many of Márton's Székely-themed paintings are part of public collections in Hungary, and a significant number of his works can be seen in public spaces in the country as well.

Fig. 6.3. István Medgyaszay's Orient-inspired building in Mátraháza. FORTEPAN ©
2010–2014 under Creative Commons CC-BY-SA-3.0 license, Gyöngyi.

The foundation of the Gödöllő Art Colony is usually linked to the relocation of painter and industrial artist Aladár Körösfői-Kriesch (1863–1920) to Gödöllő in 1901. Other artists soon joined Körösfői-Kriesch in this town located northeast of Budapest. In addition to the previously mentioned István Medgyaszay, these artists included Sándor Nagy, who had become acquainted with Körösfői-Kriesch in Paris; Árpád Juhász (1863–1914); Jenő Remsey; Zoltán Remsey; István Zichy; Ede Toroczkai Wigand; Ödön Moiret; Mariska Undi; and Carla Undi. The most distinguished Hungarian modernist architect, Lajos Kozma, also worked at the colony but—like Medgyaszay—only for a brief period. The work and activity of the artists at the Gödöllő Art Colony have been extremely well documented in exhibitions, albums, and memoirs.[25] The English Arts and Crafts movement served as the model for these artists and creators, who thus strove as the pre-Raphaelites to expand the scope of their endeavors to include industrial arts and assert their artistic principles in everyday life as well. The Tolstoyan, mystical, and socialistic ideas of the Gödöllő Art Colony's founders exercised a strong impact on resident artists, many of whom were vegetarians and wore sandals and simple clothing that they had designed themselves. These artists, who frequently slept outside, held group calisthenics, and practiced naturism, might be viewed as early hippies of a sort who were a world away from mainstream Hungarian society. Those who have written about the artists who lived and worked at the Gödöllő Art Colony often focus solely on their gravitation toward Eastern or pseudo-Eastern ideas and creeds such as Buddhism and theosophy.[26] It thus appears that the connections of these artists to Turanism or Eastern thought will remain shrouded in obscurity.

The Renaissance masters and the enormous symbolic and historical frescoes of Pierre Puvis de Chavannes greatly influenced Aladár Körösfői-Kriesch and his friends. Gödöllő Art Colony creators used these models as the foundation for their attempt to portray Hungarian ancient history, particularly Hun-Hungarian folklore, on canvas, textiles, glass, carpet, and other materials. These artists frequently used motifs that Körösfői-Kriesch and other fellow residents of the Gödöllő Art Colony had collected on trips to Transylvania, notably the Székely Land and the Kalotaszeg region, and to the town of Mezőkövesd and the surrounding area in northeastern Hungary known as the Matyóföld.[27] The collection of folk motifs was not unprecedented: beginning in the 1880s, the drawing teacher József Huszka had traveled throughout the Székely Land gathering such decorative patterns for a compilation of Hungarian ornamentation. Huszka published part of his collection in a 1930 book entitled *A magyar turáni ornamentika története* (The history of Hungarian Turanian ornamentation), the introduction and theoretical foundation of which represent an introduction to the world of Turanian-Sumerian romanticism.[28] Körösfői-Kriesch and his associates hoped that their collection of Hungarian folk motifs begun in the 1890s would lead to the tradition-based renewal of their artwork. Those who accompanied Körösfői-Kriesch on his collection tours included Árpád Juhász, Sándor Nagy, István Medgyaszay, and Ede Toroczkai Wigand, whose participation in these trips prompted him to add Toroczkai to his surname in reference to the Székely village of Torockó (Rimetea, Romania). Dezső Malonyay also took part in the collection of folk motifs with these artists, who provided the journalist and novelist who was an associate of author Zsigmond Justh with documentation and other assistance required to publish *A magyar nép művészete* (Art of the Hungarian people).[29] This five-volume work published between 1907 and 1922 represents one of the most significant reference works pertaining to Hungarian decorative folk art and has inspired several generations of artists and ethnographers.[30] As a result of their own talent and the persistent goodwill and financial support of Ministry of Religion and Public Education Art Department director Elek Koronghi Lippich, the Gödöllő Art Colony artists not only received major representative commissions (decoration of the Hungarian Parliament Building, the Academy of Music, and the Hungarian Pavilion at the Venice Biennale) but also had their weaving school declared an official training workshop of the Industrial Arts School (now known as the Moholy-Nagy University of Art and Design), thus making it eligible for government funding. Moreover, Aladár Körösfői-Kriesch and Sándor Nagy provided the iconography for the Palace of Culture in Marosvásárhely (Târgu Mureş, Romania). Árpád Zempléni was among the progressive figures who regularly visited the Gödöllő Art Colony and developed such good relations with Sándor Nagy that he asked the painter to illustrate the English-language edition of his 1910 book *Turáni dalok* (Turanian songs).[31] Although the death of Körösfői-Kriesch in 1920 is usually regarded as the event that signaled the end of the Gödöllő Art Colony, many artists continued to work at the location even after this year.[32]

Although many of those who have written about the Gödöllő Art Colony have indicated that László Endre, who became chief magistrate in 1923, generally detested the artists who lived and worked there, primary sources suggest that this was not the case.[33] In fact, Sándor Nagy and his wife, Laura Kriesch, conducted very friendly correspondence with the future Interior Ministry state secretary.[34] The territorial losses that Hungary sustained via the Treaty of Trianon apparently radicalized some of the colony's resident artists: in his memoirs, Sándor Nagy described the pain he felt when Romanian poet Octavian Goga personally rewrote the ancient Székely ballads depicted on the stained-glass windows of the Palace of Culture in Marosvásárhely in the Romanian language after the city became part of Romania.[35] Sándor Nagy illustrated Béla Szépvizi Balás's publications and provided the radical Turanist Gyöngyi Békassy with an illustration for her periodical *Hadak Útja*. Nagy furthermore expressed his viewpoints regarding Turanism in a questionnaire. Although the painter's responses were not very coherent, they are still worth quoting.

QUESTION: "What is your opinion on the Turanian issue?"

ANSWER: "The Turanian question will be decided in Asia . . . and is already being decided. In fact, it was already decided in a scientific sense when European scholars named this continent Eurasia."

QUESTION: "What are you expecting from it [Turanism] in terms of domestic (in particular integral) politics and world politics?"

ANSWER: "Hungarians can't expect anything from it in this form. However, escaping from it is difficult. 'You are not yet an Aryan and you are no longer a Hun. . . . The Aryans mistreat us, while the yellow people have long forgotten us.'"

QUESTION: "Should this idea [Turanism] be propagated and if so, how?"

ANSWER: "Only in the language of poetry and art of the highest order, which knows no tendency. All other configurations discredit it."

QUESTION: "How do you see the future of the West and within it ours?"

ANSWER: "'Western culture has sprung a leak' said one of our great bishops. Since then everybody has been able to feel the sinking. Europe is no longer a producer of culture. But a culture liquidator: it is auctioning off everything it has. Meanwhile it can live well, especially the liquidators! Hungarians! Hang on to the seven plum trees as long as you can."[36]

Jenő György Remsey, who, along with Sándor Nagy, was one of the most distinctive figures among the residents of the Gödöllő Art Colony, became a full-fledged member of the radical Hungarian Turan Alliance. In the early 1920s, Remsey participated in Hungarian Turan Alliance programs as a lecturer and later took part in organization-sponsored events, such as the official inauguration of a new chapter in his hometown of Nagykőrös for which he held an exhibition of his art. Remsey's works, such as his 1920 dramatic poem "A szent turul" (The holy turul)[37] and 1923 monumental painting *Hungária lenyűgözése* (The captivation of Hungaria), gained a certain degree of popularity among those on the far right of the Hungarian political spectrum, and at the end of the 1930s, the versatile painter and writer contributed to the József Szörtsey–edited radical right-wing weekly *Nemzeti Figyelő* (National observer).[38] However, it is important to note that the Gödöllő Art Colony's resident artists never engaged in overt political activity and never aligned themselves with any specific political force or openly supported any political party. The transformation and evolution of their artistic ideas as a result of the post–First World War collapse and the Treaty of Trianon led them to espouse their viewpoints such as they were. One may condemn these viewpoints, but this does not detract from the enduring quality of the art produced at the colony.

Before the First World War, István Medgyaszay maintained close relations with Gödöllő Art Colony artists, notably Sándor Nagy, who produced the sgraffiti on Medgyaszay's theater building in Veszprém and commissioned the architect to design his house in Gödöllő. However, Medgyaszay's contacts with these artists slackened after 1920. Medgyaszay's desire to become acquainted with the East may have existed before he became associated with the Gödöllő Art Colony: during his years of study in Vienna around the turn of the century, the young architect was temporarily a member of the club that operated at the home of Lajos Thallóczy, whom he recalled fondly even decades later.[39] As previously mentioned, Medgyaszay, who regarded the integration of Hungarian folk motifs and modern architectural procedures (such as the use of reinforced concrete) to be the main element of his artistic creed, designed many of the buildings for the military exhibition held on Margaret Island in Budapest in 1917–1918. By this time, Medgyaszay had already designed some of his emblematic buildings, such as the theaters in the cities of Veszprém and Sopron and the church in the village of Rárósmúlyad (Mul'a, Slovakia). In the 1920s, the architect's interests gradually turned toward the East and the roots of the Hungarians.[40] Although Medgyaszay came into only intermittent contact with the various Turanist organizations during this decade, he was among the founding members of both the Society of Hungarians and the Hungarian-Indian Society.[41] Medgyaszay's association with the Hungarian-Indian Society was presumably the result of his friendship with Ferenc Zajti, whose trip to India and subsequent exhibition of items collected in that country at the Industrial Arts Museum in Budapest he helped to finance.[42]

Medgyaszay also lobbied intensively, notably with Debrecen mayor István Vásáry, to have Zajti's Indian collection incorporated into that of a museum in Hungary.[43] However, Zajti—who had become deeply indebted as a result of his trip to India—demanded too much money for his collection, which thus neither the Déri Museum nor the National Museum Ethnographic Repository purchased.[44] Medgyaszay received a series of significant commissions during the second half of the 1920s: in addition to previously mentioned buildings, he designed the Reformed church in the Kelenföld district of Budapest, the adjacent residential buildings, and the pagoda-like tourist hostel in the resort village of Mátraháza in northern Hungary. In 1927, Medgyaszay began teaching at the Budapest Technical University. Zajti's experiences in India, specifically the impetus they provided for his designs, filled Medgyaszay with such great enthusiasm that he sent Reformed bishop László Ravasz a booklet entitled *Attila hunjainak Indiába telepedett ivadékairól* (On the scions of Attila's Huns who settled in India) before the prelate departed on a trip to the United States: "Perhaps evoking these ancient connections would help to unite the spiritual world of the Hungarians of America both among one another and with us as well. The consciousness of this glorious past from an ancient time that the western peoples are not able to invoke could serve to create alluring and sympathetic brotherly affection in the deepest segment of our inner world."[45] This passage from Medgyaszay's letter to Bishop Ravasz reveals that the architect regarded the Turanian past not merely as a question of ancient history but also as a vehicle for regaining national self-esteem. With an absence of commissions as a result of the Great Depression and considerable persuasion from Ferenc Zajti, Medgyaszay himself traveled to India in 1932.[46] The immediate purpose for Medgyaszay's trip to India is as follows: through the good offices of Ferenc Zajti, Parsi Zoroastrian ecclesiastical leader Jivanji Jamshedji Modi and the head of the Bombay Board of Public Works had suggested that he might be hired to design a Turanian-Iranian museum in the capital city of the Bombay Presidency of British India.[47] The somewhat dreamy Zajti believed that the museum building might also house the nucleus of a Collegium Hungaricum/Institute of Eastern Relations.[48] Medgyaszay believed that he could use an updated version of his internationally recognized, award-winning 1902 design for the never-built national pantheon in Budapest for this museum. Medgyaszay, who despite being in his midfifties, learned English in just a few months so that he would be capable of negotiating with Indian officials and prepared an architectural drawing of the proposed Turanian-Iranian museum; however, once he reached India, it became apparent that this building was unlikely to be constructed. Nevertheless, Medgyaszay traveled throughout India holding lectures and tirelessly proclaiming the notion of Hungarian-Indian kinship. At the end of his five-month stay in India, Medgyaszay bade farewell to his newly acquired Indian friends with the promise that he would soon return. The motifs and photographs that he had collected during his trip served to heighten Medgyaszay's conviction that the peoples related to the Hungarians were to be found somewhere in India.

In the 1930s, this belief led Medgyaszay to conduct lengthy correspondence with Vilmos Hevesy, a Hungarian engineer who lived in Paris and was a former colleague of the French aviator, inventor, and engineer Louis Blériot (as well as the brother of Nobel Prize–winning chemist György Hevesy).[49] In the 1920s, Vilmos Hevesy had published a book under the pen name Uxbond in which he expounded the notion of kinship between the Hungarians, the Maori, and the Munda people of northeastern India.[50] Medgyaszay lent books to Hevesy and attempted to convince "Finno-Ugrists" to accept the engineer's viewpoints regarding Hungarian kinship or, at the very least, to regard them as worthy of consideration.[51] Incidentally, József Huszka was Hevesy's drawing teacher at the Piarist High School in Budapest, a connection that may have sparked his interest in the topic of kinship. It is easy to disparage Medgyaszay's notions regarding Hungarian kinship and ancient history, though one can clearly separate these ideas from his highly original architectural designs, steadfast belief in the Eastern roots of Hungarian folk culture, and consistent and discriminating use of modern architectural principles and building materials. Eastern motifs and their Hungarian counterparts served as the inspiration for much of his work. István Medgyaszay may be regarded as the preeminent member of the trio of prominent Turanian architects active during this period (Medgyaszay, Ede Toroczkai Wigand, and Jenő Lechner) due to the relatively large number and stylistic unity of buildings that he designed and the steadiness of his architectural creed, which he clearly defined in articles and books. If Turanism or thought regarding the East continues to exercise a residual effect in Hungary, this might be felt the most acutely in the domain of culture, particularly in the arts. Medgyaszay's work may be one of the greatest contributors to this lasting impact. His use of folk-inspired forms, ideas

Fig. 6.4. István Medgyaszay–designed theater (in Sopron, 1965). FORTEPAN © 2010–2014 under Creative Commons CC-BY-SA-3.0 license, József Hunyady.

regarding vernacular architecture, and considerations surrounding the use of wood and concrete influenced one of the most acclaimed architects in Hungary during the 1980s and 1990s, Imre Makovecz (1935–2011), and other so-called organic architects. Makovecz in fact analyzed Medgyaszay's work in a book on Hungarian architecture at the turn of the nineteenth and twentieth centuries that he and two coauthors published in 1990.[52]

The career of architect Ede Toroczkai Wigand proceeded along a somewhat different course than that of Medgyaszay. Toroczkai Wigand did not become associated with the various networks and organizations that existed at the time and, as a result of his reserved nature, did not participate to such a great degree in artistic public life.[53] However, in the 1930s Toroczkai Wigand was a steadfast member of the Turanian Society's leadership, although one wonders if even any of his fellow leaders were able to understand the exalted and rambling article "Turáni öreg csillagok" (Turanian old stars) that the architect published in Turán to mark the twenty-fifth anniversary of the organization's foundation.[54] Toroczkai Wigand became associated, as did Medgyaszay, with the Turanist movement via his affiliation with the Gödöllő Art Colony and participation in the folk motif–collecting trips its resident artists made to Transylvania. The rather reclusive Toroczkai Wigand spent perhaps the most productive period of his life in Marosvásárhely, where, beginning in 1907, he designed villas, community buildings, and prototype houses in both the city and at other locations in Maros-Torda County within the framework of the government-sponsored "Székely action" and with the support of Marosvásárhely (today Târgu Mures, Romania) mayor György Bernády. Toroczkai Wigand, who had previously been engaged primarily in interior design, became a true architect during his years in Marosvásárhely. Following the First World War, Toroczkai Wigand taught at the Industrial Arts School in Budapest and thus had less time and opportunity to undertake community- and state-commissioned architectural projects. During this time, he designed a few villas, and certain residential buildings at the Pongráctelep Housing Estate constructed in Budapest to house refugees bear his signature.[55] This was also the period in which the theoretical foundation of his work took form. In articles published in the daily newspaper *Magyarság*, Toroczkai Wigand expressed his opinion on topics ranging from the construction of family houses and Lake Balaton summer cottages to rethinking the concept of the garden.[56] The novelty of his ideas, idiosyncrasy of his designs, and complexity of his buildings made Toroczkai Wigand's architecture impossible to imitate.

Toroczkai Wigand played a role in the activities of the Turanian Society until 1944 and remained a part of the organization's steering committee even after the previously mentioned leadership purge that took place in the spring of that year. He spoke on Hungarian Radio in the name of the Turanian Society, and in 1931, he published an homage in *Turán* to the recently deceased Finnish painter and personal acquaintance Akseli Gallen-Kallela, whom he had visited in Finland before the First World War.[57] Toroczkai Wigand was not a very vocal supporter of Turanism, and his connections to the movement were related primarily to the cult surrounding the Székely people that emerged in Hungary during the interwar period. Toroczkai Wigand transformed part of his residence near the tomb of Ottoman dervish poet Gül Baba in Budapest into a "Székely house," to which he invited painter Fülöp László and Turanian Society chief patron archduke Joseph Francis of Austria, among others, for tea.[58] The architect later established a Székely museum near his new home after moving to the Buda Castle district. When he was about seventy-five, Toroczkai Wigand offered his Székely collection to the National Museum Ethnographic Repository (the future Ethnographic Museum). Museum conservator Sándor Gönyei determined that the collection was very valuable but had become such an integral part of Torockai Wigand's household that it could not be moved to the ethnographic repository. Therefore, Gönyei proposed that the National Literature and Arts Council make the decision regarding the future location of Toroczkai Wigand's Székely collection, suggesting that the Vajdahunyad Castle in Budapest might serve as the most appropriate site for its safekeeping.[59] However, this collection was lost, along with the architect's papers, either at the time of the 1944–1945 Siege of Budapest or during the subsequent removal of debris from damaged buildings and infrastructure.

The third "Turanian architect" was Jenő Lechner the designer of the Industrial Arts Museum in Budapest and the nephew of the famous Art Nouveau architect Ödön Lechner (as well as the son of painter Gyula Lechner, who translated Árpád Zempléni's Turanian songs into the German language). Jenő Lechner's pathway to Turanism did not pass through Gödöllő, although he did occasionally work with Aladár Körösfői-Kreisch and Ede Toroczkai Wigand. Lechner attained a much higher position and greater public recognition than either Körösfői-Kreisch or Toroczkai Wigand: in 1928, he gained appointment as an instructor at the Fine Arts College in Budapest and two years later received a Corvin Wreath, the most prestigious cultural award in Hungary during the interwar period. Moreover, Lechner designed the chalice from which Corvin Wreath recipients drank during their collective dinners. In terms of style, Lechner's designs reflect a lesser degree of Transylvanian, Székely, and Eastern influence than those of his fellow "Turanian architects." Lechner initially regarded the Renaissance architecture found in the cities of Upper Hungary (present-day Slovakia) to be the model according to which a national architectural style could be formulated—an idea that manifested itself in his design for the Sárospatak Teacher Training College in northeastern Hungary. Lechner later decided that classicism would better serve as this paradigm, one that he used in the design of the Our Lady of Hungary Roman Catholic Church in Budapest. Lechner, who was a loyal member of the Turanian Society throughout the interwar period, expressed his viewpoints regarding the art of the Turanian peoples in articles on subjects such as the steppe legacy and Mesopotamian architecture that, if rather mechanical and extremely slapdash, were not completely devoid of insight.[60] However, he did not really apply his ideas regarding Turanian art to his extensive body of architectural designs. In the early years of the twentieth century, Jenő Lechner attempted in the course of debate regarding the "national architectural style" to make a clear distinction between Ödön Lechner and his followers, emphasizing the fact that most of the latter were Jews and that they had deviated from his uncle's design principles, which he did not, incidentally, believe had served to create a "national style."[61] Lechner attributed the popularity of Eastern motifs among the architectural disciples of his father's younger brother to their "eastern" (i.e., Jewish) origin, emphasizing that such design elements were useful and interesting but not Hungarian.[62]

All three of these "Turanian architects"—István Medgyaszay, Ede Toroczkai Wigand, and Jenő Lechner—participated in an open competition in 1923 to design buildings to house the Ethnographic Museum. As Katalin Keserü and Péter Granasztói have shown in their articles on this competition, all three architects proposed designs for these never-constructed buildings, which were to have been located in the fifth district of Budapest, that combined certain components of their previous work with Hungarian folk elements intended to promote architectural renewal. Medgyaszay's proposal was based on revised versions of his designs for the never-built national pantheon and the Margaret Island military exhibition, featuring forms characteristic of both the East and peasant culture—which were clearly regarded as obligatory architectural elements on buildings erected during the interwar period to accommodate national public institutions such as the Ethnographic Museum. Toroczkai Wigand, who entered the competition in association with Béla Jánszky, submitted a design that manifested his previous experiences in Transylvania and Finland and envisioned placing the museum in a garden, thus creating a Skansen-like effect. Only a perspective drawing of Lechner's submission has survived: this design, which the judges liked despite the fact that it contained relatively few "Turanian" architectural forms, included a domed entry hall and Gothicizing towers. Although no winner was declared in this competition, the proposed designs clearly show that these "Turanian architects" supported the Klebelsberg-advocated notion of ethnography as the paramount national science and reflected their viewpoints regarding the Eastern and Hungarian elements of their national culture.[63]

Painter Tibor Boromisza, a relative by marriage of István Medgyaszay, used Turanian themes in the visual arts.[64] Boromisza grew up in a middle-class family and initially undertook a career in the military before deciding to become a painter. He studied at the painting academies of Paris, but he was among those Hungarian artists for whom the clamor and effervescence of the city did not bring about the desire to settle there. Boromisza lived and worked at the Nagybánya (Baia Mare, Romania) Art Colony beginning in 1906 before moving to the Balaton Painting Colony in 1908.[65] He played a significant role in the foundation and development of modern Hungarian painting and was an active member of progressive fine-arts circles in Hungary. In addition to his impeccable degree of technical skill and knowledge as an artist, Boromisza—unlike most of his fellow painters—wrote both well and abundantly. He was a strong and sensitive personality who generally strove to achieve leadership status, a character trait that sometimes engendered personal and theoretical conflict of the type that prompted him to leave the Nagybánya Art Colony. Boromisza performed military service in Szatmárnémeti (Satu Mare, Romania) during the First World War, and during the Aster Revolution that took place in Hungary in the final days of the war, he served as a member of the soldiers' council. In the spring of 1919, he joined the short-lived directorate formed in Szatmárnémeti following the proclamation of the Hungarian Soviet Republic in Budapest.[66]

In 1920, Boromisza was imprisoned as a result of his political activities in 1918 and 1919. While in prison, he became familiar with Buddhism, which exercised a lasting influence over the nephew of the Catholic Bishop of Szatmár, and subsequently wrote a 150-page unpublished manuscript about the religion.[67] His interests then turned in the direction of Hungarian-origin myth. In 1928, after collecting ethnographic motifs in the Hungarian-inhabited regions of Slovakia, Boromisza exhibited his painting *Koppány emlékezete* (Koppány's memory), a lost work depicting ancient Hungarian themes. In the same year, the painter moved to the Hortobágy steppe, where he worked relentlessly until 1930. The robust former hussar officer won the confidence of local livestock herders, known as *csikós* in Hungarian, with his skilled horsemanship and his forceful personality. Boromisza, who depicted the facial features of these herdsmen in more than sixty full-size portraits, adored life on the Hortobágy, writing in a letter to István Medgyaszay with regard to the steppe that "[here] we breath the genuine open air of Asia."[68] Boromisza was loosely associated with the previously mentioned circle of Debrecen intellectuals who took an interest in the East and Turanism: in

1922, he held a joint exhibition with Ferenc Medgyessy and maintained contacts with János Sőregi, István Ecsedi, and Miklós Káplár either via mail or in person during his stays on the Hortobágy. Sőregi enthusiastically awaited the painter's first visit to the steppe in 1928: "Tibor! Those of us who cherish the soul, land and ancient world of the Hungarians believe that only you can give this to us. We await you with great longing. Come as soon as possible to create beneath the spring sky of the steppe."[69]

After 1933, Boromisza, who had wanted to establish an art colony on the Hortobágy steppe, became a founding member of the Society of Hungarian Painters along with Aladár Fáy, György Littkey, Miklós Káplár, Dezső Mokry-Mészáros, and a few lesser-known artists. Many of these painters were affiliated with the Endre Bajcsy-Zsilinszky–led National Radical Party, an originally far-right political formation that came to oppose the Horthy régime, while some of them—including Boromisza—participated in the activities of the Hungarian Community, a nationalist secret society that in organizational terms was based on the model of the Freemasons.[70] In the 1930s, Boromisza served as the art critic for the progovernment daily *Függetlenség* (Independence) and at the same time published articles in Endre Bajcsy-Zsilinszky's opposition newspapers as well. Boromisza began to sign his works using the Old Hungarian script in 1924, thus becoming the first notable Hungarian painter to do so. In 1938, he was appointed to the Great Council of the newly reconstituted Hungarian Turan Alliance. In a letter of acknowledgment to the latter organization, the painter wrote, "My general activity moves within the domain of public education—I hope that Turanism, of which I am a born partisan, can see some kind of usefulness in this."[71] In 1942, Boromisza became a full member of the Turanian Society and again proclaimed his support for Turanist principles in a letter acknowledging his admission to the organization.[72] Although Boromisza was not among the painters who were active members of the Turanian Society, his work, outlook, and even the furnishings in his home were infused with Eastern elements. His magnetic personality, indisputable talent, and receptiveness to public life almost always elevated him to positions of leadership before his "angry Hungarian" (in the words of János Sőregi) disposition sparked conflicts that served to marginalize him. Boromisza occasionally squabbled with the Turanist intellectuals of Debrecen and harbored resentment against István Medgyaszay because the latter did not immediately support him with regard to the Society of Hortobágy Painters affair.[73] Boromisza described the origin of his orientation toward the East in a letter written in 1925: "I reached the East, partially to India, partially to China, along an intuitive path as I searched for the origin of Hungarian folk art. It is not my objective to do regular research, I have neither the ability nor the means, nor the training for this. I was merely listening to the instincts stirring within me."[74]

Nearly two decades later, Boromisza lamented the lack of state and public purchases of his paintings, complaining that not even the city of Debrecen had acquired any works from his Hortobágy series. The painter noted that he had repeatedly asked his friends and acquaintances, including *Függetlenség* editor in chief Kálmán Hubay, who was executed for war crimes in 1946, to intervene on his behalf in order to secure such purchases, to no avail.[75] Boromisza described his artistic objective at this time as "the investigation of Hungarian folk art and the art of our near and distant eastern racial kin at a European level and with modern perceptions."[76] Boromisza's disregard for Christianity and enthusiasm for the East, the articles he published in the daily newspaper of the increasingly right-wing government, and his former status as a military officer and impetuous remarks invite hasty and one-sided conclusions regarding his character. Boromisza was friends with liberals and artists of Jewish origin, while at the end of the 1920s, he worked with the left-wing intellectuals affiliated with Alice Madzsar's eurhythmics school. Moreover, unlike most Hungarians on the political right, he was fond of Hungary's capital city: "Budapest is needed just the same and I myself like it," he wrote to Miklós Káplár in 1929.[77] One should regard Boromisza's anger and sensitivity against this complex backdrop. German soldiers burned Boromisza's house in Budapest to the ground during the 1944–45 Soviet siege of the city, and at the age of sixty-five and as the father of four children, he was forced to start a new life, first in Keszthely and then in Szentendre. Although a memorial room was opened in honor of the painter in the latter city in 1964, his artwork was not rediscovered until the 1990s.

Painter Dezső Mokry-Mészáros, who last appeared in this book in connection to his enthusiastic participation in a small group of intellectuals who met at the Borsod-Miskolcz Museum to study the Old Hungarian script, earned a university degree in agriculture before undertaking employment as an estate manager. Mokry-Mészáros, a native of the village of Sajóecseg in northeastern Hungary, painted during his free time in this period. After leaving his job as an estate manager, Mokry-Mészáros spent several years in Italy and France prior to the outbreak of the First World War and also made trips to Tunesia, Egypt, and Ceylon.[78] During a visit to the island of Capri, he sold one of his paintings to Maxim Gorky. Mokry-Mészáros painted a wild, bewildering, and solitary world of primordial beings, shellfish, plant forms, and even dinosaurs. He initially used microscopic organisms that he had examined as a student at the Magyaróvár Agricultural Academy as models for artistic ornamentation. Mokry-Mészáros became acquainted with Jenő and Zoltán Remsey in the early 1920s and displayed some of his paintings at an exhibition that the brothers organized in 1924 through their newly founded association known as the Alliance of Spiritual Artists. He formed a long-lasting friendship with art historian Zoltán Felvinczi Takács at this time.[79] In 1930, Mokry-Mészáros traveled to Turkey at the invitation of Imam Abdüllatif, the spiritual leader of the Muslims of Hungary—a trip that the painter described in an article published in the Endre Bajcsy-Zsilinszky–edited weekly *Előörs*.[80] Mokry-Mészáros produced his first paintings and statuettes depicting themes from Hungarian folklife at this time and also began to study the Old Hungarian script and take Japanese lessons.[81] The painter even formulated his own runic script using the branding symbols of Hortobágy herdsmen and Mongolian texts as his models.[82] Mokry-Mészáros became the vice president of the Society of Hungarian Painters but gradually distanced himself from this organization because he felt that his fellow members, most of whom were trained artists, ostracized him as a result of his autodidacticism. The self-taught painter nevertheless gained a modest degree of recognition at this time.

In 1940, Mokry-Mészáros's dissatisfaction with the existing Turanist associations in Hungary prompted him to establish the Party of Turanian Hungarians.[83] However, this party existed for just over a year before its leadership decided to continue its operations "on an intellectual plane" as a result of "the persistently troubling uncertainty of the wartime conditions."[84] During the Second World War, Mokry-Mészáros's writings appeared in publications such as the *Magyar könyv* (Hungarian book), which disseminated the works of the Turanian monotheists and radical Turanists. In 1942, Mokry-Mészáros published an article regarding Turanian cemeteries in the second volume of *Magyar könyv*, which reveals that he considered a significant portion of the Chinese population to be affiliated with the Turanian peoples.[85] During these years, Mokry-Mészáros shifted his artistic focus from painting to graphics and ceramics. He also began to struggle with permanent financial difficulties, which a few years after the Second World War forced him to move from Budapest back to the city of

Miskolc, where he lived until his death in 1970. Mokry-Mészáros's papers show that in the late 1930s, he became a militant supporter of Turanism, which went hand-in-hand with the Hungarian Community's anti-German outlook, aspiration to create an authentic Hungarian "national art," and desire to eliminate all "foreign influences."[86] The solitary, autodidactic painter's discovery of a new form of artistic expression via his turn toward the East and acquaintance with the Old Hungarian script in the early 1930s represents a sign of the times. Mokry-Mészáros was not a talentless artist: for him, the Eastern idea and the focus on the Asian origin of the Hungarian people represented means of gaining equal status with his fellow painters and renewing his formerly universal artistic themes.

The aforementioned creators reformulated the Asian aspects of what they considered to be the soul of the Hungarian people. Through their works of art and architecture, they left a visible impression on public squares and the facades of buildings in Hungary. These artists and architects have bequeathed to us the single appraisable legacy of Turanism: Asian art, or what they considered to be such, interwoven with their own inventions.

Notes

1. Frigyes Lukinich, "A néprokonsági eszme terjesztése," *Turán* 19, nos. 1–4 (1936): 55.

2. MNL OL K 28, 211. doboz, Pekár Gyula levele Bethlen István miniszterelnöknek, Budapest, 1925. december 27.

3. MNL OL P 1384, 7. doboz, Pekár Gyula átirata Klebelsberg Kunónak, 1925. május 27.

4. The introduction of Turanian education at high schools in Hungary represented one of the main objectives of the Hungarian Turan Alliance. This organization appears to have developed concrete plans regarding Turanian education already in 1921. See "A Magyarországi Turán Szövetség céljai és működése," *Turán* 4 (1921): 76.

5. MNL OL P 1384, 7. doboz, Pekár Gyula átirata Klebelsberg Kunóhoz, Budapest, 1925. május 27.

6. Győző Fehérvári, *"A dalnak új utat mutattam": A Kalevala és a Kalevipoeg összehasonlító elemzése, magyarországi fogadtatása és hatása* (Budapest: Lucidus, 2002).

7. For a historical examination of this agreement, see Halmesvirta, *Kedves rokonok*, 174–83.

8. OSZKK, Fond 446, Turáni dolgozatok 2: Turáni tanterv tervezete, n.d.

9. News reports published in the late 1920s reveal that the Hungarian Scouting Association had already begun to hold instruction in the Old Hungarian alphabet by this time. See "Don Antonio Sancho a Cserkészházban," *Pesti Hírlap*, August 13, 1929, 13; Béla Mindszenti Szvoboda, "A magyar rovásírás" *Magyar Cserkész* 19, no. 12 (March 1, 1938): 16–17. About the school experiments, see "A református egyetemes konvent befejezte tanácskozásait," *Pesti Hírlap*, April 18, 1931, 3, and Vitéz Ede Faragó, *Cserkészapród-könyv*

(Budapest: Magyar Cserkészszövetség, 1937; first published in 1931), 87–88. See also István Györffy, *Néphagyomány és nemzeti művelődés* (Budapest: Egyetemi Néprajzi Intézet, 1939), 19.

10. Zoltán Szilády, "Gyomlay László: Turáni vándorok," *Protestáns Szemle* 42, no. 3 (March 1932): 220.

11. See the following three works by János Kodolányi, *Julianus barát* (Budapest: Athenaeum, 1938); *Istenek* (Budapest: Athenaeum, 1941); and *Holdvilág völgye* (Budapest: Athenaeum, 1942).

12. Children in Hungary recited this poem at the beginning of every school day during the interwar period: "I believe in one God, I believe in one Homeland / I believe in a divine eternal truth / I believe in the resurrection of Hungary."

13. Budapest City Archives, VII. 2.e., Cg 14873, a Turán Film (Szepessy Árpád) ügyei.

14. Ibid., VII. 2.e., Cg 12813, "Turán" Szén- és Fakereskedelmi Társaság 2553 kisdoboz; Ibid., VII. 2.e., Cg 21946, a Turáni Szőnyegszövő Rt iratai.

15. Ibid., VII. 2.e., Cg 12122, 2594. kisdoboz.

16. Ibid., VII. 2.e., Cg 16089, 3055. kisdoboz.

17. Ibid., VII. 2.e., Cg 21946, a Turáni Szőnyegszövő Rt iratai, a cégbiztos 1924. március 11-én kelt véleménye.

18. Ibid., VII. 2.e., Cg 26.509, Turán Magyar Nemzeti Háziipari Szövetkezet iratai, 3465, kisdoboz Cholnoky Jenő levele a cégbírósághoz (n.d. [1926]).

19. Ibid., VII. 2.e., Cg 15641 (3326. kisdoboz), Turáni Ötvös Műterem (Kéz József cége), 1921–1923.

20. Ibid., a budapesti kir. törvényszék elutasító végzése, Budapest, 1921. október 12.

21. *Fővárosi Közlöny* 39, no. 79, December 31, 1928, 3354. In 1950, this street was renamed after a murdered member of the communist underground movement. The street regained its original name after the end of the communist era.

22. László Balogh, "Debrecen város utcanévkatasztere," *Hajdú-Bihar Megyei Levéltár közleményei* 30 (2007): 410.

23. Budapest City Archives, VII, 2.e., Cg 29775: Turánudvar Társasház-Szövetkezet iratai 1928–1934, 3678–3679. kisdoboz.

24. For the dichotomy between *Újlipótváros* and the eleventh-district *Lágymányos-Szentimreváros* (Saint Emeric Town) neighborhood, see András Ferkai, "A társasház, mint a budapesti lakóházépítés megújításának egyik módja," *Ars Hungarica* 20, no. 2 (1992): 71.

25. See Katalin Gellér and Katalin Keserü, *A Gödöllői Művésztelep* (Budapest: Cégér, 1994).

26. See, for example, Katalin Gellér, "Misztikus tanok hatása Körösfői-Kriesch Aladár művészetében," in *Körösfői-Kriesch Aladár (1863–1920) festő- és iparművész monográfiája és oeuvre katalógusa*, ed. Cecília Nagy Őriné (Gödöllő: Gödöllői Városi Múzeum, 2016), 120–26.

27. Károly Lábadi, "A gödöllőiek találkozása a nép művészetével," in *A gödöllői művésztelep 1901–1920*, ed. Katalin Gellér, Mária G. Merva, and Cecília Nagy Őriné (Gödöllő: Gödöllői Városi Múzeum, 2003), 139–43; and Cecília Nagy Őriné, ed., *A népművészet a 19–20. század fordulójának művészetében és a gödöllői művésztelepen* (Gödöllő: Gödöllői Városi Múzeum, 2006).

28. József Huszka, *A magyar turáni ornamentika története* (Budapest: Pátria, 1930). Huszka had become an embittered elderly man by the time he managed to publish this book, in which he expresses viewpoints from which Hungarian scholarly circles largely distanced themselves. Hungarian National Museum Department of Ethnography director Zsigmond Bátky had previously expressed criticism of Huszka's work in letter to Minister of Religion

and Public Education József Vass: "It is my duty to state that in the course of his activity in this regard, he [Huszka] has increasingly deviated from the sole urgent task of collection and description [and departed down] the exceedingly difficult, unpredictable and will-o'-wisp-bounded [road toward] uncovering the origin of Hungarian ornamentation" (NMI, 70/1921, Bátky Zsigmondnak a Nemzeti Múzeum Néprajzi Osztálya vezetőjének levele Vass József kultuszminiszterhez, Budapest, 1921. augusztus 22).

29. Róbert Keményfi, "Malonyay: 'A magyar nép művészete'; A gödöllőiek—helyek, emlékezetek," in *"A burgonyától a szilvafáig"*: *Tanulmányok a hetvenéves Kósa László tiszteletére*, ed. Elek Bartha (Debrecen: Debreceni Egyetem Néprajzi Tanszéke, 2012), 33–80.

30. László Kósa, "Malonyay Dezső és 'A magyar nép művészete,'" in *Nemesek, polgárok, parasztok* (Budapest: Osiris, 2003), 387–403.

31. MTAKK, Ms 1020/214, Zempléni Árpád levele Vargha Gyulának, Budapest, 1919. május 17.

32. Contrary to Sándor Nagy and Jenő Remsey, the ideas connected to Turanism did not significantly influence Aladár Körösfői-Kriesch. For relations between Sándor Nagy and Körösfői-Kriesch, see Sándor Nagy, *Életünk Körösfői-Kriesch Aladárral* (Gödöllő: Gödöllői Városi Múzeum, 2005).

33. "Szathmáry Zoltán visszaemlékezése," in *Emlékezések a gödöllői művésztelepre*, ed. Péter Polónyi (Gödöllő: Helytörténeti Gyűjtemény, 1982), 18.

34. MNL Pest Megyei Levéltár XIV.2.a., 19. doboz. 210. pallium, Nagy Sándor levelei Endre Lászlónak, Gödöllő, 1923–1938.

35. Nagy, *Életünk Körösfői-Kriesch Aladárral*, 135.

36. Béla Szépvizi Balás, ed., *Napkönyv – Turáni képes naptár és évkönyv*, vol. 1 (Gödöllő: self-published, 1925), 41. At the end of the eighteenth century, around 5 percent of the population of Hungary belonged to the nobility. Members of this class constituted a greater proportion of the population only in Poland and Spain within Europe at this time. However, the large majority of Hungarian nobles owned only a very small amount of land— and sometimes no land whatsoever—and were thus known colloquially in Hungarian as *hétszilvafás* (seven-plum-tree) nobility.

37. The *turul* is a mythical bird that serves as the totem animal of the Hungarian nation. There is debate regarding whether this bird is a saker falcon or some kind of eagle. The turul was depicted in many chronicles beginning in the Middle Ages, and during the nineteenth and twentieth centuries, it was portrayed in many public statues in Hungary as well.

38. Scholarly literature has largely ignored Remsey's Eastern orientation: MTA BTK Művészettörténeti Intézet, Adattár, MDK-C-II/377, Remsey Jenő György életrajza (1964); and Mária G. Merva, "Remsey Jenő György (1885–1980) sokoldalú munkássága," in *Remsey Jenő György festőművész, író emlékkiállítása* (Gödöllő: Gödöllői Városi Múzeum, 2010), 6–37.

39. For the relationship between Medgyaszay and Thallóczy, see István Medgyaszay, *Thallóczy Lajos művészlelke. 1937. december 3-i emlékbeszéd* (Budapest: Thallóczy Lajos Társaság, 1938).

40. For a comprehensive examination of István Medgyaszay's life and work, see Ferenc Potzner, *Medgyaszay István* (Budapest: Holnap, 2004).

41. See "Társasági ügyek," *Turán* 11, nos. 1–4 (1928): 75; and OSZKK, Fond 446 Turáni dolgozatok 1., a Magyar-Indiai Társaság közgyűlésének jegyzőkönyve, 1930. évi május 23. és uo. Turáni dolgozatok 2, a Magyarok Társasága 1930. január 20-i alapító közgyűlésének jegyzőkönyve.

42. Medgyaszay collection (private), Társaság-album, kéziratos feljegyzés, 1931. május.

43. DEENKK, Sőregi János hagyatéka, Ms 13/96, Medgyaszay István levele Vásáry Istvánnak, Budapest, 1930. június 24.

44. Déri Museum Ethnographic Archives (hereafter, DMNA), 98–70, Felvinczi Takáts Zoltán levele Ecsedi István múzeumigazgatónak, Budapest, 1930. június 25. For correspondence regarding this issue, see NMI 36/1929, Bátky Zsigmond igazgató levele Hóman Bálintnak, a Nemzeti Múzeum főigazgatójának, Budapest, 1929. április 24, and NMI 27/1930, Bátky Zsigmond igazgató Klebelsberg Kunó kultuszminiszternek ugyanebben az ügyben, Budapest, 1930. február 26.

45. Medgyaszay collection, Társaság-album, Medgyaszay István levele Ravasz Lászlóhoz, Budapest, 1929. június 3.

46. Medgyaszay kept everything that came into his possession during his trip to India, including such things as menu cards from his voyage (Medgyaszay collection, India album).

47. Medgyaszay collection, India-album, Medgyaszay István levele a vallás- és közoktatásügyi minisztériumnak, Budapest, 1931. október 28. Zajti Ferenc levele Medgyaszay Istvánnak, Bombay, 1928. december 25.; Zajti Ferenc indiai gyűjteménye. *Pesti Napló*, 1929. november 21. 12; see Potzner, *Medgyaszay István*, 23; and Katalin Keserü, "Magyar-indiai építészeti kapcsolatok," *Néprajzi Értesítő* 77, (1995): 167–82.

48. See "Közgyűlés," *Turán* 12, nos. 1–4 (1929): 62.

49. Medgyaszay collection, India album, Hevesy-Medgyaszay-levelezés, 1932–1938.

50. F. A. Uxbond, *Munda-Magyar-Maori: An Indian Link between the Antipodes; New Tracks of Hungarian Origins* (London: Luzac, 1928).

51. For example, Medgyaszay collection, Medgyaszay István levele Hevesy Vilmosnak, Budapest, 1938. január 28. In his letter to Vilmos Hevesy, Medgyaszay reported that he had presented the engineer's viewpoints to Miklós Zsirai, one of the leading Finno-Ugric linguists in Hungary.

52. See János Gerle, Attila Kovács, and Imre Makovecz, *A századforduló magyar építészete* (Budapest: Szépirodalmi, 1990).

53. For details regarding Toroczkai Wigand's life, see Katalin Keserü, *Toroczkai Wigand Ede* (Budapest: Holnap, 2008), 13–26.

54. Ede Thoroczkai Wigand, "Turáni öreg csillagok," *Turán* 19, nos. 1–4 (1936): 57–64.

55. Keserü, *Toroczkai Wigand Ede*, 23–24.

56. See, for example, Ede Thoroczkai Wigand, "Virágok," *Magyarság*, August 19, 1923; "Hogyan építsünk a Balaton partján?" *Magyarság*, April 5, 1931, 43; "Az elrontott Budapest," *Magyarság*, August 2, 1931, 26; "Az elrontott Budapest," August 9, 1931, 22; and "Az elrontott Budapest," August 30, 1931, 22.

57. On March 29, 1930, Toroczkai Wigand's wife read his essay "Turáni hagyományok népépítésünkben" (Turanian traditions in our folk architecture) on the radio. See *Magyarság*, March 28, 1930, 19. See also Ede Thorockai Wigand, "Akseli Gallén-Kallela," *Turán* 1–4 (1931): 30–40.

58. Petőfi Irodalmi Múzeum, Kézirattár, V 4715/93, Toroczkai Wigand Ede levele László Fülöpnek, Budapest, 1935. május.

59. NMI-27/1944 Gönyey Sándor jelentése Toroczkai Wigand Ede gyűjteményéről, Budapest, 1944. március 29.

60. Dr. Jenő Lechner, "A turáni népek művészete," *Turán* 5, nos. 3–4 (1922): 179–92.

61. MFM Érd, Cholnoky-hagyaték, 5. doboz, Lechner Jenő levele Cholnoky Jenőnek, Budapest, 1942. január 16. In this letter to Jenő Cholnoky dated January 16, 1942, Jenő Lechner wrote the following in reference to an article entitled "Lechner Ödön nem volt

magyar?" (Was Ödön Lechner not a Hungarian?) that he had published in the daily newspaper *Magyar Nemzet* (Hungarian nation) a few days previously (January 11, 1942, 4): "I have been very pro-German since the very beginning of the movement and indeed criticized the non-Hungarian character of the work of my uncle's followers in this spirit on racial grounds already in 1908, though the peremptory behavior of the fraternal nation in the domain of scientific research always filled me with pain."

62. Eszter Gábor, "'. . . e műemlékeinkben a történelmi magyar hangulatoknak mélységes tengerét bírjuk': Lechner Jenő kísérlete a magyar nemzeti historizmus megteremtésére," in *Sub Minervae nationis praesidio: Tanulmányok a nemzeti kultúra kérdésköréből Németh Lajos 60. születésnapjára* (Budapest: ELTE Művészettörténeti Tanszék, 1989), 180–85.

63. For further information on this competition, see Péter Granasztói, "Pajta és gimnázium között. A Néprajzi Múzeum épülete tervpályázatának története (1923)," *Néprajzi Értesítő* 97 (2015): 37–64; and Katalin Keserü, "A budapesti Néprajzi Múzeum építészeti tervei és a gödöllőiek," in *A népművészet a 19–20*, ed. Nagy Őriné (Gödöllő: Gödöllői Városi Múzeum, 2006), 136–44.

64. Medgyaszay's mother-in-law was a member of the Boromisza family.

65. For Boromisza's work at the art colony in Nagybánya, see László Jurecskó, *Boromisza Tibor nagybányai korszaka (1904-1914)* (Miskolc: MissionART, 1996). For a comprehensive examination of the painter's career, see Katalin Török and László Jurecskó, *Boromisza Tibor 1880–1960* (Szentendre: Pest Megyei Múzeumok Igazgatósága, 2012).

66. "Élet a Nemzeti Tanácsban," *Szamos*, November 7, 1918, 2; "Élet a Nemzeti Tanácsban," *Szamos*, March 29, 1919, 2; and Katalin Török, "Pályatörténet új megvilágításban," in *Boromisza Tibor önéletrajzi feljegyzései*, ed. Katalin, Török (Szentendre: Rectus, 2011), 35.

67. Török, "Pályatörténet új megvilágításban," 45–47.

68. OSZKK, Fond 25/123, Boromisza Tibor levele Medgyessy Ferencnek, Hortobágy, 1928. november 10.

69. Tibor Boromisza papers, family archives, Szentendre (hereafter, BT-CsA), Sőregi János levele Boromisza Tiborhoz, Debrecen, 1928. március 29.

70. Bajcsy-Zsilinszky regularly engaged Boromisza to write articles in his newspapers and was acquainted with other Turanist creators as well, notably István Medgyaszay, with whom he once spent his summer holiday. The nature of Bajcsy-Zsilinszky's relationship with Boromisza is reflected in a letter in which he invited the painter to attend an election rally: MDK-C-II/407, Bajcsy Zsilinszky Endre levele Boromisza Tibornak, Budapest, 1930. június.

71. MNL OL P 2249, 10. sorozat, 2. t., Boromisza Tibor Előd levele az MTSZ Nagytanácsának, Buda, 1938. április 20.

72. MNL OL P 1384, 11. doboz, 2. t. 1942-es ügyviteli iratok, Boromisza Tibor a Turáni Társaságnak, Budapest, 1942. október 20. 376. f.

73. Déri Museum Visual Arts Documentation Department (hereafter, DMKA), 82.58 Káplár Miklós levelezése, Boromisza Tibor levele Káplár Miklósnak, s. l. (Budapest?) 1929. január 9. In a letter to Miklós Káplár, Boromisza wrote, "I talked with Medgyaszay, but his faction is not capable of taking decisive measures even with regard to Hungarian things, although they declare themselves to be Scythians."

74. Török, "Pályatörténet új megvilágításban," 72–73.

75. NMI 11/1935, Hubay Kálmán levele Zichy Istvánhoz (mellékelve Visky Károly szakvéleménye), Budapest, 1934. december 31.

76. Medgyaszay collection, Társaság album, Boromisza Tibor önéletrajzi töredéke, Budapest, 1943. január 7.

77. DMKA, 82.58 Káplár Miklós levelezése, Boromisza Tibor levele Káplár Miklósnak, 1929. január 3.

78. For more detail regarding Mokry-Mészáros's life, see István Dobrik, *Mokry-Mészáros Dezső* (Miskolc: Herman Ottó Múzeum, 1985); and Attila S. Tasnády, "Adalékok Mokry Mészáros Dezső művészi pályaképéhez," in *Yearbook of the Herman Ottó Museums* 45, ed. László Veres and Gyula Viga (Miskolc: Herman Ottó Muzeum, 2006), 355–69. For a recently published book on the painter's artwork, see Anna Váraljai, *Mokry. Idegen világ—Mokry-Mészáros Dezső művészete* (Budapest: Virág Judit Galéria, 2017).

79. The friendship between Mokry-Mészáros and Felvinczi Takács is reflected in nearly three decades of correspondence: HOM, Visual Arts Archives, Dezső Mokry-Mészáros papers, 1. doboz, Mokry-Mészáros Dezső és Felvinczi Takáts Zoltán levelezése, 1930–1958, Mokry-Mészáros Dezső levele Felvinczi Takáts Zoltánnak, n.d. [1930]; and for example Felvinczi-Takáts Zoltán levele Mokry-Mészáros Dezsőnek, Budapest, 1953. szeptember 21.

80. Tibor Boromisza, "Az öreghídtól—Sztambulig," *Előörs*, June 28, 1930, 5–6.

81. For information regarding Mokry-Mészáros's study of the Japanese language, see OSZKK, Fond 25/311: Mokry-Mészáros Dezső levelezőlapja Medgyessy Ferencnek, 1939. október 15.

82. Many of these manuscripts can be found among Mokry-Mészáros's papers kept at the Ottó Herman Museum.

83. MNL OL K 149, a Belügyminisztérium reservált iratai, 81. doboz, 4. t., 6407/1940, Bejelentés és rendőrségi környezettanulmány, Budapest, 1940. február 1.

84. MDK, Mokry-Mészáros Dezső hagyatéka, C-I-39/7, a Turáni Magyarok Pártjának körlevele, Budapest, 1941. június 3.

85. Dezső Mészáros, "A turán-magyar temető," in *Magyar könyv*, vol. 2, ed. László Tarján Kállay and Károly Béla Mészáros (Budapest: Hollóssy János Könyvnyomtató Műhelye, 1942), 92–97; Dezső Mészáros, "A rovás történelmi, faji és gyakorlati jelentősége," in *Magyar könyv*, ed. Kállay and Mészáros (Budapest: Szalay Sándor könyvnyomdája, 1941), 57–61.

86. See the manuscripts of Mokry-Mészáros's lectures on Hungarian visual arts: MDK, Mokry-Mészáros Dezső hagyatéka, C-I-39/7-2-3, "Turkish-Hungarian Fraternity: Struggle for Hungarian Visual Arts"; "The Old Hungarian script." A characteristic quote from the artist is as follows: "The time of perpetual running [pilgrimage] to Paris, Berlin and Rome is over."

7

DÉVÉNY AND TOKYO

THE HIGHLIGHT OF THE FINNO-UGRIC CONFERENCE HELD IN Tallinn, Estonia, in 1936, the final such meeting of the interwar period, occurred when participants sang the Turanian anthem for which the Hungarian poet, folklorist, and translator Aladár Bán had written the lyrics and Estonian musician J. Jürgenson had composed the music:

> From the foot of the Urals and Altais,
> from the dark lap of the millennia,
> a swarm of people once set forth
> across unknown lands.[1]

However, the Finnish translation of the anthem prepared by the distinguished Finnish writer, poet, and translator Otto Manninen produced a minor controversy: not only had Manninen furnished the song with the title Uralic anthem rather than Turanian anthem, but he had also omitted the reference to the Altai Mountains in its first line, which he recast as "From the barren foot of the rugged Urals." This incident reflects the vast discrepancy in the understanding of Turanism that existed between Hungarians and their related peoples. Finnish public opinion and even those Finns who vehemently upheld their relationship with the Uralic peoples rejected any reference to purported kinship with the peoples of Central Asia, the Turks, and the Japanese.[2] At the same time, some Turkish Turanists, such as the Pan-Turkic followers of Ziya Gökalp, were unwilling to regard the Hungarians, not to mention the Finns and Japanese, as kin.[3] Hungarian Turanism was therefore the only variant of the movement that embraced all of these kinship relations and thus lacked the power to gain their broader acceptance.

As previously mentioned, the primary objective of diplomats from Hungary after 1920 was to rebuild the traditional Western orientation of the country's foreign policy. Therefore, between 1919 and 1921 the various governments of Hungary established diplomatic missions in London, Rome, Paris, Berlin, and the capitals of neighboring states—Vienna, Prague, Bucharest, and Belgrade. During this period Hungary also opened foreign missions in cities located in neutral countries that played a prominent role in international affairs such as Geneva, Bern, The Hague, and Stockholm. As a result of the belated conclusion of the post–First World War peace agreement between the United States and Hungary, the Hungarian diplomatic mission in Washington, D.C., began operating only in 1922. During these years, Hungary opened only one foreign mission in a "Turanian" capital city—Sofia. In 1923, Hungarian diplomats were posted in Tallinn, which at this time was still known by its German name Reval as well. Tallinn was particularly important to Hungary, not as a result of Finno-Ugric kinship, but because the capital of Estonia served as one of the principal sites for Hungarian-Soviet talks regarding the release of prisoners of war withheld in the Soviet Union. In 1928, the Hungarian diplomatic mission in Tallinn was moved to Helsinki, though Finland did not dispatch a permanent envoy to Budapest until 1933. Finnish political official Eemil Setälä, a longtime kinship-movement activist who maintained good connections in Hungary, had urged Hungarian foreign minister Miklós Bánffy—once an ardent member of the Turanian Society—to establish a diplomatic mission in Helsinki, but Bánffy rejected the request on financial grounds.[4] Hungary considered Kemalist Turkey to be a potential ally and established diplomatic relations with the country in 1924 after the Treaty of Lausanne had made it possible to do so the previous year. In fact, in December 1923, the newly proclaimed Republic of Turkey signed its first international treaty with Hungary.[5]

As a result of Japan's initial lack of interest in Hungary following the First World War, diplomatic relations between the two countries were for many years conducted at the Japanese legation in Vienna. However, the subsequent strengthening of Japanese-Hungarian relations, Hungary's positive stance toward the Anti-Comintern Pact, and, especially, the incorporation of Austria into the German Reich via the Anschluss prompted Japan to move the country's diplomatic mission in Vienna to Budapest in 1938. The following year, Japan sent a plenipotentiary minister to Hungary for the first time ever.[6] Also in 1939, the first independent Estonian foreign mission was established in Hungary, although by this time Richard Jöffert had been serving as Estonia's chargé d'affaires in the country for four years.[7]

Hungary's formal contacts with countries inhabited by peoples considered to be related to the Hungarians were thus rooted in the previously described diplomatic relations with Finland, Estonia, Bulgaria, Turkey, and Japan. However, the Turanian spirit did not always govern the actions of Hungarian diplomats posted in these countries. For example, Sándor Nemeskéri Kiss, a veteran of the Hungarian foreign service who had opened the embassy of Hungary in Sofia after the First World War and been appointed as the country's ambassador to Finland in 1933, was quoted anonymously—though quite identifiably—in the daily newspaper *Pesti Napló* as saying, "Without the Swedes, the Finns would today be an insignificant Finno-Ugric tribe of the Russian Bolshevik empire, just as the Voguls or the Ostyaks."[8] This quote so infuriated Finnish officials that they asked the Hungarian Foreign Ministry to recall envoy Nemeskéri Kiss.

Political considerations in many cases exercised a negative impact on public opinion in Finland toward Hungary. Finns affiliated with left-wing, liberal, and agrarian parties regarded the political regime in Hungary with skepticism as a result of its conservative, even reactionary, nature and believed that it was insufficiently democratic, lacked social awareness, and failed to modernize ossified conditions in the country. However, Finnish agrarians nevertheless supported the concept of Finno-Ugric kinship. Some of Finland's envoys in Budapest during the interwar years were associated with the political left, a circumstance that manifested itself in their diplomatic reports and thus often determined official Finnish policies toward Hungary. Finns on the political right were much less critical of the Hungarian political and social system, although they were still unwilling to support all of the aims of the Turanian movement.[9] The observation that Finland's ambassador to Hungary, Karl Gustaf Idman, made in 1922 very accurately describes Finnish-Hungarian relations during the interwar period regardless of the political considerations described here: "In Hungary they devote greater attention to the kinship of our peoples than we do at home."[10]

In 1927, Eemil Setälä became Finland's envoy to Hungary in place of Idman, who had carried out the duties connected to this office from Copenhagen. Setälä, a veteran of the kinship movement who had begun to make regular visits to Budapest in the late nineteenth century, maintained contacts with radical Turanists in Hungary, although he did not embrace their extreme ideas.[11] In 1934, Onni Talas succeeded Setälä as envoy, a position that he held until 1940. Talas regularly participated in events related to

Finno-Ugric kinship, became a popular figure in Budapest social circles, and even married his Finnish bride in the city.

Although Hungarian Turanists and kinship specialists expressed sympathy for the Finnish claim to East Karelia, which the newly independent Finland had been forced to relinquish to the Soviet Union in 1920, this solidarity was based primarily on the corresponding feeling of injustice that Hungarians had felt after Hungary had lost two-thirds of its pre–First World War territory to neighboring states via the Treaty of Trianon the same year. However, this sympathy was not enough to persuade activists affiliated with the Association of Finnish Culture and Identity (Suomalaisuuden Liitto) or the Academic Karelia Society (Akateeminen Karjala-Seura)—who reciprocated Hungarian support for Finnish irredentism through their endorsement of Hungarian revisionism—to espouse the notions of Turanian kinship or blood relations with the Turks and Mongols. Not even Eemil Setälä was willing to countenance these ideas. The reluctance of Finns to underscore their Asian origin was partially the product of Finland's emancipatory struggles against Sweden. Although in the 1930s Finland's diplomats in Hungary regularly attended Turanian Society–sponsored events, neither they nor the many Finnish intellectuals who visited Budapest proved willing to embrace Turanist concepts that transcended the kinship movement. This situation did not change during the period of "brotherhood in arms" at the time of the Second World War, when Finnish voices calling for the liberation of the Finno-Ugric peoples and the creation of a Greater Finland became stronger, though neither public opinion nor official circles in Finland became more receptive to the concept of far-reaching kinship. During a visit to Budapest in January 1943, Parliament of Finland Second Deputy Speaker Edwin Linkomies, who became the head of the Finnish government two months later, appeared to be totally unresponsive to the fulminations of his Hungarian interlocutors regarding the proletariat, Slavic imperialism, and "Swedish capitalism," and even the reference of Prime Minister of Hungary Miklós Kállay to Finnish-Hungarian "racial kinship" visibly failed to impress Linkomies. The second deputy speaker of the Finnish parliament expressed gratitude for the assistance that Hungary had provided Finland during the Winter War (1939–1940) and highlighted the importance of their common struggle against Bolshevism but refused to go even one inch farther than this. Linkomies was furthermore somewhat taken aback when Regent Horthy, who had otherwise made a positive impression on the future prime minister of Finland, expressed support for the fanciful Pan-Finno-Ugric notion that the blood of the Hungarian people might be refreshed through the settlement of Finnish men in Hungary following the end of the war in order to marry Hungarian women.[12]

The Estonians were somewhat more inclined than the Finns to make declarations that went beyond kinship, particularly in the early 1920s as they attempted to abolish Russian and Baltic German cultural hegemony, though this tendency was neither enduring nor profound. However, the vast array of publications, translations, scholarships, and cultural events connected to the relationship between the Hungarian, Estonian, and Finnish peoples in the 1920s and 1930s reveal that the interwar years can nevertheless be regarded as the golden age of Finno-Ugric kinship. An astonishingly large number of Estonian and Finnish works were published in Hungary during this period, while Budapest theaters staged Estonian plays and Finnish artists participated in cultural forums in the city or spoke on Hungarian Radio. As the result of the committed efforts of a few intellectuals, the presence of Hungarian culture in Estonia and Finland was also widespread. Between 1913 and 1944, more than fifteen hundred articles dealing with the theme of kinship appeared in the Turanian Society periodical *Turán*, while more than seventy newsreels were produced in Hungary during this period that pertained to Hungarian-Estonian and Hungarian-Finnish relations. In addition, Hungarian Radio broadcast nearly sixty thematic presentations regarding Estonia and Finland from the station's foundation in 1925–1944.[13] Following the Soviet occupation of Estonia in 1940, leaders of the Turanian movement came up with the idea of settling Estonian intellectuals and professionals, primarily physicians, in Hungary in order to alleviate the shortage of specialists that had emerged in the country partially as a result of the 1938–1939 Jewish Laws. According to the proponents of this idea, these Estonian intellectuals and professionals—as native speakers of a related language—would learn Hungarian quickly and could also use their knowledge of Russian to communicate with the non-Hungarian peoples living in the region of Subcarpathia that Hungary had reacquired shortly before the outbreak of the Second World War.[14] During the interwar years, the focus in Hungary on Finno-Ugric kinship manifested itself in other ways as well, such as the Estonian-language brochures that both the IBUSZ (Idegenforgalmi Beszerzési Utazási és Szállítási Rt) travel agency and the Budapest Central Health and Holiday Resort Committee published during this period, which is quite unthinkable today. Therefore, Horthy-era Hungary, which many consider to have constituted the prototype of a "Christian-nationalist" state, paradoxically championed a concept such as Finno-Ugric kinship that was branded "anti-national" after the communist period.[15]

The Hungarian-Bulgarian connection represents one of the least investigated domains of Turanian kinship relations during this period. The territorial losses that both Hungary and Bulgaria sustained via the post–First World War peace treaties served as a "common fate" that brought the countries close to one another during the interwar years. Available documents suggest that Bulgarian government officials were receptive to the notion of Turanian kinship: Bulgarian diplomats were members of the Turanian Society, presumably a reflection of the increasing amount of research that was taking place in Bulgaria regarding the Turkish-Turkic origin of the Bulgarian people.[16] However, Turanist notions regarding common Turkish origin touched on delicate aspects of the Bulgarian national identity even if examination of Byzantine-Bulgar-Turkish relationships greatly inspired Hungarian ancient-history researchers during the interwar period.[17]

The reception of Hungarian Turanism in Turkey was even more complex than in the countries inhabited by Finno-Ugric peoples. Hungarian Turanists had long maintained good relations with Turkish intellectuals, many of whom were affiliated with the Young Turks political party that supported both Pan-Turkism and the ideas associated with Turanism. Hungarian Turanists may have believed that the collapse of the Ottoman Empire would bring political officials who sympathized with them to power in the new Turkey. However, the deaths of the "Three Pashas" who led the Young Turks—Enver, Talaat, and Djemal—shortly after the First World War and the rise of Mustafa Kemal Atatürk dashed any such hopes. By late 1921, Atatürk indicated that he intended to transform Turkey into a secular state for ethnic Turks and was not interested in any kind of nebulous, transnational ideology.[18] Moreover, in the 1920s, Turkey required support from the Soviet Union in order to carry out postwar reconstruction of the country and thus could not participate in plans promoting the independence of Turkic peoples living in the USSR. In 1925, the Soviet Union and Turkey signed an agreement in which the Turkish government pledged to prohibit any kind of support to Pan-Turkic organizations. The Turkish apostles of the prewar Turanian and Pan-Turkic movement either managed to more or less adapt to the new system, as Yusuf Akçura, Ziya Gökalp, and Munis Tekinalp did, or were forced to go into internal or external exile. The notorious Young Turks leader Enver Pasha, who had served as the Ottoman

Empire's minister of war from 1914 to 1918, died in combat against Soviet forces in 1922 on the territory of the current-day country of Tajikistan in the course of the struggle to create a Greater Turkestan in Central Asia. However, the Turkish government in fact tolerated Pan-Turkic movements, which no longer posed a significant threat to the internal stability of Turkey, in spite of its nominal prohibition of them. Not only were Pan-Turkic newspapers allowed to appear, but they even published Turkish state advertising. Pan-Turkic organizations were nevertheless banned from time to time and their members either imprisoned or placed under police surveillance.[19]

In the 1930s, this relative tolerance paved the way for the emergence of the second generation of Turkish Turanists, who were much more focused on racial protection than their predecessors had been, sometimes espoused fascist precepts (antisemitism, military society, racial purification), and were not at all interested in the alleged Turanian origin of the Hungarians. The new generation of Turkish Turanists did not include Hungarians in their conception of "Turanian union" and sometimes disparaged them in their writings. Pan-Turkic intellectuals, most prominently the poet and author Nihâl Atsız (1905–1975), who coalesced around the newspapers *Orhun, Bozkurt,* and *Atsız Mecmua* came to the forefront of Turkish public life during the Second World War with the help of significant financial support from the German embassy. Despite strenuous protests from the neutral government of Turkey, many writings were published in the country during the conflict on the eastern front between Axis forces and the Soviet Union regarding the fate of Turkic peoples in southern Russia, the Caucasus, and Central Asia. In May 1944, the aspiration of the Turkish government to maintain its neutrality, preserve the benevolence of the Soviet Union, and quell the unrest surrounding the trial of Nihâl Atsız that had resulted in several mass demonstrations in Ankara and Istanbul prompted it to abolish Pan-Turkic organizations through the prosecution of activists associated with the "Turanian–racial protectionist" movement that resulted in long prison sentences for around two dozen of them.[20] Among those imprisoned at this time was the university professor Zeki Velidi Togan (1890–1970), a Bashkir brother-in-arms of Enver Pasha in the struggle for an independent Turkestan who, in 1929, became an honorary member of the Turanian Society in Budapest along with Yusuf Akçura.[21] Although the concept of Turanism was perhaps as strong in Turkey as it was in Hungary in an intellectual sense, as a result of the difference in religion, Turkish Turanist leaders were reluctant to accept Hungarian ideas regarding the guiding principles of the movement and always focused on the Turkic peoples in Europe and Asia rather than the Japanese, Finns, or Hungarians.

Diplomatic relations between Hungary and Turkey were very steady and cordial during most of the interwar period, at least until 1934.[22] Hungarian and Turkish political officials conducted mutual official visits on several occasions and signed a series of bilateral agreements. Hungarian prime ministers István Bethlen and Gyula Gömbös both made official trips to Turkey during which the latter inaugurated the Tekirdağ Hungarian House, the former residence of the exiled leader of the 1703–1711 uprising against Habsburg rule, Ferenc Rákóczi, that has remained under the ownership of the state of Hungary and the administration of the Hungarian National Museum ever since. In addition, around six hundred Hungarian specialists and advisors participated in the postwar reconstruction of Turkey, working either on building projects in Ankara or as employees of the Turkish state apparatus. President Kemal Atatürk did not hesitate to refer to Turkish-Hungarian kinship and the resulting community of interests between Turkey and Hungary during his meetings with Hungarian political officials, though one of the latter remarked that "they [the Turks] would not gladly see the Turanian Society operating [in Turkey], because this would immediately awaken the belief among our enemies that they want to pursue greater Turanian policies."[23] It is important to note that both Pan-Turkism and Turanism, movements that are often conflated, were both present within the intellectual life of the new, post–First World War Turkey, although Pan-Turkism undoubtedly aroused the enthusiasm of a greater number of people in the country. Although the Kemalist government did not pursue active Pan-Turkic foreign policies, which would not have even pertained to Hungary in the first place, it firmly supported cultural Pan-Turkism at the domestic level. From the official interwar Turkish perspective, the superiority of the nomadic Turkic culture of the steppes was indisputable. The second Pan-Turkic renaissance occurred in the late 1960s, when the newly founded Nationalist Movement Party (Milliyetçi Hareket Partisi) and affiliated intellectuals and organizations synthesized Pan-Turkism and Islam. Nationalist Movement Party leader Alparslan Türkeş (1917–1997), a former Turkish army colonel, had been sentenced to prison during the 1944 purge of Turanists in Turkey and later received training in the United States as a result of his ardent anticommunism.[24]

Diplomats from Hungary and Japan raised the subject of Hungarian-Japanese kinship only in the course of unofficial small talk and did not take the notion that they were related peoples seriously. The concept of kinship constituted a less important factor in the rapprochement between the two countries during the interwar period than mutual fear of the Soviet Union. The latter common concern prompted Japan to place increasing pressure on Hungary beginning in 1937 to assent to the reciprocal opening of diplomatic missions. Japanese officials believed that Hungary might become part of a pro-Japanese Central European bloc that would be based on the notion that "we must jointly defend ourselves against the Soviet threat."[25] Hungarian diplomatic and military officials were interested primarily in the degree to which a potential conflict between Japan the and Soviet Union might divert the attention of the Red Army away from Romania and the other two members of the Little Entente. The chiefs of staff of the Hungarian army were so interested in the ramifications of possible warfare between Japan and the Soviet Union that beginning in 1933, they had detailed reports and maps prepared every three months regarding the military situation in the Far East. In the 1920s and 1930s, Japan supported Hungary in various disputes with neighboring countries regarding the determination of borders and various litigation regarding property rights, while Hungary needed the backing of even such a distant power as Japan in order to achieve its revisionist objectives.[26] Although Japanese intellectuals, political officials, and journalists frequently articulated pro-Hungarian viewpoints and participated in events aimed at promoting relations between Japan and Hungary or propagating the notion of Turanian kinship, the ideas associated with Turanism were much less prevalent within Japanese society than they were within Hungarian society.

During the interwar period, Hungarian-Japanese contacts were generally confined to superficial events such as the formal conferral of cherry-tree sprigs or samurai swords. Only at the time of the Second World War did relations between Japan and Hungary begin to produce more significant concrete results such as the foundation of the Japanese-Hungarian Cultural Institute in Tokyo, the functions of which the war circumscribed to a great degree. The Japanese-Hungarian Cultural Institute did nevertheless publish sixteen issues of a periodical, each of which was around fifty pages in length, containing articles regarding the culture, literature, and history of Hungary. The previously mentioned Yuichiro Imaoka was the propelling force guiding the operations of the Japanese-Hungarian Cultural Institute, while the Hungarian envoy to Japan and the famous Japanese patron Baron Takaharu Mitsui served as the organization's president. The palpable lack of dynamism in relations between Japan and Hungary despite such initiatives was primarily the result of the great distance separating the two countries but was also due to the relative indifference of both the Japanese and Hungarian governments toward bilateral contacts. The activities of zealous intellectuals—such as Imaoka; Viscount Naokazu Nabeshima, the founder of the Tokyo Liszt and Petőfi societies; and Nándor Metzger, the longtime resident of Japan—and various Hungarian diplomats who attempted to highlight their own importance in reports to foreign-ministry officials in Budapest may have created the impression that many Japanese were interested in strengthening relations with Hungary.[27]

Naturally there were some Turanists in Japan: in 1929–1931, Tokyo lawyer Tomoyoshi Sumioka published a periodical that dealt extensively with Hungary and Turanian brotherhood. Sumioka's interest in Hungary presumably stemmed from his friendship with Vilmos Pröhle. After ceasing publication of this periodical, Sumioka expressed pessimism in a letter to Yuichiro Imoaka regarding the prospects for Turanism in Japan: "The Turanian movement requires a great amount of dedicated work, though this work has not resulted in success. I do not believe that this [success] will be realized in my lifetime." Sumioka nevertheless founded the Japanese Turanian Society in 1932 and the Greater Japan Turanian Youth Alliance in 1934. At the same time, the decision of the Japanese government following its establishment of the puppet state of Manchukuo in 1932 to pursue further expansion in China and Southeast Asia rather than in the "Turanian"-inhabited Mongolian People's Republic and region of Siberia in order to preserve Soviet neutrality served to weaken official support for Turanist endeavors in Japan. In general, pragmatic political factors determined the course of relations between Hungary and Japan during the interwar period rather than Turanism or some other kind of Eastern creed. Hungarian Turanism-based initiatives were successful when they emphasized cultural connections between Japan and Hungary, as in the case of choir meetings and student exchanges. However, Hungarian diplomats and decision makers were not sure how to handle the concept of Turanian kinship reaching back to the distant past, and the Hungarian public did not take note of efforts to strengthen relations with Japan. The fact that leading Hungarian Turanists such as Gyula Pekár, Alajos Paikert, and Zoltán Felvinczi Takács had to conduct correspondence with their Japanese counterparts in either French or, less frequently, English because they did not know Japanese is very revealing.

Almost all connections between "Turanian" countries passed through Hungary. Although the Turanian Society periodical *Turán* published enthusiastic articles about the visit of a Turkish delegation to Finland and an Estonian military officer's words of praise regarding Turkey, the notion that such transversal relations—that is, those not involving Hungary—might begin to prosper was mere wishful thinking.[28] In fact, Finnish and Estonian advocates of the kinship movement were generally not eager to make the acquaintance of their non-Finno-Ugric "Turanian" kin. There were a very small number of Turkish Turanists who showed interest in the Japanese based on the concept of their common Tungusic origin. The staunch anticommunism of Turkish Turanists and their ambition to liberate the Turkic peoples of the Soviet Union inspired intellectuals such as the Crimean Tatar Muharrem Feyzi Togay (1877–1947). Togay, who had fled to Turkey from the Crimea after the First World War, published a large number of articles regarding Turkish-Japanese kinship and relations and maintained contacts with Yuichiro Imoaka after the latter returned to Japan that were founded on their common conviction that the advance of Chinese and Russian communism had to be contained in order to achieve the liberation of the Turkic peoples of Central Asia. The association between Togay and Imaoka represented the only discernable connection between Turkish and Japanese Turanism. Togay, incidentally, was among those imprisoned as a result of the 1944 Turanist trials in Turkey.[29]

Turanism received woefully bad press, which was the result of the movement's illusory ambitions, the activities of affiliated radicals, and the Catholic Church's vigorous condemnation of Turanist precepts. Moreover, British, French, and American diplomats regarded Turanism as a dangerous pan-nationalist ideology and, in the case of Hungary, a vehicle for achieving revanchist objectives. In 1919, France's ambassador to Romania noted during a short stay in Budapest that a local informant had told him that Pál Teleki, who became prime minister of Hungary the following year, had maintained "Pan-Islamic, Pan-Turanian, and Pan-German" plans during the First World War and thus should not be permitted to play a role in Hungarian politics.[30] The notion of Turanism as a grand movement embracing an entire continent was a Hungarian invention that gained little support from the leaders and people of countries regarded as part of the Turanian kinship network and exercised very little influence in Europe.[31]

Notes

1. Aladár Bán, "Uráliak himnusza," *Turán* 19, nos. 1–4, (1936): 41.
2. Halmesvirta, *Kedves rokonok*, 20–31.
3. Oláh, "A török és a magyar turanizmus kapcsolata a 20. század első felében," 74–75.

4. MNL OL, Mikrofilmtár, X 9062, E. N. Setälä levelezése, 31134. tekercs, Bánffy Miklós levele E. N. Setälänek, Budapest, 1921. augusztus 3 (microfilmed source from the National Archives of Finland).

5. For information regarding the Hungarian diplomatic service during the interwar period, see Pál Pritz, ed., *Iratok a magyar külügyi szolgálat történetéhez 1918–1945* (Budapest: Akadémiai 1994), 430–42.

6. Gergely Pál Sallay and Péter Wintermantel, "A magyar-japán diplomáciai kapcsolatok története, 1918–1945," in *Tanulmányok a magyar–japán kapcsolatok történetéből*, ed. Farkas et al. (Budapest: ELTE Eötvös, 2009), 121–33.

7. Emese Egey, *A két világháború közötti magyar-finn-észt kapcsolatok történetéből: Társasági, diplomáciai, katonai együttműködés*, Specimina fennica Savariae 15 (Szombathely: NYME SEK Uralisztikai Tanszék, 2010), 65–69.

8. János Kodolányi, "A svéd kérdés," *Pesti Napló*, October 24, 1936, 10.

9. Vesa Vares, "A romantikus távoli rokon: Finnország és Magyarország kapcsolatai, illetve a finnek Magyarország-képe a két világháború között," *Iskolakultúra* 8, no. 5 (1998): 56–66.

10. Ibid., 60.

11. Setälä's moderate Turanism is reflected in his correspondence with Hungarian friends and acquaintances such as Benedek Baráthosi Balogh, Sándor Ispánovits, István Ecsedi, Alajos Paikert, and Vilmos Hevesy, MNL OL, Mikrofilmtár, X 9062, E. N. Setälä levelezése, 31134. tekercs, especially Baráthosi Balogh Benedek levele Eemil Setälä-nek, 1930. február 25.; Ispánovits Sándor levele Eemil Setälä-nek, 1929. október 10.; 1930. január 30.

12. For the 1943 visit of Linkomies to Hungary, see Matti Turtola, "Linkomies, Horthy and Mannerheim: Some Aspects of Linkomies's 'State Visit' to Hungary in January 1943," *Hungarologische Beiträge* 7 (1996): 136; cf. "'Szabadság és függetlenség nélkül minden földi lét értelmetlen'—Szinyei Merse kultuszminiszter és Linkomies finn professzor pohárköszöntője," *Pesti Hírlap*, January 20, 1943, 3. For Prime Minister Kállay's ideas regarding the centuries-long struggle against Slavic imperialism and the intimate feelings among the "kindred types" that would produce a happier future, see "Kállay Miklós miniszterelnök előszava a finn miniszterelnök budapesti előadásához," *Pesti Hírlap*, May 1, 1943, 5.

13. Emese Egey and Enikő Szijj, eds., *A Turán című folyóirat 1913, 1917–1918, 1921–1944 finnugor mutatója* (Budapest: Tinta, 2002), and Egey, *A két világháború közötti magyar-finn-észt kapcsolatok* történetéből, 140–190.

14. MNL OL K 28, a Miniszterelnökség II, Kisebbségi Osztályának iratai, 205. doboz, 389. t. "a Magyar-Észt Társaság iratai": 1941-A-18204, Jeney Endre memoranduma a Magyar-Észt Társaság elnökéhez, Petri Pálhoz, Debrecen, 1941. március 17.

15. For Hungarian-Estonian relations during the interwar period, see Egey, *A két világháború közötti magyar-finn-észt kapcsolatok történetéből*, and András Bereczki, "A két háború közötti magyar-észt kapcsolatok történetéről," *Jogtörténeti Szemle* 18, no. 1 (2004): 58–67.

16. For information regarding the role that Turanian Society–associated archaeologist Géza Fehér played in interwar Hungarian-Bulgarian cultural and scientific relations, see Alexander Gjurov, "Fehér Géza helye a bolgár-magyar kulturális és tudományos kapcsolatokban a két világháború között," *Somogy* 20, no. 3 (1992): 68–73.

17. See, for example, Zoltán Gombocz, "Bolgárok és magyarok," *Új Magyar Szemle* 2, no. 2 (1920): 176–83; and Bálint Hóman, *Ősemberek, ősmagyarok* (Budapest: Kairosz, 2002),

200–208. (The latter work is composed of a manuscript and notes that had been previously unpublished due to Hóman's death in 1951.)

18. See Oláh, "A török és a magyar turanizmus kapcsolata a 20. század első felében," 79–82; and Landau, *Pan-Turkism*, 74–81.

19. Landau, *Pan-Turkism*, 74–107.

20. Ibid., 111–20.

21. For Velidi's speech in Budapest and the context in which it took place, see Zaur Gasimov and Wiebke Bachmann, "Transnational Life in Multicultural Space: Azerbaijani and Tatar Discourses in Interwar Europe," in *Muslims in Interwar Europe: A Transcultural Historical Perspective*, ed. Bekim Agai, Umar Ryad, and Mehdi Sajid (Leiden: Brill, 2015), 216–17.

22. This issue is examined in the following work: Péter Kövecsi-Oláh, "Török-magyar diplomáciai kapcsolatok a két világháború között (1920–1945)" (PhD diss., Eötvös Loránd University, Budapest, 2018).

23. Quoted in Oláh, "A török és a magyar turanizmus kapcsolata a 20. század első felében," 79.

24. Landau, *Pan-Turkism*, 148–79. For the evolution of the whole milieu, see Ilker Aytürk, "The Racist Critics of Atatürk and Kemalism, from the 1930s to the 1960s," *Journal of Contemporary History* 46, no. 2 (April 2011): 308–35.

25. MNL OL K 63, 115. cs. 15/7. t. 33pol-1939. Napijelentés a japán nagykövettel folytatott beszélgetésről. Róma, 1939. február 26.

26. Wintermantel and Sallay, "A magyar-japán diplomáciai kapcsolatok története, 1918–1945," 124–48.

27. For information regarding Imaoka, see Yuko Umemura, *A Japán-tengertől a Duna-partig. Imaoka Dzsúicsiró életpályája a magyar-japán kapcsolatok tükrében* (Budapest: Gondolat, 2006).

28. See "Hírek," *Turán* 9, no. 1 (1926): 56; and B. A. "Észt katonatiszt a turanizmusról," *Turán* 9, no. 2–3 (1926): 93–95.

29. For information regarding Turkish-Japanese Turanist relations, see Sinan Levent, "Common Asianist Intellectual History in Turkey and Japan: Turanism," *Central Asian Survey* 35, no. 1 (2016): 121–35.

30. M. Saint-Aulaire, "minister de France à Bucarest à M. Pichon, minister des affaires étrangères, Bucarest, le 28 octobre 1919," in *Documents diplomatiques français sur l'histoire du bassin des Carpates*, vol. 2, ed. Magda Ádám (Budapest: Akadémiai, 1995), n. 94.

31. See Harold Nicolson, *Peacemaking* (London: Constable, 1933), 21. Nicolson, who served as a member of the British delegation at the 1919 Paris Peace Conference, wrote about Hungarians: "I confess that I regarded and I still regard that Turanian tribe with acute distaste. Like their cousins the Turks, they had destroyed much and created nothing." However, it is important to note that Nicolson's father was British consul general in Budapest and Nicolson passed painful years in Budapest as a child.

8

WAITING FOR THE WINDS TO CHANGE

HUNGARY LARGELY AVOIDED THE RAVAGES OF THE SECOND World War until the German occupation of the country in March 1944. Although Hungarian troops had been fighting against the Red Army on the eastern front under supreme German command since 1941, the Allies had not bombed Hungary, public provision was adequate in spite of the introduction of the ration-card system, the increasing demand for military equipment and supplies generated economic growth, wages rose, domestic tourism underwent yearly expansion beginning in 1939, the Hungarian movie industry produced a steady stream of films, opposition parties were active in the National Assembly, and the press reflected a fairly broad range of political opinion. Moreover, although Jewish men had been conscripted into labor battalions in which they were often exposed to inhumane treatment and several discriminatory Jewish Laws had been adopted, Jews in Hungary did not face immediate threat to their physical well-being and were not confined to ghettos; however, after Hitler discovered that the Hungarian government had initiated cautious attempts to conclude a separate-peace agreement with the Allies, the führer ordered the German military to occupy Hungary. On March 19, 1944, the Wehrmacht invaded Hungary and replaced the country's pro-British government with a pro-German cabinet under the leadership of the longtime Hungarian envoy to Germany. The Gestapo arrested many opposition political officials and deported them to concentration camps in Mauthausen and other locations. Following Germany's occupation of Hungary, Nazi officials working with the ready cooperation of the Hungarian public administration quickly forced Jews to move into ghettos from which they were deported to the Auschwitz-Birkenau concentration and extermination camps. In slightly over two months, more than 437,000 Jews were deported from Hungary to these camps, where between 80 and 90 percent of them were murdered.[1] The Allies began to bomb

Hungary, and Hungarian citizens became acquainted with the horrors of war. In late August 1944, the Red Army reached the expanded frontier of Hungary at the Carpathian Mountains and one month later crossed the interwar borders of the country. The Battle of Budapest, one of the largest and most forgotten instances of urban warfare during the Second World War, took place from late November 1944 to mid-February 1945. On Christmas Eve 1944, Soviet troops fully encircled Budapest, whose one million residents had not been evacuated and were, therefore, forced to endure the siege in shelters of various types. On February 11, 1945, Hungarian and German troops defending the city were annihilated during an unsuccessful attempt to break out of the Soviet military blockade.[2] The Soviet army gained control over the entire territory of Hungary in early April 1945 and continued to advance westward.

The depredations of the Second World War devastated the Hungarian Turanist community. Allied bombs killed Turanian Society general secretary Elemér Virányi, his wife, and their one-year-old son at their home in Budapest on January 25, 1945. Benedek Baráthosi Balogh also perished in Budapest during the Soviet siege, while Ede Toroczkai Wigand died in the city on January 22, 1945, from bomb wounds suffered during an air raid.[3] Both Béla Vikár and former Hungarian Turan Alliance grand vizier Antal Szentgáli died in 1945, although several months after the end of the war. Jenő Cholnoky and his wife took refuge from the advancing Red Army in Balatonfüred on the north shore of Lake Balaton. However, after the Soviet military occupied the town, soldiers raped Cholnoky's wife, who died of injuries sustained during the assault.[4] Meanwhile, Cholnoky's house in Budapest was ransacked.[5] Many Hungarian Turanists emigrated to western Europe and North America after the Second World War. Vilmos Pröhle fled to Germany, where he died in Berchtesgaden in 1946.[6] The sons of Alajos Paikert settled in the United States, while diplomat Félix Pogrányi Nagy, who served as the Turanian Society's Sumerian- and Etruscan-language instructor, wound up in Argentina. In 1949, the former managing director of the Hungarian Turan Alliance, László Túrmezei, moved to New Zealand after living for a few years in the British zone of occupation in Austria.[7] Túrmezei participated actively in the Turanian movement in exile until his death in 1978 and was a member of the Hungarian Communion of Friends (Magyar Baráti Közösség)—a circle of exiled intellectuals with moderate political views—that was founded in the United States in the late 1960s and has continued to function until the present day. László

Békássy, the former head of Hungary's consulate in Berlin, settled on his family estate west of Budapest following a short period of internment at the end of the Second World War. Here Békássy and his sister Gyöngyi Békássy came into the crosshairs of the communist political police known as the State Protection Authority (ÁVH). In 1950, the ÁVH sent László Békássy's dossier to Soviet advisors with the ominous note "for General Slepnov!" attached to it.[8] Although the former Horthy-era diplomat and Szálasi-government official was never arrested, Fejér County police kept him under surveillance until 1964 and closed his dossier, which reveals a shattered life interspersed with family tragedy, only after he died in 1977. A 1950 police report stated that Gyöngyi Békássy was living on a small parcel of land that the chief forester of her former estate was cultivating for her. Nothing else is known regarding the postwar life and activities of the former feminist and radical Turanist.[9] Journalist Iván Nagy, who had been an active member of the Turanian Society's Finno-Ugric wing and had served as the head of the foreign ministry press department in the Szálasi administration, fled before the advancing Soviets to Austria, where the United States Army took him into custody in September 1945 and handed him over to Hungarian authorities the following month. In 1946, Nagy was sentenced to two years in prison and deprived of his political rights for five years after being found guilty of crimes against the people for his affiliation with the Arrow Cross Party, implementation of the Szálasi government's press censorship policies, and membership in the Scientific Racial Protection Society.[10] In 1951, Nagy—as well as former *Turán* editor in chief Aladár Bán and Turanian Society general secretary Frigyes Lukinich—were among the members of the former "ruling classes" expelled from the city of Budapest after having their homes confiscated.[11] Nagy subsequently settled in the village of Solymár, where he earned his living as a language teacher. State-security organizations continued to keep tabs on Nagy during his residency in Solymár, though he never again faced retribution for his previous affiliation with right-wing political and scientific organizations. Information regarding an informant contained in a 1957 state-security report reveals the probable reason for this: "Solymár resident Dr. Iván Nagy, agent of the Pest County Political Department. His liaison, Lt. Comrade János Pató."[12]

Others who had been affiliated with the Turanist movement such as Vilma Mányoki, who had served as Béla Vikár's assistant in the La Fontaine Literary Society, and Hungarian Turan Alliance librarian György

Boér were subjected to criminal prosecution following the Second World War as well. Mányoki was charged in connection with several articles she had published in *Turán* regarding women's national defense organizations in Finland, but she was exonerated due to lack of evidence, testimony from numerous people regarding her actions to rescue Jews during the war, and the fact that she herself was partly Jewish—which in the context of the post–Second World War period served to exclude individuals from the possibility of having propagated fascist ideology.[13] Accusations against Boér were based on antisemitic references contained in the Polish language book that he had published shortly before the war; however, a 1948 presidential amnesty prevented him from facing punishment for this offense.[14]

In 1945–1946, most Turanists who held state positions were placed under examination to determine if their wartime and prewar political activities disqualified them from public employment. Those who underwent such screening included law professor István Csekey, entomologist Gyula Krepuska, art historian Zoltán Felvinczi Takács, and composer Gábor Gergelyffy, who had been the director of the Turanian Society during the last eight years of the organization's existence.[15] The examination committee determined that the violinist Mrs. Félix Ávedik, whose maiden name was Alice Felvinczi Takács, was "unsuitable to hold office" because she had "belonged to the right-wing segment of musical life" and had played in the same orchestra as the wife of Arrow Cross government justice minister László Budinszky.[16] Mrs. Félix Ávedik petitioned to have this decision overturned, but there is no information available regarding the outcome of her appeal. The daughter of Zoltán Felvinczi Takács was part of the small Turanism-inspired intellectual circle to which the painter and graphic artist Gyula Szörényi belonged and became the godmother of the latter's youngest son, Levente, the future singer and songwriter for the rock group Illés who played a key role in the birth of Hungarian rock music in the 1960s. Szörényi recalled the influence that his godmother had exercised over his musical and intellectual development in a 2015 biography:

> At home we had earlier learned to play an instrument from my godmother, "auntie" Alice Felvinczi Takács. It is true that this was the violin. Auntie Alice's father was Zoltán Felvinczi Takács, the founder and director of the East Asian Museum and a noted art historian during the prewar period. One of his books was on my shelf when I was a kid among my old man's books. The figure on the cover was so frightful that I didn't ever look at it. At least not then. However, as an adult the book, *Buddha útján a Távol-Keleten* [On the pathway of Buddha in the Far East], meant a lot to me.[17]

Former Church of Turanian Monotheists leader Zoltán Bencsi did not pass through the Hungarian Bar Association's screening process.[18] Bencsi's son Attila was interned at the infamous Recsk Labor Camp in northern Hungary a few years after his father's death in June 1947.[19] Although none of those mentioned here—perhaps with the exception of Bencsi, whose vetting documentation has been lost—were prosecuted for their affiliation with Turanism, the movement gained such a bad reputation following the Second World War that those subjected to political screening during the postwar years almost always avoided mentioning their previous participation in Turanist organizations and activities. Only Vilma Mányoki openly stated that she had "been a member of the Turanian Society since 1937," although she noted that this organization was "not the same as the chauvinist Turanian Alliance" and was able to refer to the fact that a presumably left-wing people's prosecutor had hidden her Jewish mother during the 1944–1945 Hungarian Holocaust.[20] Available evidence suggests that retired commercial school teacher and longtime proponent of Turanism Lajos Sassi Nagy was the only person whose earlier Turanist pursuits entailed legal repercussions. In August 1945, police in the small town of Maglód detained Sassi Nagy based on a criminal complaint connected to the book *A turánizmus, mint nemzeti, faji és világeszme* (Turanism as a national, racial, and world concept) that he had published in 1918 and republished in 1942 with updated sections pertaining to ideas such as the establishment of a "German-Turanian World Alliance." Police released Sassi Nagy after he made the following statement: "My fanatical Hungarianness and my belief in the Turanist idea alone guided me in my act. . . . Through the affirmation of this idea I attempted merely to promote the restoration of Greater Hungary as a state complex based on the geographical unity of the Carpathian Basin. I am not nor have ever been a member of a political party. For a few years I was a member of the Turanian Alliance, which was an association established exclusively for the purpose of research regarding races and peoples and did not deal with daily political affairs."[21] Although the office of the people's prosecutor indicted the seventy-eight-year-old Sassi Nagy, his wife shortly thereafter informed authorities that her husband had "unfortunately died."[22]

Many believed that the presence of Soviet troops in Hungary and neighboring countries was only temporary. The political system that functioned in Hungary between 1945 and 1947–1948 can be characterized as a semidemocracy: during this period, the moderate right-wing Independent

Smallholders Party won a National Assembly election, the government implemented land reform, and the press represented a wide range of opinions even if criticism of the Soviet Union or the Soviet military and vindication of the pre-1945 political systems were taboo. However, in late 1946 and early 1947, the Hungarian Communist Party, which had received only 17 percent of the vote in the first postwar general election, began to build a dictatorial regime similar to those in other states of east-central Europe with the support of the Soviet Union. Beginning at this time, the Hungarian Communist Party–controlled Interior Ministry and political police began to arrest officials from non-left-wing parties and stage show trials, and many sectors of Hungary's economy underwent nationalization. In 1947, Prime Minister Ferenc Nagy was forced to resign and remain abroad, and the Hungarian Communist Party won a National Assembly election in which it obtained only 22 percent of the vote in spite of engaging in open fraud. In 1945, many still believed that the Soviet army would remain in Hungary only until the conclusion of the postwar peace treaty and that the USSR would refrain from forcing the countries of central and eastern Europe to adopt its political system.

On August 14, 1945, with the process of vetting Turanists in full swing, former Turanian Society executive president Domokos Szent-Iványi submitted a request to the Interior Ministry for permission to resume the organization's activity.[23] Ministry of Religion and Public Education advisor Géza Paikert, the son of Turanian Society founder Alajos Paikert and himself a former member of the Turanian Society's board, unsurprisingly petitioned Interior Ministry officials to approve this request.[24] On September 21, 1945, former Turanian Society officials convened to elect new organizational leaders. Just over one year later, in October 1946, the Turanian Society resumed operations at its former location in the Hungarian Parliament Building under the name Hungarian People's Kinship Society. Domokos Szent-Iványi conducted the initial meeting of the reconstituted Turanian Society at which Turkologist and university professor Gyula Németh was appointed to serve as the organization's president in place of Jenő Cholnoky.[25] Németh, who had worked as an editor of the Turanian Society periodical *Turán* during the First World War, had refrained from participating in the organization's activities during the interwar period and the Second World War because, according to the minutes of the meeting, "later [after the First World War] tendencies with which he could not identify himself prevailed within the Society. . . . He notes that the Society has recently behaved in very sensible fashion." Németh remarked that many people had shunned the Turanian Society because they associated it with the more extreme elements of the Turanist movement that harbored Eastern dreams and advocated breaking away from the West. Németh stated that the objectives of the Hungarian People's Kinship Society should be to investigate previously neglected themes regarding the Uyghurs, Kazakhs, and Turks; to present the culture of related peoples; to establish contacts with associations operated by these peoples; to maintain connections with scientific organizations such as the Hungarian Academy of Sciences and the Kőrösi Csoma Society; and to continue to conduct language courses. The newly appointed president emphasized that the organization must be careful to avoid sponsoring the viewpoints of dilettantes and warned that he was prepared to vacate his position if things did not go well.

Németh furthermore expressed the hope that the Hungarian People's Kinship Society would receive government financial support that it could use to pay for the publication of grammar books, the translation of literature, and the granting of scholarships. Németh's references to related peoples clearly pertained to those who spoke Mongolic, Tungusic, and Turkic languages as well as those who spoke Uralic languages and Bulgarian, which he considered to be close to Hungarian though of different linguistic origin. The Turkologist stated that although the Hungarian-Japanese and Hungarian-Korean linguistic relationship had not been proven, he had "left open" the possibility that such connections existed. However, with regard to alleged kinship between Hungarians and Etruscans, Sumerians, South Asian Indians, and Chinese, he asserted that "those who proclaim [these relationships] are chasing illusions." Finally, Németh declared that the Hungarian People's Kinship Society must "acquaint national public opinion with research surrounding related peoples because the unique character of our national life can be accentuated in this way."[26] The list of the organization's leaders contains the names of all the old veterans of the Turanist movement, including the ailing Alajos Paikert as honorary president for life, who had remained in Hungary and not compromised themselves politically as well as those of individuals affiliated with the previously mentioned Hungarian Community and the Independent Smallholders' Party and some former students of Pál Teleki. Officials from the communist-controlled Interior Ministry surely noticed that the Turanian Society had reconstituted itself in the spirit of "business as usual." Although the Hungarian People's Kinship Society attempted to pacify possible suspicion regarding its political orientation through the cooption of some influential members of the new regime as well as left-wing or even communist intellectuals, several prominent Turanists—such as Domokos Szent-Iványi and Miklós Majthényi, the final president of the Hungarian Turan Alliance—became implicated in the Hungarian Society affair beginning in early 1947.[27] In March of that year, the Interior Ministry asked the Budapest police to dissolve the "Hungarian People's Kinship Association–Turanian Society" and requested that the dreaded ÁVH open a file on the organization.[28] The ÁVH seized the organization's premises and books, while conversations that Gyula Németh held with political-police authorities led him to conclude by at least early 1948 that revival of the Turanist association was inopportune from every standpoint.[29]

However, the ÁVH somewhat surprisingly did not appear to focus significant attention on Turanism, and those affiliated with the movement were not portrayed as enemies of the people during the Hungarian Community trial or at any other time. State-security reports regarding the Turanist movement and its adherents were brief, amateurish, and full of errors, often failing to make the proper distinction between the Turanian Society, the Hungarian Turan Alliance, and the Turanian Hunters.[30] During research for this book, the author discovered only one source referring to communist-era political-police action against a Turanist organization—an ÁVH dossier from the early 1950s regarding an attempt to weaken the remnants of the National Association of Turanian Hunters network in Hungary. According to this file, subversion of the Turanian Hunters would serve to compromise the Hungarian Community and, perhaps, National Assembly representative Mrs. Endre Bajcsy-Zsilinszky, one of the main exponents of the cult that had emerged surrounding her late husband, the anti-Nazi resistance leader Endre Bajcsy-Zsilinszky, whom Arrow Cross authorities had sent to the gallows in December 1944. Moreover, the ÁVH could thereby prevent the National Association of Turanian Hunters from carrying through with its plan to ensure that in the event of a rebellion against communist rule, "armed groups composed of Turanist members would be capable of action."[31] There is no evidence suggesting that the ÁVH ever implemented the measures envisaged in the file.

Authorities also took an interest in local Turanist organizations based in cities such as Csepel, Balassagyarmat, and Miskolc.[32] However, their reliance on information from the residents of these cities sometimes led to false conclusions, such as those contained in a police report on the Balassagyarmat branch of the Turanian Society, which had been one of the most dynamic chapters of the organization in provincial Hungary in 1930–1933, stating that it had never been truly active.[33] The story of Orosháza resident Mihály Virasztó, who went by the name Koppány Virrasztó, is a prime example of what happened to those who continued to publicly espouse Turanist ideas during the communist era.[34] Virrasztó studied electrical engineering in Pozsony (Bratislava, Slovakia) and worked as a technician for the Hungarian postal service in Budapest before returning to Orosháza in the southeastern part of Hungary, where he opened a radio-repair workshop in 1942 after an unsuccessful attempt to earn a living in agriculture. In the mid-1930s, Virrasztó organized the Orosháza branch of one of the many small National Socialist parties that functioned in Hungary during this period, thus prompting local officials to initiate at least a dozen legal proceedings against him for offenses ranging from traffic violations—for which police confiscated his bicycle—to religious incitement in an attempt to restrain his political activity.[35] At the same time, Virrasztó became one of the most active disciples of the Church of Turanian Monotheists in provincial Hungary, where he disseminated Chief Shaman Zoltán Bencsi's previously mentioned publications as well as the sect's periodical *Turáni Roham*. Moreover, Virrasztó was presumably the Church of Turanian Monotheist bonze who had been the subject of a widely reported April 1936 canard regarding the incision of an infant's face with a knife as part of an initiation ritual, sensational news that likely contributed to the decision of the National Socialist party with which he was affiliated to expel him from its ranks the same month.

However, Virrasztó was not the type of person who allowed such setbacks to deter him, defiance reflected in his scolding of Endre László after the powerful Gödöllő chief magistrate had failed to call on him during a stay in Orosháza but did visit the local magistrate of "Romanian race."[36] Virrasztó was found guilty of a series of transgressions that included the defamation of judges and failure to pay the church tax and served a four-and-a-half-year prison sentence in Szeged.[37] Following the Second World War, authorities monitored Virrasztó's activities and kept him under constant surveillance after discovering an unauthorized weapon in his house in Orosháza following the 1956 revolution.[38] He nevertheless continued to publicly denounce communists, Jews, and priests and conducted brisk correspondence with former Church of Turanian Monotheists associates and members of the ancient-history subculture.[39] Virrasztó also wrote both signed and unsigned letters to state organizations and daily newspapers and transformed his radio-repair workshop into an information hub of sorts after the renewal of his trade permit in 1960. According to state-security reports, he otherwise lived the life of a respectable citizen, relaxing at the local steam bath every Sunday and spending evenings at a pastry shop exchanging news with friends and acquaintances. However, state-security officials decided to take drastic action against Virrasztó after he failed to heed several warnings to change his ways (one operative stated in a report that he had a "cantankerous, wise-guy nature").[40] As early as the 1930s, doubts had surfaced regarding Virrasztó's sanity.[41] In 1938, authorities ordered personnel at the Szeged prison at which Virrasztó was incarcerated to monitor his state of mind after he had declared during his trial: "This has been the Hungarian fate for 900 years, prison and the gallows are the places for true Hungarians. This is the fate of all true Hungarians, Habsburg intrigues drove Széchenyi to Döbling."[42] In 1963, a specialist determined in the course of legal proceedings that had been launched against Virrasztó in connection with his aforementioned letters that he suffered from "mental illness characterized by delusions" and was unaware of the danger that his actions posed to society. Virrasztó was subsequently forced to undergo psychiatric treatment.[43] After completing a second mandatory stint at a mental hospital in 1968, Virrasztó was placed under the legal guardianship of his wife, and his state-security dossier was closed.

Authorities also harassed Turanists who lived in Budapest, though to a somewhat lesser degree than they did those in provincial Hungary. In 1965, for example, retired Hungarian Royal Army lieutenant colonel Vilmos Simsay, a convicted Second World War criminal who made his living through odd jobs and the sale of books, was prosecuted for disseminating "banned literature" among his friends. Although Simsay got off with a warning, the judge who presided over the retired military officer's case ordered the confiscation of his books and other literature, including an article entitled "A turáni eszme gyakorlati értéke" (The practical value of the Turanian concept) that he had published in the *Katonai Közlöny* (Military gazette) in 1926.[44]

Post–Second World War legal procedures such as those described here highlighted certain rifts that had developed within the Turanist movement. Although influential Turanists such as Mihály Kmoskó, Benedek Baráthosi Balogh, and Alajos Paikert had advocated the concept of Hungarian-Sumerian kinship beginning in the 1910s, the Turanian Society did not officially endorse this notion. It did, however, publish articles supporting the purported relationship between the Hungarians and the Sumerians in its periodical *Turán*.[45] Furthermore, the survival of Finno-Ugric linguistics in the new postwar regime as a result of the connection between Finno-Ugric kinship and the Soviet Union / communism served to intensify the longtime conflict between linguists and those who opposed their methods and conclusions. In 1963, for example, László Bendefy made the following statement in a letter to former fellow Turanist Lajos Marjalaki Kiss: "It is extremely fortunate that the linguists have begun to be pushed aside. They caused a million problems!"[46]

In 1960, the First International Finno-Ugric Conference was held in Budapest. This conference not only embodied the significance that Finno-Ugric scholarship had attained in communist Hungary but also marked the return and unofficial rehabilitation of the eighty-eight-year-old Turanist Aladár Bán, whose translation of the Estonian national epic *Kalevipoeg* was republished for the event.[47] However, Aladár Bán died before the republication of his translation of *Kalevipoeg*, and the Finno-Ugric conference was a great disappointment to some longtime Turanist Finno-Ugrists such as former Turanian Society general secretary Frigyes Lukinich, who complained in a letter to Bán's widow that while attending the conference he had felt like a holdover from a bygone era "whose work was not interesting and which they had happily forgotten." Lukinich noted in the letter that he would have gladly spoken at the conference about the Livonians, though nobody had asked him to do so, even though he and "my dear old Aladár" had for fifteen years organized contacts with members of this Finnic ethnic group. The former Turanian Society general secretary, who, like Bán, had been among those expelled from Budapest in the early 1950s, added with regard to the way in which he was treated under the new regime: "I received the highest awards in the fraternal states while here at home I was persecuted, then deported and lived for more than two years in a stable in Csanádapáca on the Great Hungarian Plain with my elderly mother and my daughter. They took away our home, over which I have now regained ownership rights on the grounds that a mistake was made."[48] Former members of the Turanian Society, such as the architect Jenő Lechner, the blood-group researcher Endre Jeney, and the anthropologist Lajos Bartucz, who had survived the Second World War and remained in Hungary were forced to gloss over their previous activities as part of the organization in order to reintegrate themselves into the postwar system. Less compliant

Turanists were subjected to persecution and ostracism. The architect István Medgyaszay, for example, was forced to endure extreme poverty and
continual harassment throughout the 1950s. Although Medgyaszay and his
family members were surprisingly allowed to continue living in their house
in Budapest, they were compelled to share the residence with other ten-
ants.[49] The ailing Medgyaszay may have found some degree of solace in an
article praising his work that Lechner published in honor of his eightieth
birthday in the periodical *Magyar Építőművészet* (Hungarian architecture)
in 1957.[50] According to Medgyaszay's son-in-law, the elderly architect spoke
on his deathbed about the windows on the Shah-i-Zinda Necropolis in Samarkand and how much he would like to travel to the regions lying beyond
the city.[51]

Other Turanists, such as the painter-librarian Ferenc Zajti, seemed not
to notice the change in political winds. Following the Second World War,
Zajti continued to pursue his interests in painting and Hungarian-Indian
kinship after being forced to retire from his position at the Municipal Library in Budapest as a partial result of his alleged participation in far-right
activities in 1944.[52] Zajti maintained contacts with like-minded intellectuals, which along with his visits to the embassy of India in Budapest drew
the attention of the ÁVH. In 1952, Zajti attempted to prevent the threatened
withdrawal of his pension by noting that in 1945 he had donated a portrait of Tolstoy to a Moscow gallery and that in 1949 he had held a lecture
at the Franz Liszt Academy of Music in Budapest entitled "The Cultural
Contacts of the Ancient Soviet-Russian Lands with India in Antiquity and
the Middle Ages."[53] In 1955, Zajti presented Deputy Minister of People's
Culture Ernő Mihályfi with a comprehensive plan for the establishment
of an Indian-Hungarian cultural institute, which stipulated, among other
details, that espresso and pilaf be served at the institute's cafeteria.[54] In
this proposal, Zajti expressed his belief in Hungarian-Hun-Gurjar kinship, supporting this notion with photographs that whimsically included
a portrait of the elderly Jenő Cholnoky as a representation of the "ancient
Hungarian type." Zajti's plan for the Hungarian-Indian institute resembled
that prepared for the Collegium Hungaricum in Bombay in 1929 but replaced the nationalist phraseology used in the latter with quotes from Soviet scientists and scholars.[55] This was not a manifestation of opportunism:
Zajti was willing to deal with officials affiliated with any political ideology
as long as they promoted his profound convictions regarding Hungarian
kinship and ancient history.

Former Hungarian-Nippon Society executive vice president István Mezey, who had also served as a longtime member of the Turanian Society's board of directors, was able to continue to practice law during the period of communist rule in Hungary and in 1963 was even permitted to publish a work of juvenile fiction regarding the East entitled *Kelet magyar vándorai* (Hungarian wanderers of the East). When Mezey died in 1970, he was still working as a lawyer and as a legal advisor to the embassy of Sweden in Budapest.[56] The preservation of Finno-Ugric scholarship in Hungary following the Second World War served to revitalize unconventional theories regarding the origin of the Hungarian language that even some Turanists had rejected before 1945, imbuing them with the status of "national science" and the spirit of opposition to the new regime. These unorthodox theories flourished primarily among radical Turanists, such as Sándor Szöllőssy, Sándor Hajnóczy, Barna Kósa, Sándor Zsuffa, Sándor Széll, and Adorján Magyar, who had emigrated following the war and published articles presenting their ideas in periodicals such as the Buenos Aires–based *Turán* and *A Nap Fiai* (Sons of the sun). Some publications expounding alternative versions of Hungarian ancient history surprisingly cited the works of former minister of justice and minister of foreign affairs Erik Molnár (1894–1966), a staunch communist and director of the Institute of History of the Hungarian Academy of Sciences who did not discount the possibility of a Hungarian ancient homeland in Central Asia.[57]

The concept of Hungarian-Sumerian kinship was the most prevalent alternative ancient-history theory within the Hungarian émigré community following the Second World War. Dr. Ida Bobula (1900–1981), who had earned a PhD in history from Budapest University and been one of the most prominent advocates of Christianity-based women's liberation in Hungary during the interwar period, was one of the leading proponents of Hungarian-Sumerian kinship.[58] It would be a mistake to regard Bobula as an inherent partisan of the extreme right. She was of Slovak origin through her grandfather, the noted architect and political official János Bobula, and as the director of the Catholic Sarolta College, she sheltered Polish refugees in Hungary during the Second World War and was thus able to serve as one of the primary witnesses for the defense of former ministerial advisor Iván Nagy during his people's tribunal hearing.[59] Shortly after the Second World War, Ida Bobula emigrated to the United States, where she had lived for several years in the 1920s. In the United States, she filled auxiliary positions at various educational institutions and conducted research to support the hypothesis that the Hungarian and Sumerian languages were related to one another. In 1948, Bobula wrote enthusiastically to her former professor Sándor Domanovszky that "we must ask for a retrial [because] back at that time [the interwar period] the Hungarian scientific world impetuously discarded the issue of the Sumerian-Hungarian connection."[60] After receiving an "incredulous" response from her erstwhile mentor, Bobula dispatched a letter to Géza Paikert, who had also emigrated to the United States, asking him to forward a summary of her ideas regarding Hungarian-Sumerian kinship to his gravely ill father, Alajos Paikert, in Budapest: "Send this copy to your father along with my very respectful greetings," Bobula wrote, adding that "It will soon become clear that they were totally and perfectly correct with their Turanian fancies." Géza Paikert sent the recapitulation to his father along with the following exuberant note: "Bobula's research is a landmark in the history of Turanism! Your theories have in every way been vindicated and here in the USA the most serious scientific circles have already acknowledged them. Bobula has highlighted your name everywhere in the most loyal fashion. Bravo, I offer you my hearty congratulations!"[61] However, Alajos Paikert died at the end of July 1948, just a few weeks after his son wrote these lines. Ida Bobula was therefore compelled to search for another patron.

Bobula eventually found Debrecen Sumerologist and theology professor Zsigmond Varga to support her effort to promote the idea of Hungarian-Sumerian linguistic affinity.[62] In 1915, a prominent linguist published criticism of Varga's viewpoints regarding the Hungarian-Sumerian linguistic relationship in the periodical *Magyar Nyelvőr* (Hungarian language guardian) that served to impede his habilitation at the university in Kolozsvár and employment at the university in Debrecen.[63] However, Varga—who had studied for years at the best universities in Germany and was one of the few experts on Sumerian civilization who had actually attained proficiency in the Sumerian language—nevertheless received a teaching position at the Debrecen Royal Hungarian University in 1921 as a result of his excellent qualifications and eventually rose to occupy various important academic offices at the institution. Although Varga's extensive publications regarding the history of religion, notably the Old Testament, have remained useful to this day, many Hungarian scholars regarded his Sumerological research with skepticism by the 1920s.[64] Zsigmond Varga was not directly engaged in the Turanist movement, but he did serve on the board of the Hungarian-Indian Society. Nor was he affiliated with the group of Debrecen intellectuals and academics, such as István Ecsedi, János Sőregi, Ferenc Medgyessy, Jenő Darkó, Rezső Milleker, Géza Lencz, and István Rugonfalvi Kiss, who espoused the Eastern idea. Varga's lack of active participation in Turanist organizations and social circles was presumably due to the paralysis from which he suffered as a result of a neurological disease. Following the Second World War, Varga's physical and emotional distress intensified as a result of this progressive paralytic disorder and the 1945 death of his son, a Reformed pastor, at one of the Gusen concentration camps. In December 1948, Ida Bobula wrote a letter to Debrecen university literature professor János Hankiss in which she inquired about the possibility of contacting the sixty-two-year-old Varga: "I am immensely interested to know what the old gentleman wrote in [his book]: as far as I know, he was the last of the Mohicans who amid general disapproval proclaimed Sumerian-Hungarian kinship and all of us urgently neglected to read his book. Is the old gentleman still alive and is it possible to talk to him? I would like to repentantly ask him for forgiveness in the name of all of us because I now see that he was right and in a couple of years everybody will certainly see this."[65] In February 1949, Bobula wrote in a letter to Varga:

> The Sumerians have not become extinct and they shall never perish. . . . It is my hope that with this clue [one of Varga's books] we will be able to determine not only the origin of certain words, but the old secret of the origin of the Hungarian nation as well. And I have devoted my own life to this just as Sándor Kőrösi Csoma and my good professor did. The result is in the hands of God. I am very alone here [in the United States] with my work. The Philadelphia Sumerologists [and] neo-Halévy school don't even want to hear about common descent. . . . I think with inexpressible gratitude about the decades in which the good professor steadfastly upheld the sacred Hungarian truth of a theory that in an environment of icy indifference had become unpopular and ridiculous. I had to come across the ocean in order to see the significance and importance of that, but I now see it.[66]

Over the following six years, Bobula and Varga conducted regular correspondence that included the exchange of scientific viewpoints, clothing, coffee, and drawings of flowers and birds. In 1955, Varga asked Bobula to coauthor a book entitled *Magyar mitológia* (Hungarian mythology); however, the intellectual environment that prevailed amid the dictatorship in Hungary and the elderly professor's death in 1956 impeded its publication.

In the meantime, Bobula was writing independent works in the United States, some of them in English. In 1951, she published the book *Sumerian Affiliations: A Plea for Reconsideration.* Bobula also presented her ideas regarding the Hungarian-Sumerian connection at the annual conferences of various archaeological, historical, and Orientalist associations. The response of convention guests—few if any of whom were familiar with both the Hungarian and Sumerian languages—to Bobula's theories was mixed. However, her lectures occasionally met with strong approval, such as when she spoke to a Hungarian audience in New York: "I held a lecture regarding the Sumerian question at the request of the New York Transylvanian Alliance. It was a major success, the audience tumultuously applauded the idea of Sumerian kinship. Two people quibbled and contradicted. The only reason the audience didn't clobber them was because they ridiculed them. Soon we shall reap what we have sown."[67] Bobula published a half dozen more books regarding Sumerian-Hungarian linguistic affinity over the remaining decades of her life, which she spent amid relative privation. Bobula's scholarly activity in the United States linked via the person of Zsigmond Varga the sporadic pre-1918 manifestations of the Hungarian-Sumerian kinship tradition with certain ideas that became prevalent within the Hungarian émigré community following the Second World War.[68] Her work also served as a point of reference for researchers, such as Tibor Baráth, Viktor Padányi, and Ferenc Badiny Jós, who revived the Turanism-associated notion of Sumerian-Hungarian linguistic kinship in postcommunist Hungary.

Tibor Baráth (1906–1992), who, like Ida Bobula, had studied history under Professor Sándor Domanovszky in Budapest, spent the 1930s living in Paris before receiving a teaching position at the university in Kolozsvár after the city was transferred back to Hungary along with the northern section of Transylvania in 1940. Baráth, who had gravitated steadily toward the radical right, then became an official in the Ministry of Religion and Public Education at the time of the Arrow Cross government in late 1944.[69] Following the Second World War, Baráth first returned to France before moving to Canada in the early 1950s. After settling in Canada, he began to deal seriously with Hungarian ancient history and between 1968 and 1974 published a three-volume book entitled *A magyar népek őstörténete* (The ancient history of the Hungarian peoples). In this work, Baráth attempted to synthesize the diverse theories regarding the ancient Hungarian homeland, which he placed in a broad area extending from the Caucasus through Mesopotamia to Egypt. Baráth estimated in this book that in the thirteenth century BC, around thirty million people belonged to Hungarian tribes known by various names.[70]

Viktor Padányi earned a PhD in history in 1943 and subsequently worked for a short time as a high school teacher, eventually becoming an active member of the far-right Party of Hungarian Renewal (Magyar Megújulás Pártja) in the city of Szeged. In 1945, he fled from Hungary to Austria, where he lived for several years before emigrating to Australia. After settling permanently in the latter country, Padányi published many books on Hungarian history as well as poetry and plays. Padányi's works included *Dentu-Magyaria*, a history of the Hungarians before their arrival to the Carpathian Basin that appeared shortly before his death in 1963. In this book, Padányi cited Ida Bobula's previous research to support the thesis of Sumerian-Hungarian kinship and his conclusion that the ancient Hungarian homeland was located in the southern Caucasus. Padányi was among the early proponents of the notion that the Finno-Ugric language family was a Habsburg machination contrived to inhibit the development of the Hungarian national identity.

Ferenc Badiny Jós (1909–2007) published articles such as "Pilóták korszerű kiképzése" (Modern pilot training) after undertaking a career as an officer in the Hungarian Royal Army. However, he was forced to leave the military due to injuries suffered during a skiing accident and thereafter earned his living as a crop wholesaler and guest house manager in the town of Hévíz along Lake Balaton.[71] After the Second World War, Badiny Jós emigrated to Argentina, where, under the influence of former diplomat and Turanian Society Etruscan-language instructor Félix Pogrányi Nagy, he began to deal intensively with Sumerology and, beginning in the 1960s, published many books on the subject that moved beyond the idea of Sumerian-Hungarian kinship.[72] Badiny Jós also launched a Chinese friendship movement and wrote a book in which he argued that Jesus was Parthian rather than Jewish based on propositions that closely resembled those on which Ferenc Zajti had based his claim that Jesus was of Scythian origin in his 1936 work *Zsidó volt-e Krisztus?* (Was Christ a Jew?). As a professor at a Jesuit university in Argentina, Badiny Jós had the opportunity to present his unconventional theses on ancient history at several international conferences in the 1960s and 1970s. In 1973, he founded the still-published periodical *Ősi Gyökér* (Ancient root) as a vehicle for propagating his ideas. Following the end of the communist era, Badiny Jós returned to Hungary, where in his eighties and nineties, he popularized his interpretation of ancient history in articles and television interviews and had his previous works republished. Badiny Jós also played a significant role in the foundation of the King Lajos the Great Private University in Miskolc, an institution that specializes in the instruction of esoteric ancient-history theories and at which the papers of the maverick historian and Sumerologist are kept.[73] Statues, commemorative plaques, and memorial rooms have recently been dedicated in honor of Badiny Jós in Losonc (Lučenec, Slovakia), Balassagyarmat, and Hévíz.

During the period of state socialism, the previously cited works circulated among a small group of intellectuals in Hungary, and following the years of repression in the 1950s, Turanists who had remained in the country reconstituted their networks of connections, social circles, and chains of solidarity. Former military officer Sándor Zsuffa, who had published articles in *Turán* before 1944, disseminated a manuscript entitled *A magyarországi szumír probléma állása különböző korokban* (The status of the Sumerian problem in Hungary during various periods) that represented a frontal attack against Finno-Ugric linguistic kinship and was among the first works to portray nineteenth-century linguists József Budenz and Pál Hunfalvy as agents of Habsburg intrigue and to denounce dual monarchy–era minister of religion and public education Ágoston Trefort as a proponent of Finno-Ugrism.[74] In 1976, Mrs. György Hary Gizella Némethy published an article entitled "Kiegészítések egy nyelvvita történetéhez" (Addenda to the history of a linguistic dispute) in the Society for Dissemination of Scientific Knowledge periodical *Valóság* (Truth) that presumably based the following assertion regarding Trefort's alleged promotion of Finno-Ugric linguistic kinship on information from Sándor Nemesdedinai Zsuffa's book: "In 1876, Education Minister Ágoston Trefort called together Hungarian linguists and, according to the minutes, at the end of the conference declared that 'we need European, not Asian, relatives' and therefore in the future only those who pursue studies supporting Finnish-Hungarian kinship will be eligible for state scholarships, college placement and foreign study trips."[75] This anecdote circulated widely and to this day is frequently cited in arguments challenging the validity of Finno-Ugric kinship, although not even meticulous research has uncovered its factual basis and the quote attributed to Trefort is most likely apocryphal. Mrs. György Hary Gizella Némethy worked as a secretary at a historical institute and was associated with the theosophical subculture that reconstituted itself during the darkest period of dictatorship in postwar Hungary and subsequently became so active that in 1969 or 1970 state-security officials started a dossier on it under the name "contemplators" and initiated operations aimed at weakening the group.[76]

Némethy, who, in addition to conducting research on ancient history, translated books on theosophy and foot massage into Hungarian, belonged to a group of people who focused on the issue of Sumerian-Hungarian linguistic kinship that had coalesced around András Zakar (1912–1986), the former secretary of Cardinal József Mindszenty, the archbishop of Esztergom. Mindszenty was imprisoned on fabricated charges following a show trial in 1949. He was released from prison during the anticommunist popular revolt in Hungary in October 1956 and following the suppression of the uprising took refuge in the United States Embassy in Budapest. After spending the following fifteen years at the embassy, Mindszenty was permitted to leave for Austria, where he died in 1971. András Zakar was condemned to a six-year prison term in 1949 but remained in Hungary following his release and surprisingly managed to obtain a certain degree of rehabilitation in 1970. The extraordinarily dynamic Zakar, who had earned a university degree in engineering, organized and galvanized those in his environment.[77] He managed to have some articles propounding Sumerian-Hungarian kinship published in respected scholarly journals, though international Sumerologists and Assyriologists uniformly rejected his arguments in support of this theory.[78] The large number of state-security reports on Zakar reveal that he voiced antisemitic opinions in conversation with his associates, describe how he was able to smuggle his manuscripts out of Hungary, and detail his relations with Hungarian émigrés who held similar beliefs, particularly those affiliated with the *Magyar Történelmi Szemle* (Hungarian historical review) published in New York. Némethy enthusiastically exchanged books with Zakar.

In 1975, Némethy wrote to geodetic surveyor, geologist, historian, and author László Bendefy that she intended to send three Károly Pálfi–authored books on Hungarian ancient history and several articles to Zakar and Béla Oláh, a former cooperative director who was also an active member of the network of Turanists who had remained in Hungary. In this letter, Némethy remarked: "An anonymous article appeared in yesterday's *Esti Hírlap* [Evening news] entitled '*Hakasz-Minuszunszki medence—Itt jártak a szkíta hadak*' [The Khakass-Minusinsk hollow: The Scythian armies were here] in which the author introduces the findings of Soviet scholars and asserts at the end of the article that they confirm the ancient unity of the Asian, European and American peoples." The elderly Némethy, referring to a newspaper article entitled "Vámbéry, a nyelvész," concluded that the ideas presented in this article represented a trend: "What is this if not the slow preparation of public opinion for a new turning point?"[79] Némethy's letter is important for two reasons: on the one hand, it highlights the inclination of proponents of esoteric concepts regarding ancient history to interpret any minor indication of greater acceptance of their theories as a major breakthrough; on the other hand, its recipient was one of the scholars, along with ethnographer Gábor Lükő and Turkologist István Mándoky Kongur, who sustained Turanist/Eastern thought in Hungary during the period of state socialism and incorporated various elements of it into the Hungarian collective consciousness in the postcommunist period.[80] László Bendefy, whose papers preserved at the National Széchényi Library in Budapest provide a clear depiction of this network of intellectuals in spite of the fact that they have been redacted in order to eliminate politically sensitive subject matter, initially studied to become an engineer based on career advice obtained from Jenő Cholnoky during a meeting with the grand vizier of the Hungarian Turan Alliance shortly before graduating from high school in the town of Szentgotthárd in 1922.[81] Bendefy—who as an adult changed his surname from the Slavic-sounding *Benda*—earned a PhD in geology in 1929 but subsequently continued to pursue his ardent interests in history and geography. Bendefy spent his entire professional career engaged in activities related to geodesy and water management. In addition to reorganizing the Hungarian geodesic service following the Second World War, Bendefy edited a geodesic bibliography and compiled an enormous bibliography of the hand-drawn maps that are kept at various archives and museums in Hungary.

Moreover, in the 1930s, he began to conduct tireless research on the Eastern origins of the Hungarians. Bendefy not only was a member of the Turanian Society but also served as the organization's librarian and contributed regularly to *Turán*.[82] He also published several articles and other works on the roots of the Hungarians in the Caucasus, including three books that appeared between 1941 and 1945: *Kunmagyaria: A kaukázusi magyarság története* (Kunmagyaria: History of the Caucasian Hungarians); *A magyarság kaukázusi őshazája: Gyeretyán országa* (The Caucasian ancient homeland of the Hungarians: The realm of Gyeretyán); and *A magyarság és a Közép-Kelet* (The Hungarians and the Middle East). However, Bendefy published his most influential work, *Az ismeretlen Julianus* (The unknown Julian), several years before the Second World War—in 1936. This book, which was based on previously unknown or little-known Vatican documents and described the expedition that a group of Brother Julian–led Dominican friars made to the Southern Urals in the first half of the thirteenth century in order to find Hungariäns who had remained in the ancient homeland, inspired author János Kodolányi to write his 1938 novel *Julianus*.[83] Bendefy also published shorter works and bibliographies regarding Brother Julian and was among those who initiated the erection of a statue of the Dominican friar amid religious ceremony on Castle Hill in 1937 (and it can currently be found still standing next to the Budapest Hilton).[84] He was also involved in the tortuous effort to raise a statue in honor of Sándor Kőrösi Csoma to commemorate the one hundredth anniversary of the famous Hungarian Orientalist's death. In 1942, Bendefy wrote a letter to Jenő Cholnoky asking his mentor for assistance in this endeavor, remarking, "I have on one occasion already helped Your Honor to realize one of his dreams, the Julian statue."[85] Later that year, Transylvanian Reformed Church district chief clerk Sándor Tavaszy expressed dissatisfaction with the completed statue of Kőrösi Csoma, noting that district officials "adhere to the notion of highlighting Csoma's Székely-Hungarian character and do not regard the Buddhist-priest habit to be propitious."[86] In 1984, state and local government organizations finally approved the erection of the Kőrösi Csoma statue, which had been lying in storage at a warehouse in Budapest for decades, in the garden of the Hungarian Geographical Museum in Érd. However, the inscription on the statue makes no reference to the role that the Turanian Society played in its inception.[87]

Although Bendefy continued to collect ethnographic and archaeological data regarding the ancient history and Eastern connections of the Hungarians throughout the 1950s and 1960s, he essentially quit publishing works on these subjects after the Second World War; however, his correspondence reveals that after 1945, he attempted to serve as an intermediary between the Turanists who had remained in Hungary and members of the official academic establishment. Scholars who dealt with Hungarian history, Eastern research, and ethnography in the postwar period generally maintained a benevolent attitude toward Bendefy but attempted to keep a certain distance from him. However, one contributor to the periodical *Egyetemes Philologiai Közlöny* (Universal philological gazette) was not so charitable, calling Bendefy's competence as a scholar into question in an article entitled "Egy 'őstörténész' latin tudása" (The Latin knowledge of an "ancient historian").[88] Moreover, Bendefy's former Turanian Society associate Aladár Bán expressed public skepticism regarding his contention that a Hungarian principality had existed in the Caucasus until the fourteenth century: "The main task in the elucidation of this question would be for us to indisputably establish the authenticity and scientific usefulness of the records surrounding the city called *Magyar*. Without this, the entire complex of questions is only a series of legends, a collection of tales."[89] Most of those who were active in relevant fields of scholarship acknowledged that Bendefy's work regarding the Eastern origins of the Hungarians contained many astute and useful insights in addition to major misinterpretations.[90] Bendefy strove to maintain contacts with distinguished and/or somewhat dissident Turkologists, historians, and archaeologists during the communist era and in the 1960s and 1970s conducted correspondence with Sándor Zsuffa, Mrs. György Hary Gizella Némethy, Lajos Marjalaki Kiss, Old Hungarian script researcher László Pataky, and even former Pest County chief recorder Lajos Blaskovich, who had gone into internal exile.[91] Almost the entire network of museums in Hungary made use of Bendefy's irrefutable knowledge and comprehensive familiarity with source materials, thus providing him with a relatively broad platform from which to proclaim his ideas.

Ethnographer Gábor Lükő, one of the people with whom László Bendefy corresponded following the Second World War, moved to Romania during his university years under the influence of the ideas of poet Endre Ady and composer Béla Bartók regarding fraternity among the peoples of the Danube basin. Lükő subsequently learned the Romanian language and, in association with research groups under the direction of noted University of Bucharest sociologist Dimitrie Gusti, spent a long period of time living among the Csangó Hungarians of Moldavia in the early 1930s, publishing a comprehensive book regarding this ethnic group in 1936.[92] After returning to Hungary, Lükő began working at the Déri Museum in Debrecen and in 1942 published another book, *A magyar lélek formái* (Forms of the Hungarian soul), that drew extensively on Gyula Mészáros's Chuvash collections.[93] In this book, Lükő examined the Eastern equivalents of Hungarian folk symbols and spatial and temporal perception, although the volume did not use the term *Turanian* even once. The work reflects the author's orientation toward the East and his convictions that Hungarian and Eastern symbolism was superior to Western symbolism in terms of abundance, complexity, and diversity and that Eastern culture was healthier and more metaphysical than Western culture. Lükő likewise venerated Hungarian folk music and poetry, stating in an interview conducted in 1997, "The fact that not only our language, but our music proved to be a traceable ancient legacy had an enormous impact on me."[94] The titles of public lectures that Lükő held during and shortly after the Second World War—"Skita hagyományok művészetünkben" (Scythian traditions in our art) in 1942 and "Az ázsiai és a dunatáji lélek egyezései" (The concord between the Asian and Danubian souls) in 1948—suggest that he was engaged in a comprehensive investigation of the Eastern temperament and spiritual nature of the Hungarians during this period.[95] Following the communist takeover in Hungary, Lükő was forced to leave Debrecen in order to work at small local museums in Gyula, Baja, and Kiskunfélegyháza. While living in these towns, Lükő continued to publish works dealing with Eastern tradition and relations between the Hungarians and other peoples of the Carpathian Basin, primarily the Romanians. Lükő's charisma and ostracism elevated him to a position of prominence within a certain segment of the Hungarian ethnographic community. His influence is reflected in the nearly nine-hundred-page book that was published to commemorate his ninetieth birthday in 1999.[96] Following the end of the communist era, Lükő republished his works in a series of short books entitled *Gyökereink* (Our roots). In these books, he also postulated that the ancient Hungarians had practiced Buddhism—an idea that is similar to some of the notions that Turanists espoused with a greater apparatus at their service in the 1920s and 1930s.[97] Lükő died in Budapest in 2001, just a few weeks after having received the most prestigious state cultural award in Hungary, the Kossuth Prize.

István Mándoky Kongur (1944–1992) was born and raised in the city of Karcag in eastern Hungary and then moved to Budapest, where he studied under Turkologist Gyula Németh at Eötvös Loránd University and maintained a friendship with Gábor Lükő, who served as the witness for his second wedding. Mándoky Kongur's strong Cuman self-identity served as a great source of inspiration for him throughout his career.[98] During the 1980s, he traveled extensively in Soviet Central Asia, where he established contact with intellectuals who were already preparing for the post-Soviet national awakening in the region. Mándoky Kongur died in Makhachkala during a trip to Dagestan in 1992 and was buried at the Kensai Cemetery in Almaty, Kazakhstan. In 2005, a school was named after him in Almaty, and his library was donated to the International Turkic Academy in Astana, Kazakhstan. Mándoky Kongur's most significant work, *A kun nyelv magyarországi emlékei* (Traces of the Cuman language in Hungary), was published one year after his death.[99] He played a key role in the revival of Cuman identity in Hungary beginning in 1990 and kept the issue of the

Central Asian Turkic nomad legacy of the Hungarians on the agenda during the early postcommunist years. According to one of Mándoky Kongur's friends and university classmates, the "overestimation of the Turkic nomad [element]" and its placement above the settled peoples were "for him a fundamental conviction."[100] Unlike Gábor Lükő, who believed in the supremacy of Eastern and peasant culture, Mándoky Kongur regarded the culture of the steppe nomads to be paramount. As a result of the nonconformism of both Lükő and Mándoky Kongur and their relegation to the periphery of Hungarian academic life, they came to represent an alternative scientific orientation in the years of one-party communist rule, while László Bendefy focused his activity during this period on the preservation of pre-1945 Turanist networks. There were others who strove to perpetuate various elements of Eastern thinking between 1948 and 1990, though the efforts of Lükő, Mándoky Kongur, and Bendefy clearly exemplify the alternative pathways and dilemmas associated with the academic history of this era.

Adorján Magyar was a very unique figure even among the many other Turanists who had extraordinary lives and careers. After the First World War, Magyar assumed the duty of managing a family hotel in Zelenika, Montenegro, from his father and lived the rest of his life on the shores of the Adriatic. As a young hussar officer, he had dealt extensively with Hungarian ornamentation and ancient history even before the war, writing to folklorist Gyula Sebestyén in 1914 that "my soul knows no greater delight than to occupy myself with these ancient Hungarian things and to try to resurrect them."[101] Magyar published a large number of works on a diverse array of topics from his home in Yugoslavia and conducted intensive and frequently provocative correspondence with the editors of Hungarian-language publications around the world.[102] He also attempted to catalog ancient Hungarian motifs based on Eastern examples. In the 1920s, Magyar—who was an excellent drawer and painter—devised his own runic script and became one of the primary proponents of the notion of Hungarian autochthony in the Carpathian Basin, which he considered the cradle of civilization. He wrote his principal work, *Ősműveltség* (Ancient culture), twice, the second time because the original eleven-thousand-page manuscript for the book was lost during the First World War.

Magyar's writings appeared in radical Turanist publications such as the previously mentioned *Napsugár*, *Hadak Útja*, *Turáni Roham*, and *A Nap Fiai* both before and after the Second World War. Advertisements for his hotel, which was nationalized after the war, generally accompanied his articles in these periodicals ("No Mosquitos"; "No Cooking with Olive Oil"; "Italian-Dalmatian Dishes upon Request"). Magyar often wrote letters to scholars engaged in fields of study that interested him, such as previously shown in the case of Lajos Marjalaki Kiss. When Magyar was nearly eighty years old, he wrote to university professor Gyula Németh with regard to an article he had written about the Bashkirs: "All this Asianizing and nomadizing is nothing more than a Hermann Wamberger [Ármin Vámbéry]–devised Austrian imperial and Jewish fabrication for which no evidence can be found anywhere, but being under Russian military dictatorship you must derive your origins from Russia, for example Bashkiria, and continue to call yourselves a mixed people that collected one word from here and another from there, etc."[103] Magyar thus articulated a theory that he had espoused for four decades—namely, that the Carpathian Basin was the ancient homeland of the Hungarians and that peoples with whom they were said to be related had descended from them. With regard to these ideas, Magyar declared in his letter to professor Németh that "ascertaining, voicing and writing them are not allowed."[104] While Magyar may have been unconventional, the complexity of his thought and his profound erudition and knowledge of languages were well above average among scholars active in his field. The republication of Magyar's works and the formation of a circle of followers associated with the World Federation of Hungarians, an organization composed of primarily radical right-wing members, have served to sustain his influence to the present day.[105]

Scholars in Hungary endeavored in their own way to address the problematic ideas pertaining to Hungarian ethnogenesis and linguistic kinship, most of which had endured among Hungarian émigré communities abroad. Whereas historian Géza Komoróczy's 1976 book *Sumér és magyar?* (Sumerian and Hungarian?) alternately utilized the weapons of ridicule and scientific reasoning to refute these notions, linguist János Pusztay employed various means of persuasion in an attempt to achieve this objective in his 1977 book *Az "ugor-török háború" után* (After the "Ugrian-Turkish War"). Archaeologist and historian Gyula László (1910–1998), who devised the highly contested hypothesis of the two-phase Hungarian settlement of the Carpathian Basin, sought instead to reconcile the various theories and concepts regarding the origin and ethnolinguistic affiliation of the Hungarian people.[106] László's recently digitized papers reveal that the scholar, who was also an accomplished artist, strove to treat those who supported alternative versions of Hungarian ancient history in an equitable manner even while adhering to scientific norms, perhaps precisely because his fellow historians and archaeologists had subjected his "dual settlement" thesis to such intense criticism.[107] However, the efforts of Komoróczy, Pusztay, and László in this regard were frequently dismissed as invalid products of the dictatorship in which they originated.

This was the state of public and intellectual life in Hungary at the beginning of the country's democratic transition. Over the previous four decades, a permanent breach appears to have developed between viewpoints regarding Hungarian kinship. Proponents of Finno-Ugric kinship became irreversibly separated from Eastern thought, which had become firmly fixed on national and political foundations. Moreover, the thinking of those who dealt with the issues of Hungarian ancient history and kinship in Hungary during the communist era reveals that the distortions of dictatorship affect the reasoning of even those who strive to retain their intellectual independence. In addition to the malevolence of informants, this circumstance provides an explanation for the antisemitism, receptivity to conspiracy theories, and dictatorial responses to the challenges of dictatorship reflected in the letters of Turanists who remained in Hungary after the Second World War and the intelligence reports written about them. It is also evident that the end of the Stalinist reign of terror in Hungary following the 1956 revolution allowed advocates of certain Turanist/Eastern ideas to reconstitute their communication networks.

Even if Turan did not exist, even if the Turanian Society had been disbanded and could not be revived, the concepts that had spurred the Turanist movement survived.

Notes

1. See Ignác Romsics, *Hungary in the Twentieth Century* (Budapest: Osiris-Corvina, 1999), 210–16.

2. See Krisztián Ungváry, *Battle for Budapest* (London: Tauris, 2012).

3. The author obtained the information regarding the deaths of Elemér Virányi, Benedek Baráthosi Balogh, and Ede Toroczkai Wigand from Budapest district death certificates. For Virányi, see Budapest District I, Halotti anyakönyvek, 1945, március, 1945. június 4-i bejelentés, 799–800, 802. bejegyzés, 134 (via the familysearch.org database, uploaded on October 23, 2018). For Baráthosi Balogh, see Budapest District XIV, Halotti anyakönyvek, 1944–1945, 1945. február 5-i bejelentés, 375. bejegyzés, 63 (note that Baráthosi Balogh's cause of death is listed as "heart weakness, asthma"). For Toroczkai Wigand, see Budapest District I, Halotti anyakönyvek, 1945. június 11-i bejelentés, 820. bejegyzés, 137.

4. "Cholnoky Jenő önéletrajza," *Vár Ucca Tizenhét* 17, no. 2 (1998): 329.

5. For a list of items stolen from Cholnoky's house at this time, see MFM, Cholnoky-hagyaték, 5. doboz, statisztikai adatfelvételi ív, n.d. (1945).

6. MTAKK, Ms 2748/13, Emlékezés Dr. Pröhle Vilmos (1879–1946) utolsó hónapjaira, Testvérei számára feljegyezte Pröhle Ingeborg.

7. Andover-Harvard Theological Library, Harvard Divinity School Repository, Unitarian Service Committee, Case Files, 1938–1951. Box 25, Folder 8, Laszlo, Turmezei 1948–1949, accessed October 23, 2018, http://id.lib.harvard.edu/ead/d /901f9d56-d7d4-4b57-9ecc-b7089316fdd8/catalog. See Túrmezei's obituary in the periodical of the Hungarian Communion of Friends: "Meghalt Túrmezei László," *Itt-Ott* 12, no. 1 (1979): 12–14.

8. Historical Archives of the Hungarian State Security (hereafter, ÁBTL), P-110, Adatgyűjtés a Békássy családra vonatkozóan, Békássy László levele Moór Oszkárnak, Budapest, 1939. június 13.

9. Ibid., Környezettanulmány, n.d. [1950].

10. BFL, XXV. 1.a, Nb. 4366/1945 (0132078), Budapesti Népbíróság, Nagy Iván ügye, kihallgatási jegyzőkönyvek. Ítélet: ibid., Budapest, 1946. április.

11. ÁBTL, A-290, kitelepítések Borsod és Szabolcs megyébe, 31. (Bán Aladár).

12. ÁBTL, O-12310/1/61 "Levelezők," Várszegi Rudolf rendőrnyomozó hadnagy jelentése, 1957. október 21.

13. BFL, XXV. 2.b, 1466/1947, Budapesti Népügyészség eljárása Rafael Viktorné Mányoki Vilma tanárnő ellen.

14. Ibid., 8450/1947, Budapesti Népügyészség eljárása Gyalui Boér György ellen, Az eljárás megszüntetése, Budapest, 1948. május 29. In 1941, Boér published a short book in which he proposed that a Turanian-Sumerian capital city called Bojár be built in the southeastern part of the Great Hungarian Plain around the cities of Gyula and Békéscsaba. See György Gyalui Boér, *Bojár* (Nagybánya [Baia Mare, Romania]: Self-published, 1941).

15. BFL, XVII.1513–1945, Budapesti "143/b. sz. Igazolóbizottság" (Magyar Nemzeti Múzeum) iratai, Krepuska Gyula igazolási ügye, 1945–1946; ibid., XVII.1514–1945, "145/a. sz. Igazolóbizottság (Magyar Szövegírók, Zeneszerzők és Zeneműkiadók Szövetkezete) iratai," Gergelyffy Gábor igazolási ügye, 1945; ibid., XVII.1709, 455.b/1945, Budapesti kisebb igazolóbizottsági fondok levéltári gyűjteménye, a kolozsvári egyetem, a kassai és az újvidéki főiskola tanárainak ügyei, Felvinczi Takáts Zoltán igazolása, 1945. október 13; ibid., XVII. 1709., 455.b/1945, Csekey István igazolása, Szeged, 1945. június 27.

16. BFL, XVII.1518–1945, Ávedik Félixné Felvinczi Takács Alice igazolási ügye, az Államilag Engedélyezett Magánzeneiskolák Országos Szövetségének igazoló bizottságának határozata, Budapest, 1946. május 23.

17. András Stumpf, *Szörényi—Rohan az idő* (Budapest: Helikon, 2015), 34–35.

18. BFL VII.180, Barcs Ernő közjegyző iratai, 275/1947, Bencsi Zoltán póthagyatéki ügye. Supplementary inheritance procedures reveal that Bencsi's heritors were forced to pay for "exhumation costs," thus revealing that the initial burial of the former Turanian monotheist leader had not been conducted according to his family's wishes.

19. See the website of the Recsk Federation (*Recski Szövetség*), accessed October 23, 2018, http://www.recskiszovetseg.hu/about_b_II.html.

20. BFL XXV. 2.b, 1466/1947, Budapesti Népügyészség eljárása Rafael Viktorné Mányoki Vilma ellen, Mányoki Vilma vallomása, n.d.

21. BFL, XXV.1.a, 3439/1945, Sassi Nagy Lajos vallomása, Maglód, 1945. augusztus 16.

22. Ibid., özv. Sassi Nagy Lajosné bejelentése a népbíróságnak, 1945. november.

23. MNL OL, Belügyminisztérium iratai, XIX-B-1-h, 131. cs. 490655/1948. Szentiványi Domokos levele a belügyminisztériumnak, Budapest, 1945. augusztus 14.

24. Ibid., Paikert Géza levele a belügyminisztériumnak, Budapest, 1945. szeptember 6.

25. Ibid., az 1946. október 16-i újjáalakuló ülés jegyzőkönyve.

26. Ibid.

27. For the history of the Hungarian Community, see Nóra Szekér, *Titkos társaság: A Magyar Testvéri Közösség története* (Budapest: Jaffa, 2017). For the role that Miklós Majthényi played in this organization, see ÁBTL, 3.1.9. V-2000/12, Horváth Lőrinc vallomása, and V-2000/28/236., Kiss Károly: A Magyar Közösség által használt jelzések.

28. MNL OL BM, XIX-B-1-h, 13. cs., 495747/1947. Szebenyi Endre miniszteri osztályfőnök átirata a Magyar Államrendőrség budapesti főkapitánysága vezetőjének, 1947. március 14.

29. Ibid., Bajkó Mihály rendőrnyomozó hadnagy jelentése Németh Gyula kihallgatásáról, Budapest, 1948. február 16.

30. See, for example, ÁBTL, A-456/1 Turáni Vadászok Egyesülete (előadásszöveg), n.d.

31. ÁBTL, V-104/018, Vizsgálati dosszié, Gerezsdi István vallomása, Budapest, 1953. augusztus 26.

32. MNL OL, XIX-B-1-h, 37. cs. 437907/1947, Gálffy Imre miskolci polgármester a belügyminisztériumnak, Miskolc, 1947. április 15; ibid.,. 112. cs. 487149/1948. Pest-Pilis-Solt-Kiskun vármegye alispánjának jelentése a belügyminisztériumnak a Turáni Vadászok csepeli csoportjáról, Budapest, 1948. február 21.

33. MNL OL, XIX-B-1-h, 20. cs. 431353/1947, Szarvassy Imre próbarendőr jelentése, Balassagyarmat, 1947. szeptember 28.

34. The pagan leader Koppány was the greatest political rival of King Stephen I, the founder of the Hungarian state. Stephen had Koppány drawn and quartered in 997. Koppány has become the emblematic figure for Hungarians who look toward the East and has served as an inspiration for many works of Hungarian literature.

35. See chapter 5, note 71.

36. MNL PML, XIV.2.a. Endre László iratai, magánlevelezés, 27. doboz, 313. dosszié, Virasztó Mihály levele Endre Lászlónak, Orosháza, 1935. június 15.

37. See "A 'turáni táltost' a tábla öthónapi fogházra ítélte a bírák és ügyeszek rágalmazásáért," *Délmagyarország*, February 12, 1942, 5; and "Virasztó Koppány tizenötödik büntetése," *Délmagyarország*, September 5, 1941, 7.

38. For details surrounding the surveillance of Virrasztó, see ÁBTL, 0-14980/18 Virasztó Mihály dossziéja.

39. Ibid., Sóshalmi ügynök jelentése, 1959.

40. Ibid., "Pákozdi" fedőnevű ügynök jelentése Galsi Károly századosnak, Orosháza, 1960, október 6.

41. "A 'turáni táltost' a tábla öthónapi fogházra ítélte a bírák és ügyeszek rágalmazásáért," *Délmagyarország*, February 12, 1942, 5.

42. Szécsényi, "Virrasztó Koppány és társai," 360. Count István Széchenyi (1791–1860) was one of the central figures of the Reform era in Hungary and served as one of the primary promoters of modernization in the country. Count Széchenyi is associated specifically with the construction of the Chain Bridge spanning the Danube River in Budapest, the foundation of the Hungarian Academy of Sciences, and the establishment of the Hungarian banking system. He was a minister in the first independent Hungarian government formed following the 1848 revolution. Széchenyi subsequently suffered a breakdown and spent the last decade of his life living at a mental hospital in Döbling, Austria, near Vienna.

43. ÁBTL, O–14980/18 Virasztó Mihály dossziéja.

44. BFL, XXV. 44.b, 1965/23515, Simsai Vilmos és Füzesséry Istvánné bűnügye.

45. See Benedek Baráthosi Balogh, *Szumirok, szittyák, ősturánok* (Budapest: Self-published, 1929); Mihály Kmoskó, "A sumirek," *Turán* 1, no. 1 (1913): 15–27; Alajos Paikert, "Turáni múlt, turáni jövő," *Turán* 19, nos. 1–4 (1936): 6–10; and Sándor Márki, "A turáni népek története," *Turán* 5, no. 1 (1922): 25–26.

46. HOM Történeti Tár 73.911.2, Marjalaki Kiss Lajos levelezése 2, Bendefy László levele Marjalaki Kiss Lajosnak, Budapest, 1963. február 17.

47. For correspondence regarding this episode, see Gyula Krúdy Library, Várpalota, papers of Aladár Bán, "Bán Aladár–Jegyzetek–1958."

48. Gyula Krúdy Library, Várpalota, papers of Aladár Bán, "Levelezés," Lukinich Frigyes levele özv. Bán Aladárnénak, Budapest, 1961. december 21.

49. Information from interview with Medgyaszay's granddaughter, Mrs. Gabriella Ládonyi Bartha, conducted in Budapest in the spring and summer of 2016.

50. Jenő Kismarty-Lechner, "A 80 éves Medgyaszay István," *Magyar Építőművészet* 6, nos. 5–6 (1957): 175–76. Lechner wrote to the Hungarian Architects' Alliance asking it to commemorate the eightieth birthday of his friend Medgyaszay. See Medgyaszay collection, Társaság-album: Lechner Jenő levele a Magyar Építőművészek Szövetségéhez, Budapest, 1957. augusztus 15.

51. Eötvös Loránd University Library, manuscript and rare documents archive, G 872, Bartha Zoltán: Fehér Könyv Medgyaszay alkotásai védelme érdekében, 1959–82, 3.

52. Katsányi Sándor, *A főváros könyvtárának története 1945-ig* (Budapest: Fővárosi Szabó Ervin Könyvtár, 2004), 340, 344.

53. Hopp Museum Documentation Department, papers of Ferenc Zajti, L084/2004, Zajti Ferenc levele az Országos Nyugdíjintézetnek, Budapest, 1952. március 5.

54. MTAKK, Ms 4395/26 Zajti Ferenc: A Kőrösi Csoma Sándor Collegum Hungaricum létesítésének tervezete. Budapest, 1955.

55. See "Társasági ügyek," *Turán* 12, nos. 1–4 (1929): 62; "Az indiai magara népnél," *Budapesti Hírlap*, April 26, 1929, 5; and Ferenc Zajti, *Magyar évezredek (Skytha-hun-magyar faji azonosság)* (Budapest: Self-published, 1939), 52.

56. For Mezey's obituary, see Mezey István gyászjelentése, accessed October 27, 2018, https://dspace.oszk.hu/handle/123456789/424006#.

57. MTAKK, Ms 4395/26 Zajti Ferenc: A Kőrösi Csoma Sándor Collegium Hungaricum; and ÁBTL 3.1.2. M-39112/2, Vitéz fedőnevű ügynök munkadossziéja, "Vitéz" jelentése Szebeni őrnagynak, Budapest, 1971. május 6.

58. See Ida Bobula, "Az egyetemi nőkérdés Magyarországon," *Napkelet* 6, no. 8 (April 15, 1928): 581–95; Ida Bobula, "El kell-e bocsátani a férjes tisztviselőnőket?" *Katolikus Szemle* 48, no. 4 (1934): 247–48; and Ida Bobula, "A Nemzetpolitikai Társaság ankétja a női választójogról," *Magyarság*, February 4, 1938, 7.

59. BFL XXV. 1.a, Nb. 4366/1945 (0132078), Budapesti Népbíróság, Nagy Iván ügye, Bobula Ida vallomása.

60. MMGM SZE, Paikert Alajos hagyatéka, 2012.21.1–30.1, Bobula Ida levele Domanovszky Sándornak, New Brunswick, 1948. május 5.

61. MMGM SZE, Paikert Alajos hagyatéka, 2012.21.1–30.1, Paikert Géza levele Paikert Alajosnak, 1948. június 21.

62. For information regarding Zsigmond Varga, see István Gábor Kovács, ed., *Hit, tudomány, közélet: A Debreceni Tudományegyetem Református Hittudományi Kara (1914–1950)*

professzorainak életrajzi adattára és életútleírása (Budapest: ELTE Eötvös Kiadó, 2014), 142–46; and Béla Levente Baráth, "Varga Zsigmond teológia professzor, a debreceni m. kir. Tisza István Tudományegyetem 1932/33: Évi rector magnificusa," *Gerundium* 9, no. 1 (2018): 3–22.

63. See Gyula Zolnai, "Tudománytalan nyelvhasonlítások," *Magyar Nyelvőr* 44, no. 4 (1915): 151–63, 194–206; and Gyula Zolnai, "Felelet a tudománytalan nyelvhasonlítások ügyében," *Magyar Nyelvőr* 44, no. 4 (1915): 268–71.

64. See, for example, Library of the Trans-Tisza Reformed Diocese in Debrecen (hereafter, TTREK), manuscript archive, R2450 Munkácsi Bernát Varga Zsigmondnak, Nagykanizsa, 1925. december 27.

65. MTAKK, Ms 5993/59, Bobula Ida levele Hankiss Jánosnak, New York, 1948. december 3.

66. TTREK, Varga Zsigmond hagyatéka, R 2845/10, Bobula Ida levele Varga Zsigmondnak, New York, 1949. február 20.

67. Ibid., R 2889/27, Bobula Ida levele Varga Zsigmondnak, s.l., 1954. január 19.

68. See Knüppel, "Zur ungarischen Rezeption der sumerisch-turanischen Hypothese in der zweiten Hälfte des 20," 93–107; and Pálfi and Tanos, "A sumer-magyar hit és a sumerológia," 100–106.

69. For more information regarding Tibor Baráth, see Rudolf Paksa, "A történetírás mint propaganda: Baráth Tibor útja a szaktörténetírástól a mítoszgyártásig," *Kommentár* 1, no. 5 (2006): 69–79. For Baráth's political transformation, see Balázs Ablonczy, "Ördögszekéren: Baráth Tibor párizsi évei (1930–1939)," *Történelmi Szemle* 58, no. 3 (2016): 429–50.

70. Tibor Baráth, *A magyar népek őstörténete*, 3 vols. (Montreal: Self-published, 1968–74).

71. See Ferenc Jós, "Pilóták korszerű kiképzése," *Magyar Katonai Szemle* 3, no. 2 (1933): 128–32; "Az önálló légi háború bombázásairól," *Magyar Katonai Szemle* 4, no. 2 (1934): 120–22.

72. For more information regarding Badiny Jós, see Kovács, "A diaszpóra visszavándorlásának ideológiai vonatkozásai Közép-Kelet Európában," 284–304. For Pogrányi Nagy's influence on him, see Ferenc Badiny Jós, *Messze az édes hazától* (Budapest: Magyar Ház, 2006), 168.

73. Kovács, "A diaszpóra visszavándorlásának ideológiai vonatkozásai," 291.

74. Sándor Zsuffa, *A magyarországi szumír probléma állása különböző korokban*, Institute of Hungarian Studies website, accessed October 28, 2018, http://www.magtudin.org/Szumir %20problema.htm.

75. Citation from Ferenc Kanyó, "A Habsburgok és a magyar őstörténet," toriblog.blog .hu, March 17, 2009, accessed August 12, 2016, http://toriblog.blog.hu/2009/03/17/mitoszok _nyomaban_i_a_habsburgok_es_a_magyar_ostortenet.

76. ÁBTL, O-13711, "Elmélkedők" (1969–70), illetve: uo. 3.1.2. M-39112/2, "Vitéz" fn. ügynök munkadossziéja (1969–1971).

77. ÁBTL 3.1.2. M-39112/2, Vitéz fn. ügynök munkadossziéja. A state-security agent who was a trained psychologist began monitoring Zakar in 1971.

78. András Zakar, "Sumerian-Ural-Altaic Affinities," *Current Anthropology* 12, no. 2 (April 1971): 215–25. See also the responses and comments of Miguel Civil, Mridula Adenwala Durbin, William H. Jacobsen Jr., Johann Knobloch, W. P. Lehmann, A. Leo Oppenheim, Robert L. Oswalt, Herbert. H. Paper, Joe. E. Pearce, Elaine K. Ristenen, Francis Lee Utley, and H. J. Cowan to Zakar's article.

79. OSZKK, Fond 170, Bendefy László hagyatéka, Levelezés H-J, Hary Györgyné levele Bendefy Lászlónak, Budapest, 1975. január 14.

80. See the following book regarding László Bendefy: Márta Sragner, ed., *A száz éve született Bendefy László élete és művei* (Marosvásárhely [Târgu Mureş]: Mentor, 2004).

81. MFM, Cholnoky-hagyaték, 3. doboz, tudományos és hivatalos levelezés (1929–31, 1924, 1910–11, 1920–21), Benda Laci levele Cholnoky Jenőnek, Szombathely, 1922, április 10.

82. Some of the articles that László Bendefy published in the Turanian Society periodical are as follows: "Az ércbeöntött Julianus," *Turán* 20–21, nos. 3–4 (1937–38): 53–57; "Aeneas Sylvius Piccolomini magyarjai," *Turán* 20–21, nos. 7–10 (1937–38): 138–55; "Magyer, Jaretány fejedelem székvárosa I" *Turán* 22, no. 6 (1939): 132–39; "Magyer, Jaretány fejedelem székvárosa II," *Turán* 23, no. 1 (1940): 29–36; "A csegemvölgyi szkita szarvas," *Turán* 23, no. 3 (1940): 126–29; and "A kunszentmiklósi 'kamenai baba,'" *Turán* 23, no. 3 (1940): 160.

83. János Kodolányi, *Julianus* (Budapest: Athenaeum, 1938).

84. "Julian barát szobra," *Budapesti Hírlap*, June 27, 1937, 10.

85. MFM, Cholnoky Jenő hagyatéka, 5. doboz, 1942-es levelek dosszié, Bendefy László levele Cholnoky Jenőnek, Budapest, 1942. január 7.

86. Ibid., 7. doboz, A Kőrösi Csoma-szoborral kapcsolatos külön dosszié, Jakab Miklós vallástanár levele Cholnoky Jenőhöz, 1942. március 11.

87. For further information regarding this statue, see János Kubassek, "Kőrösi Csoma Sándor szobra Érden," *Földrajzi Múzeumi Tanulmányok* 1, no. 1 (1985): 11–16.

88. Emil Scheitz, "Egy 'őstörténész' latin tudása," *Egyetemes Philológiai Közlöny* 67 (1943): 239–40.

89. Aladár Bán, "dr. Bendefy László: A magyarság kaukázusi őshazája. Gyeretyán országa," *Ethnographia* 53, nos. 1–2 (1942): 160.

90. From interview with Eötvös Loránd University Department of Turkic Studies Professor Emeritus István Vásáry, July 22, 2016.

91. See OSZKK, Fond 121, Németh Gyula hagyatéka, Bendefy László levele Németh Gyulának, Budapest, 1948. december 18.; Ibid, Fond 170, Bendefy László hagyatéka, rendezetlen levelezés, 1944–1977 (3 doboz), Zsuffa Sándor levelei Bendefy Lászlónak, Budapest, 1965. július 21. and július 29.Marjalaki Kiss Lajos levele Bendefy Lászlónak, Miskolc, 1963. február 14.

92. Gábor Lükő, *A moldvai csángók* (Budapest: Pázmány Péter Tudományegyetem Néprajzi Intézete, 1936).

93. Gábor Lükő, *A magyar lélek formái* (Budapest: Sylvester, 1942). Lükő frequently cited Gyula Mészáros in this book: see pages 19, 27, 30, 50, and 72, among others.

94. DMNA, 2881/98, Vajda Mária beszélgetése Lükő Gábor néprajzkutatóval, Budapest, 1997. október 10. 3.

95. The author found an invitation to the latter lecture among István Medgyaszay's papers. See Medgyaszay-gyűjtemény, Társaság album, Budapest, 1948. november 5, and DEENK, Sőregi János hagyatéka, Ms 13/18, Napló 1941–1942: 1942. március 5.

96. Péter Pozsgai, ed., *Tűzcsiholó: Írások a 90 éves Lükő Gábor tiszteletére* (Budapest: Táton, 1999).

97. Gábor Lükő, "A múló időben: Buddhista korszakunk halvány emlékei," *Gyökereink*, vol. 7 (Debrecen: Debreceni Egyetem Társaslélektani Intézete, 1998), 107–54.

98. The Cumans are a Turkic people who settled in Hungary in the thirteenth century. They maintained certain medieval privileges, traces of which exist to this day, for centuries after their linguistic assimilation with the Hungarians.

99. István Mándoky Kongur, *A kun nyelv magyarországi emlékei* (Karcag: Karcag Város Önkormányzata, 1993).

100. István Vásáry, "A turkológus Mándoky Kongur István," in *Kőember állott a pusztán*, ed. Ágnes Birtalan and Dávid Somfai Kara (Budapest: L'Harmattan, 2008), 13.

101. EA 13148, Sebestyén Gyula hagyatéka, Levelek-M, no. 3203. Magyar Adorján levele Sebestyén Gyulának, Zelenika, 1914. május 4.

102. For more information regarding Adorján Magyar, see Dr. Zoltán Magyar, *Volt egyszer egy pesti polgárcsalád* (Budapest: Biró, 2011); and "Magyar Adorján élete," accessed October 28, 2018, http://www.magyaradorjan.com/007/doc/eletrajz.html.

103. OSZKK, Fond 121/1077, Németh Gyula hagyatéka, Magyar Adorján levele Németh Gyulának, Zelenika, 1966. május 7.

104. Ibid.

105. For an appraisal of Adorján Magyar's work, see Klára Sándor, "Européer rovásírás," Nyelv és Tudomány, June 26, 2014, accessed October 28, 2018, https://www.nyest.hu/hirek /europeer-rovasiras.

106. See Gyula László, "Más megoldás is elképzelhető?" *Életünk* 17, no. 4 (1979): 273–89.

107. MTA BTK, László Gyula Digitális Archívum, Levelezés, accessed October 29, 2018, http://lgyda.btk.mta.hu/levelezes. See specifically: "László Gyula levele Kászonyi Ferencnek," Budapest, February 1, 1962; "László Gyula levelei Zsuffa Sándornak," Budapest, May 21 and July 5, 1963; "Baráth Tibornak," April 1, 1975; "Badiny Jós Ferencnek," Budapest, December 22, 1976, and Kecskemét, February 23, 1977; "Magyar Adorjánnak," September 22, 1978; "Hary Györgynének," Budapest, May 3, 1977, and May 25, 1981; and "Fehér Jenő Mátyásnak," Budapest, May 15 and June 10, 1972.

9

RENAISSANCE AND MANNERISM

FOLLOWING THE CHANGE OF REGIME IN HUNGARY IN 1989–1990, for a time the importance of the so-called East dwindled in Hungarian thinking. The East referred more to the communist great powers, the fallen Soviet Union on the one hand and China (still very present) on the other, and these states represented entities and ideologies from which the Hungarian wider public and narrower political elite yearned to be free. In the 1994 parliamentary elections, the Hungarian Socialist Party campaigned with a platform based in part on a promise to regain the "eastern markets," but this pledge was more an attempt to win votes by giving hope to the broad segment of Hungarian society that was suffering from high unemployment rates than it was an effort to revive any interest in the Eastern origins of the Hungarians.[1]

Authors who had left Hungary and, living abroad, had cherished and nurtured the Eastern element of Hungarian identity soon appeared. A tiny book by Tibor Baráth, who had left Hungary for Canada, was published in Hungary before Baráth's death.[2] A publishing house in Veszprém that has since closed published one of Baráth's narratives of the prehistory of the Hungarians, as well as one of the works of Viktor Padányi. The first books written by Ferenc Badiny Jós, who was living in Argentina, were published in Hungary, though they met with very little response, and Badiny Jós, a noncommissioned air force officer almost ninety years of age at the time who often traveled to Hungary, complained of this.[3] A breakthrough came, from the perspective of the familiarity of the wider public with his work, in 2004, when Magyar Ház Kiadó (Hungarian House Publishers), working closely with the right-wing weekly *Demokrata*, published all of his works as a series and made them widely available.[4] The views expounded in his book *Jézus Király, a pártus herceg* (King Jesus, the Parthian prince) met with harsh criticism in Catholic and Calvinist circles (he contended that

Jesus was a "proto-Hungarian" and prince of the region of Parthia), but the "Sumerologists" in academic life (i.e., scholars who contend that Hungarians are the descendants of the ancient Sumerians) reflected only tepidly and in relatively narrow circles on Badiny Jós's ideas, which were slowly but surely spreading.[5] For the most part, the critical reviews relied on a work by Géza Komoróczy written in the 1970s.[6]

In the 1990s, the Private University of King Lajos the Great Private University was founded in Miskolc, and initially it entertained hopes of gaining official accreditation. The university offered a home or nest to esoteric teachings on prehistory and new interpretations of the Eastern elements of Hungarian history and identity. Several publishing houses began to republish works by authors who earlier had been prohibited from publishing or at least kept quiet, so soon the works of authors like Ida Bobula and Adorján Magyar began to find a small but nonetheless respectable market. After the change of regime, the works of Sándor Forrai on the Székely script were published one after the other. With the passing of time, Forrai had increasingly come to accept the notion of a relationship between the Hungarian and Sumerian languages and, thus, peoples, and he himself had begun to play a central role in the world of people interested in (or beguiled by) the Old Hungarian script, in no small part due to the Forrai Sándor Rovásíró Kör (Sándor Forrai Runic Script Circle) and the competitions it organized. A series of presentations for the wider public were held by popular lecturers who accepted either in part or entirely the radical views that were being brought into Hungary by people returning from lives spent abroad. The Zurich Hungarian Historical Society, which was founded in 1985, was very active in attempts to tie up some loose ends and, in addition to getting out the works of serious scholars, it also helped historians who were drawn to Turanist teachings and even simple amateurs to reach the larger public.[7]

In 1998, the periodical *Turán* went into publication again. Archaeologist Gyula László became president of the editorial board of the periodical, which was, according to its subtitle, "a journal of the sciences dealing with research on the origins of the Hungarians." The editorial board included architect György Csete (1937–2017), composer and rock musician Levente Szörényi, and Sándor Forrai. In the first issue, the journal referred to *Turán*, the periodical by the same name that had been in publication until 1944, and the editor's introduction made it quite clear that the new journal regarded itself as the bearer of the legacy of its namesake, even if the profile of the Turanian Society was not narrowly focused on research concerning the origins of the Hungarians.[8] The editorial board alluded to the example set by Pál Teleki, a scholar and historian who twice served as prime minister of Hungary and committed suicide in 1941, in support of its contention that "for a successful future, one must know the past." Their goal, they claimed, was to spread knowledge of Hungarian prehistory "with no obfuscation, no false humbuggery or calculated deceit." And they cautiously noted that they sought to offer an alternative to the canonized narratives of the academia and university scholars. Their goal, they contended, was "to provide space for research on our origins that is different in its approach" in "scientific but widely comprehensible articles." The introductory text expressed its disdain for language-based research concerning "ethnic" origins, and it lamented the fact that "the official Hungarian science of history stubbornly insists on the notion of Finno-Ugric descent." In its first issue, the journal included an article on the Hungarian-Celtic "link," of which the editorial board delicately expressed its skepticism. In general, the writings of respectable representatives of scholarship on the East were published alongside works by people eager to spread their ideas among the wider public and representatives of completely unscholarly views. In 2009, the company that published the journal began to face financial problems, and in 2011, publication was suspended.[9] At a press briefing held in December 2015, the Society of Eurasian Treasures (Eurázsia Kincsei Egyesület) announced that it would begin to publish the journal again in mid-2016, and it would give the issues a new numbering, but would also explicitly refer to and associate itself with the first incarnation of the journal, launched in 1913. Ultimately, the journal went into publication in 2017 under a different name, *Kelet kapuja* (Gate to the East). Its editor in chief, Borbála Obrusánszky, a historian specializing in Mongol studies and a consultant for the radical right-wing political party Jobbik, has taken part in numerous debates concerning the prehistory of the Hungarians. Actually, the last issue of the publication came out in mid-2020, since its editor in chief became the Hungarian ambassador to Mongolia.

In order for these various interests, which came from various sources and seemed pointed in various directions, to meet and become a genuine "issue" in the first decade of the new millennium, laying the foundations for the so-called Eastern Opening in Hungary (a political stance announced by the government in the wake of the 2010 elections), three or four processes had to converge. The selection of new officers for the World Federation of Hungarians may initially seem to be the least significant of these processes. The World Federation of Hungarians (Magyarok Világszövetsége, or MVSZ) was founded in 1938 to represent the interests and concerns of Hungarians who had left the country for political or economic reasons. Following the communist takeover, it did not cease to function. Rather, for four decades it served as a propaganda and intelligence organ of the Hungarian government in its efforts to obtain information on and spread propaganda to Hungarians living in Western Europe and the rest of the world. Following the fall of communism, Sándor Csoóri (1930–2016), one of the founders of the Hungarian Democratic Forum political party and a poet who earlier had been part of the opposition, became the president of the World Federation of Hungarians. After his withdrawal in 2000, much to everyone's surprise, Miklós Patrubány, a forty-eight-year-old Transylvanian IT entrepreneur, rose to the head of the MVSZ instead of the government's candidate. The new president pushed the organization into the world of extreme right-wing political sects, and through his active use of the media and his assertive portrayals of certain themes, from time to time he put himself in the focus of public life, for instance the referendum held in 2004 on dual citizenship. (The referendum, which was launched by the MVSZ, asked citizens whether the Hungarian government should grant Hungarian citizenship to ethnic Hungarians living outside Hungary, primarily in the neighboring states. The right-wing opposition led by Fidesz supported the referendum. Ultimately, it failed due to a low voter turnout.)

However, thanks to the organizational infrastructure (a network that stretched across continents) and Patrubány's unquestionably skillful organizational work, a series of demands formulated by the individuals and organizations presented earlier became focal points for the activities of the World Federation of Hungarians. In 2004, the MVSZ organized the Sixth World Congress of Hungarians, at which Patrubány opened the conference on the prehistory of Hungarians with the following statement: "The World Federation of Hungarians believes that the time has come to turn our gaze towards the ancient homeland of the Hungarian people. In the direction in which almost a billion people consider us friends, relatives, talented siblings torn westwards."[10] This statement harmonizes well with the Turanist discourse of the interwar period in Hungary. This was one of the first such declarations in Hungarian public life since the change of regime, and the so-called Movement for a Better Hungary, or Jobbik, which began to gain prominence and political presence in 2003, presumably borrowed the Turanian idea from here and made it the focal point of its foreign policy platform, at least until 2014. Jobbik was founded in 1999 by radical right-wing university students, and in 2003, it became a political party. In the 2006 general election, Jobbik did not reach the threshold of votes to get into parliament, but the political scandals and economic crisis that came in the wake of the elections and the shrill anti-Roma and often antisemitic rhetoric embraced by the party had a strong influence on its fortunes. In 2009, the party got almost 15 percent of the votes in the European Parliament election, giving it three representatives in Brussels. In the national and European Parliamentary elections held since 2010, Jobbik has received between 15 and 20 percent of the votes, and it has regularly been in second place in public opinion surveys.[11]

Another circumstance that has favored political discourses drawing on references to the Eastern element of Hungarian identity is the domestic political war that was fought fiercely between 2002 and 2010 and the almost permanent state of political crisis. I do not intend to offer a penetrating analysis of this here (as it would stretch the framework of my inquiry), but I would hazard the contention that the disappointment that followed Hungary's accession to the European Union in 2004 (a disappointment caused largely because of financial concerns), the political crisis that broke out in 2006, and the global economic crisis of 2007–2008 gave a stronger voice and stronger public presence to people who demanded a turn away from Western political models and a political platform based at least in part on some notion of ethnic identity or belonging—but not the notion of Finno-Ugric belonging. The foundations had been laid by that time for the presentation of the notion of the Finno-Ugric origins of the Hungarian people as a "Jewish-communist-Habsburg scheme and fabrication." In this fragile time of crisis, another series of cultural phenomena were taking hold of the public imagination that were also (allegedly) tied to prehistoric Hungarian culture, such as so-called *baranta* (supposedly an ancient Hungarian martial art), a runic script (allegedly) used by the Hungarians before the adoption of the Latin alphabet, and equestrian archery, also thought of as part of Hungarian "tribal" culture (i.e., dating back to the period before the shift from nomadism to a settled way of life).

The third circumstance that contributed to the emergence of "Turanism" in public discourse in Hungary was the rise of Jobbik as an increasingly significant political party and its relative successes in the 2009 and 2010 European Parliament and national elections, after which it became a presence in both. In Jobbik's 2010 political program (both in its foreign and domestic policy sections), in a chapter entitled "Our Ancient Roots and

Historical Bonds," the party made very clear what it meant when it spoke of a shift in the "one-sided Euro-Atlantic orientation": "We have not exploited the potentials latent in the fact that to this day the Turkic peoples of Inner Asia unquestionably consider us to be relatives. Our bond to them is an organic part of our ancient national consciousness, and the most recent findings of scholarly research convincingly prove this."[12] And so, should the party rise to power, it pledged "to lay the groundwork for political and economic relations in the case of the Turkic peoples of Inner Asia by building cultural relations resting on ancient kinship ties. We will develop closer economic and political cooperation, based on bonds of kinship and shared economic interests, with Turkey, which has taken a resolute diplomatic turn and shown dynamic economic growth."[13]

Jobbik's 2014 program ("We Name It, We Solve It") was considerably more cautious in its phrasing, and while it contained a passing reference to the development of "closer foreign policy ties with the countries of Inner Asia, which are (and consider themselves) to be bound by ties of kinship to the Hungarian people on the basis of culture and descent," emphasis had shifted palpably to relations with Germany, Russia, and Turkey and an envisioned Polish-Croatian-Hungarian axis.[14] Jobbik politicians made innumerable statements in which the overtones of Turanism were clearly audible, and they made other important gestures. Party president and floor leader Gábor Vona (b. 1978), for instance, made trips to Turkey, and the hand sign (a fist with two fingers raised to resemble a wolf) used by the so-called Grey Wolves (Ülkü Ocakları), a terrorist organization with close ties to the Turkish far-right Nationalist Movement Party, is featured on Jobbik's website. I will cite two of the more dramatic and revealing declarations. In the summer of 2011, Jobbik vice president and member of the European Parliament Csanád Szegedi made the following statement during a trip to the Székely Land in Romania: "We must free ourselves of the North Atlantic system of alliances, which is foreign to the Hungarian people, and we must return to the system of alliances of the Turanian peoples, which unites our kind, who number almost one billion." Similarly, in connection with a Turkish-Hungarian national soccer match, Jobbik president Vona wrote the following to the Turkish fans in 2012 (the statement was issued in Turkish and Hungarian): "There may have been many battles between us in the course of history, and we may have spilled each other's blood, and perhaps we worship the One Lord by different names, but we are nonetheless siblings: the sons of Turan. . . . We are all the grandchildren of Attila!"[15]

In the years that have passed since 2014, Jobbik's political strategy has palpably changed. In the party's characterizations of its foreign policy stance, the adjective *Eurasian* has largely supplanted the term *Turanian*. In the summer of 2016, while visiting the Transylvanian Hungarian Youth camp in Gyergyószentmiklós (Gheorgheni, Romania), Vona spoke of the "Eurasian peoples" and made the contention that, through the ties maintained with them, "there are tremendous geopolitical potentials in the Attila myth."[16] On the one hand, this statement reveals a kind of postmodern relativism in Vona's views that earlier would have been unthinkable, as he characterizes the notion of the common ethnogenetic origin of the Turkic peoples as a myth. On the other hand, the Jobbik president clearly refers to the purely political instrumentalization of this myth, uncoupling it from the idealism that, particular in the case of this kind of belief, is characteristic of Jobbik's value system. After Jobbik's poor performance in Hungary's 2018 parliamentary election, Vona withdrew from politics and the party adopted a more moderate political stance. This pushed Jobbik into a deep political crisis and some right-wing intellectuals of Turanist orientation shifted toward the governing Fidesz party. While Jobbik's rise has been the political breakthrough of the past decade, the Kurultáj event has in fact achieved a similar success in the contested terrain of the politics of ethnic origins. In 2006, a Hungarian-Kazak expedition pursued research on the Madjar tribe in the Torgaï region of northwestern Kazakhstan. Hungarian anthropologist András Zsolt Bíró, who works at the Hungarian Museum of Natural Science, was one of the people who took part in the expedition. On the basis of the genetic patterns found among the Madjars, Bíró, working together with other scholars, later published the findings in English-language scientific journals. According to these findings, Bíró concluded that the Hungarians and the Madjars are related.[17]

Thanks to his assiduous efforts, Hungary was represented (a total of twenty Hungarians took part) at the 2007 Great Kurultáj, a cultural event launched in 2007. The Great Kurultáj is intended to strengthen the sense of unity among Hungarians and the nomadic peoples of Central Asia (the word *kurultáj* in Hungarian is allegedly based on old Turkic roots and means "meeting of the tribes"). Emboldened by what he saw at the event, Bíró, along with others who shared his views, decided to hold similar festivals in Hungary intended to serve as celebrations of prehistoric Hungarian tribal culture and Hungary's cultural bonds to the peoples of Central Asia. The first Kurultáj held in Hungary was in 2008 in Bösztörpuszta, near

Kunszentmiklós.[18] Ferenc Vukics and people belonging to his circle took part in the organization of the event at the time. Vukics, a military officer, had played a prominent role in popularizing baranta, the aforementioned martial art that was becoming increasingly popular, in no small part because it was considered an ancient Hungarian form of fighting. The Kurultáj festivals were held once every two years, and in order to make the organizational background more stable, in 2009 the organizers created the Hungarian Turanian Foundation and the Hungarian Turanian Alliance, which work together in close symbiosis. In the meantime, Vukics and his circle had begun to become politically active, founding the Alliance of Hungarians (Magyarok Szövetsége) and parting ways with Kurultáj. Initially, they organized the National Gathering of Hungarians (Magyarok Országos Gyűlése) in Bösztörpuszta and then Apajpuszta (in 2010, for instance, at almost the same time as that year's Kurultáj).

After only a few years, however, the latter event was no longer organized, while Kurultáj remained (and remains). In uneven years, the Hungarian Turanian Society organizes the so-called Day of Our Ancestors (Ősök napja), also in Bugac (it was held in 2019 for the fifth time). Since 2012, thanks to the support of Sándor Lezsák, a Fidesz parliamentary representative and (also since 2012) deputy speaker of the National Assembly of Hungary, the event has enjoyed the support of the government in the form of considerable subsidies (70 million forints in 2014, roughly US$260,000 at the time). In 2014 and 2016, the people invited from twenty-seven different countries for the event were given a welcome in the Hungarian parliament, which offers a clear sign of the importance of the occasion. Between 2013 and 2015, Lezsák organized educational programs as part of a so-called Eastern Opening Collegium at the People's College (Népfőiskola) in Lakitelek, which was also founded by Lezsák. The program was a clear reflection of his interest in the Eastern element of Hungarian identity (for instance, it included instruction in several Central Asian languages).[19] According to the organizers, in 2016, 180,000 people took part in the three-day Kurultáj festival, which enjoyed the support of local governments in Hungary and the Turkish Cooperation and Coordination Agency (TIKA), and the event was also attended by several ambassadors and representatives of official agencies in Central Asia. Kurultáj included an array of engaging programs. An archery competition, a horse procession, sports competitions, and the events organized by so-called tradition preservers (*hagyományőrzők*) clearly offered an unforgettable experience for tens of thousands of people and also presented less familiar sides of the culture of the Hungarian people on the steppes of Central Asia before arriving to the Carpathian Basin, thus providing a kind of heritage tourism experience. In television shows and newspaper articles in Western Europe, the festival is presented as a somewhat alarming curiosity, while in Turkey and Central Asia, it has met with a remarkably positive reception.[20] It has also become considerably tamer. While in earlier years, the Hungarian Turanian Society took part in political events that could hardly have been considered part of "preservation of tradition" (for instance, a protest in 2012 against an attorney who took part in the reprisals taken after the 1956 revolution), this is no longer the case today. The presentations and lectures that are held as part of Kurultáj for the most part concern scholarly questions, and indeed, some of the representatives of more esoteric (and less scientific) narratives of Hungarian prehistory have taken exception to this. At the same time, to this day the right-wing literature coming out of Hungary finds a good market at the festival. Jobbik has consistently supported the idea behind the event, and in 2013, it awarded the main organizer of Kurultáj the so-called Gergely Pongrátz Cross of Merit, an award created by the party itself.[21]

The relationship, however, changed over the course of the past years, that is, since the shift in Jobbik's rhetoric concerning the East. Despite all efforts to establish a moderate political discourse, it is nonetheless worth noting and reflecting on the fact that András Zsolt Bíró and representatives of the Hungarian Turanian Foundation regularly speak of "the falsified account of Hungarian history." Their outbursts are directed against the scientific community supported by the Hungarian Academy of Sciences and, more narrowly, linguists, and they issue social demands in connection with the ideas they promote (insisting, for example, on "healthy public life and public education").[22] They strive, furthermore, to structure their discourse around the notion of the Hunnic roots of the Hungarians, and they envision the erection of a tremendous Attila statue in Budapest. Gradually, the whole affair has come to resemble quite strikingly the radical demands of the so-called Turanists who were active in the interwar period. On the one hand, today's Turanists regularly organize a festival that, in the name or under the pretext of nurturing the legacy of the past, creates a ritual presence and a forum in which to fashion a sacral vision of the national past—for the most part successfully, at least in the eyes of the participants. On the other hand, the organizers peddle a message that is by no means new (and they may very well be aware of this), the roots of which are found in the Hungarian Turanism of the interwar period.

Fig. 9.1. Kurultáj in 2014. Attribution: Derzsi Elekes Andor: Metapolisz DVD line under Creative Commons CC-BY-SA-3.0 license.

In 2010, the spread in public life of rhetorical reflexes based on notions of the Eastern elements of Hungarian identity prompted Fidesz, which had won a decisive parliamentary majority and was preparing to assume its place as the governing party, to express its views on the question. In its campaign platform, the party had already used the phrase "Eastern Opening" ("We need a new global economic opening, which includes an opening to the East, while maintaining the advantages we enjoy as a member of the European Union").[23] The government platform had already embellished this with talk of Hungary as "the border of the East" and the "new railway silk road."[24] In the period between 2010 and 2014, Prime Minister Viktor Orbán and, first and foremost, Péter Szijjártó (who at the time was state secretary of foreign affairs and who has since become minister of foreign affairs) took frequent trips to the East and made frequent statements that helped give some sense of what the term meant and put it in a larger context. As was and remains his habit, Prime Minister Orbán was not sparing with imaginative comparisons in his efforts to explain the background and essence of the Eastern Opening: "A Western brother [came to join] his Eastern brother" (in connection with a trip to Kazakhstan); "Hungary understands the message of the East" (when presenting distinctions to Lebanese businessmen); "We sail under a Western flag, but in the global economy the Eastern wind blows" (at the Hungarian Permanent Conference); and "Among half-Asian peoples like us, this is how things are done" (addressing Hungarian entrepreneurial leaders).[25]

In general, Szijjártó represented this stance more in dry numbers (for instance, in a speech held in Gödöllő, Hungary, in September 2013 for honorary Hungarian consuls). In his more technocratic explanations, the idea of kinship with the peoples of the East generally plays a smaller role. Szijjártó considered the Eastern Opening important from four perspectives, as emphasized in his exposé held in 2013: the strengthening of economic ties to Russia and the countries of the Far East, more active relations with the countries of the Caucasus, new foundations for ties to the Arab world, and the strengthening of Hungary's presence in the western Balkans.[26] It is worth noting that he did not mention the countries of Central Asia in his speech. In contrast, János Martonyi, who served as minister of foreign affairs from 2010 to 2014, and the whole Foreign Ministry under his direction stuck tenaciously to the "global opening" formula, and Martonyi spoke of the Eastern Opening as a kind of subsystem of this idea.[27] He did this perhaps first and foremost because Western partners, who were critical of the Orbán government from the outset, were noticing with increasing irritation and disapproval allusions to the alleged "crisis of the West" (yet another incarnation of Oswald Spengler's notion of the decline of the West, which one might have hoped not to see being recycled again) in the talk of an Eastern Opening, and they sensed a turn away, in Hungarian politics and public thinking, from the system of Euro-Atlantic relations. János Lázár, Fidesz floor leader at the time, tried to resolve this with the formula "keleti nyitás, nyugati tartás," which could be translated as something like "opening to the East, remaining in the West."[28] The Hungarian trade houses, positions as foreign trade attachés, and the new government scholarship program (Stipendium Hungaricum), all of which were tools in this enthusiastically promoted undertaking, were calibrated to meet the exigencies of this process of "opening," as were the foundation of new Hungarian cultural institutes and the strengthening of a network of instructors in these countries.

As part of these efforts, Hungarian cultural institutes were opened in Beijing, Belgrade, and Zagreb, and a government resolution and joint declaration were issued concerning the opening of Hungarian institutes in Baku and Teheran. (They were never actually opened, and the Baku institute was dropped from the agenda.) The ultimate fruits of the Eastern Opening in numbers were mixed: while Hungarian exports to China grew dramatically (from 318 billion forints to almost 500 billion forints between 2010 and 2014), exports to Central Asia and the countries of the Caucasus fluctuated, and the sanctions against Russia brought about a drastic drop in bilateral trade.[29] In the meantime, however, trade with the West grew, so the proportions of foreign trade did not change much. This consisted in large part of sales to the Far East by multinational companies that had set up factories in Hungary, like Mercedes and Audi. Furthermore, the Eastern Opening was accompanied by scandals, such as the extradition to Azerbaijan in 2012 of Ramil Safarov, an Azerbaijani military officer who had been convicted of murdering Armenian army lieutenant Gurgen Margaryan in Budapest in 2004 (Safarov was immediately pardoned upon his return and set free by the Azerbaijani president, much to the outrage of Armenia and the international community), or anomalies in the operations of the trade houses, which similarly did not put the initiative in a good light. Presumably, the announcement of a "Southern opening" toward Africa and South America in 2015 was necessary in part as a way of dropping talk about the East.

An attempt by a country to reorient its foreign policy and international relations and find new markets while using various rhetorical tropes and figures to facilitate and nurture support for this endeavor is in and of itself understandable and legitimate. And the "Eastern Opening" in Hungary is not or was not, in and of itself, a Turanist political idea. Neither Viktor Orbán nor Péter Szijjártó is a Turanist, and indeed in all likelihood, Gábor Vona is not one either. They do not consider it their mission to redeem the West or turn Hungary to the East. For the most part, they have a grasp of the history of the project of modernization in Hungary, and their upbringing and worldviews tie them to the Western world. The most recent turn in Jobbik's platform and Vona's increasingly frequent statements concerning the descent of the party into an instrument of populism and attempts to stifle antisemitic voices suggest that he himself does not take Turanism terribly seriously anymore (if he ever did). Nonetheless, in their discourses, these politicians use elements of the rhetoric of Turanism. For the moment, the influence of this rhetoric is limited. According to the 2017 assessment of Eurobarometer, the population of Hungary is, on average, more satisfied with the European Union than that of other EU member states (46 percent in Hungary compared with the European average of 42 percent). More than two-thirds of the population would vote to remain in the European Union if a referendum were held, compared with only 17 percent who would vote to leave. The majority of Hungarian citizens envision Hungary's future within Western frameworks (the EU and NATO). Only a small fraction of the population supports a turn to the East, and the number of people who adopt a "neither Eastward nor Westward" stance is significant.[30]

It would be an oversimplification to say that Turanism is an illusion, halfway between small-state imperialism and a Hungarian mirage. The situation is much more complex. Turanism may be a specific response to the tension between the notion that the Hungarians come from the East but follow the example of the West, and this would make it a distinctly or specifically Hungarian phenomenon, of interest only in the Hungarian context. But it is not an isolated phenomenon in eastern Europe. Some of its elements can also be discerned in Polish Sarmatism, Russian Eurasianism, and Pan-Turkism.[31] Turanism was the pillar of a vision of triumphant Hungarian imperialism before 1918—that is, the notion that the Hungarian state and nation should play a leading role in the cultural, political, and economic scene in the Balkans, eastern Europe, and perhaps even the Middle East. After the First World War, Turanism became the ideology of loss and frustration, and internal tensions broke up the movement. At the same time, the government cherry-picked whichever elements it deemed useful, and this paved the way for the emergence of the idea of "kindred peoples." The concept built on the Turanist understanding of the scientifically demonstrable shared roots of the Finnish, Estonian, and Hungarian peoples, and thus, it sought first and foremost to create a cultural and educational bridge between Hungarians and their "relatives."

One fundamental motive for this was the yearning to address Hungary's diplomatic isolation after the Treaty of Trianon. Since the elites of the nations concerned seemed to be interested in the concept of Turanism in a broad sense (i.e., reaching as far as Asia) and did not need the mediation of the Hungarian state, the majority of Turanist associations were self-contained and strove to maintain their positions by organizing pseudo-events. The Turanian Society, the most prominent Hungarian Turanist organization, generally failed when entrusted with tasks beyond its traditional functions. Superfluity, however, is not synonymous with irrelevance: although members of Orientalist Academic circles tended to withdraw from Turanist associations, the organization was ensured a place in Hungarian public life and the Hungarian Parliament Building (its actual seat) by the presence of university instructors, intellectuals, and government officials in high places.

By the late 1930s and early 1940s, new views had emerged among radical Turanists, views that drew on radical anti-Habsburg, anti-German stances and calls for independence, as well as the notion of the superiority of the Hungarians over the neighboring peoples and nations. They drew, furthermore, on frustrations with the world of academia and the universities and anticommunism tinged with racist notions of protecting the purity of the Hungarian people. After 1945, in certain circles of the émigré community, these views gave an additional thrust to notions of "kindred peoples," especially to assertions concerning the alleged kinship between the Sumerians and the Magyars. In the Hungarian public sphere under state socialism, intellectuals susceptible to these approaches tended to be marginal. They voiced their views among friends and in private gatherings, and they lent and borrowed books on the subject to and from one another. On the periphery of the academic world, some served as "bridge-builders" (to use the epithet ascribed to István Széchenyi, the nineteenth-century Hungarian statesman who had the first permanent bridge built linking Pest and Buda), seeking to preserve their ideas for a later day, after the fall of socialism. After 1990, there was a general turn away from the East in Hungary. Two factors that led to the increasingly palpable emergence of these ideas and the return of some of its elements to public discourse were a growing dissatisfaction with the promises of the prosperity that would come with integration into the Euro-Atlantic system and the permanent political crisis of the early 2000s. These ideas also gained currency, of course, because political figures who espoused them attained prominence and made them increasingly acceptable in political and public life.

This manner of speaking is worthless at this point if anyone wishes to use it as a foundation for a political platform in Hungary. It is worthless not because it is for some reason inappropriate to take an interest in the Eastern roots of Hungarian culture or the Hungarian people or to explore the contradictions between Hungary's place in Europe as a country with a distinctive language and history and the larger project of Western modernization and integration. But for the past two centuries, the Hungarian national project has consisted essentially of efforts on the part of the Hungarian elites to bring European forms (for instance, cultural, scientific, and political institutions) to Hungary. This has been seen as the precondition of success, prosperity, and liberty.[32] The great liberal generations of the nineteenth century believed that they were creating the legal and infrastructural framework for Western-style modernization, in other words civic associations (kaszinók), a banking system, the regulation of the Tisza River, the aforementioned Chain Bridge, national industry, general taxation, and (increasingly) general suffrage. If the framework were established, they believed the people of the Hungary would behave like the people of England and the Netherlands. They would be burgers, citizens, and bourgeois all at once. Things did not quite turn out this way, but that is another story. Nonetheless, the past two centuries have had tremendous weight. The various models began to appear in Hungarian society, if at times in jumbled or distorted form. "Modernization" and "reform" became stone cliffs so unmovable in public thinking that even the communists had to make appeals to them from time to time. For most Hungarians, the ideal society is, fundamentally (if also with self-contradictions), Western society. In a best-case scenario, the turn to the East is something with an exotic appeal. The Turanian idea has had some relevance in the arts. In the case of talented artists, the interest in Eastern artistic traditions is not merely another incarnation of Orientalism or simply playing with form. The buildings of István Medgyaszay, the interiors of Ede Toroczkai Wigand, and the sculptures of Ferenc Medgyessy are clear examples of the influence of this artistic concept, and they may well be among the most enduring forms of cultural reflection on the question of origins.

As early as 1841, only a few years after the emergence of the term *Turanism* in the journal *Kelet népe* (People of the East), Széchenyi, who remains perhaps the most formative figure of Hungarian thinking, raised a comment about Hungarian modernization and the origins of the Hungarian people: "The burgeoning and rise of the Hungarian people, a heterogeneous Eastern swarm so separated and isolated in Europe, to a flowering nation is not quite as simple as many people with a good disposition and warm humor think."[33] Certainly, the events of even the recent past suggest that Széchenyi was all too prescient.

Notes

1. See a statement made by László Békesi, who later served as minister of finance for the Hungarian Socialist Party: "We cannot permit ourselves to make unfounded promises,"

Népszabadság, April 19, 1994, 17. See also the democratic-opposition economic policy platforms: "Magyar Szocialista Párt (MSZP)," *Társadalmi Szemle* 49, no. 4 (1994): 15.

2. Tibor Baráth, *Tájékoztató az újabb magyar őstörténeti kutatásokról* (Veszprém-Győr: Turul, 1989).

3. For one of the first scholarly discussions of his work, see Nóra Kovács, "A diaszpóra visszavándorlásának ideológiai vonatkozásai Közép-Kelet Európában: Badiny Jós Ferenc Magyarországon," *Néprajzi Látóhatár* 16, nos. 1–4 (2017): 284–304.

4. Ferenc Badiny Jós, *Művei: I-XX* (Budapest: Magyar Ház Kiadó, 2003–2009).

5. See Péter Nemeshegyi, "Pártus herceg volt-e Jézus Krisztus?" *Távlatok* 17 (2007): 300–313; István Jelenits, "'Minden lehetséges?'—Az is, hogy Jézus pártus hercegnek született?" *Turán* 3, no. 6 (2000–2001): 103–19. On the reactions of the academic world, see Zoltán Pálfi and Bálint Tanos, "A sumer-magyar hit és a sumerológia," *Ókor* 5, nos. 3–4 (2006): 100–106; and Michael Knüppel, "Zur ungarischen Rezeption der sumerisch-turanischen Hypothese in der zweiten Hälfte des 20. Jahrhunderts," *Zeitschrift für Balkanologie* 42, nos. 1–2 (2006): 100–103.

6. Géza Komoróczy, *Sumér és magyar?* (Budapest: Magvető, 1976).

7. Zürichi Magyar Történelmi Egyesület, accessed January 19, 2021, zmte.webnode.hu.

8. See "Beköszöntő," *Turán* 1, no. 3 (1998): 1.

9. "Magyar Őstörténeti Kutató és Kiadó Kft felszámolás alatt," *Cégközlöny*, no. 29, July 21, 2011.

10. Géza Varga, "Mozog a föld. Gyorsjelentés a Magyarok Világszövetsége által a Magyarok VI. Világtalálkozója keretében rendezett 'Magyarság és kelet' őstörténeti konferenciáról," accessed September 11, 2016, http://ikint.uw.hu/mozog_a_fold.htm.

11. For an overview of the rise of Jobbik and the explanations for its rise, see András Kovács, "The Post-Communist Extreme Right: the Jobbik Party in Hungary," in *Right-Wing Populism in Europe: Politics and Discourse*, ed. Ruth Wodak, Majid Khosravinik, and Brigitte Mral (London: Bloomsbury, 2013), 223–34. On the historical roots of this phenomenon, see Balázs Ablonczy and Bálint Ablonczy, "L'extrême droite en Hongrie: Racines, culture, espace," in *L'extrême droite en Europe*, ed. Béatrice Giblin (Paris: La Découverte, 2014), 49–75.

12. "Radikális változás: A Jobbik országgyűlési választási programja a nemzeti önrendelkezésért és a társadalmi igazságosságért," 75, accessed January 19, 2021, http://docplayer.hu/158036-Radikalis-valtozas-a-jobbik-orszaggyulesi-valasztasi-programja-a-nemzeti-onrendelkezesert-es-a-tarsadalmi-igazsagossagert.html. The English version of the program did not use such terms; see accessed October 17, 2017, http://www.jobbik.com/sites/default/files/Jobbik-RADICALCHANGE2010.pdf.

13. Ibid.

14. For Jobbik's 2014 program, see "Kimondjuk, megoldjuk: A Jobbik országgyűlési választási programja a nemzet felemelkedéséért," 85, accessed September 11, 2017, https://de.slideshare.net/JobbikLadany/jobbik-programja. The English version avoided such phrasing: "We Name It, We Solve It," accessed October 17, 2017, https://drive.google.com/file/d/oB-HgDIa59TRmTTdrX3laNVhMYms/edit.

15. During his tour of the Székely Land, Csanád Szegedi again took a stand in support of the self-determination of the Székely ethnic group in Romania. See kuruc.info, June 27, 2011, accessed September 11, 2017, https://kuruc.info/r/3/81179/, and Gábor Vona, "Nagy megtiszteltetés ért," alfahir.hu, October 17, 2012, accessed September 11, 2017, http://alfahir.hu/vona_gabor_nagy_megtiszteltetes_ert-20121017.

16. Gábor Vona, "El kell menni és nemmel kell szavazni," mno.hu, August 13, 2016, accessed September 11, 2017, https://mno.hu/belfold/vona-el-kell-menni-es-nemmel-szavazni -1356683.

17. See A. Z. Biró et al., "A Y-Chromosomal Comparison of the Madjars (Kazakhstan) and the Magyars (Hungary)," *American Journal of Physical Anthropology* 139, no. 3 (2009): 305–10.

18. The website for the event is kurultaj.hu.

19. Under the "Kollégiumok" menu point on the Lakitelek People's College website, see the Eastern Opening collegium, accessed January 19, 2021, https://nepfolakitelek.hu/index .php?option=com_content&view=category&layout=blog&id=46&Itemid=225.

20. See "Les 'guerriers' des steppes se déferlent sur la Hongrie," L'Express, August 30, 2013, accessed September 11, 2017, http://www.lexpress.fr/actualites/1/culture /les-guerriers-des-steppes-deferlent-sur-la-hongrie_1277300.html; and Emel Akçalı and Umut Korkut, "Geographical Metanarratives in East-Central Europe: Neo-Turanism in Hungary," *Eurasian Geography and Economics* 53, no. 5 (2012): 596–614.

21. The award was named after a key figure in the 1956 Hungarian Revolution who died in 2005. Pongrátz took part in the foundation of Jobbik. See Chris Moreh, "The Asianization of National Fantasies in Hungary: A Critical Analysis of Political Discourse," *International Journal of Cultural Studies* 19, no. 3 (2016): 341–53.

22. "Hamis történelemszemlélet: A Barikád interjúja Bíró András Zsolttal," kurultaj.hu, July 20, 2012, accessed September 11, 2017, http://kurultaj.hu/2012/07 /hamis-tortenelemszemlelet-a-barikad-interjuja-biro-andras-zsolttal/.

23. "Nemzeti ügyek politikája," 46, fidesz.hu, accessed on January 19, 2021, https://www .slideshare.net/Mariabloghu/fidesz-vlasztsi-program-2010. The citation is found in the section entitled "Itt az idő, hogy talpra állítsuk a magyar gazdaságot!" (Now is the time to put the Hungarian economy on its feet!).

24. "A Nemzeti Együttműködés Programja," 39, parlament.hu, accessed September 11, 2016, http://www.parlament.hu/irom39/00047/00047.pdf.

25. For Viktor Orbán's declarations, see "Orbán: keleti szél fúj," index.hu, November 5, 2010, accessed October 17, 2017, http://index.hu/belfold/2010/11/05/orban_keleti_szel_fuj/. For more on this, see "Orbán Viktor miniszterelnök a Magyar Érdemrend kitüntetést adományozta Adnan és Adel Kassar uraknak," accessed October 17, 2017, https://bejrut.mfa .gov.hu/news/orban-viktor-miniszterelnoek-a-magyar-erdemrend-kituentetest-adomanyozta -adnan-es-adel-kassar-uraknak; and "Orbán: veszekedős félázsiai nép a magyar," accessed September 11, 2017, http://24.hu/belfold/2012/07/26/orban-veszekedos-felazsiai-nep-a-magyar/.

26. Speech held by State Secretary Péter Szijártó, Gödöllő, September16, 2013, accessed September 11, 2017, http://konzuliszolgalat.kormany.hu/download/0/ad/80000 /Szijjartobeszed_tbkonzkonf.pdf.

27. "Magyar külpolitika az uniós elnökség után," Budapest, December 9, 2011, accessed September 11, 2017, http://2010-2014.kormany.hu/download/a/cb/60000/kulpolitikai _strategia_20111219.pdf.

28. "Lázár János: A keleti nyitás nem jelent nyugati zárást," *Népszabadság*, April 17, 2013, accessed October 17, 2017, http://nol.hu/belfold/lazar_janos__a_keleti_nyitas_nem_nyugati _zaras-1380501.

29. For the trade data, see "Külkereskedelem, 2014," Hungarian Central Statistical Office, accessed October 17, 2017, https://www.ksh.hu/docs/hun/xftp/idoszaki/kulker/kulker14.pdf.

30. For more on this see "Public Opinion in the European Union," Standard Eurobarometer 87: Annex, May 2017, accessed October 17, 2017, http://ec.europa.eu /commfrontoffice/publicopinion/index.cfm/ResultDoc/download/DocumentKy/79557, and http://index.hu/tudomany/2017/04/13/a_fideszesek_a_legnagyobb_oroszbaratok_de_a _tobbseg_szerint_nyugaton_a_helyunk/.

31. On "Sarmatism," see *Teksty drugie* 26, no. 1 (2015). For Eurasianism, see Marlène Laruelle, *Russian Eurasianism: An Ideology of Empire* (Baltimore: Johns Hopkins University Press, 2012). See also Landau, *Pan-Turkism*.

32. On the history of ideas in Hungary in the nineteenth century, see Balázs Trencsényi, et al., *A History of Modern Political Thought in East Central Europe*, vol. 1, *Negotiating Modernity in the "Long Nineteenth Century"* (Oxford: Oxford University Press, 2016), particularly chapters 1 and 2.

33. István Széchenyi, *A Kelet népe* (Pest: Trattner Károly, 1841), 373.

BIBLIOGRAPHY

Turanist Periodicals

A Magyar-Bosnyák és Keleti Gazdasági Központ Közleményei (1917–18)
A Nap Fiai (Buenos Aires, 1967–70)
Atilla (Komádi, 1937–39)
Északi rokonaink (1939–44)
Hadak Útja (1928–29)
Kelet (1920–21)
Keleti Szemle (1900–18)
Kőrösi Csoma Archívum (1920–37)
Napkönyv (Gödöllő, 1925–26)
Napsugár (Gödöllő, 1927–29)
Turán (1913–14, 1917–18, 1921–44)
Turán (1998–2011)
Turáni Értesítő (1939)
Turáni Nép (Miskolc, 1933–34)
Turáni Roham (1934–39)
Turáni Vadászok Évkönyve (1942–44)

All other periodical publications not listed here but figuring in the notes come from the digital collection Arcanum (adtplus.arcanum.hu).

Books

Ablonczy, Balázs. *Pal Teleki (1879–1941): The Life of a Controversial Hungarian Politician.* Wayne, NJ: CHSP, 2006.
Ágoston, Gábor, and Sudár, Balázs. *Gül baba és a magyarországi bektasi dervisek.* Budapest: Terebess, 2002.
Almásy, György. *Vándor-utam Ázsia szívébe.* Budapest: Kir. M. Természettudományi Társulat, 1903.
Az 1935. évi április 27-ére hirdetett országgyűlés képviselőházának naplója. 19. kötet. Budapest: Athenaeum, 1938.
Badiny Jós, Ferenc. *Messze az édes hazától.* Budapest: Magyar Ház, 2006.
Badiny Jós, Ferenc. *Művei: I-XX.* Budapest: Magyar Ház Kiadó, 2003–2009.
Bálint, Sándor. *A szögedi nemzet: A szegedi nagytáj népélete.* Szeged: Móra Ferenc Múzeum, 1975.
Bálint, Varga. *Monumental Nation: Magyar Nationalism and Symbolic Politics in Fin-de-siècle Hungary.* New York: Berghahn, 2016.
Balkányi, Kálmán. *Arcok, harcok, kudarcok.* Budapest: Pesti Lloyd Társulat, 1934.
Balogh, István. *Ecsedi István élete és munkássága.* Folklore and Ethnography 20. Debrecen: KLTE Néprajzi Tanszék, 1985.

Balogh, László. *Debrecen város utcanévkatasztere*. Debrecen: Hajdú-Bihar Megyei Levéltár, 2007.

Baráth, Tibor. *A magyar népek őstörténete*. 3 vols. Montreal: Self-published, 1968–74.

———. *Tájékoztató az újabb magyar őstörténeti kutatásokról*. Veszprém-Győr: Turul, 1989.

Baráthosi Balogh, Benedek. *Szumirok, szittyák, ősturánok*. Budapest: Self-published, 1929.

Batu. *A turáni egyistenhívők egyszerű istentiszteletének szertartása*. Budapest: n.p., 1936.

Békássy, Gyöngyi. *A turáni eszme*. Budapest: Göncöl, 1920.

———. *A vércsoportok kutatásának faji jelentősége*. Budapest: Reé, 1937.

Bencsi, Zoltán. *Koppány-e vagy István?* Budapest: Gyarmati Ferenc könyvnyomtató műhelye, Atilla Urunk 1504, esztendejében [1938].

———. *Ősi hitünk* [Our Ancient Faith]. Toronto: Magyar Church of Canada, 1987.

Bendefy, László. *Kunmagyaria: A kaukázusi magyarság története*. Budapest: Cserépfalvi, 1941.

———. *Magyarország és a Középkelet*. Budapest: Aquincum, 1945.

Benkő, Samu, ed. *Édes Idám! Kós Károly levelei feleségéhez, 1911–1918, 1946–1948*. Kolozsvár (Cluj-Napoca): Polis, 2011.

Bíró, Ferenc. *A nemzethalál árnya a XVIII. századvég és a XIX. századelő magyar irodalmában*. Pécs: Pro Pannonia, 2012.

Birtalan, Ágnes, and Dávid Somfai Kara, eds. *"Kőember állott a pusztán": Tanulmánykötet Mándoky Kongur István emlékére*. Budapest: L'Harmattan, 2008.

Blaskovich, Lajos. *Őshaza és Kőrösi Csoma Sándor célja*. Budapest: Stádium, 1942.

Bobula, Ida. *Sumerian Affiliations: A Plea for Reconsideration*. Washington, DC: Self-published, 1951.

Boér, György Gyalui. *Boját*. Nagybánya (Baia Mare, Romania): Self-published, 1941.

Csanády, György. *A májusi nagy áldozat*. Budapest: Szefhe, 1941.

Csetri, Elek. *Kőrösi Csoma Sándor*. Kolozsvár (Cluj-Napoca): Kriterion, 2002.

Csiki, Ernő. *Csiki Ernő állattani kutatásai Albániában*. Vol. 1. Balkán-kutatások, 1. Budapest: MTA, 1923.

———. *Csiki Ernő állattani kutatásai Albániában*. Vol. 2. Balkán-kutatások I, 2. Budapest: MTA, 1940.

Darkó, Jenő. *A turáni kultúra jellemvonásai és jelentősége*. Budapest: A Magyar Tanítók Könyvtára, 1936.

Déry, Attila. *Nemzeti kísérletek építészetünk történetében*. Budakeszi: Terc, 1995.

Diószegi, Vilmos. *Sebestyén Gyula*. Budapest: Akadémiai, 1972.

Dobrik, István. *Mokry-Mészáros Dezső*. Miskolc: Herman Ottó Múzeum, 1985.

Domokos, Péter. *Szkítiától Lappóniáig: A nyelvrokonság és az őstörténet kérdéskörének visszhangja irodalmunkban*. Budapest: Universitas, 1998.

Duka, Theodore. *Life and Works of Alexander Csoma de Kőrös*. London: Trübner, 1985.

Ecsedi, István. *A bolgárok földjén: Útirajzok*. Debrecen: Tiszántúli Könyv- és Lapkiadó Rt., 1929.

———. *A Hortobágy puszta és élete*. Debrecen: Debreczen Sz. Kir Város Könyvnyomda-vállalata, 1914.

Egey, Emese. *A két világháború közötti magyar-finn-észt kapcsolatok történetéből: Társasági, diplomáciai, katonai együttműködés*. Szombathely: NYME SEK Uralisztikai Tanszék, 2010.

Egey, Emese, and Enikő Szíj, eds. *A Turán című folyóirat 1913, 1917–1918, 1921–1944 finnugor mutatója*. Budapest: Tinta, 2002.

Fajcsák, Györgyi, and Zsuzsanna Renner, eds. *A Buitenzorg-villa lakója—A világutazó, műgyűjtő Hopp Ferenc (1833–1919)*. Budapest: Hopp Ferenc Múzeum, 2008.

Faragó, Ede. *Cserkészapród-könyv*. Budapest: Magyar Cserkészszövetség, 1937. First published in 1931.

Farkas, Ildikó, István Szerdahelyi, Yuko Umemura, and Péter Wintermantel, eds. *Tanulmányok a magyar-japán kapcsolatok történetéből*. Budapest: ELTE Eötvös, 2009.

Fazekas, Csaba. *Kisegyházak és szektakérdés a Horthy-korszakban*. Budapest: TEDISZ-Szent Pál Akadémia, 1996.

Fehérvári, Győző. *"A dalnak új utat mutattam": A Kalevala és a Kalevipoeg összehasonlító elemzése, magyarországi fogadtatása és hatása*. Budapest: Lucidus, 2002.

Gall, Anthony. *Kós Károly műhelye/The Workshop of Károly Kós*. Budapest: Mundus, 2002.

Gebhardi, Lajos Albert, József Hegyi, and István Kultsár. *Magyar Országnak históriája*. Vol. 2. Pest, 1803.

Gellér, Katalin, and Katalin Keserü. *A Gödöllői Művésztelep*. Budapest: Cégér, 1994.

Gellér, Katalin, Mária G. Merva, and Cecília Nagy Őriné, eds. *A gödöllői művésztelep 1901–1920/The Artists' Colony of Gödöllő*. Gödöllő: Gödöllői Városi Múzeum, 2003.

Gerle, János, Attila Kovács, and Imre Makovecz. *A századforduló magyar építészete*. Budapest: Szépirodalmi, 1990.

Gerlóczy, Gedeon, and Lajos Németh, eds. *Csontváry-emlékkönyv*. Budapest: Corvina, 1976.

Goldziher, Ignác. *Napló*. Edited by Sándor Scheiber. Budapest: Magvető, 1984.

Györffy, István. *Néphagyomány és nemzeti művelődés*. Budapest: Egyetemi Néprajzi Intézet, 1939.

Halmesvirta, Anssi. *Kedves rokonok: Magyarország és Finnország 1920–1945*. Budapest: Cédrus Művészeti Alapítvány-Napkút, 2014.

Haraszti, György, ed. *Vallomások a holtak házából—Ujszászy István vezérőrnagynak, a 2. vkf. osztály és az Államvédelmi Központ vezetőjének az ÁVH fogságában írott feljegyzései*. Budapest: Corvina-ÁBTL, 2007.

Hóman, Bálint. *Ősemberek, ősmagyarok*. Budapest: Kairosz, 2002.

Hübner, János, ed. *Mostani és régi nemzeteket, országokat, tartományokat, városokat, emlékezetre méltó mezővárosokat, helységeket, folyókat, tavakat, tengereket, öblöket, fokokat, szigeteket, hegyeket, erdőket, barlangokat, pénzeket, mértékeket, 's t. e. f. esmértető lexicon*. Vol. 1. Pest: Trattner János, 1816.

Huszka, József. *A magyar turáni ornamentika története*. Budapest: Pátria, 1930.

Ikvai, Nándor, ed. *Gödöllőiek, szentendreiek: Művészettörténeti tanulmányok*. Studia Comitatensia 10. Szentendre: Pest Megyei Múzeumok Igazgatósága, 1982.

Illés, György. *A katolikus turáni eszme hőse és vértanuja: Wilfinger József magyar apostoli hithirdető élete és működése Kínában*. Szombathely: Szombathelyi Papnövendékek Szent Ágoston Egylete, 1936.

Ipolyi, Arnold. *Magyar mythologia*. Pest: Heckenast Gusztáv, 1854.

Jungerth-Arnóthy, Mihály. *Moszkvai napló*. Edited by Péter Sipos and László Szűcs. Budapest: Zrínyi, 1989.

Jurecskó, László. *Boromisza Tibor nagybányai korszaka (1904–1914)*. Miskolc: MissionART, 1996.

Jurecskó, László, and Katalin Török. *Boromisza Tibor 1880–1960*. Szentendre: Pest Megyei Múzeumok Igazgatósága, 2012.

Juzbašić, Dževad, Imre Ress, and Andreas Gottsmann, eds. *Lajos Thallóczy, der Historiker und Politiker*. Sarajevo: Akademia der Wissenschaften und Küste von Bosnien-Herzegowina-Ungarischen Akademie der Wissenschaften, Institut für Geschichte, 2010.

Kállay, László Tarján, and Károly Béla Mészáros, eds. *Magyar könyv.* Vol. 2. Budapest: Hollóssy, n.d. [1942].

Katsányi, Sándor. *A főváros könyvtárának története 1945-ig.* Budapest: Fővárosi Szabó Ervin Könyvtár, 2004.

Keserü, Katalin. *Toroczkai Wigand Ede.* Budapest: Holnap, 2007.

Kincses Nagy, Éva, ed. *Őstörténet és nemzettudat, 1919–1931.* Szeged: JATE Magyar Őstörténeti Kutatócsoport, 1991.

Kiszely, Mária. *Turániak.* Budapest: Bárd Ferenc és Fia, 1944.

Kodolányi, János. *Emese álma regényfolyam: Istenek.* Budapest: Athenaeum, 1941.

———. *Holdvilág völgye.* Budapest: Athenaeum, 1942.

———. *Julianus barát.* Budapest: Athenaeum, 1938.

Komoróczy, Géza. *Sumér és magyar?* Budapest: Magvető, 1976.

Kopin, Katalin. *Kilenc évtized a művészet vonzásában. Pirk Jánosné Remsey Ágnes (1915–2010) és a Remseyek.* Szentendre: PMMI, 2011.

Kósa, László. *A magyar néprajz tudománytörténete.* Budapest: Osiris, 2001.

———. *A Magyar Néprajzi Társaság története 1889–1989.* Budapest: Magyar Néprajzi Társaság, 1989.

Kovács, István Gábor, ed. *Hit, tudomány, közélet: A Debreceni Tudományegyetem Református Hittudományi Kara (1914–1950) professzorainak életrajzi adattára és életútleírása.* Budapest: ELTE Eötvös Kiadó, 2014.

Kovács, Sándor Iván, ed. *Batu kán pesti rokonai.* Pozsony (Bratislava): Kalligram, 2001.

Kozma, Andor. *Turán: Ősrege.* Budapest: MTA, 1922.

Landau, Jacob M. *Pan-Turkism: From Irredentism to Cooperation.* London: Hurst and Company, 1995.

Lange, Britta. *Die Wiener Forschungen an Kriegsgefangenen 1915–1918.* Vienna: Verlag der ÖAW, 2013.

Langó, Péter. *Turulok és Árpádok: Nemzeti emlékezet és a koratörténeti emlékek.* Budapest: Typotex, 2017.

Laruelle, Marlène. *Russian Eurasianism: An Ideology of Empire.* Baltimore: Johns Hopkins University Press, 2008.

Lechner, Jenő. *A turáni népek művészete.* Budapest: Magyar Tudományos Társulatok Sajtóvállalata Rt., 1923.

Lóczy, Ludwig [Lajos]. *Geologische Studien im westlichen Serbien.* Balkán-kutatások 2. Berlin: Walter de Gruyter, 1924.

Lukinich, Frigyes. *A lív föld és népe.* Budapest: Egyetemi Nyomda, 1935.

Lükő, Gábor. *A magyar lélek formái.* Budapest: Sylvester, 1942.

———. *A moldvai csángók.* Budapest: Pázmány Péter Tudományegyetem Néprajzi Intézete, 1936.

Magyar, Zoltán. *Volt egyszer egy pesti polgárcsalád.* Budapest: Biró, 2011.

Malcolm, John. *Geschichte Persiens von der früesten Periode an bis zur jetzigen Zeit.* Leipzig: Hartleben, 1830.

Mandler, David. *Arminius Vambéry and the British Empire: Between East and West.* Lanham, MD: Lexington Books, 2016.

Mándoky Kongur, István. *A kun nyelv magyarországi emlékei.* Karcag: Karcag Város Önkormányzata, 1993.

Marjalaki Kiss, Lajos. *Anonymus és a magyarság eredete.* Miskolc: Miskolci Könyvnyomda, 1929.

Márki, Sándor. *Turáni tanulmányok*. Máriabesnyő: Attraktor, 2014.

Medgyaszay, István. *Thallóczy Lajos művészlelke. 1937. december 3-i emlékbeszéd*. Budapest: Thallóczy Lajos Társaság, 1938.

Mészáros, Gyula. *A másfélezeresztendős magyar nemzet: Néptörténelmi tanulmány*. New York: New York-i Magyar Irodalmi Kör, n.d.

Mit kíván a Magyar-Keleti Gazdasági Központ. Budapest: Márkus Samu Könyvnyomdája, 1916.

Nagy, Géza. *A skythák: Székfoglaló értekezés*. Budapest: MTA, 1909.

Nagy, Norbert. *A Konstantinápolyi Magyar Tudományos Intézet története (1916–1918)*. Balkán Füzetek 7. Pécs: PTE TTK FI Kelet-Mediterrán és Balkán Tanulmányok Központja, 2010.

Nagy, Sándor. *Életünk Körösfői-Kriesch Aladárral*. Gödöllő: Gödöllői Városi Múzeum, 2005.

Németh, József. *Hét év (1914–1921)*. Budapest: Magvető, 1993.

Nicolson, Harold. *Peacemaking*. London: Constable, 1933.

Őriné, Cecília Nagy, ed. *A népművészet a 19–20. század fordulójának művészetében és a gödöllői művésztelepen*. Gödöllő: Gödöllői Városi Múzeum, 2006.

Ormos, István. *Egy életút állomásai: Kmoskó Mihály (1876–1931)*. Budapest: METEM, 2017.

Padányi, Viktor. *Dentumagyaria*. Budapest: Püski, 2000.

Polónyi, Péter, ed. *Emlékezések a gödöllői művésztelepre*. Gödöllő: Helytörténeti Gyűjtemény, 1982.

———. *Remsey Jenő György 1885–1980 festőművész, író születésének 100. évfordulójára*. Gödöllő: Városi Helytörténeti Gyűjtemény, 1985.

Potzner, Ferenc. *Medgyaszay István*. Budapest: Holnap, 2004.

Pozsgai, Péter, ed. *Tűzcsiholó: Írások a 90 éves Lükő Gábor tiszteletére*. Budapest: Táton, 1999.

Pritz, Pál, ed. *Iratok a magyar külügyi szolgálat történetéhez 1918–1945*. Budapest: Akadémiai, 1994.

Pusztay, János. *Az "ugor–török háború" után*. Budapest: Magvető, 1977.

Remete, László. *A Fővárosi Szabó Ervin Könyvtár története*. Budapest: Fővárosi Szabó Ervin Könyvtár, 1966.

Romsics, Ignác. *Clio bűvöletében—Magyar történetírás a 19–20. században, nemzetközi kitekintéssel*. Budapest: Osiris, 2011.

———. *Hungary in the Twentieth Century*. Budapest: Osiris-Corvina, 1999.

Rubinyi, Mózes, ed. *Zempléni Árpád emlékezete*. Budapest: Lafontaine Irodalmi Társaság, 1940.

Sándor, Klára. *A székely írás nyomában*. Budapest: Typotex, 2014.

Snyder, Louis L. *Macro-Nationalisms: A History of the Pan-Movements*. London: Praeger, 1984.

Sőregi, János. *A szkíta-magyar kontinuitás elméletének jogosultsága a turáni szellem keretében*. Karcag: Kertész József könyvnyomdája, 1927.

Sragner, Márta, ed. *A száz éve született Bendefy László élete és művei*. Marosvásárhely (Târgu Mureş): Mentor, 2004.

Staud, Géza. *Az orientalizmus a magyar romantikában*. Budapest: Terebess, 1992.

Stumpf, András. *Szörényi—Rohan az idő*. Budapest: Helikon, 2015.

Szabó, Miklós. *Az újkonzervativizmus és a jobboldali radikalizmus története (1867–1918)*. Budapest: Új Mandátum, 2003.

Széchenyi, Béla. *Gróf Széchenyi Béla keletázsiai utazásának (1877–1880) tudományos eredményei*. 3 vols. Budapest: Kilián, 1890–97.

Széchenyi, István. *A Kelet népe*. Pest: Trattner Károly, 1841.

Szekér, Nóra. *Titkos társaság: A Magyar Testvéri Közösség története*. Budapest: Jaffa, 2017.

Szendrei, László. *A turanizmus: Definíciók és értelmezések 1910-től a II. világháborúig*. Máriabesnyő: Attraktor, 2010.

Szendrei, László, ed., *Márki Sándor: Turáni tanulmányok*. Máriabesnyő: Attraktor, 2014.

Szépvizi Balás, Béla, ed. *Napkönyv—Turáni képes naptár és évkönyv*. Vol. 1. Gödöllő: Self-published, 1925.

Szerdahelyi, István, and Péter Wintermantel, eds. *Japanológiai körkép*. Budapest: ELTE Eötvös, 2007.

Szörényi, László. *Hunok és jezsuiták: Fejezetek a magyarországi latin hősepika történetéből*. Budapest: Nap, 2018.

Teleki, Pál, ed. *Finnek, észtek—A magyarok északi testvérnépei*. Budapest: Királyi Magyar Egyetemi Nyomda, 1928.

Teleki, Pál, ed. *Finnek, észtek—A magyarok északi testvérnépei*. Budapest: Királyi Magyar Egyetemi Nyomda, 1928.

———. *A Turáni Társaság eddigi és jövendő működése: Megnyitó beszéd az 1914. január 31-i közgyűlésre*. Budapest, 1914.

———. *Válogatott politikai írások és beszédek*. Edited by Balázs Ablonczy. Budapest: Osiris, 2000.

Teleki Pál, and Ernő Csiki, eds. *Adatok Albánia flórájához / Additamenta ad floram Albaniae*. Balkán-kutatások 3. Budapest: MTA, 1926.

Török, Katalin, ed. *Boromisza Tibor önéletrajzi feljegyzései*. Szentendre: Rectus, 2011.

Trencsényi, Balázs, Maciej Janowski, Monika Baar, Maria Falina, and Michal Kopecek, eds. *A History of Modern Political Thought in East Central Europe*. Vol. 1, *Negotiating Modernity in the "Long Nineteenth Century."* Oxford: Oxford University Press, 2016.

Tubay, Tiziano. *A székely írás kutatásának története*. Budapest: OSZK, 2015.

Túrmezei, László. *A Turán sajtóiroda története*. Budapest: Magyarországi Turánok Baráti Köre, 1935.

Umemura, Yuko. *A Japán-tengertől a Duna-partig: Imaoka Dzsúicsiró életpályája a magyar-japán kapcsolatok tükrében*. Budapest: Gondolat, 2006.

Ungváry, Krisztián. *Battle for Budapest*. London: Tauris, 2012.

Uxbond, F. A. *Munda-Magyar-Maori: An Indian Link between the Antipodes; New Tracks of Hungarian Origins*. London: Luzac, 1928.

Vámbéry, Ármin. *Küzdelmeim*. Budapest: Franklin, 1905.

———. *A magyarság bölcsőjénél*. Budapest: Athenaeum, 1914.

Vámbéry, Arminius. *His Life and Adventures*. London: T. Fisher Unwin, 1886.

Váraljai, Anna. *Mokry. Idegen világ—Mokry-Mészáros Dezső művészete*. Budapest: Virág Judit Galéria, 2017.

Varga, Ildikó P., ed. *"Finnország leglelkesebb diplomatája itt több mint 50 éven keresztül": Vikár Béla levelei*. Kolozsvár (Cluj-Napoca): Erdélyi Múzeum Egyesület, 2017.

Vásáry, István. *Magyar őshazák és magyar őstörténészek*. Budapest: Balassi, 2008.

Vincze, Zoltán. *A kolozsvári régészeti iskola a Pósta Béla-korszakban (1899–1919)*. Kolozsvár (Cluj-Napoca): EME, 2014.

Virányi, Elemér. *A finn-ugor népek élettere*. Budapest: Stádium, 1941.

Wesselényi, Miklós. *Szózat a' magyar és szláv nemzetiség' ügyében*. Pest: Ottó Wigand, 1843.

Zajti, Ferenc. *A hun—magyar őstörténelem*. Budapest: Self-published, 1928.

———. *Kapcsolataink Indiával*. Budapest: Magyar Nemzeti Szövetség, 1929.

———. *Magyar évezredek (Skytha-hun-magyar faji azonosság)*. Budapest: Self-published, 1939.

Zarycki, Tomasz. *Ideologies of Eastness in Central and Eastern Europe*. BASEES/Routledge Series on Russian and East European Studies, no. 96. London: Routledge, 2014.

Zempléni, Árpád. *Turáni dalok: Mondai és történelmi hős-énekek*. Budapest: Franklin, 1910.

Zichy, Jenő. *Harmadik ázsiai utazása*. vols. 1–6. Budapest-Leipzig: Hornyánszky-Hiersemann, 1900–1905.

———. *Kaukázusi és közép-ázsiai utazásai*. 2 vols. Budapest: Gusztáv Ranschburg, 1897.

———. *Oroszországi és keletázsiai expeditiójának beszámolója*. Budapest: Hornyánszky, 1899.

Articles and Chapters

Ablonczy, Balázs. "'Lándzsahegy', néprokonság, small talk—Turanizmus és keleti gondolat a két világháború közötti magyar külpolitikai gondolkodásban." In *Magyar külpolitikai gondolkodás a 20. században*, edited by Pál Pritz, 87–106. Budapest: Magyar Történelmi Társulat, 2006.

———. "Ördögszekéren." Baráth Tibor párizsi évei (1930–1939)." *Történelmi Szemle* 58, no. 3 (2016): 429–50.

———. "Székely identitásépítés Magyarországon a két világháború között." In *Székelyföld és a Nagy Háború. Tanulmánykötet az első világháború centenáriuma alkalmából*, edited by Zsolt Orbán, 467–85. Csíkszereda [Miercurea Ciuc]: Csíkszereda Kiadóhivatal, 2018.

Ablonczy, Balázs, and Bálint Ablonczy. "L'extrême droite en Hongrie: Racines, culture, espace." In *L'extrême droite en Europe*, edited by Béatrice Giblin, 49–75. Paris: La Découverte, 2014.

Akçalı, Emel, and Umut Korkut. "Geographical Metanarratives in East-Central Europe: Neo-Turanism in Hungary." *Eurasian Geography and Economics* 53, no. 5 (2012): 596–614.

Angyal, Endre. "Lengyel és magyar barokk." In *Tanulmányok a lengyel-magyar irodalmi kapcsolatok köréből*, edited by László Sziklay, Lajos Hopp, István Csapláros, and Jan Reychman, 211–44. Budapest: Akadémiai, 1969.

Arbanász, Ildikó, and György Csorba. "Magyar kutatók az isztambuli levél- és könyvtárakban a második világháború előtt." In *A kísérlet folytatódik*, vol. 2, *Nemzetközi Vámbéry-konferencia*, edited by Mihály Dobrovits, 7–46. Dunaszerdahely [Dunajská Streda]: Lilium Aurum, 2005.

Avar, Gyula [Lajos Gogolák]. "Miért veszedelmes a turanizmus?" *Vigilia* 1, no. 1 (1935): 178–86.

Aytürk, Ilker. "The Racist Critics of Atatürk and Kemalism, from the 1930s to the 1960s." *Journal of Contemporary History* 46, no. 2 (April 2011): 308–35.

Bálint, Sándor. "Maróthy István orvos, Vörösmarty diákkori barátja." Az Országos *Orvostörténeti Könyvtár Közleményei*, no. 43 (1967): 113–22.

Baráth, Béla Levente. "Varga Zsigmond teológia professzor, a debreceni m. kir. Tisza István Tudományegyetem 1932/33. évi rector magnificusa." *Gerundium* 9, no. 1 (2018): 3–22.

Bartha, Júlia. "Györffy István balkáni és törökországi kutatásai." In *Társadalom, kultúra, természet: tanulmányok a 60 éves Bellon Tibor tiszteletére*, edited by Gábor Barna, 289–300. Szolnok: Jász-Nagykun-Szolnok Megyei Múzeumok Igazgatósága, 2001.

Bereczki, András. "A két háború közötti magyar-észt kapcsolatok történetéről." *Jogtörténeti Szemle* 18, no. 1 (2004): 58–67.

Biezanis, Lowell. "Volga-Ural Tatars in Emigration." *Central Asian Survey* 11, no. 4 (1992): 29–74.

Bincsik, Mónika. "Felvinczi Takács Zoltán (1880–1964): A magyar orientalista művészettörténet-írás megalapítója." *Enigma* 17, no. 83 (2010): 83–100.

Bíró, A. Z., A. Zalán, A. Völgyi, and H. Pamjav. "A Y-Chromosomal Comparison of the Madjars (Kazakhstan) and the Magyars (Hungary)." *American Journal of Physical Anthropology* 139, no. 3 (July 2009): 305–10.

Blazovich, László. "A Tripartitum és forrásai." *Századok* 141, no. 4 (2007): 1011–23.

Bori, Imre. "Zempléni Árpád." *Híd* 63, no. 11 (1999): 687–91.

"Cholnoky Jenő önéletrajza." *Vár Ucca Tizenhét* 6, no. 2 (1998): 187–339.

———. "hozzászólása." In *A zsidókérdés Magyarországon. A Huszadik Század körkérdése,* 2nd ed., 71–76. Budapest: Társadalomtudományi Társaság, 1917.

Csáki, Tamás. "A finn építészet és az 'architektúra magyar lelke' Kultúrpolitika, építészet, publicisztika a századelő Magyarországán." *Múltunk* 51, no. 1 (2006): 200–230.

Csaplár-Degovics, Krisztián. "Lajos Thallóczy und die Historiographie Albaniens." In *Südost-Forschungen,* vol. 68, edited by Ulf Brunnbauer and Konrad Clewing, 205–46. Regensburg: Oldenbourg, 2009.

Csirkés, Ferenc. "Nemzeti tudomány és nemzetközi politika." Vámbéry Ármin munkásságában. *Magyar Tudomány* 174, no. 8 (2013): 944–51.

Csorba, György. "Történész a történelem viharában: Karácson Imre az 1908–1911 közötti törökországi eseményekről." *Keletkutatás* (Spring 2012): 87–101.

Csörsz, Édua. "Az 'ősmagyar mítosz' posztmodern rítusai Bugacon: A Kurultáj és az Ősök Napja." In *Már a múlt sem a régi . . . Az új magyar mitológia multidiszciplináris elemzése,* edited by László Attila Hubbes and István Povedák, 207–25. Szeged: MTA-SZTE Vallási Kultúrakutató Csoport, 2015.

Dévényi, Kinga. "Levelek, napló, emlékbeszéd: adalékok Goldziher Ignác és Vámbéry Ármin kapcsolatához." *Keletkutatás* (Autumn 2014): 101–14.

Fajcsák, Györgyi. "Keleti művészeti kiállítás: Keleti magángyűjtemények, kínai tárgyak a két világháború között Budapesten." *Tanulmányok Budapest múltjából,* no. 34 (2009): 185–208.

Farkas, Gyula. "A magyar antropológia története a kezdettől 1945-ig." In *A Móra Ferenc Múzeum Évkönyve 1987,* 81–118. Szeged: Móra Ferenc Múzeum, 1988.

Farkas, Ildikó. "A Magyar-Nippon Társaság." In *Tanulmányok a magyar-japán kapcsolatok történetéből,* edited by Ildikó Farkas, István Szerdahelyi, Yuko Umemura, and Péter Wintermantel, 226–47. Budapest: ELTE Eötvös Kiadó, 2009.

———. "A magyar turanizmus török kapcsolatai." *Valóság* 50, no. 6 (2007): 31–48.

———. "A török-tatár népek turanizmusa." *Világtörténet* 28, no. 2 (2006): 52–63.

———. "A turánizmus." *Magyar Tudomány* 54, no. 7 (1993): 860–68.

———. "A turanizmus és a magyar-japán kapcsolatok a két világháború között," *Folia Japonica Budapestininensia* 1 (2001): 28–44.

Ferkai, András. "A társasház, mint a budapesti lakóházépítés megújításának egyik módja," *Ars Hungarica* 20, no. 2 (1992): 61–76.

Fettich, Nándor. "Szkíták-szittyák." *Magyar Szemle* 4, no. 12 (1928): 338.

Filep, Tamás Gusztáv. "Turáni dalok." In *Az ellenállás vize: Jegyzetek, kísérletek, portrévázlatok,* by Tamás Gusztáv Filep, 14–17. Budapest: Széphalom, 1993.

g-y. "dr. Bencsi Zoltán: Ősi hitünk." *A Fehér Barát* 2, no. 3 (September 1939): 45–46.

Gaál, László. "Műkedvelők a magyar őstörténeti kutatásban." *Magyar Szemle* 12, no. 5–8 (1931): 262–72.

Gábor, Eszter. "'. . . e műemlékeinkben a történelmi magyar hangulatoknak mélységes tengerét bírjuk': Lechner Jenő kísérlete a magyar nemzeti historizmus megteremtésére." In *Sub Minervae nationis praesidio: Tanulmányok a nemzeti* kultúra kérdésköréből Németh Lajos 60. születésnapjára, 180–85. Budapest: ELTE Művészettörténeti Tanszék, 1989.

Garázda, Péter [Béla Zolnai]. "Turáni kótyag." Széphalom 3, no. 3–4 (1929): 144–47.

Gasimov, Zaur, and Wiebke Bachmann. "Transnational Life in Multicultural Space: Azerbaijani and Tatar Discourses in Interwar Europe." In Muslims in Interwar Europe: A Transcultural Historical Perspective, edited by Bekim Agai, Umar Ryad, and Mehdi Sajid, 205–24. Leiden: Brill, 2015.

Gellér, Katalin. "Misztikus tanok hatása Körösfői-Kriesch Aladár művészetében." In Körösfői-Kriesch Aladár (1863–1920) festő- és iparművész monográfiája és oeuvre katalógusa, edited by Cecília Nagy Őriné, 120–26. Gödöllő: Gödöllői Városi Múzeum, 2016.

Germanus, Gyula. "Turán." Magyar Figyelő 6, no. 1 (1916): 405–20.

———. "Turán II." Magyar Figyelő 6, no. 2 (1916): 23–37.

Gjurov, Alexander. "Fehér Géza helye a bolgár-magyar kulturális és tudományos kapcsolatokban a két világháború között." Somogy 20, no. 3 (1992): 68–73.

Godinek, Ibolya. "Fajvédő eszme A Cél című folyóiratban." Valóság 57, no. 2 (2014): 40–58.

Gombocz, Zoltán. "Bolgárok és magyarok." Új Magyar Szemle 2, no. 2 (1920): 176–83.

Granasztói, Péter. "Pajta és gimnázium között: A Néprajzi Múzeum épülete tervpályázatának története (1923)." Néprajzi Értesítő 97 (2015): 37–64.

Győry, János. "Turánizmus után exotizmus." Magyar Szemle 26, no. 3 (1936): 276–78.

Heiss, Johann, and Johannes Feichtinger. "Distant Neighbors: Uses of Orientalism in the Late Nineteenth-Century Austro-Hungarian Empire." In Deploying Orientalism in Culture and History: From Germany to Central and Eastern Europe, edited by Johannes Feichtinger, James Hodkinson, John Walker, and Shaswati Mazumdar, 148–65. Rochester, NY: Woodbridge, Boydell, and Brewer, 2013.

Hoppál, Mihály. "Egy elfelejtett magyar sámánkutató: Baráthosi Balogh Benedek élete és munkássága." Keletkutatás (Autumn 1996/Spring 2002): 185–202.

Horváth, Iván. "A székely rovásírás és a latin-magyar ábécé." In A magyar irodalom történetei, vol. 1., edited by Mihály Szegedy-Maszák, 36–48. Budapest: Gondolat, 2007.

Jäschke, Gotthard. "Der Turanismus der Jungtürken. Zur osmanischen Außenpolitik im Weltkriege." Die Welt des Islams 23, nos. 1–2 (1941): 1–54.

Kállay, Ferencz. "Szónyomozások." Tudománytár 5 (1835): 147–74.

Keményfi, Róbert. "Malonyay: 'A magyar nép művészete'; A gödöllőiek—helyek, emlékezetek." In "A burgonyától a szilvafáig": Tanulmányok a hetvenéves Kósa László tiszteletére, edited by Elek Bartha, 31–80. Debrecen: Debreceni Egyetem Néprajzi Tanszék, 2012.

Kersken, Norbert. "Geschichtsbild und Adelsrepublik: Zur Sarmatentheorie in der polnischen Geschichtsschreibung der frühen Neuzeit." Jahrbücher für Geschichte Osteuropas 52, no. 2 (2004): 235–60.

Keserü, Katalin. "A budapesti Néprajzi Múzeum építészeti tervei és a gödöllőiek." In A népművészet a 19–20. század fordulójának művészetében és a gödöllői művésztelepen, edited by Cecília Nagy Őriné, 136–44. Gödöllő: Gödöllői Városi Múzeum, 2006.

———. "Finn-kép a magyar művészeti életben a századelőn." Hungarologische Beiträge 1, no. 1 (1993): 209–17.

———. "A Gödöllői Művésztelep történetének kronológiája." Vár ucca tizenhét 7, no. 2 (1999): 75–79.

Knüppel, Michael. "Zur ungarischen Rezeption der sumerisch-turanischen Hypothese in der zweiten Hälfte des 20. Jahrhunderts." *Zeitschrift für Balkanologie* 42, nos. 1–2 (2006): 93–107.

Kolta, Dóra. "A Kelet-motívum újjáéledése: Orientalista motívumok Ady prózájában." *Napút* 12, no. 6 (2010): 103–14.

Koós, Judith. "Akseli-Gallen Kallela (1865–1931) és a finn-magyar művészeti kapcsolatok kezdetei." *Művészettörténeti Értesítő* 16, no. 1 (1967): 44–66.

Kósa, László. "Györffy István öröksége." In *Nemesek, polgárok, parasztok*, 404–23. Budapest: Osiris, 2003.

———. "Malonyay Dezső és 'A magyar nép művészete,'" In *Nemesek, polgárok, parasztok*, 387–403. Budapest: Osiris, 2003.

Kovács, András. "The Post-Communist Extreme Right: The Jobbik Party in Hungary." In *Right-Wing Populism in Europe: Politics and Discourse*, edited by Ruth Wodak, Majid KhosraviNik, and Brigitte Mral, 223–34. London: Bloomsbury, 2013.

Kovács, Nóra. "A diaszpóra visszavándorlásának ideológiai vonatkozásai Közép-Kelet Európában: Badiny Jós Ferenc Magyarországon." *Néprajzi Látóhatár* 16, nos. 1–4 (2017): 284–304.

Kövér, György. "'Minden tekintetben megfelelő combinatio . . .' Egy keresztény középosztályi fiatalember párválasztási dilemmái a 19–20. század fordulóján." In *Biográfia és társadalomtörténet*, 351–72. Budapest: Osiris, 2014.

Kubassek, János. "Kőrösi Csoma Sándor szobra Érden." *Földrajzi Múzeumi Tanulmányok* 1, no. 1 (1985): 11–16.

Kund, Attila. "Méhelÿ Lajos és a magyar fajbiológiai kísérlete (1920–1931)," *Múltunk* 57, no. 4 (2012): 239–89.

Lábadi, Károly. "A gödöllőiek találkozása a nép művészetével." In *A gödöllői művésztelep 1901–1920*, edited by Katalin Gellér, Mária G. Merva, and Cecília Nagy Őriné, 139–49. Gödöllő: Gödöllői Városi Múzeum, 2003.

Laruelle, Marlène. "La question du 'touranisme' des Russes: Contribution à une histoire des échanges intellectuels Allemagne–France–Russie au XIXe siècle." *Cahiers du monde russe* 45, no. 1 (2004): 241–66.

Levent, Sinan. "Common Asianist Intellectual History in Turkey and Japan: Turanism." *Central Asian Survey* 35, no. 1 (2016): 121–35.

Liipola, Yrjö. "Akseli Gallen-Kallela Magyarországon." *Művészettörténeti Értesítő* 28, no. 1 (1979): 48–50.

Lothrop, Stoddard T. "Pan-Turanism." *American Political Science Review* 11, no. 1 (February 1917): 12–23.

Lükő, Gábor. "A múló időben: Buddhista korszakunk halvány emlékei." *Gyökereink* 7 (1998): 107–54.

Lükő, Gábor. "Moldvai emlékeim." *Honismeret* 29, no. 3 (2001): 68–71.

Marjalaki Kiss, Lajos. "Új úton a magyar őshaza felé [Új eredet-teória]," *Nyugat* 23, no. 1 (1930): 899–913.

Maszanori, Kondó. "A szibériai magyar hadifoglyok és Japán." In *Tanulmányok a magyar-japán kapcsolatok történetéből*, edited by Ildikó Farkas, István Szerdahelyi, Yuko Umemura, and Péter Wintermantel, 177–85. Budapest: Eötvös, 2009.

"Meghalt Túrmezei László." *Itt-Ott* 12, no. 1 (1979): 12–14.

Merva, Mária G. "Remsey Jenő György (1885–1980) sokoldalú munkássága." In *Remsey Jenő György festőművész, író emlékkiállítása*, 6–37. Gödöllő: Gödöllői Városi Múzeum, 2010.

Mestyan, Adam. "'I Have to Disguise Myself': Orientalism, Gyula Germanus, and Pilgrimage as Cultural Capital, 1935–1965." In *The Hajj and Europe in the Age of Empire*, vol. 5, edited by Umar Ryad, Leiden Studies in Islam and Society, 217–39. Leiden: Brill, 2017.

———. "Materials for a History of Hungarian Academic Orientalism: The Case of Gyula Germanus." *Die Welt des Islams* 54, no. 1 (2014): 4–33.

Mészáros, Dezső. "A rovás történelmi, faji és gyakorlati jelentősége." In *Magyar könyv*, edited by László Tarján Kállay and Károly Béla Mészáros, 57–61. Budapest: Szalay Sándor könyvnyomdája, 1941.

———. "A turán-magyar temető." In *Magyar könyv*, vol. 2, edited by László Tarján Kállay and Károly Béla Mészáros, 92–97. Budapest: Hollóssy János Könyvnyomtató Műhelye, 1942.

Moreh, Chris. "The Asianization of National Fantasies in Hungary: A Critical Analysis of Political Discourse." *International Journal of Cultural Studies* 19, no. 3 (2016): 341–53.

Móricz, Zsigmond, "A magyar költő—Zempléni Árpád halálára," *Nyugat* 12, nos. 14–15 (1919): 991–98.

Molnár, Antal. "A Szentszék, a magyar jezsuiták és egy törökországi tudományos intézet alapításának terve (1930–1934)." In *Magyarország és a Szentszék diplomáciai kapcsolatai 1920–2015*, edited by András Fejérdy, 173–210. Budapest: Balassi Intézet–Római Magyar Akadémia—METEM, 2015.

Nagy, Árpád Miklós. "Hekler Antal (1882–1940): Pont—ellenpont; Hekler Antal, a klasszika archeológus." *Enigma* 13, no. 47 (2006): 161–77.

Nagy, Zsolt. "In Search of a Usable Past: The Legacy of the Ottoman Occupation in Interwar Hungarian Cultural Diplomacy." *Hungarian Studies Review* 42, no. 1–2 (Spring–Fall 2015): 27–52.

Nemeshegyi, Péter. "Pártus herceg volt-e Jézus Krisztus?" *Távlatok* 17 (2007): 300–313.

Németh, Gyula. "A magyar turánizmus." *Magyar Szemle* 11, no. 2 (February 1931): 132–39.

O'Sullivan, Michael. "A Hungarian Josephinist, Orientalist, and Bibliophile: Count Karl Reviczky, 1737–1793" *Austrian History Yearbook* 45 (2014): 61–88.

———. "A török-magyar kapcsolatok alakulása egy diplomata szemével—Tahy László ankarai követ munkássága (1924–1933)." *Keletkutatás* (Spring 2015): 93–103.

Ormos, István. "Adalékok Pröhle Vilmos alakjához." *Keletkutatás* (Spring 2012): 33–65.

Paikert, Alajos. "Életem és korom." (Közzéteszi: Takáts Rózsa). *A Magyar Mezőgazdasági Múzeum Közleményei* 17 (1998/2000): 159–218.

Paksa, Rudolf. "Márki Sándor." *Korunk* 22, no. 5 (2011): 60–65.

———. "A történetírás mint propaganda. Baráth Tibor útja a szaktörténetírástól a mítoszgyártásig." *Kommentár* 1, no. 5 (2006): 69–79.

Pálfi, Zoltán, and Bálint Tanos. "A sumer-magyar hit és a sumerológia." *Ókor* 5, nos. 3–4 (2006): 100–106.

Pallag, Zoltán. "Pósta Béla és a magyar keleti archeológiai intézet terve." In *A Debreceni Déri Múzeum Évkönyve 2002–2003*, 117–32. Debrecen: Déri Múzeum, 2003.

Petruccelli, David. "Banknotes from the Underground: Counterfeiting and the International Order in Interwar Europe." *Journal of Contemporary History* 51, no. 3 (2016): 507–30.

Pirint, Andrea. "Mokry asztala: Rovásírók Miskolcon a két világháború között." In *A rovás megújítói: Mokry-Mészáros Dezső és Verpeléti Kiss Dezső*, edited by Tamás Rumi, 4–50. n.p: Rovás Alapítvány, 2018.

Pomozi, Péter. "A Tartui Egyetem és Magyarország." *Zempléni Múzsa* 3, no. 3 (2003): 16–28.

Pröhle, Wilhelm. "Studien zur Verleichung des Japanischen mit den uralischen und altaischen Sprachen," *Keleti Szemle* 17, nos. 1–3 (1916–17): 147–83.

Pulszky, Ferencz. "Irán és Turán." *Athenaeum* 6, no. 18 (September 1, 1839): 273–79.

Rady, Martin. "The Prologue to Werbőczy's Tripartitum and its Sources." *English Historical Review* 121, no. 490 (February 2006): 104–45.

Richly, Gábor. "Magyar katonai segítségnyújtás az 1939–40-es finn–szovjet háborúban." *Századok* 130, no. 2 (1996): 403–44.

Riikonen, H. K. "Sustaining Kinship in Wartime: Finnish-Hungarian Contacts in the Light of the Yearbook *Heimotyö*, 1937–1944." *Hungarologische Beiträge* 4, no. 7 (1996): 61–77.

R-k. "Az orthodox turanizmus." *Magyar Szemle* 30, no. 6 (June 1937): 182–85.

Romsics, Ignác. "A magyar birodalmi gondolat." In *Múltról a mának*, 121–58. Budapest: Osiris, 2004.

Ruttkay-Miklián, Eszter. "Die uralischen forschungen des Ungarn Benedek Baráthosi Balogh." In *Europa et Sibiria: Gedenkband für Wolfgang Veenker*, vol. 51, edited by C. Hasselblatt and P. Jääsalmi-Krüger, 373–80. Wiesbaden: Veröffentlichungen der Societas Uralo-Altaica, 1999.

Saint-Aulaire, M. "minister de France à Bucarest à M. Pichon, minister des affaires étrangères, Bucarest, le 28 octobre 1919." In *Documents diplomatiques français sur l'histoire du bassin des Carpates*, vol. 2, edited by Magda Ádám. Budapest: Akadémiai, 1995.

Sallay, Gergely Pál, and Péter Wintermantel. "A magyar–japán diplomáciai kapcsolatok története, 1918–1945." In *Tanulmányok a magyar–japán kapcsolatok történetéből*, edited by Ildikó Farkas, István Szerdahelyi, Yuko Umemura, and Péter Wintermantel, 115–76. Budapest: ELTE Eötvös, 2009.

Sárközy. Miklós. "Arminius Vámbéry and the Baha'i Faith." *Bahai Studies Review* 18, no. 1 (2012): 55–82.

———. "Gaál László, az iranista." In *A Jászkunság tudósai*, edited by Julianna Örsi, 374–86. Szolnok: Jász-Nagykun-Szolnok Megyei Tudományos Egyesület, 2015.

———. "Személyiség és keletkutatás: Vámbéry Ármin és identitásai." In *Nyelv, kultúra, identitás: A Károli Gáspár Református Egyetem 2015-ös évkönyve*, edited by Enikő Sepsi, Kornélia Deres, Anita Czeglédy, and Csaba Szummer, 31–47. Budapest: KRE–L'Harmattan, 2015.

———. "A szittya Zarathustrától a gudzsárokon keresztül az ind Jézusig—Zajti Ferenc mint orientalista." In *Okok és okozat: A magyar nyelv eredetéről történeti, szociálpszichológiai és filozófiai megközelítésben*, edited by Marianne Bakró-Nagy, 77–109. Hungarian Academy of Sciences Department I series. Budapest: Gondolat Kiadói Kör, 2018.

Scheitz, Emil. "Egy 'őstörténész' latin tudása," *Egyetemes Philológiai Közlöny* 67 (1943): 239–40.

Senga, Toru. "Bálint Gábor, Pröhle Vilmos és a japán-magyar nyelvhasonlítás története." *Magyar Nyelv* 90, no. 2 (1994): 200–207.

Seres, István. "'Gyöngyös kám'-tól 'Batu mongol–magyar hadjárata'-ig (Abulgázi Bahadir és Rasidaddin krónikáinak első magyar kutatói)." In *A kísérlet folytatódik. II. Nemzetközi Vámbéry-konferencia*, edited by Mihály Dobrovits, 164–225. Dunaszerdahely [Dunajská Streda]: Lilium Aurum, 2005.

Sezer, Yavuz. "Hungarian Orientalism, Turanism and Karoly Kos's *Sztambul* (1918)." *Centropa* 7, no. 2 (2007): 136–52.

Sinor, Dénes. "Emlékezés Pröhle Vilmosra." *Magyar Nyelv* 91, no. 1 (1995): 100–103.

Sümegi, György. "'Az etnográfus mindenütt talál tanulmányozni valót' (Györffy István levelei Lükő Gábornak, 1931–1933)." *A Herman Ottó Múzeum Évkönyve* 41 (2002): 379–87.

Szabó, Dezső. "A turánizmus," *Élet és Irodalom* 1, no. 1 (1923): 14–22.

Szabó, Lilla. "Zajti Ferenc festőművész és Medgyaszay István építész magyarságkutatásai." *A Herman Ottó Múzeum Évkönyve* 46 (2007): 447–70.

Szalai, Miklós. "Az 1916. évi VII. törvénycikk." *Történelmi Szemle* 52, no. 4 (2010): 593–601.

Szécsényi, Mihály. "Virrasztó Koppány és társai: A Turáni Egyistenhívők és a hatalom az 1930-as évek második felében." In *Felekezeti társadalom—felekezeti műveltség*, edited by Anikó Lukács. Rendi társadalom—polgári társadalom 25, edited by Anikó Lukács, 349–62. Budapest: Hajnal István Kör, 2013.

Szekfű, Gyula. "A turáni-szláv parasztállam." *Magyar Szemle* 5, no. 1 (January 1929): 30–37.

Szíj, Enikő. "A finnugor néprokonsági eszme az 1920-30-as években." In *Őstörténet és nemzettudat 1919-1931*, edited by Éva Kincses Nagy, 72–88. Szeged: JATE Magyar Őstörténeti Kutatócsoport-Balassi, 1991.

———. "Pánfinnugor és antifinnugor elméletek, mozgalmak." In *125 éves a budapesti finnugor tanszék*, edited by Péter Domokos and Márta Csepregi, 145–52. Budapest: ELTE Finnugor Tanszék, 1998.

Szilágyi, Miklós. "A nagykun öntudat." *Regio* 7, no. 1 (1996): 44–63.

Szörényi, László. "Perzsául a magyar költészetben." *Tempevölgy* 8, no. 1 (March 2016): 66–71.

Tasnády, Attila S. "Adalékok Mokry Mészáros Dezső művészi pályaképéhez." *A Herman Ottó Múzeum Évkönyve* 45 (2006): 355–69.

———. "Mokry Mészáros Dezső az alkalmazott művészetek területén." In *Ars perennis— Fiatal művészettörténészek II. konferenciája*, edited by Anna Tüskés, 201–5. Budapest: CentrArt Egyesület, 2010.

Tazbir, Janusz. "Polish National Consciousness in the Sixteenth to the Eighteenth Century." *Harvard Ukrainian Studies* 10, nos. 3-4 (December 1986): 316–35.

Toldi, Éva. "Egy ellentmondásos Babits-vers: A Turáni induló." *Híd* 60, nos. 5-7 (1996): 482–90.

"A Turáni Társaság tagjainak névsora." Budapest: FSZEK, n.d. [1911].

Turtola, Matti. "Linkomies, Horthy and Mannerheim: Some Aspects of Linkomies's 'State Visit' to Hungary in January 1943." *Hungarologische Beiträge* 4, no. 7 (1996): 133–36.

Üstel, Füsun. "Les 'Foyers turcs' et les 'Turcs de l'extérieur.'" *Cahiers d'études sur la Méditerranée orientale et le monde turco-iranien* 8, no. 16 (July–December 1993): 47–61.

Vági, Zoltán. "Endre László: Fajvédelem és bürokratikus antiszemitizmus." In *Tanulmányok a Holokausztról*, vol. 2, edited by Randolph L. Braham, 81–154. Budapest: Balassi, 2002.

Vámbéry, Ármin. "halálának 100. évfordulóján." *Magyar Tudomány* 174, no. 8 (2013) (whole issue).

Vámbéry, Ármin. "A tatárok kultur-törekvései," *Budapesti Szemle* 35, no. 131 (1907): 348–76.

Vares, Vesa. "A romantikus távoli rokon: Finnország és Magyarország kapcsolatai, illetve a finnek Magyarország-képe a két világháború között." *Iskolakultúra* 8, no. 5 (1998): 56–66.

Vásáry, István. "Magyar őstörténet és orientalisztika mint 'nemzeti tudomány.'" In *A nemzeti tudományok historikuma*, edited by Ferenc Kulin and Éva Sallai, 243–56. Budapest: Kölcsey Intézet, 2008.

———. "A 'megalkotott hagyomány': Szittyák és hunok." *Magyar Tudomány* 175, no. 5 (2014): 566–71.

———. "A turkológus Mándoky Kongur István." In *Kőember állott a pusztán*, edited by Ágnes Birtalan and Dávid Somfai Kara, 9–16. Budapest: L'Harmattan, 2008.

Waktor, Andrea. "'Kegyelmes Büzérnagy! . . . Én ábrándozom a bécsi szép napokról': Thallóczy Lajos és köre Bécsben." *Budapesti Negyed* 46, no. 4 (2004): 435–56.

Wasko, Andrzej. "Sarmatism or the Enlightenment: The Dilemma of Polish Culture." *Sarmatian Review* 17, no. 2 (April 1997). Accessed January 20, 2021. http://www.ruf.rice .edu/~sarmatia/497/wasko.html.

Wilhelm, Gábor. "Baráthosi Balogh Benedek néprajzi gyűjtései." *Néprajzi Értesítő* 88 (2006): 131–42.

Wintermantel, Péter. "Szemere Attila hagyatékának orientalisztikai vonatkozású anyagai." *A Herman Ottó Múzeum Évkönyve* 38 (1999): 793–814.

Zakar, András. "Sumerian-Ural-Altaic Affinities." *Current Anthropology* 12, no. 2 (April 1971): 215–25.

Manuscripts

Alaattin, Oguz. "The Interplay between Turkish and Hungarian Nationalism: Ottoman Pan-Turkism and Hungarian Turanism." MSc thesis, Middle East Technical University, 2005.

Bincsik, Mónika. "Japán műtárgyak gyűjtéstörténete Magyarországon a 19. század második felében—kitekintéssel a nemzetközi összefüggésekre." PhD dissertation, Loránd Eötvös University, 2009.

Fajcsák, Györgyi. "Keleti tárgyak gyűjtése Magyarországom, kitekintéssel Kínára, a 19. század elejétől 1945-ig, a Hopp Ferenc Kelet-Ázsiai Művészeti Múzeum tárgyainak tükrében." PhD dissertation, Loránd Eötvös University, 2005.

Farkas, Ildikó. "A turanizmus." PhD dissertation, Loránd Eötvös University, 2001.

Kerepeszki, Róbert. "Darkó Jenő bizantinológus élete és munkássága." MA thesis, University of Debrecen, 2006.

Kessler, Joseph A. "Turanism and Pan-turanism in Hungary: 1890–1945." PhD dissertation, University of California, Berkeley, 1967.

Kiss, Attila. "Magyar Kelet-politika a rokonság jegyében: Az őstörténet, mint társadalom- és gazdaságpolitikai tényező 100 éve és ma." Pallas Athéné Domus Animae Foundation, 2015.

Kolozsi, Ádám. "Social Constructions of the Native Faith: Mytho-historical Narratives and Identity-Discourse in Hungarian Neo-paganism." MA thesis, Central European University, 2012.

Kövecsi-Oláh, Péter. "Török-magyar diplomáciai kapcsolatok a két világháború között (1920–1945)." PhD dissertation, Eötvös Loránd University, Budapest, 2018.

Websites

"Abdu'l Bahá Budapesten." bahai.hu. Accessed September 19, 2016. http://www.bahai.hu /a-bahai-hit/magyarorszagi-tortenet/abdul-baha-budapesten/.

Andover-Harvard Theological Library. Harvard Divinity School Repository. Unitarian Service Committee. Case Files, 1938–1951. Accessed January 20, 2021. https://iiif.lib .harvard.edu/manifests/view/drs:13830189$1i.

Arcanum Digitális Tudománytár. Accessed January 29, 2021. adtplus.arcanum.hu.

Bosworth, C. E. "Turan." Encyclopaedia Iranica online. Accessed July 2, 2018. http://www .iranicaonline.org/articles/turan.

Debreczeni-Droppán, Béla. "Toldi buzogánya." A Magyar Nemzeti Múzeum blogja. March 21, 2017. Accessed July 22, 2018. https://mnm.hu/hu/cikk/toldi-buzoganya.

FamilySearch. Accessed January 20, 2021. familysearch.org.

"Gigantikus Attila-szobor és a Koppány torony: turáni építészet Budapesten." Falanszter Blog, June 22, 2011. Accessed January 20, 2021. https://falanszter.blog.hu/2011/06/22 /gigantikus_attila_szobor_es_koppany_torony_turani_epiteszet_budapesten?layout= 1%3Fdesktop.

Kanyó, Ferenc. "A Habsburgok és a magyar őstörténet." toriblog.blog.hu. March 17, 2009. Accessed August 12, 2016. http://toriblog.blog.hu/2009/03/17/mitoszok_nyomaban_i _a_habsburgok_es_a_magyar_ostortenet.

"Kimondjuk, megoldjuk: A Jobbik országgyűlési választási programja a nemzet felemelkedéséért." Accessed September 11, 2017. https://jobbik.hu/sites/default/files /cikkcsatolmany/kimondjukmegoldjuk2014_netre.pdf.

"Kurultáj." Accessed January 20, 2021. kurultaj.hu.

"Magyar Adorján élete." Accessed October 28, 2018. http://www.magyaradorjan.com/007/doc /eletrajz.html.

"Magyar Adorján és Tömöry Zsuzsa levelezése." Accessed January 20, 2021. https://web .archive.org/web/20190114104134/http://tomoryzsuzsa.weebly.com/malevelezeacutese .html.

Marton Veronika. "Emlékképek Badiny Jós Ferencről." Marton Veronika blogja. November 25, 2016. Accessed October 27, 2018. https://martonveronika.blog.hu/2016/11/25 /emlekkepek_badiny_jos_ferencrol.

MTA BTK, László Gyula Digitális Archívum, Levelezés, 1962–1988. Accessed October 29, 2018. http://lgyda.btk.mta.hu/levelezes.

"A Nemzeti Együttműködés Programja" parlament.hu. Accessed Septermber 11, 2016. http:// www.parlament.hu/irom39/00047/00047.pdf.

"Nemzeti ügyek politikája." fidesz.hu. Accessed January 21, 2021. https://www.slideshare.net /Mariabloghu/fidesz-vlasztsi-program-2010.

Nyelv és Tudomány. Accessed January 20, 2021.nyest.hu.

"Radikális változás: A Jobbik országgyűlési választási programja a nemzeti önrendelkezésért és a társadalmi igazságosságért." Accessed January 20, 2021. http://docplayer.hu /158036-Radikalis-valtozas-a-jobbik-orszaggyulesi-valasztasi-programja-a-nemzeti -onrendelkezesert-es-a-tarsadalmi-igazsagossagert.html.

Recski Szövetség honlapja. Accessed October 23, 2018. http://www.recskiszovetseg.hu/about _b_II.html.

Sándor, Klára. "Européer rovásírás." Nyelv és Tudomány. June 26, 2014. Accessed October 28, 2018. https://www.nyest.hu/hirek/europeer-rovasiras.

Tenczer, Gábor. "Ennél izgalmasabb torony nincs Budapesten." index.hu. February 21, 2015. Accessed August 19, 2018. https://index.hu/belfold/budapest/2015/02/21 /a_turani_atok_sujtotta_pogany-torony/.

Varga, Géza. "Mozog a föld. Gyorsjelentés a Magyarok Világszövetsége által a Magyarok VI. Világtalálkozója keretében rendezett 'Magyarság és kelet' [című] őstörténeti konferenciáról." Accessed September 11, 2016. http://ikint.uw.hu/mozog_a_fold .htm.

Vámbéry, Ármin. "(1832–1913): Kelet-kutató és hagyatéka a Magyar Tudományos Akadémia Könyvtárában website, 'Az "ugor-török háború."'" Accessed July 2, 2018. http:// vambery.mtak.hu/hu/09.htm.

Zegernyei. "Max Müller és a turáni átok." Nyelv és Tudomány. July 8, 2011. Accessed January 20, 2021. https://www.nyest.hu/renhirek/max-muller-es-a-turani-atok.

"Zichy Jenő gróf ázsiai expedíciói." Rénhírek. June 4, 2010. Accessed July 2, 2018. http://
   renhirek.blogspot.com/2010/06/zichy-jeno-grof-azsiai-expedicioi.html.
Zsarátnok folyóirat. Accessed January 20, 2021. zsaratnok.org.
Zsuffa, Sándor. "A magyarországi szumir probléma állása különböző korokban."
   Magyarságtudományi Intézet honlapja. October 28, 2018. Accessed October 28, 2018.
   http://www.magtudin.org/Szumir%20problema.htm.
Zürichi Magyar Történelmi Egyesület. Accessed January 20, 2021. zmte.webnode.hu.

INDEX OF NAMES

INDEX OF TERMS

BALÁZS ABLONCZY is Associate Professor at Eötvös Loránd University
(Budapest, Hungary) and Senior Research Fellow at the Center for
Humanities, Institute of History, Budapest. He is author of *Pál Teleki
(1874–1941): The Life of a Controversial Hungarian Politician.*

Printed in the USA
CPSIA information can be obtained
at www.ICGtesting.com
LVHW092045191123
764181LV00006B/247